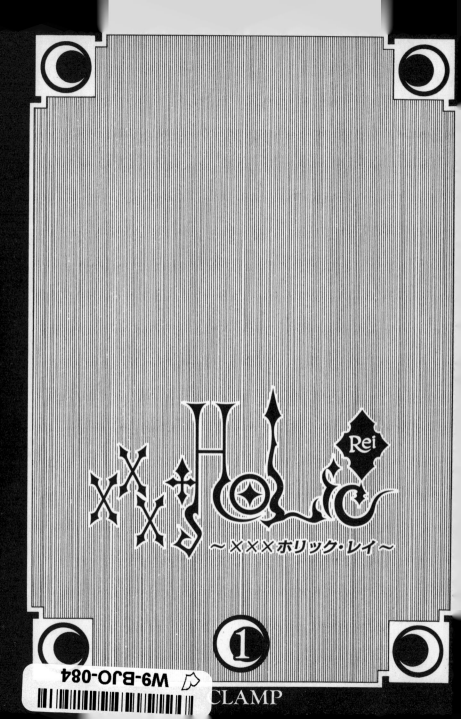

xxxHOLiC Rei
Rei
～×××ホリック・レイ～

①

CLAMP

TITLE & DESIGN BY CLAMP

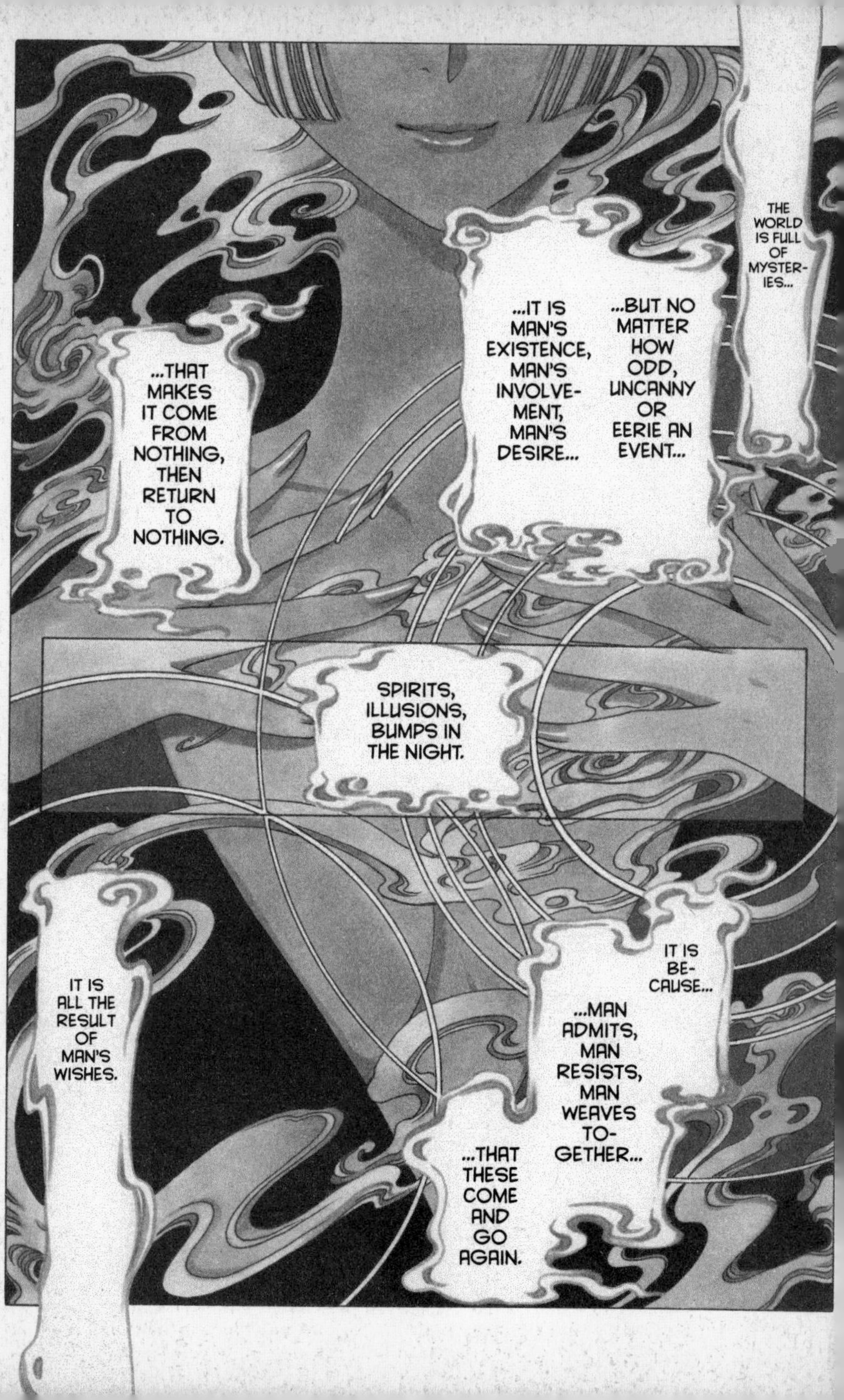
THE WORLD IS FULL OF MYSTER-IES...
...BUT NO MATTER HOW ODD, UNCANNY OR EERIE AN EVENT...
...IT IS MAN'S EXISTENCE, MAN'S INVOLVE-MENT, MAN'S DESIRE...
...THAT MAKES IT COME FROM NOTHING, THEN RETURN TO NOTHING.
SPIRITS, ILLUSIONS, BUMPS IN THE NIGHT.
IT IS BE-CAUSE...
...MAN ADMITS, MAN RESISTS, MAN WEAVES TO-GETHER...
...THAT THESE COME AND GO AGAIN.
IT IS ALL THE RESULT OF MAN'S WISHES.

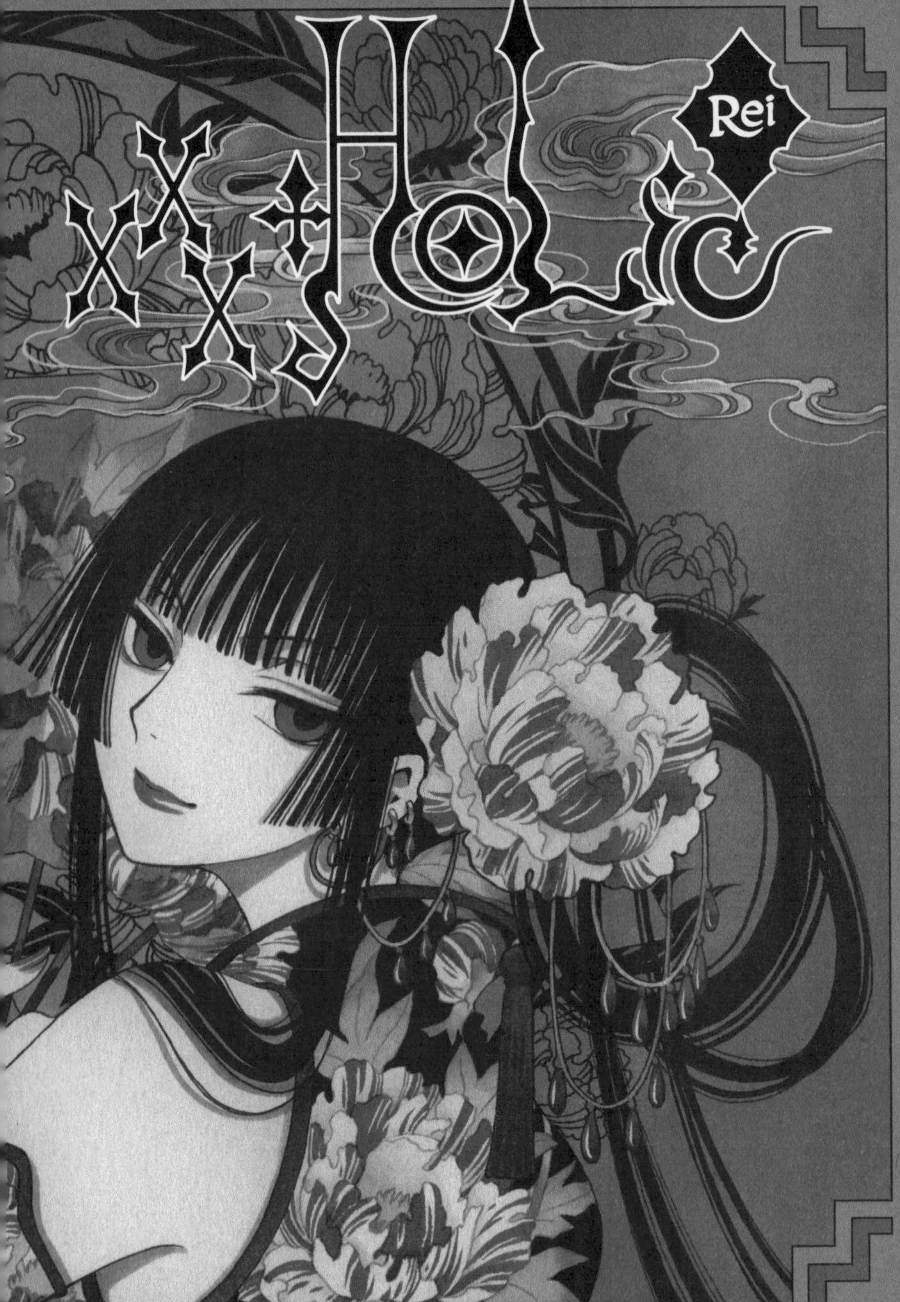
xxxHolic
Rei

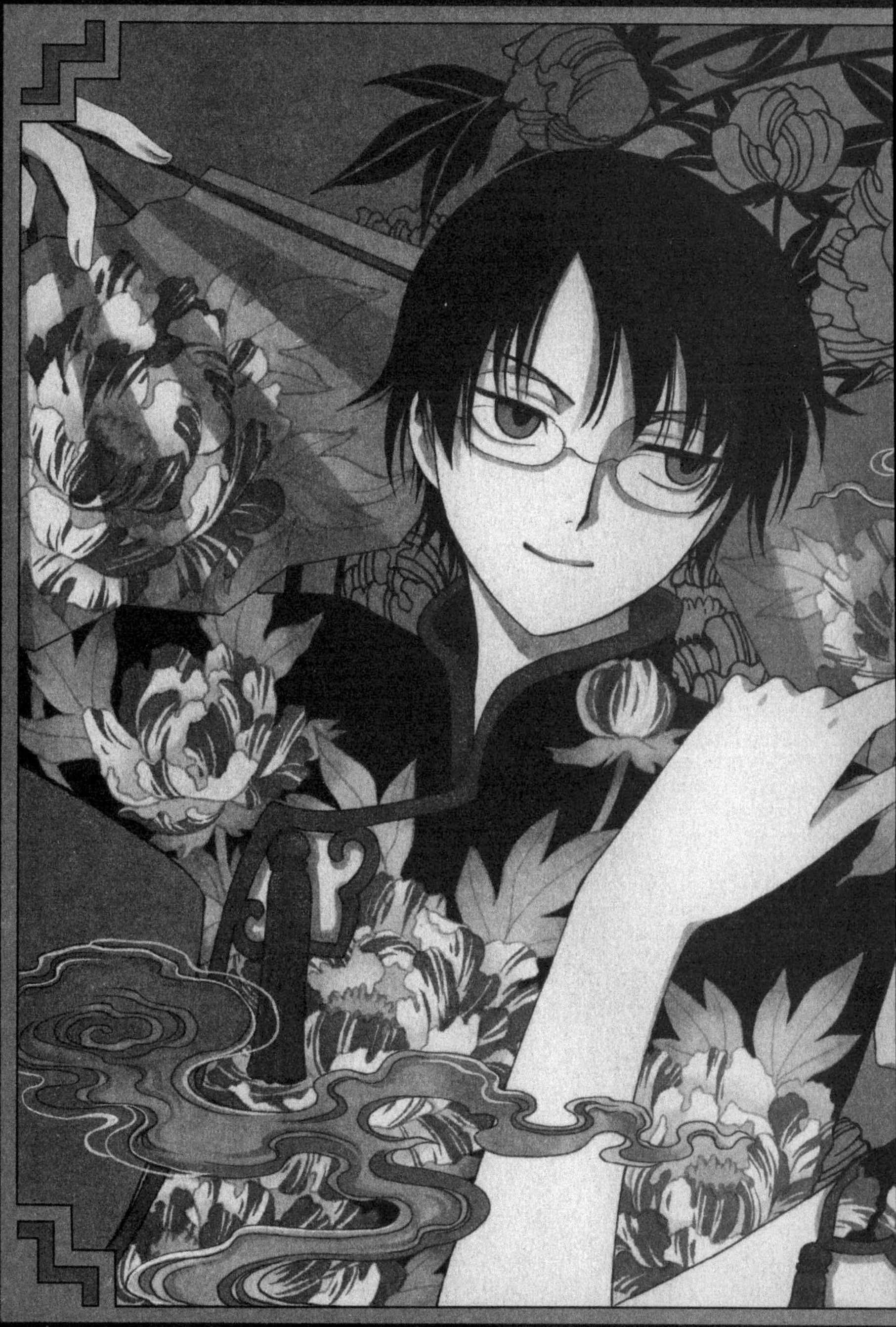

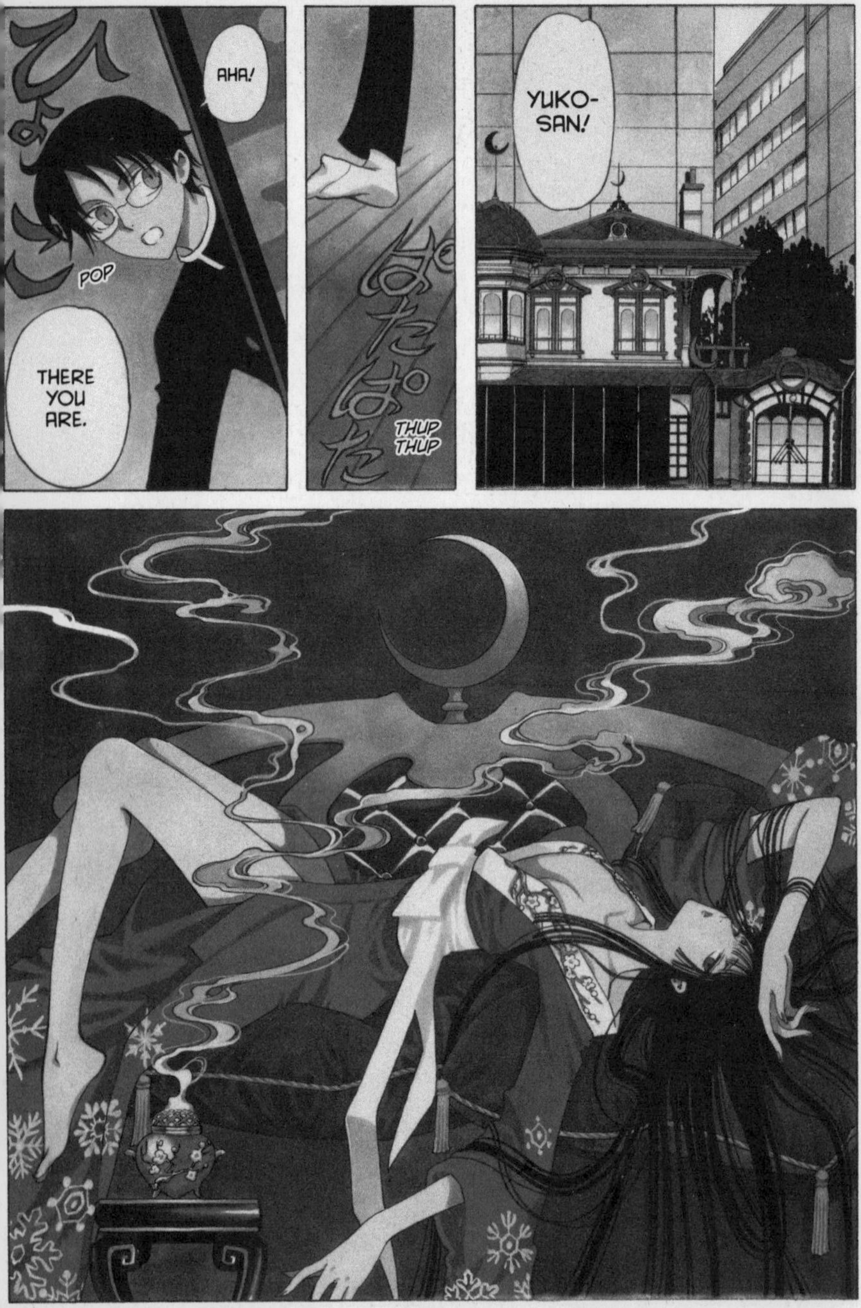
YUKO-SAN!
ぱたぱた
THUP THUP
AHA!
POP
THERE YOU ARE.

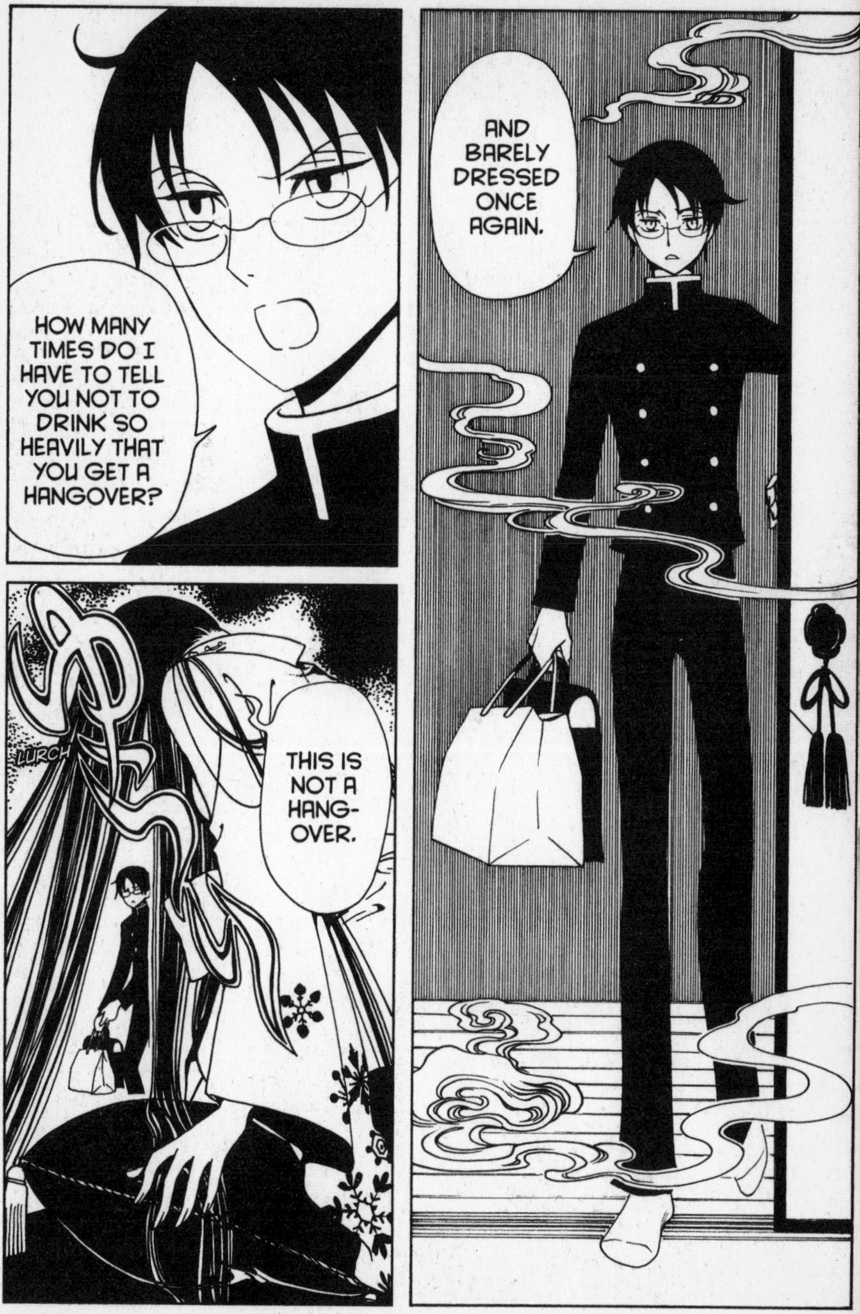
AND BARELY DRESSED ONCE AGAIN.
HOW MANY TIMES DO I HAVE TO TELL YOU NOT TO DRINK SO HEAVILY THAT YOU GET A HANGOVER?
THIS IS NOT A HANG-OVER.
LURCH

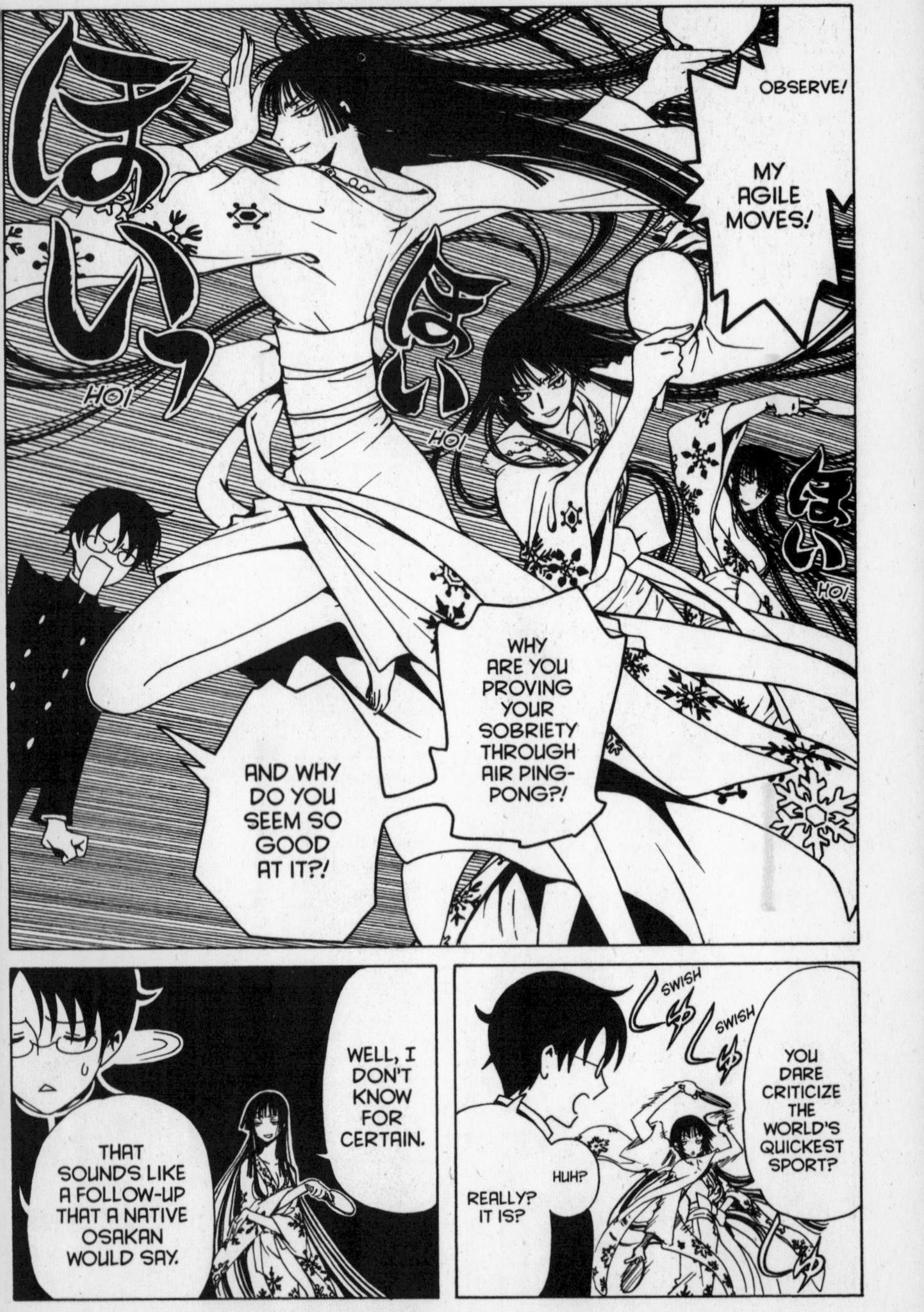
OBSERVE!
MY AGILE MOVES!
ほい
HOI
WHY ARE YOU PROVING YOUR SOBRIETY THROUGH AIR PING-PONG?!
ほい
HOI
ほい
HOI
AND WHY DO YOU SEEM SO GOOD AT IT?!
SWISH
SWISH
YOU DARE CRITICIZE THE WORLD'S QUICKEST SPORT?
HUH?
REALLY? IT IS?
WELL, I DON'T KNOW FOR CERTAIN.
THAT SOUNDS LIKE A FOLLOW-UP THAT A NATIVE OSAKAN WOULD SAY.

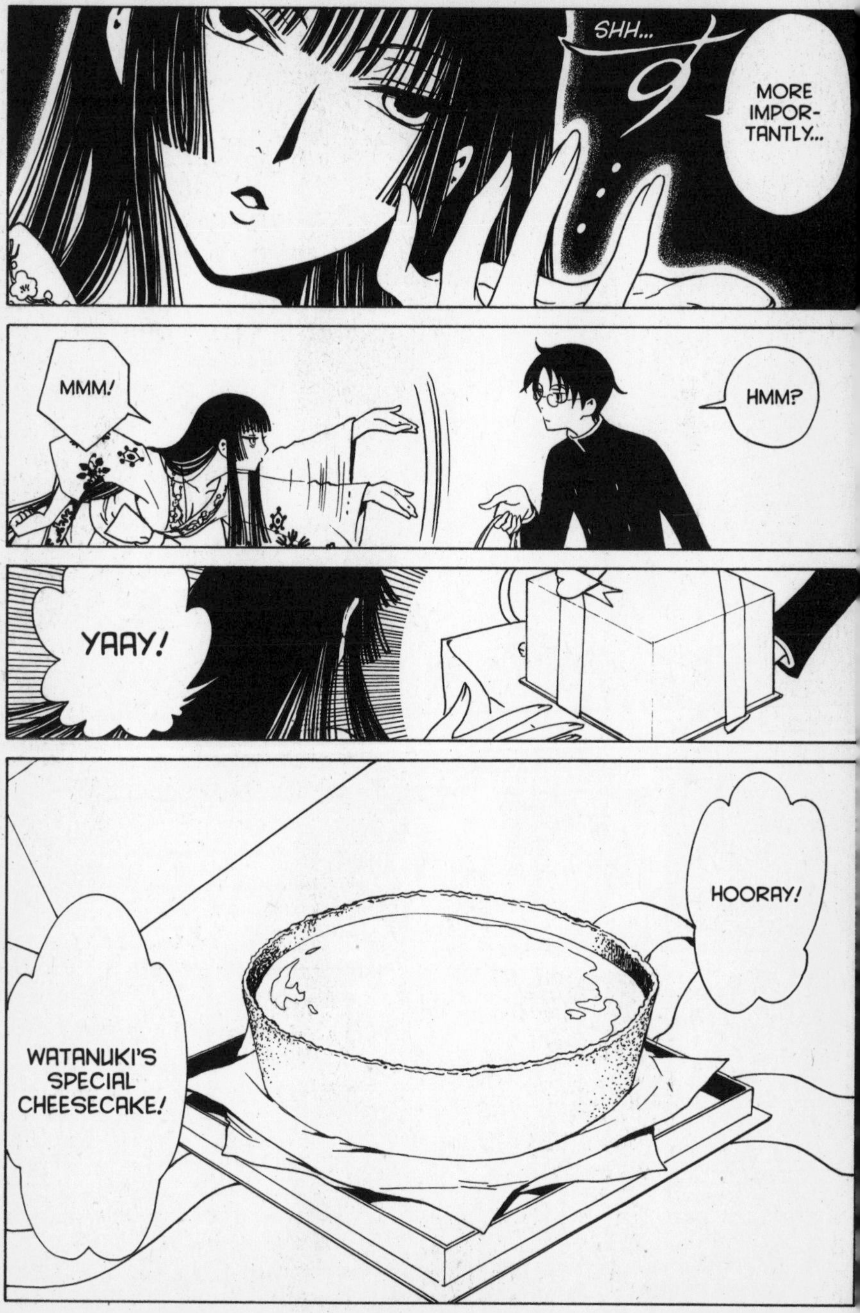
MORE IMPORTANTLY...
SHH...
HMM?
MMM!
YAAY!
HOORAY!
WATANUKI'S SPECIAL CHEESECAKE!

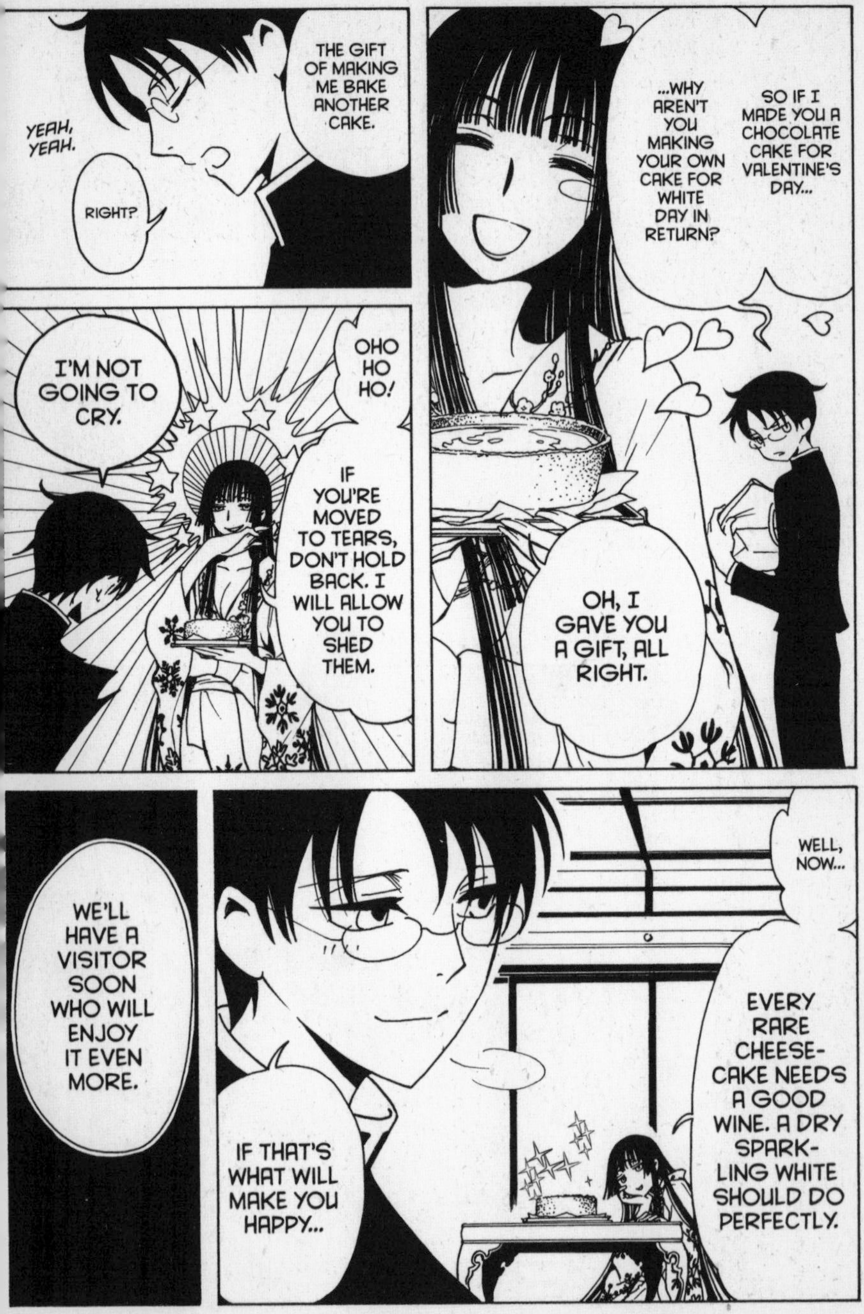
SO IF I MADE YOU A CHOCOLATE CAKE FOR VALENTINE'S DAY...
...WHY AREN'T YOU MAKING YOUR OWN CAKE FOR WHITE DAY IN RETURN?
OH, I GAVE YOU A GIFT, ALL RIGHT.
THE GIFT OF MAKING ME BAKE ANOTHER CAKE.
RIGHT?
YEAH, YEAH.
OHO HO HO!
IF YOU'RE MOVED TO TEARS, DON'T HOLD BACK. I WILL ALLOW YOU TO SHED THEM.
I'M NOT GOING TO CRY.
WELL, NOW...
EVERY RARE CHEESE-CAKE NEEDS A GOOD WINE. A DRY SPARK-LING WHITE SHOULD DO PERFECTLY.
IF THAT'S WHAT WILL MAKE YOU HAPPY...
WE'LL HAVE A VISITOR SOON WHO WILL ENJOY IT EVEN MORE.

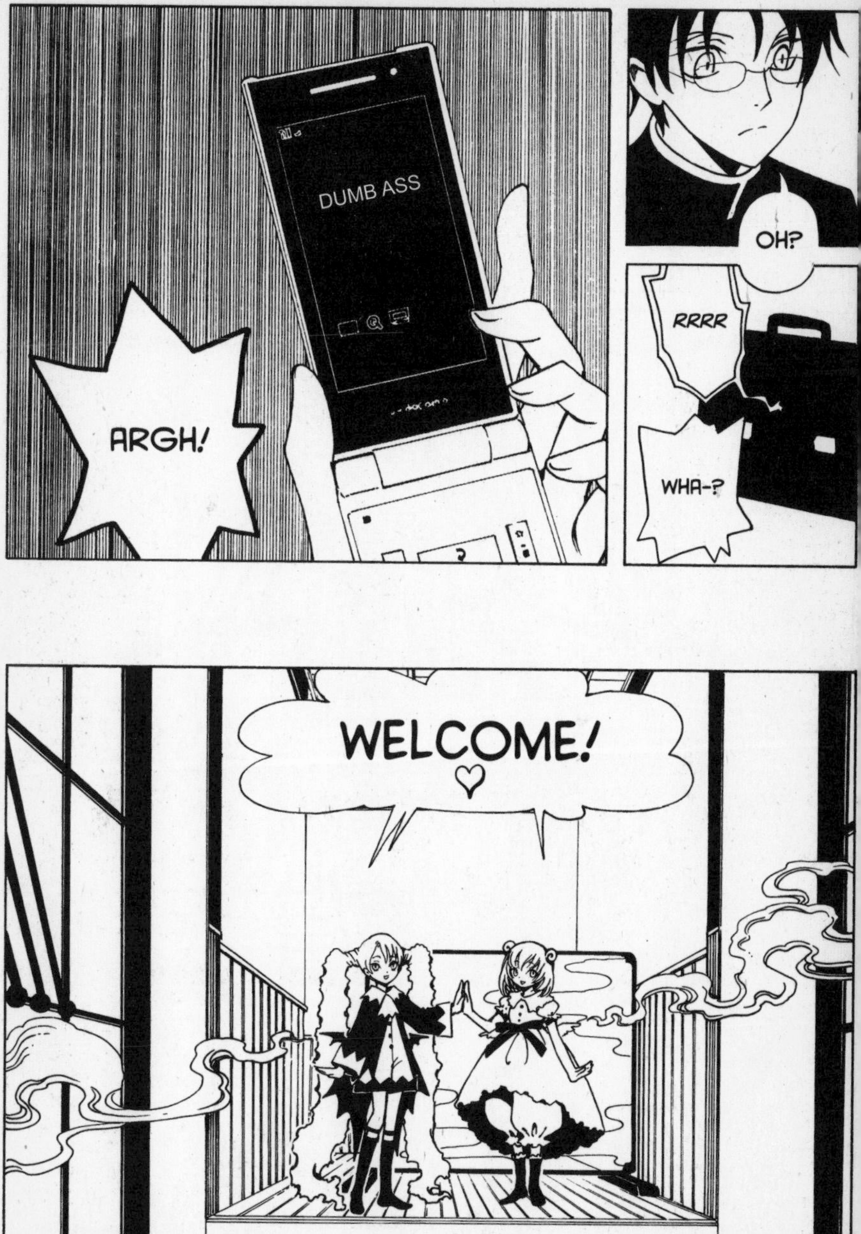
OH?
RRRR
WHA-?
DUMB ASS
ARGH!
WELCOME!

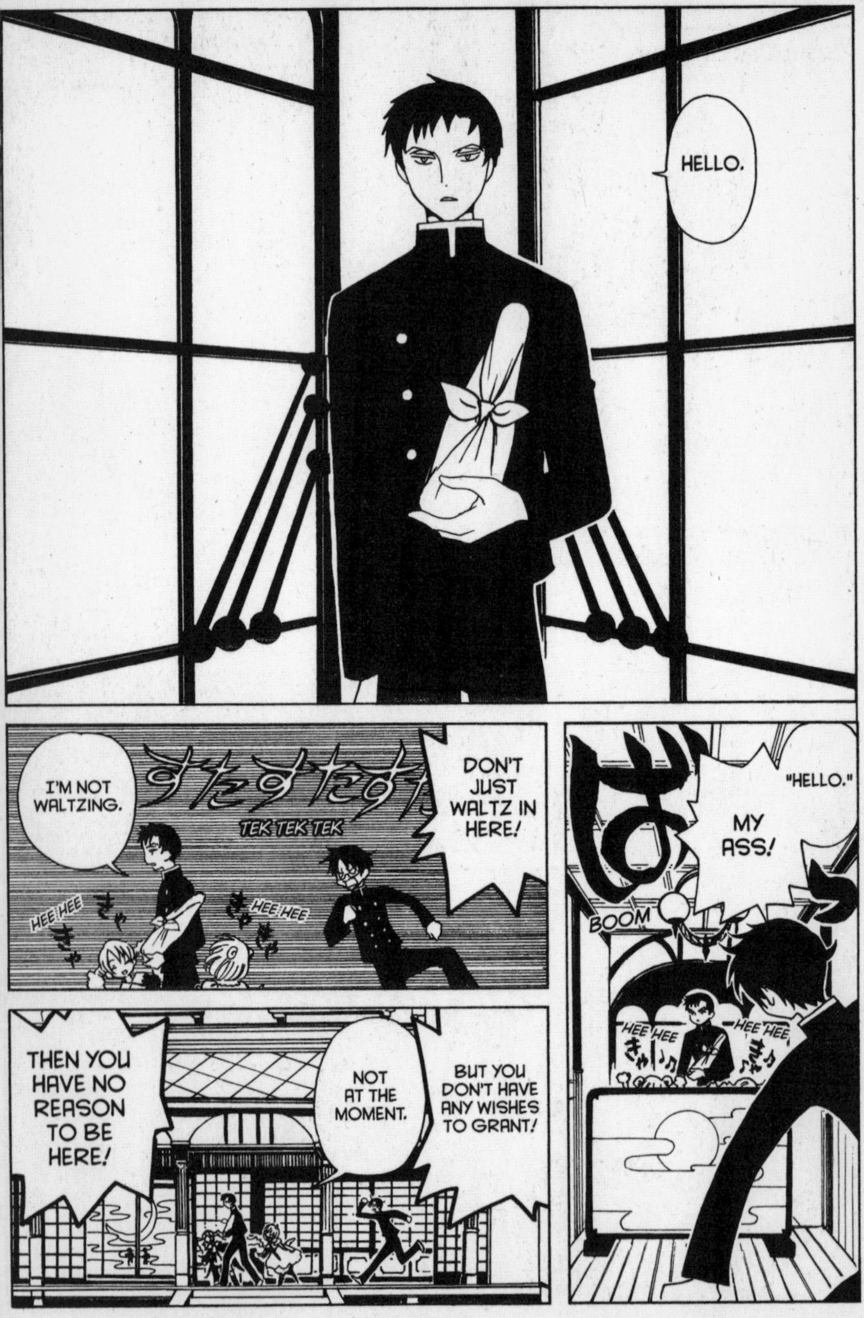
HELLO.
"HELLO."
MY ASS!
BOOM
HEE HEE
HEE HEE
DON'T JUST WALTZ IN HERE!
TEK TEK TEK
I'M NOT WALTZING.
HEE HEE
HEE HEE
BUT YOU DON'T HAVE ANY WISHES TO GRANT!
NOT AT THE MOMENT.
THEN YOU HAVE NO REASON TO BE HERE!

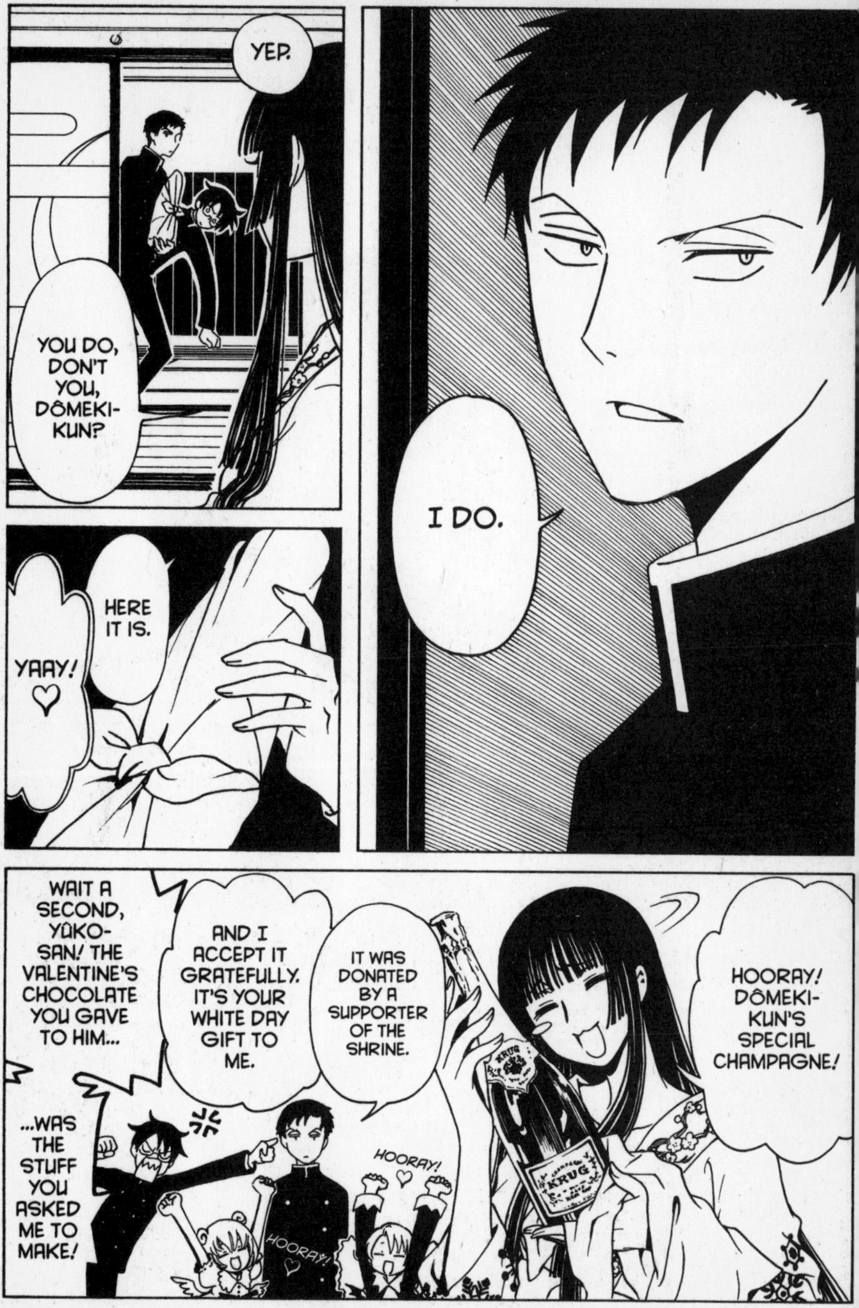
I DO.
YEP.
YOU DO, DON'T YOU, DÔMEKI-KUN?
HERE IT IS.
YAAY! ♡
HOORAY! DÔMEKI-KUN'S SPECIAL CHAMPAGNE!
IT WAS DONATED BY A SUPPORTER OF THE SHRINE.
AND I ACCEPT IT GRATEFULLY. IT'S YOUR WHITE DAY GIFT TO ME.
WAIT A SECOND, YÛKO-SAN! THE VALENTINE'S CHOCOLATE YOU GAVE TO HIM...
...WAS THE STUFF YOU ASKED ME TO MAKE!
HOORAY! ♡
HOORAY! ♡
KRUG
KRUG

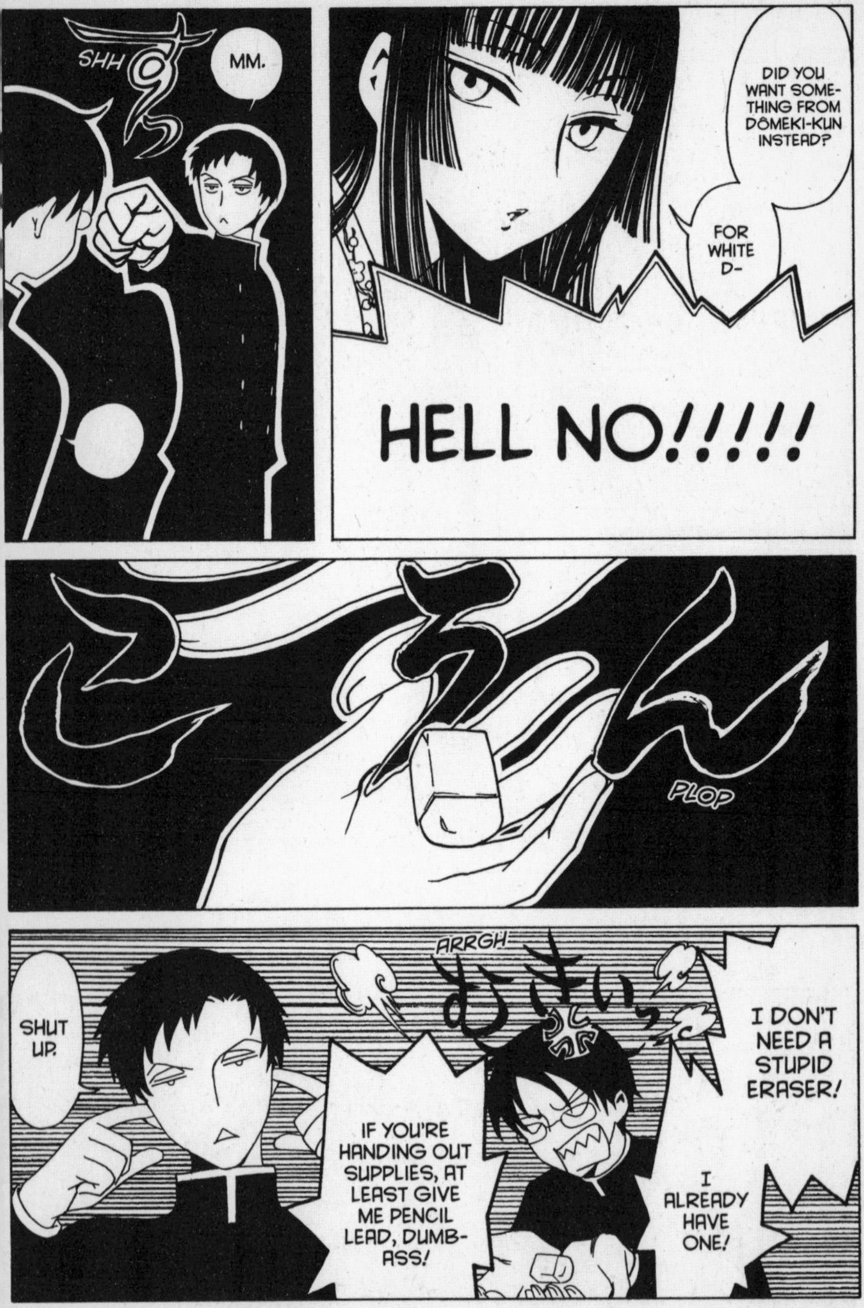
DID YOU WANT SOME-THING FROM DÔMEKI-KUN INSTEAD?
FOR WHITE D-
HELL NO!!!!!
MM.
SHH
PLOP
I DON'T NEED A STUPID ERASER!
ARRGH
I ALREADY HAVE ONE!
IF YOU'RE HANDING OUT SUPPLIES, AT LEAST GIVE ME PENCIL LEAD, DUMB-ASS!
SHUT UP.

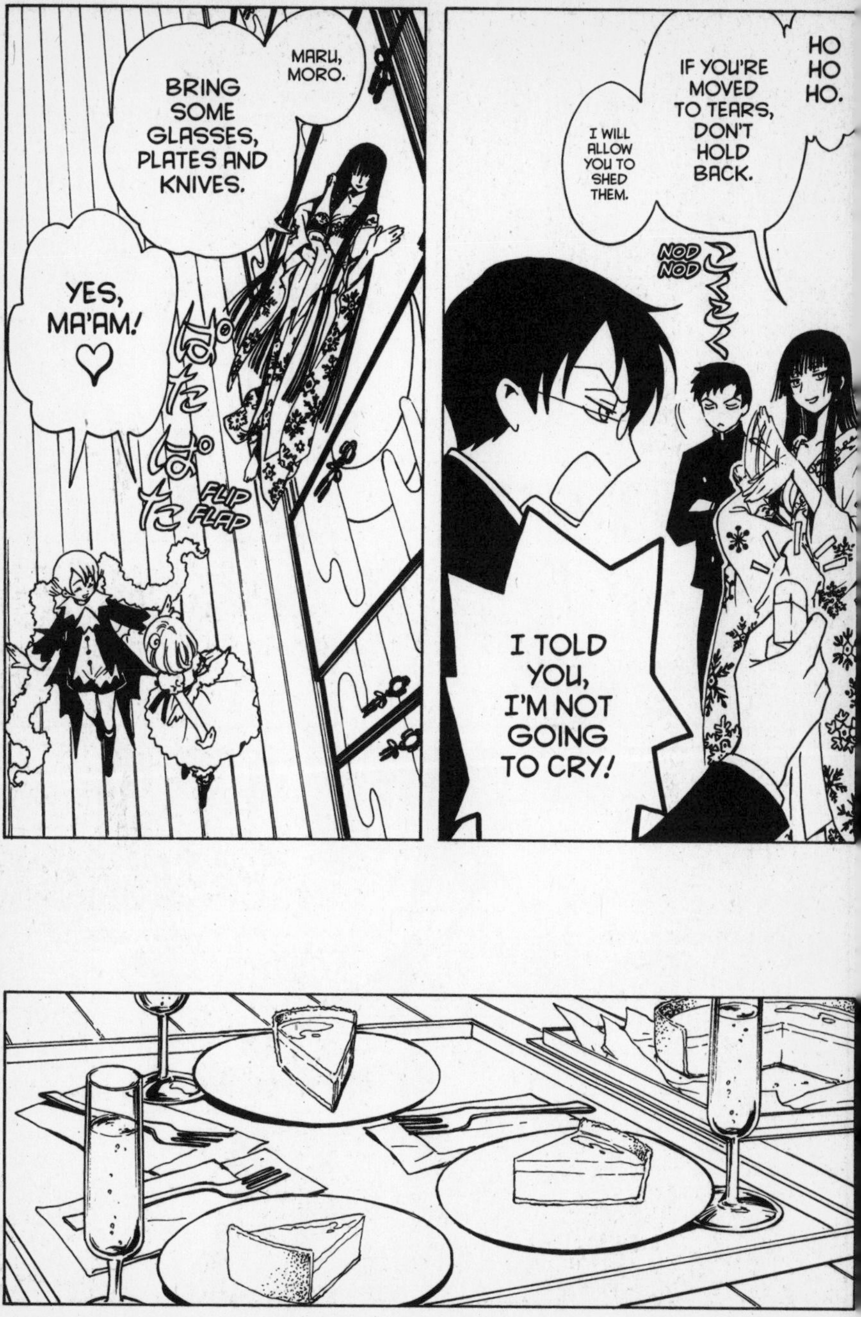
HO HO HO.
IF YOU'RE MOVED TO TEARS, DON'T HOLD BACK.
I WILL ALLOW YOU TO SHED THEM.
NOD NOD
I TOLD YOU, I'M NOT GOING TO CRY!
MARU, MORO.
BRING SOME GLASSES, PLATES AND KNIVES.
YES, MA'AM! ♥
ぱたぱた
FLIP FLAP

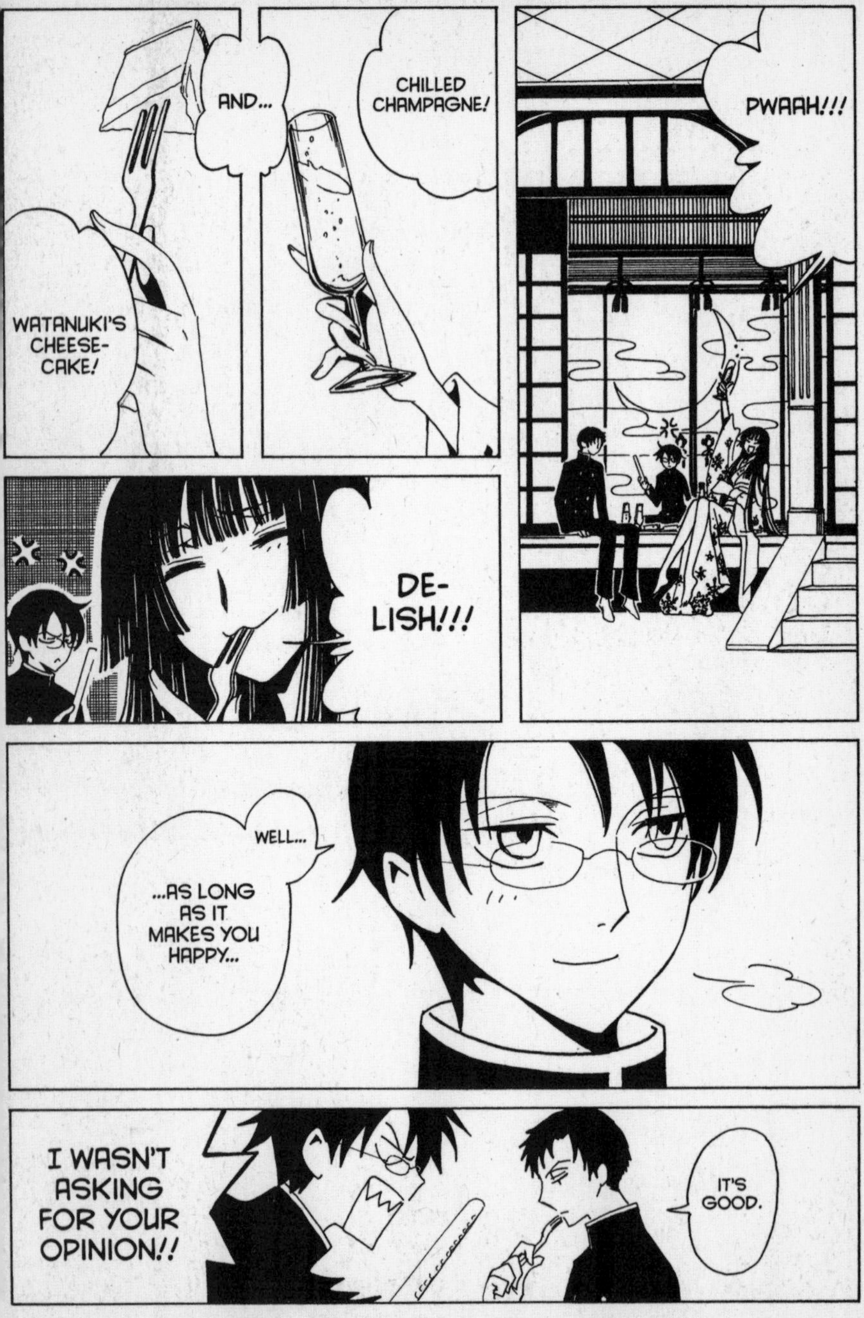
PWAAH!!!
CHILLED CHAMPAGNE!
AND...
WATANUKI'S CHEESE-CAKE!
DE-LISH!!!
WELL...
...AS LONG AS IT MAKES YOU HAPPY...
IT'S GOOD.
I WASN'T ASKING FOR YOUR OPINION!!

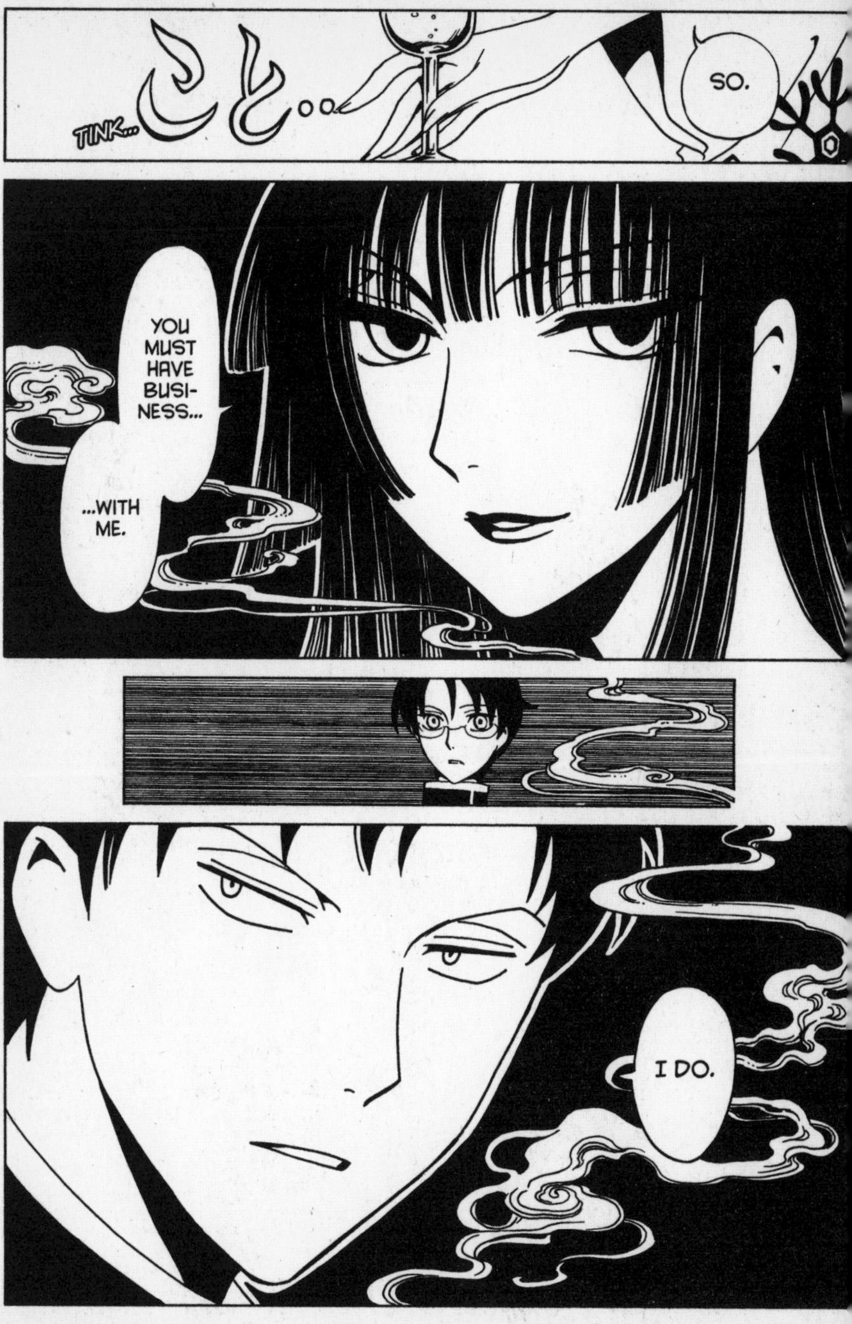
SO.
TINK...
YOU MUST HAVE BUSINESS...
...WITH ME.
I DO.

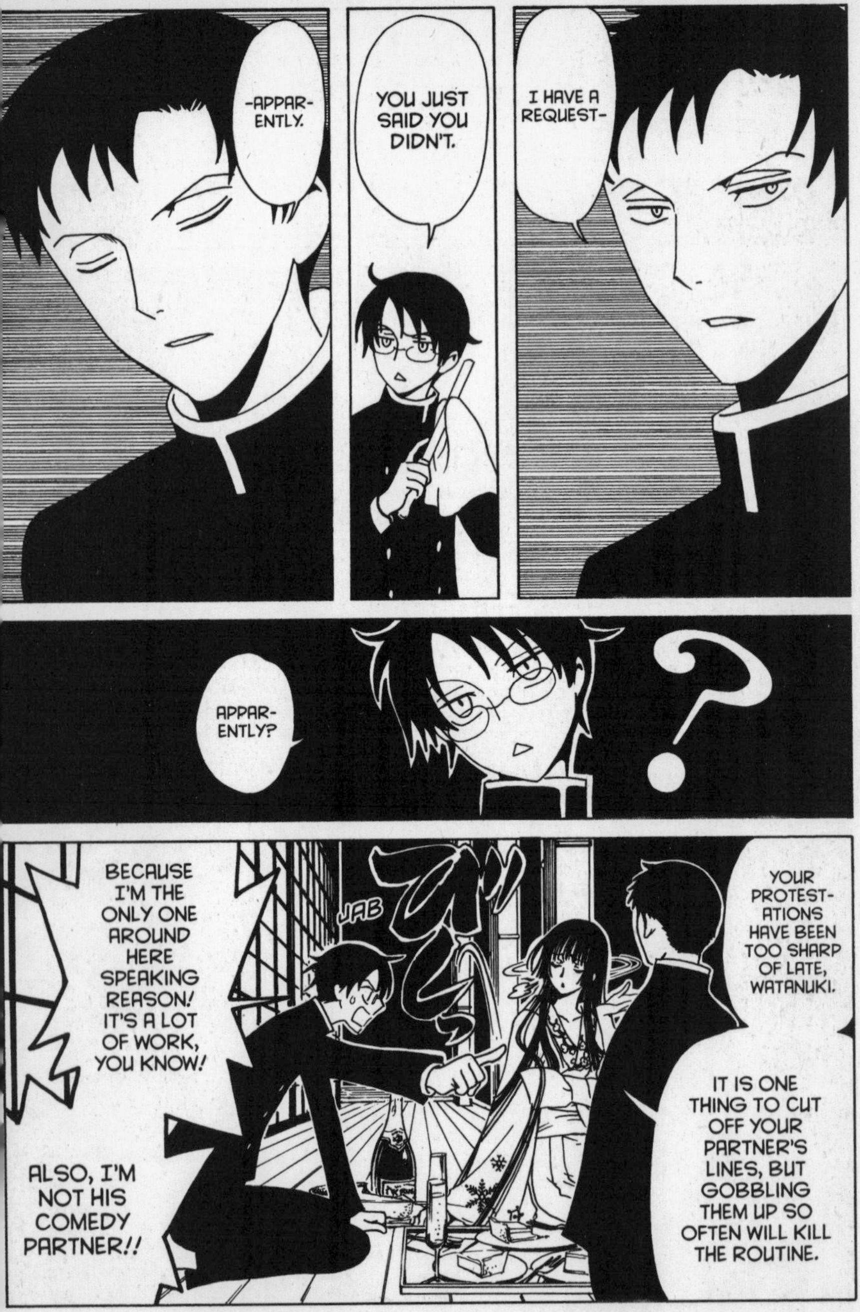
I HAVE A REQUEST-
YOU JUST SAID YOU DIDN'T.
-APPARENTLY.
APPARENTLY?
YOUR PROTESTATIONS HAVE BEEN TOO SHARP OF LATE, WATANUKI.
IT IS ONE THING TO CUT OFF YOUR PARTNER'S LINES, BUT GOBBLING THEM UP SO OFTEN WILL KILL THE ROUTINE.
BECAUSE I'M THE ONLY ONE AROUND HERE SPEAKING REASON! IT'S A LOT OF WORK, YOU KNOW!
JAB
ALSO, I'M NOT HIS COMEDY PARTNER!!

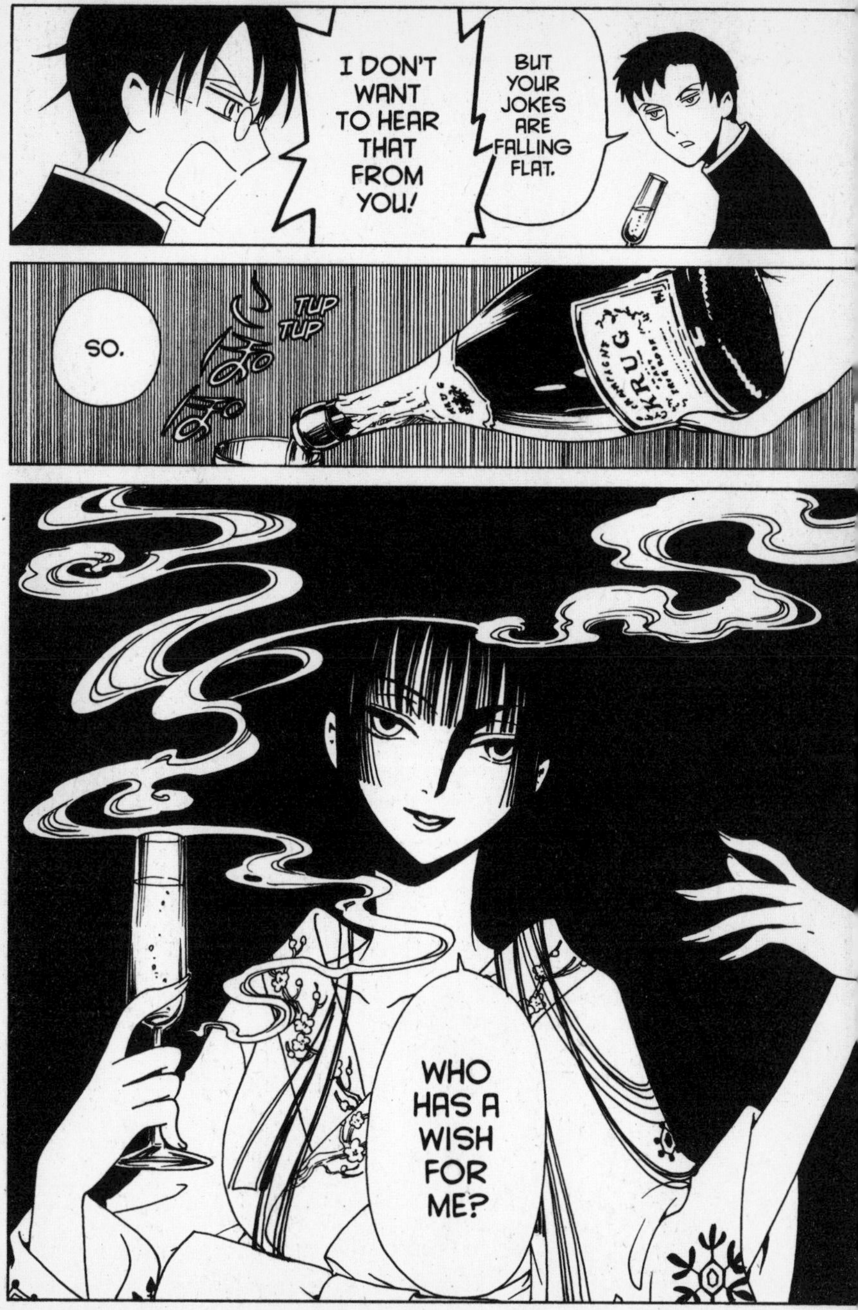
BUT YOUR JOKES ARE FALLING FLAT.
I DON'T WANT TO HEAR THAT FROM YOU!
TUP TUP
SO.
KRUG
WHO HAS A WISH FOR ME?

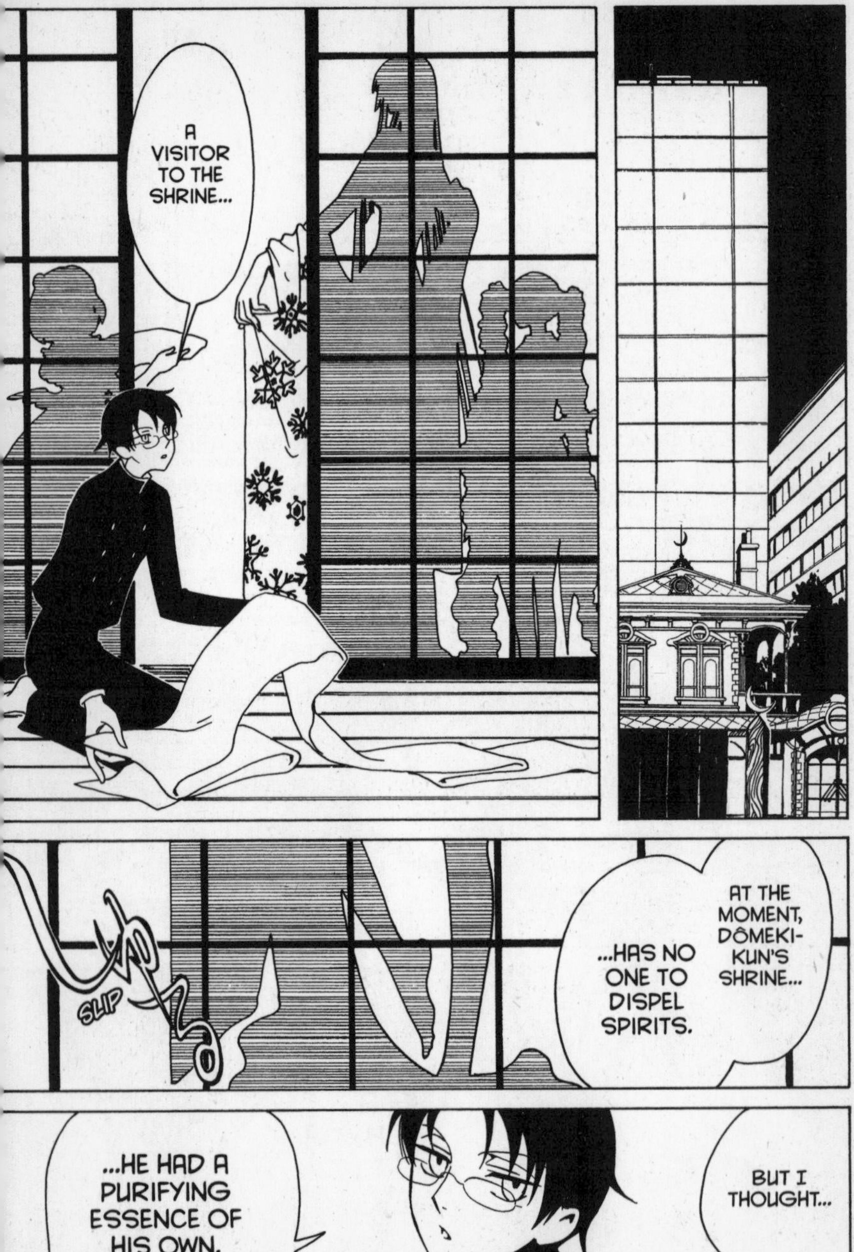
A VISITOR TO THE SHRINE...
AT THE MOMENT, DÔMEKI-KUN'S SHRINE...
...HAS NO ONE TO DISPEL SPIRITS.
SLIP
BUT I THOUGHT...
...HE HAD A PURIFYING ESSENCE OF HIS OWN.

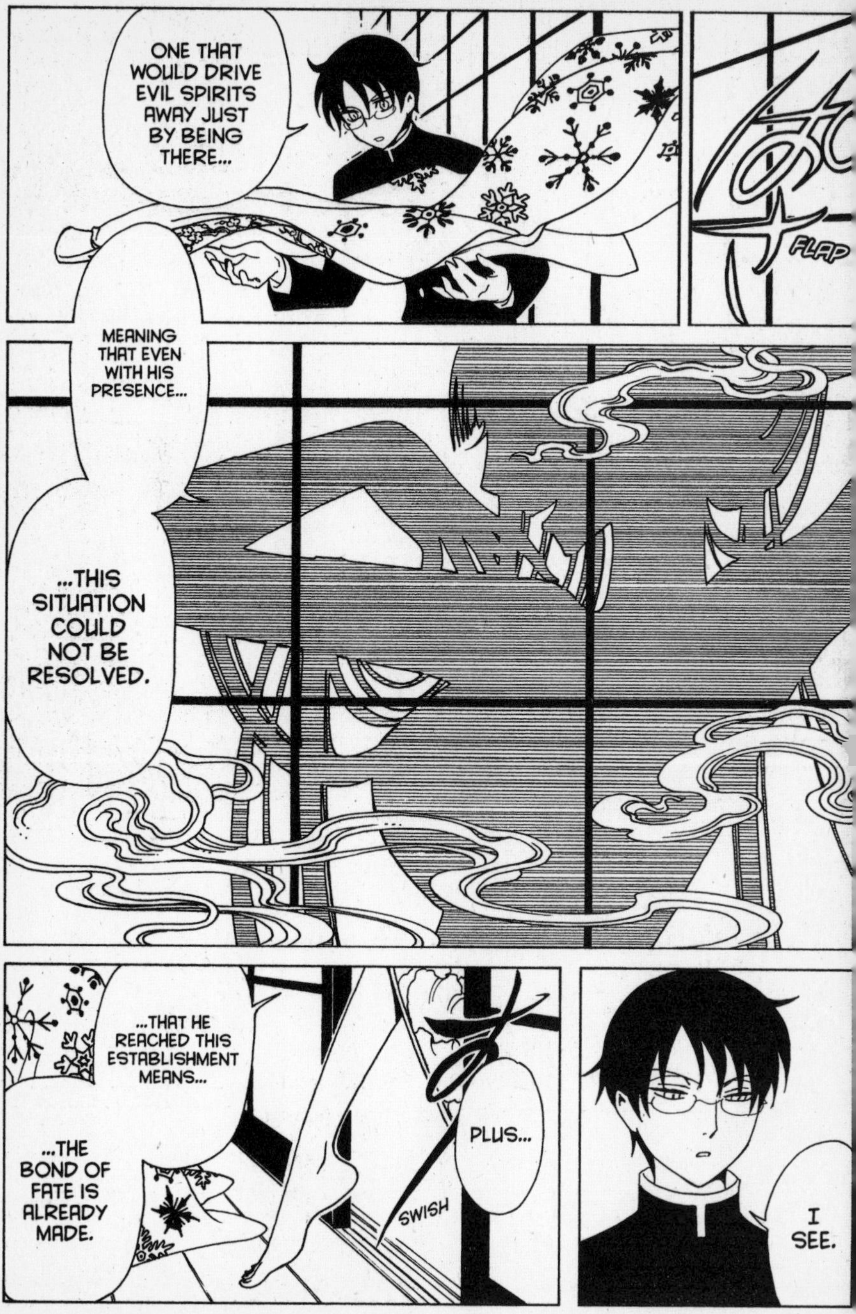
FLAP
ONE THAT WOULD DRIVE EVIL SPIRITS AWAY JUST BY BEING THERE...
MEANING THAT EVEN WITH HIS PRESENCE...
...THIS SITUATION COULD NOT BE RESOLVED.
I SEE.
PLUS...
...THAT HE REACHED THIS ESTABLISHMENT MEANS...
...THE BOND OF FATE IS ALREADY MADE.
SWISH

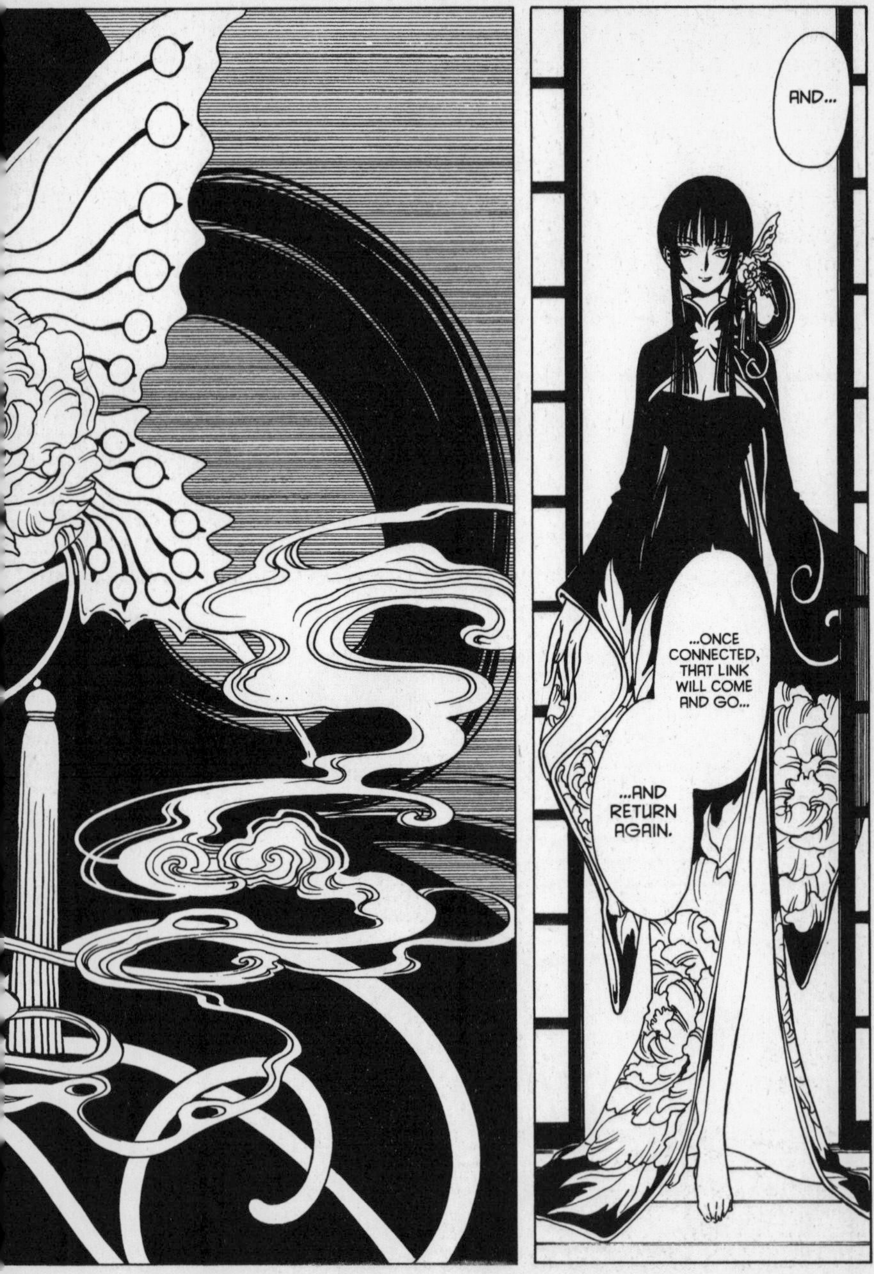
AND...
...ONCE CONNECTED, THAT LINK WILL COME AND GO...
...AND RETURN AGAIN.

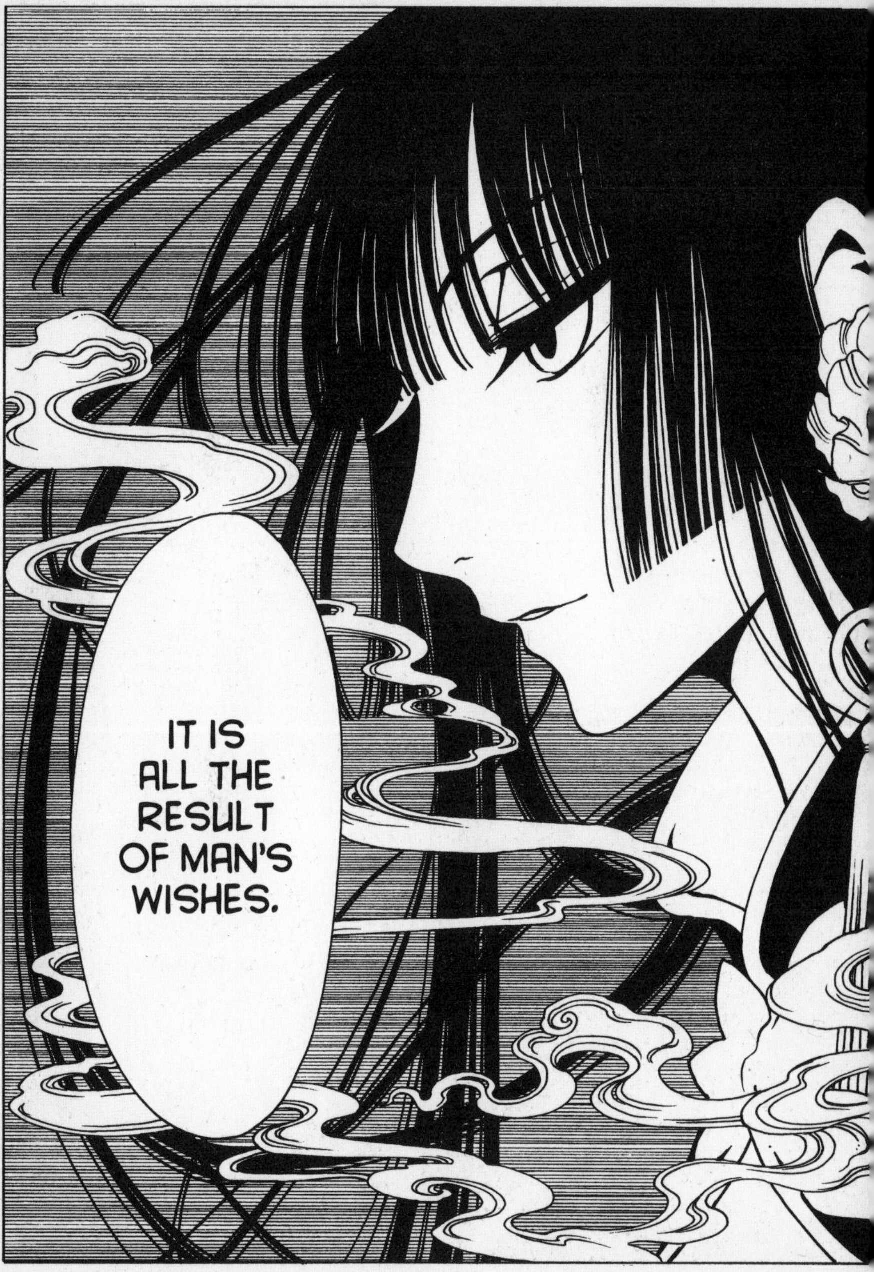
IT IS ALL THE RESULT OF MAN'S WISHES.

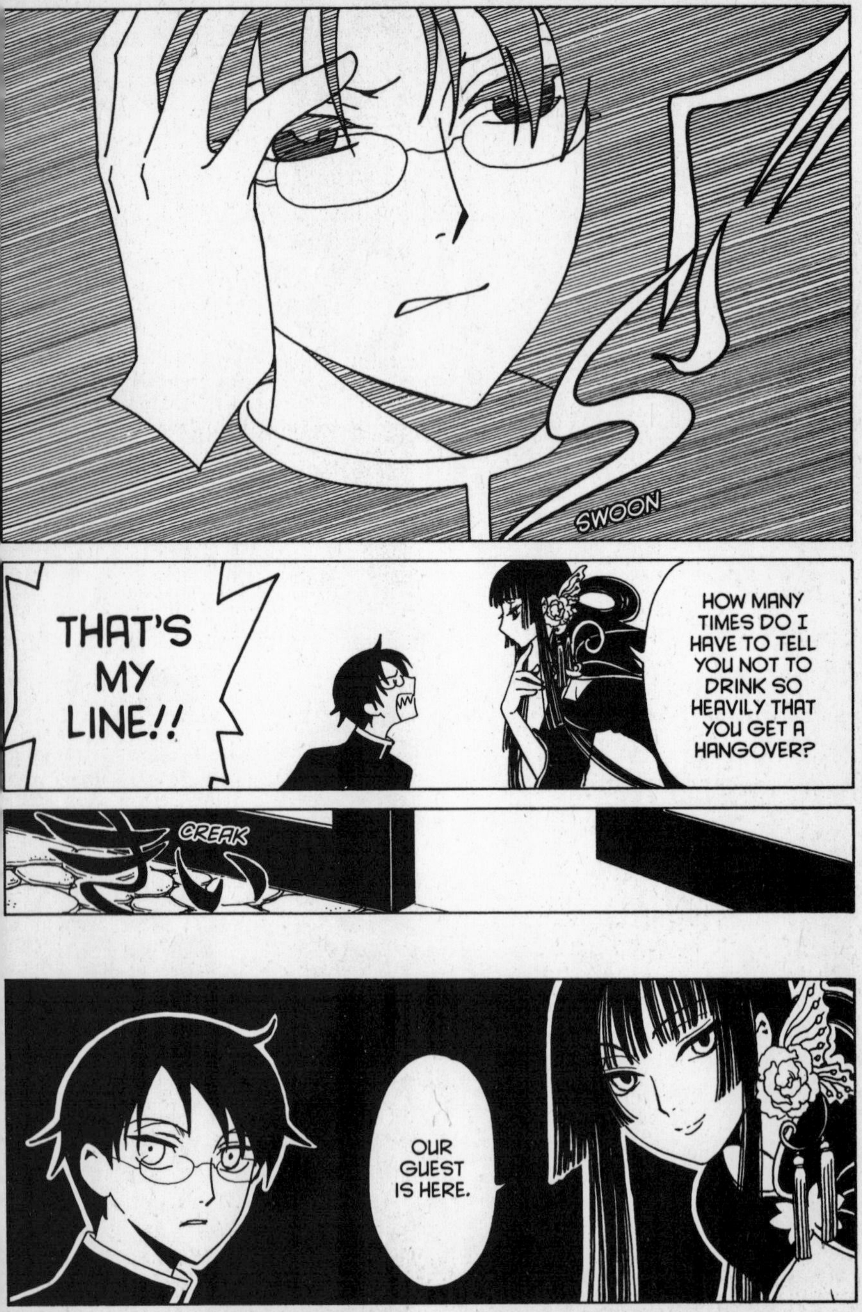
SWOON
HOW MANY TIMES DO I HAVE TO TELL YOU NOT TO DRINK SO HEAVILY THAT YOU GET A HANGOVER?
THAT'S MY LINE!!
CREAK
OUR GUEST IS HERE.

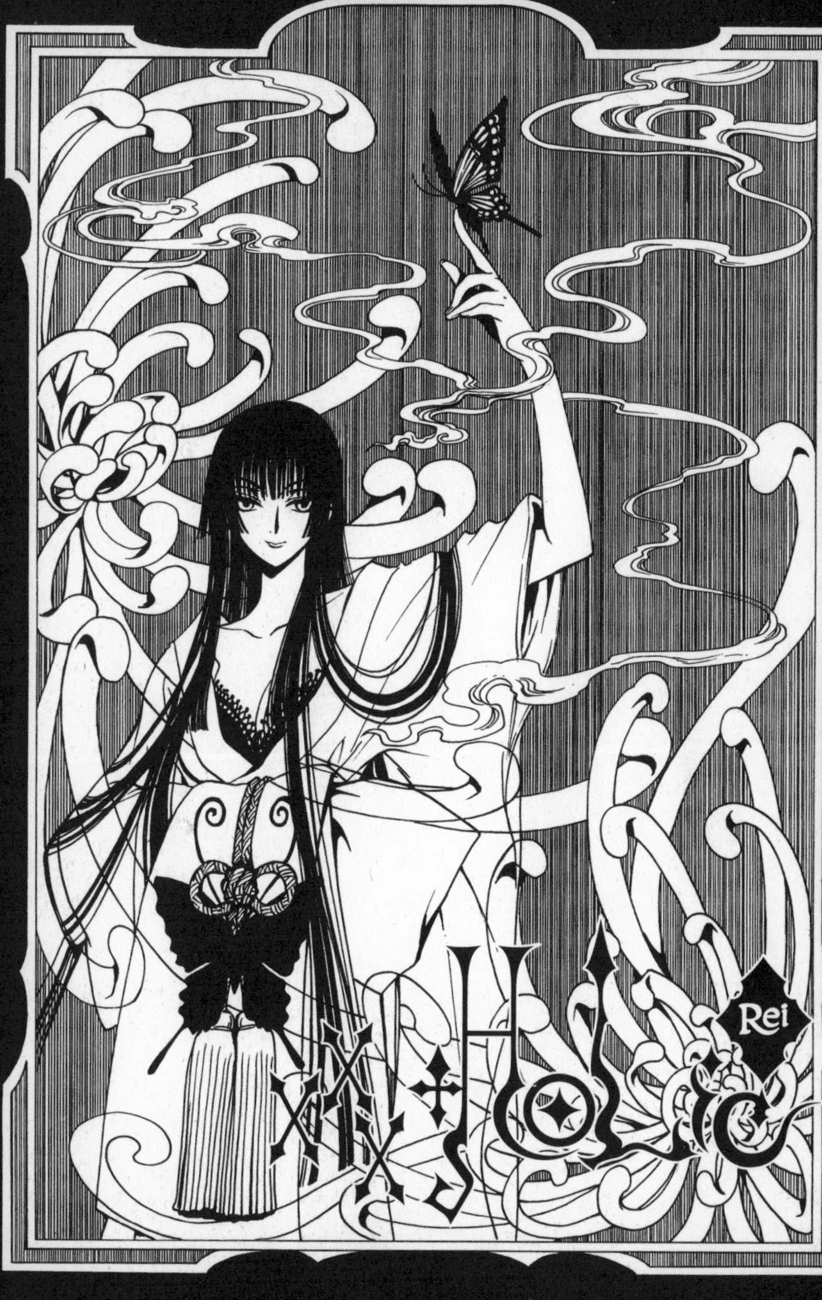
xxxHOLiC
Rei

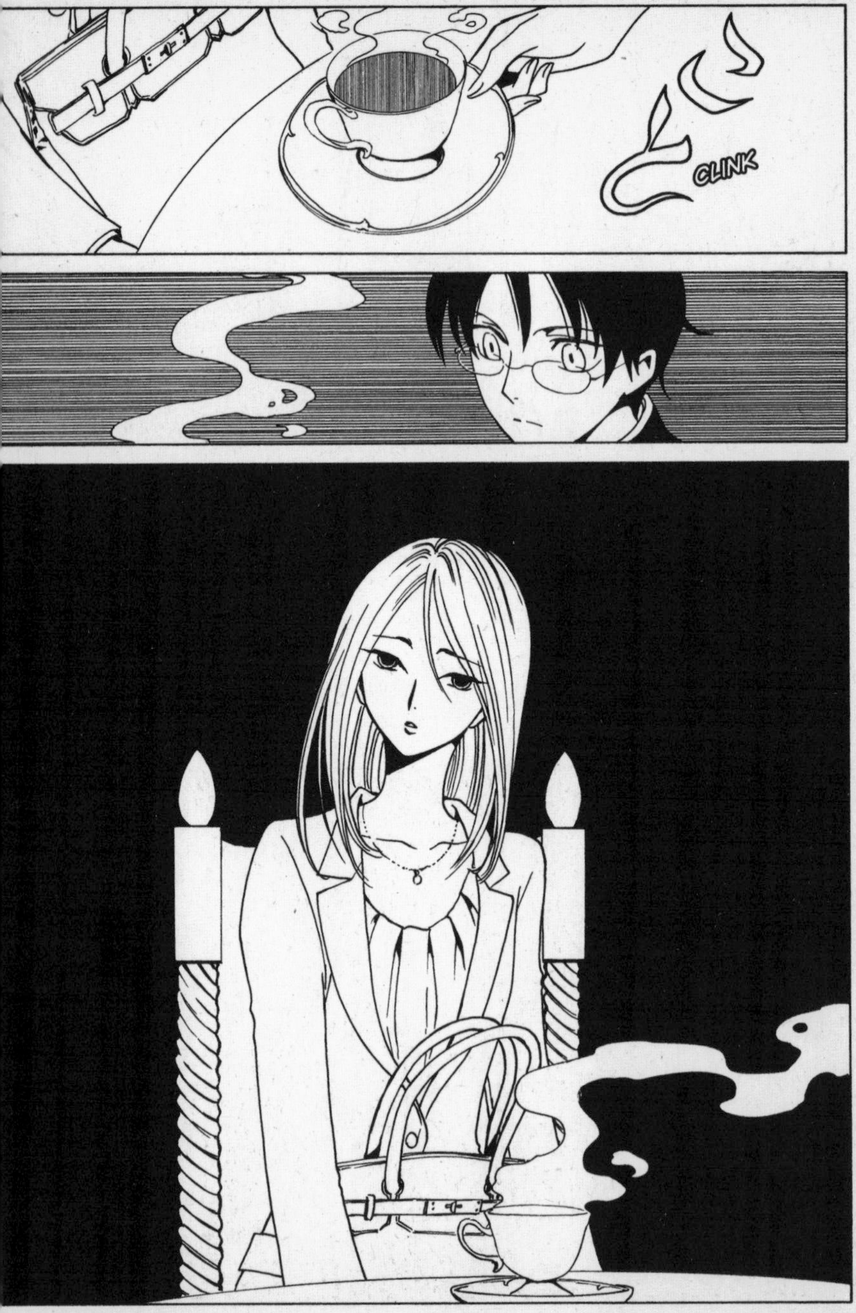
CLINK

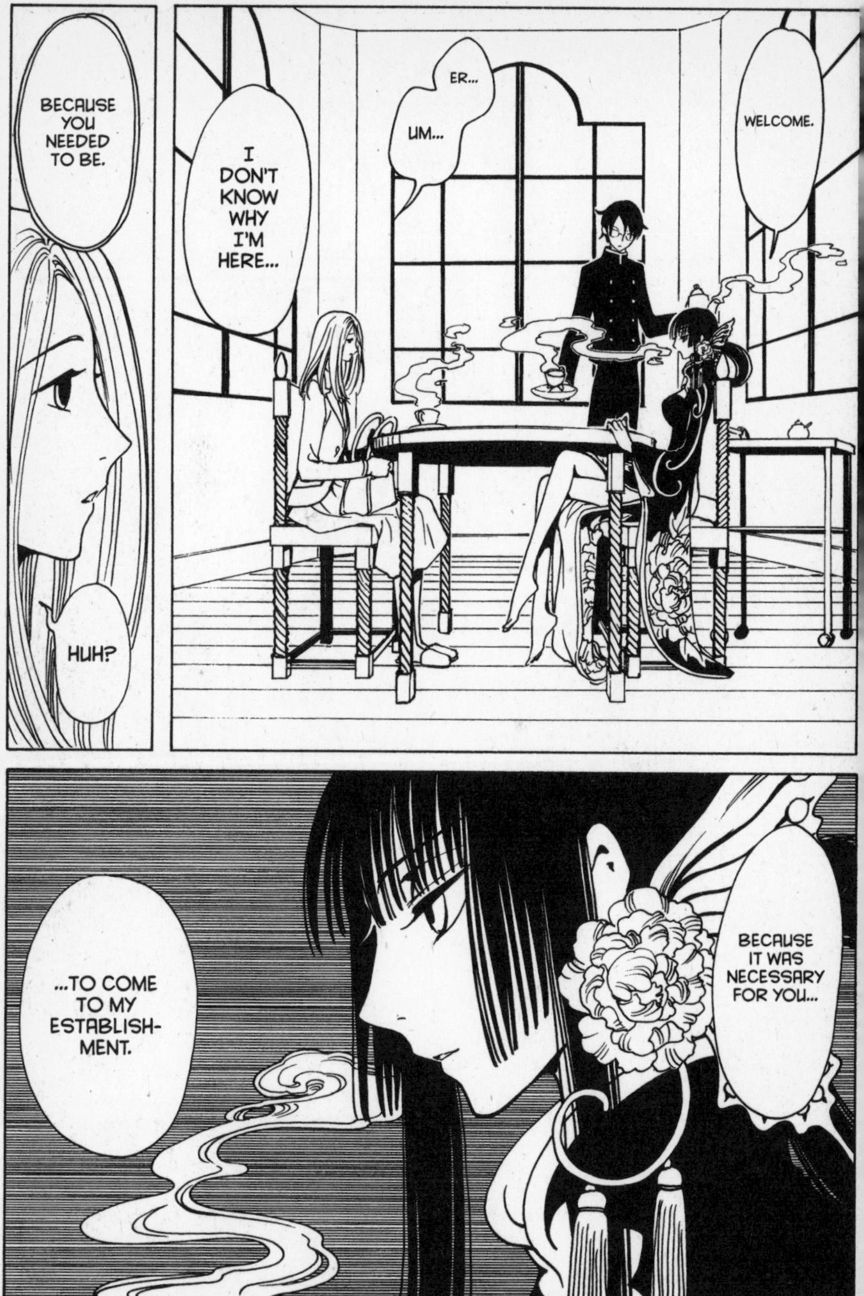
WELCOME.
ER...
UM...
I DON'T KNOW WHY I'M HERE...
BECAUSE YOU NEEDED TO BE.
HUH?
BECAUSE IT WAS NECESSARY FOR YOU...
...TO COME TO MY ESTABLISH-MENT.

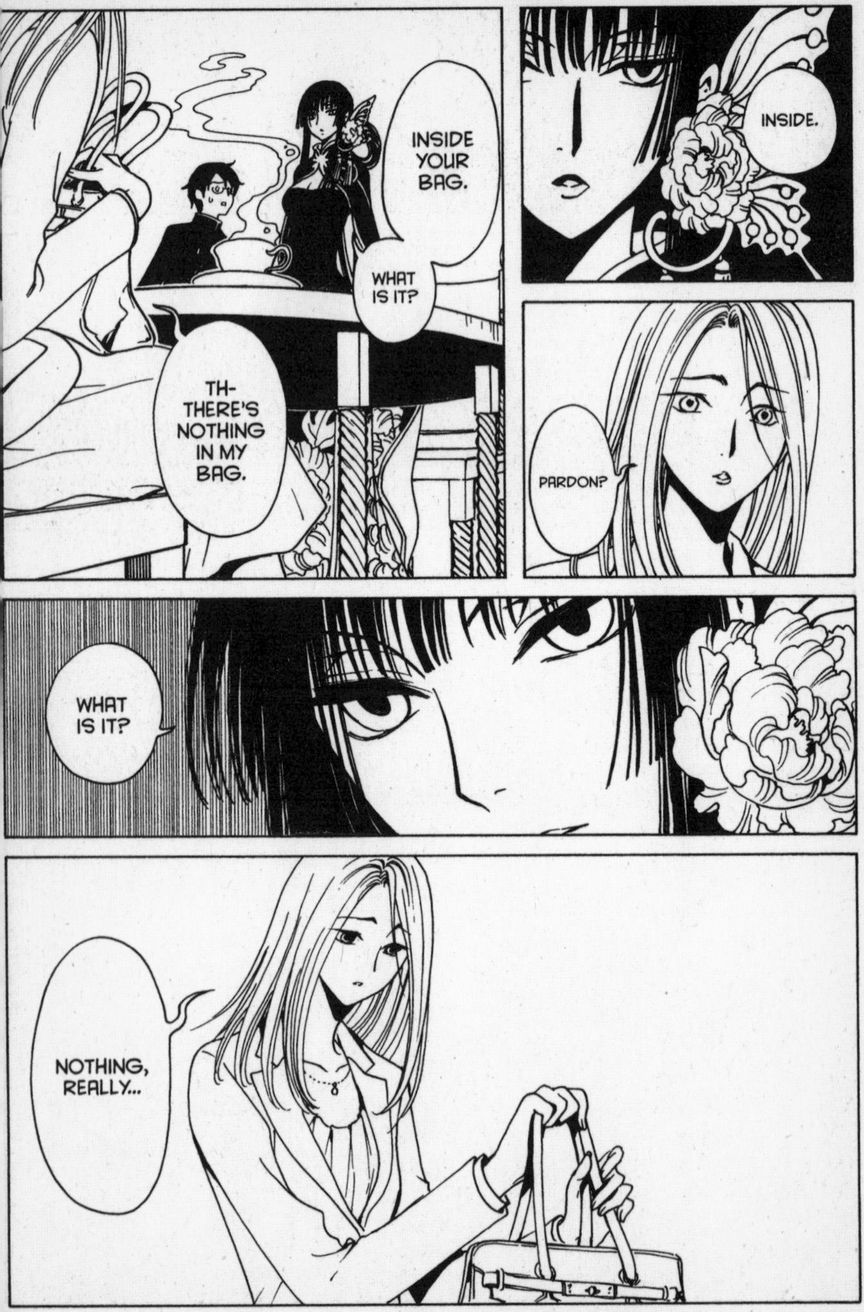

INSIDE.
PARDON?
INSIDE YOUR BAG.
WHAT IS IT?
TH- THERE'S NOTHING IN MY BAG.
WHAT IS IT?
NOTHING, REALLY...

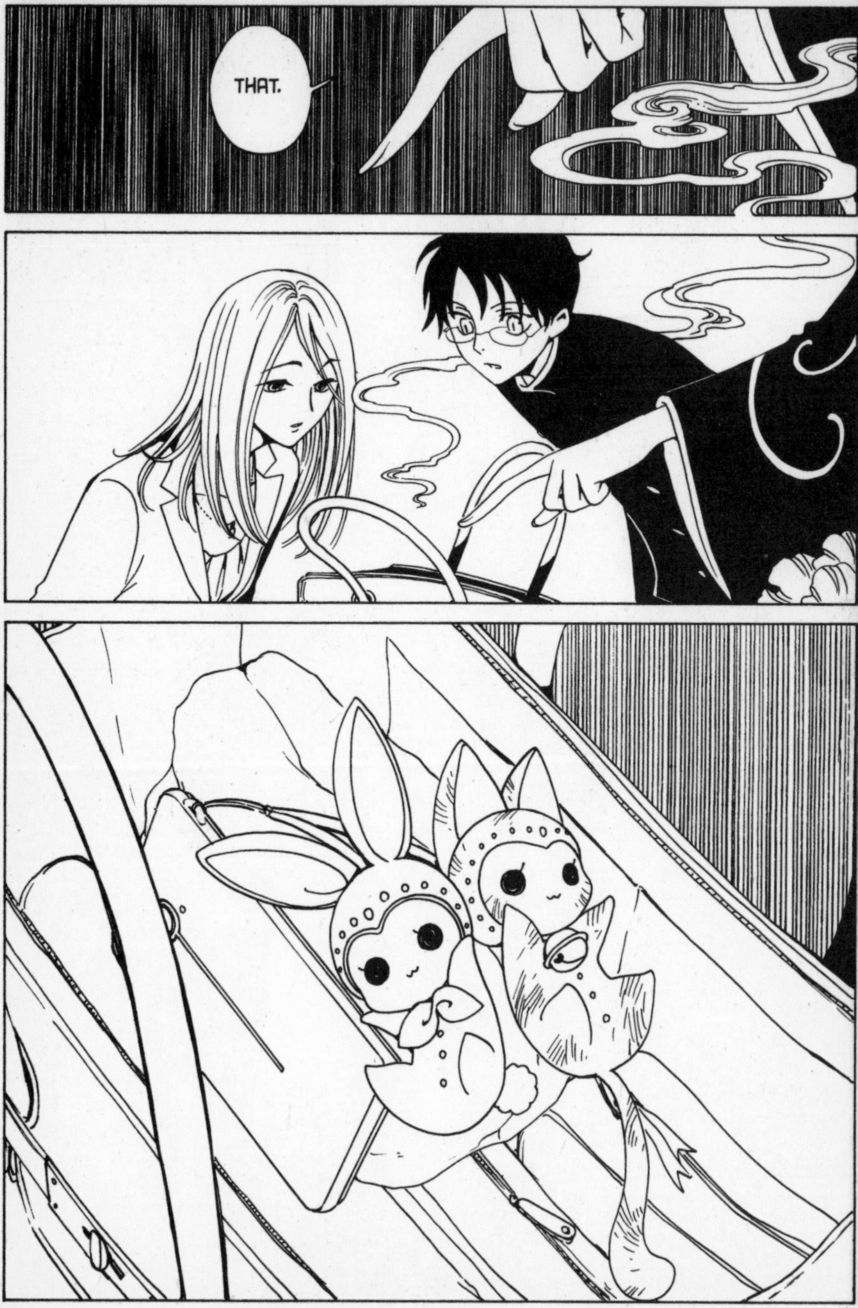
THAT.

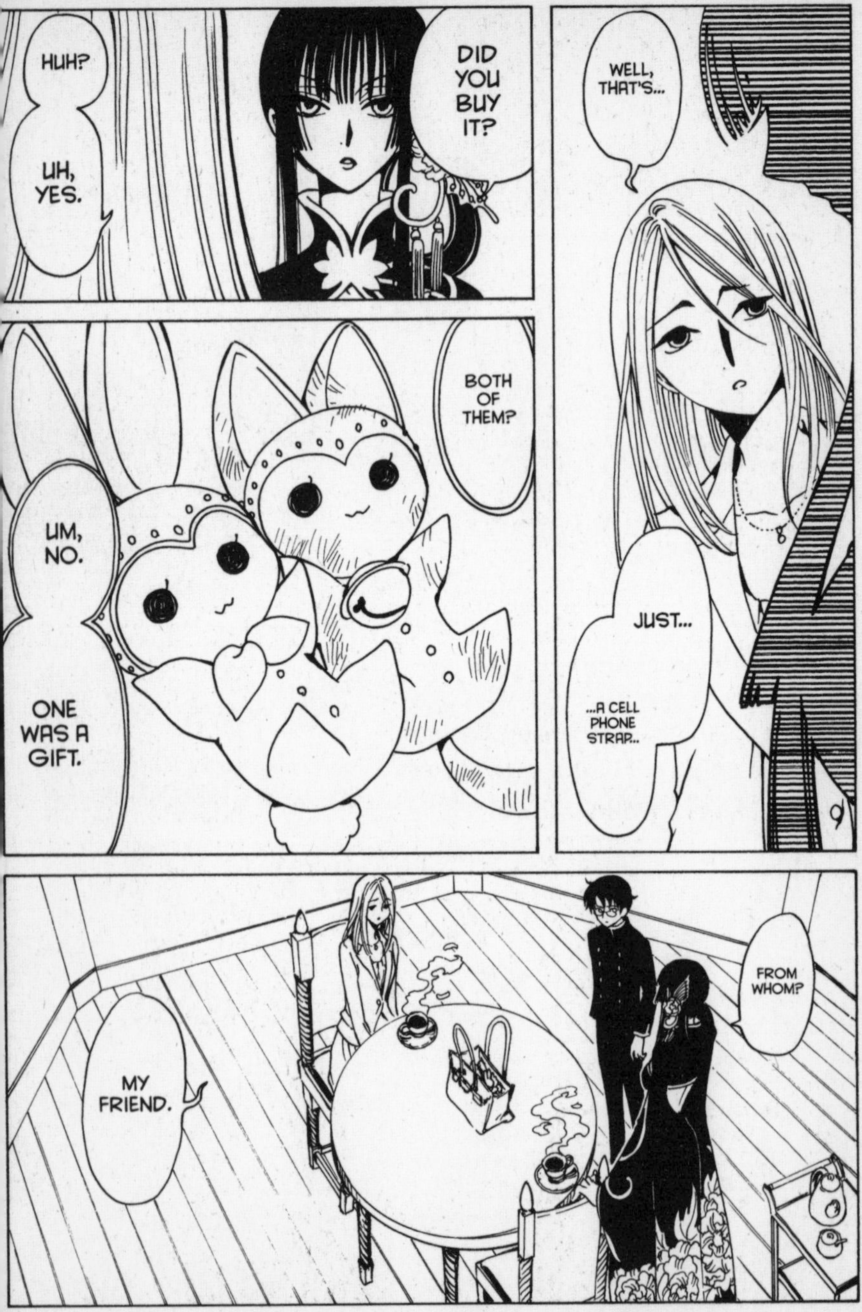
WELL, THAT'S...
JUST...
...A CELL PHONE STRAP...
DID YOU BUY IT?
HUH?
UH, YES.
BOTH OF THEM?
UM, NO.
ONE WAS A GIFT.
FROM WHOM?
MY FRIEND.

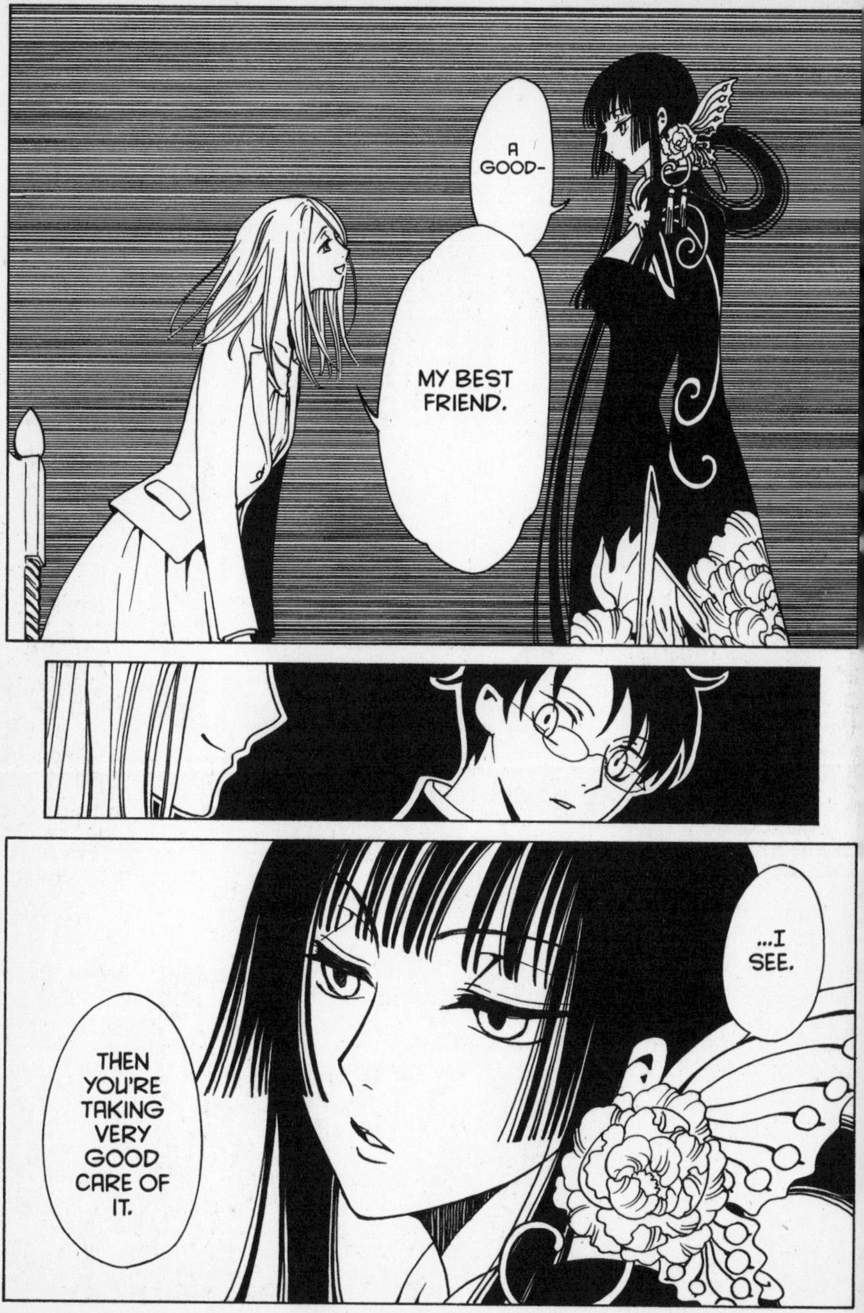
A GOOD-
MY BEST FRIEND.
...I SEE.
THEN YOU'RE TAKING VERY GOOD CARE OF IT.

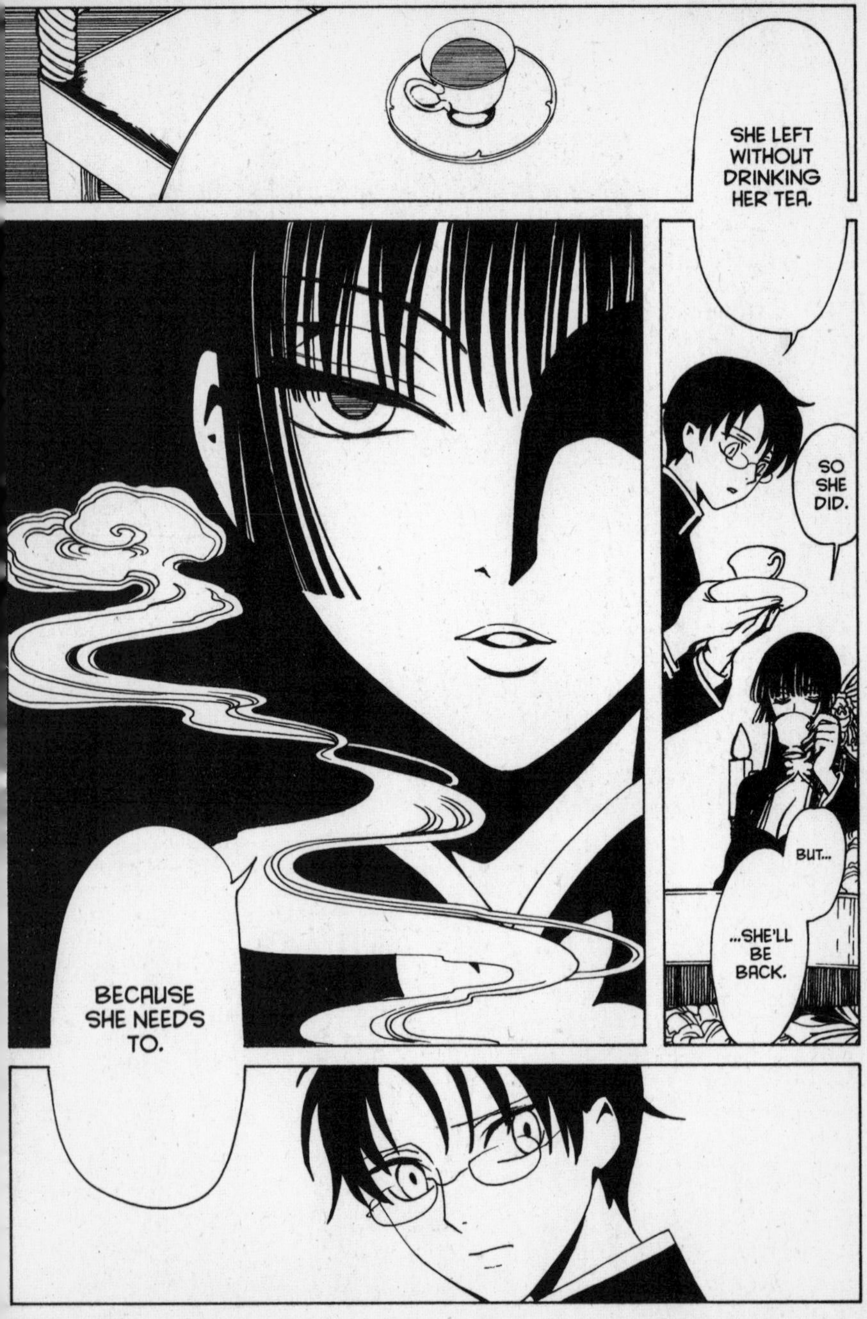
SHE LEFT WITHOUT DRINKING HER TEA.
SO SHE DID.
BUT...
...SHE'LL BE BACK.
BECAUSE SHE NEEDS TO.

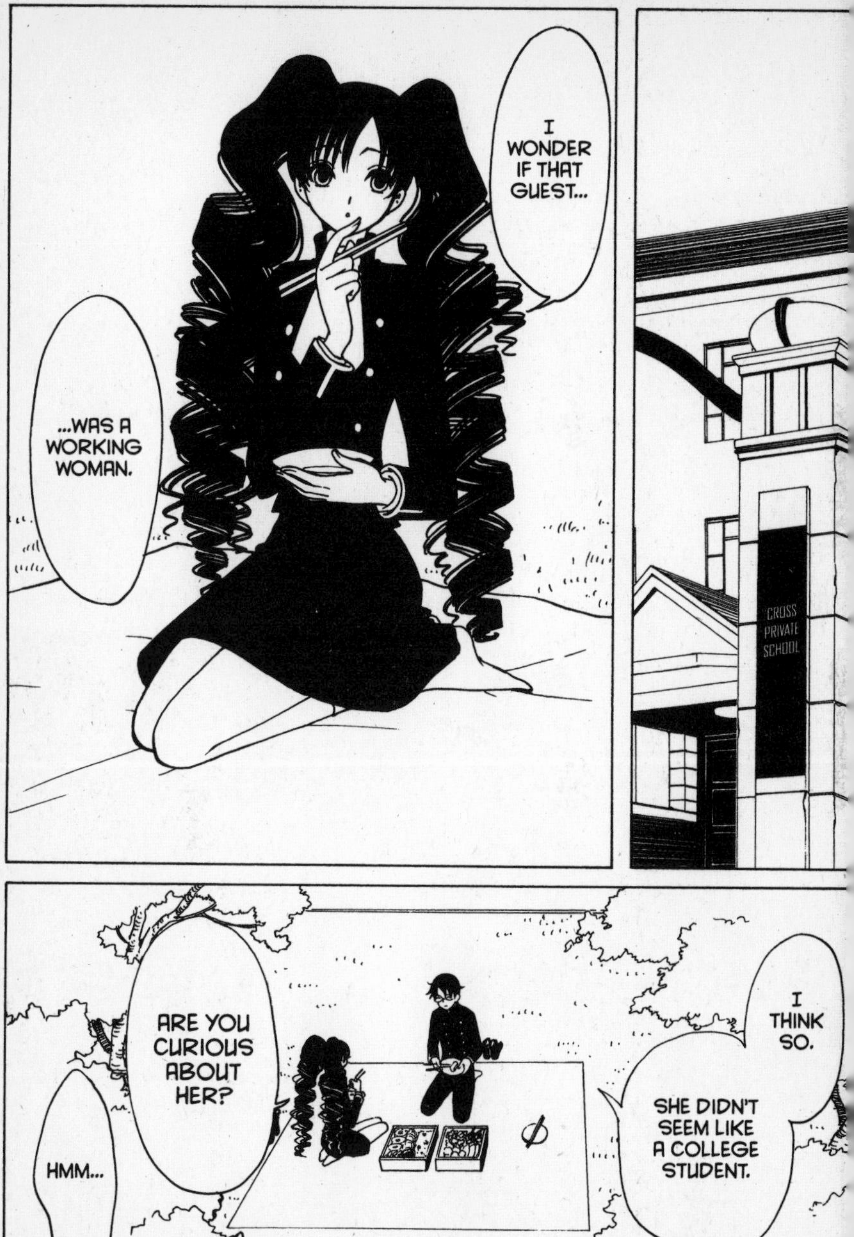
CROSS PRIVATE SCHOOL
I WONDER IF THAT GUEST...
...WAS A WORKING WOMAN.
I THINK SO.
SHE DIDN'T SEEM LIKE A COLLEGE STUDENT.
ARE YOU CURIOUS ABOUT HER?
HMM...

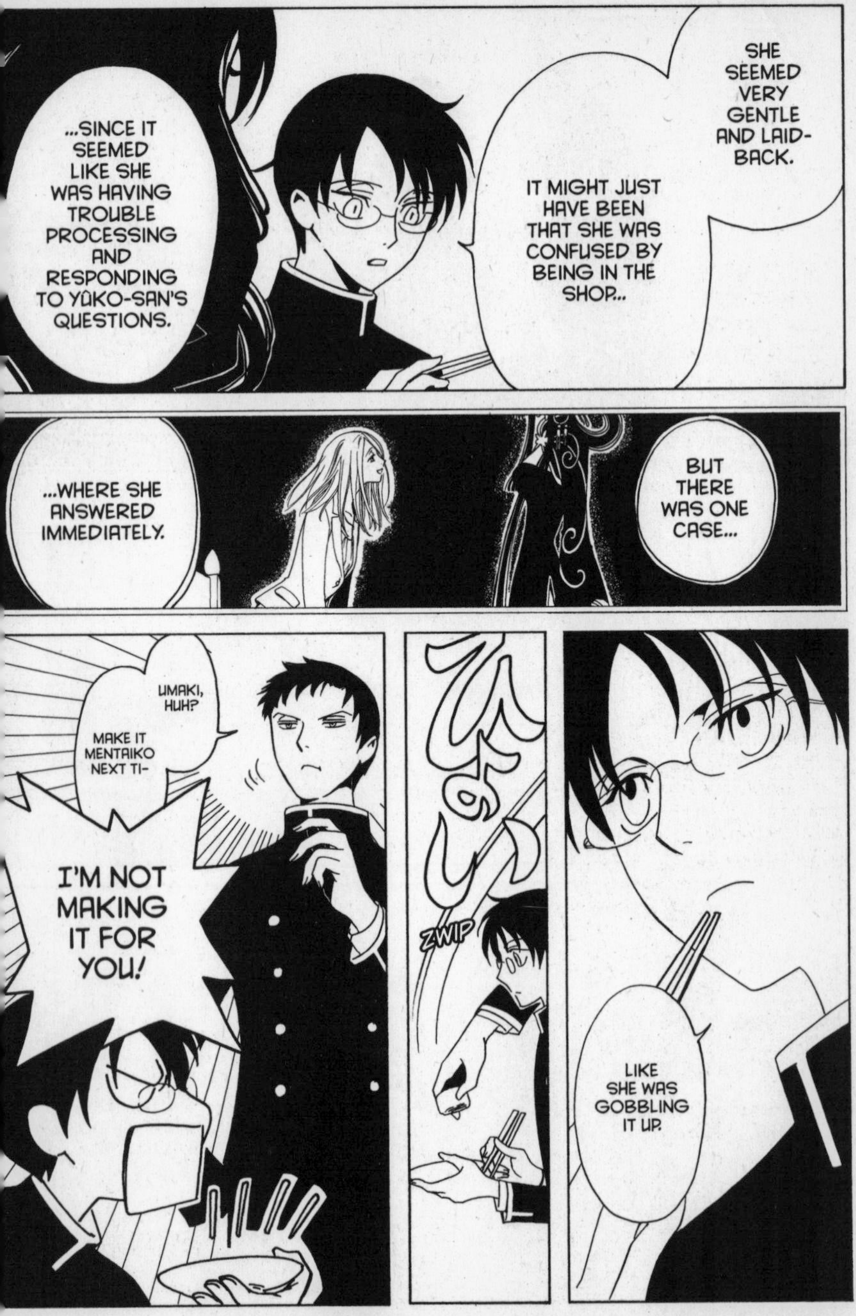
SHE SEEMED VERY GENTLE AND LAID-BACK.
IT MIGHT JUST HAVE BEEN THAT SHE WAS CONFUSED BY BEING IN THE SHOP...
...SINCE IT SEEMED LIKE SHE WAS HAVING TROUBLE PROCESSING AND RESPONDING TO YÛKO-SAN'S QUESTIONS.
BUT THERE WAS ONE CASE...
...WHERE SHE ANSWERED IMMEDIATELY.
LIKE SHE WAS GOBBLING IT UP.
ZWIP
UMAKI, HUH?
MAKE IT MENTAIKO NEXT TI-
I'M NOT MAKING IT FOR YOU!

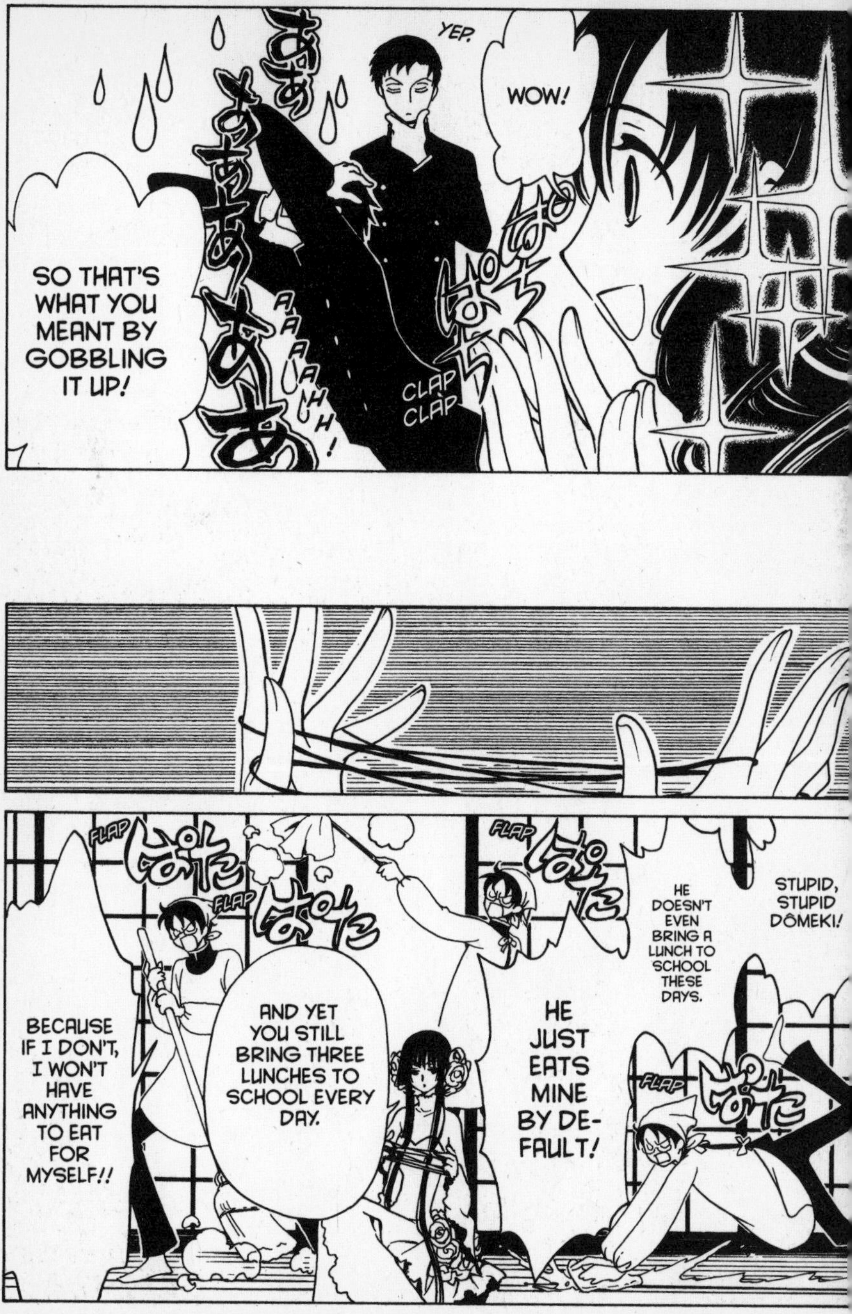

YEP.
WOW!
ぱちぱち
CLAP CLAP
ああああああ
AAAAAHH!
SO THAT'S WHAT YOU MEANT BY GOBBLING IT UP!
STUPID, STUPID DÔMEKI!
FLAP
ぱた
HE DOESN'T EVEN BRING A LUNCH TO SCHOOL THESE DAYS.
HE JUST EATS MINE BY DE-FAULT!
FLAP
ぱた
AND YET YOU STILL BRING THREE LUNCHES TO SCHOOL EVERY DAY.
FLAP
ぱた
FLAP
ぱた
BECAUSE IF I DON'T, I WON'T HAVE ANYTHING TO EAT FOR MYSELF!!

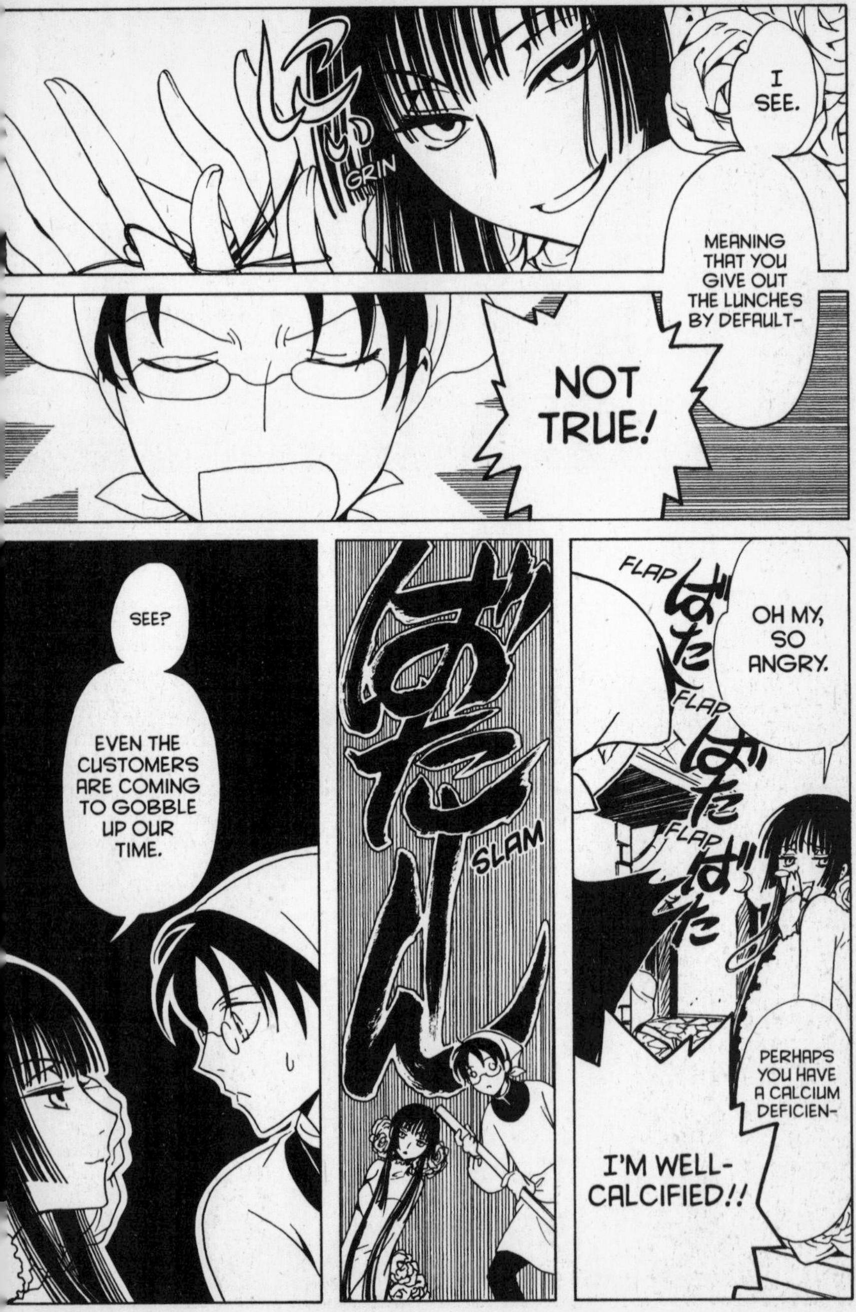
GRIN
I SEE.
MEANING THAT YOU GIVE OUT THE LUNCHES BY DEFAULT-
NOT TRUE!
FLAP
FLAP
FLAP
OH MY, SO ANGRY.
PERHAPS YOU HAVE A CALCIUM DEFICIEN-
I'M WELL-CALCIFIED!!
SLAM
SEE?
EVEN THE CUSTOMERS ARE COMING TO GOBBLE UP OUR TIME.

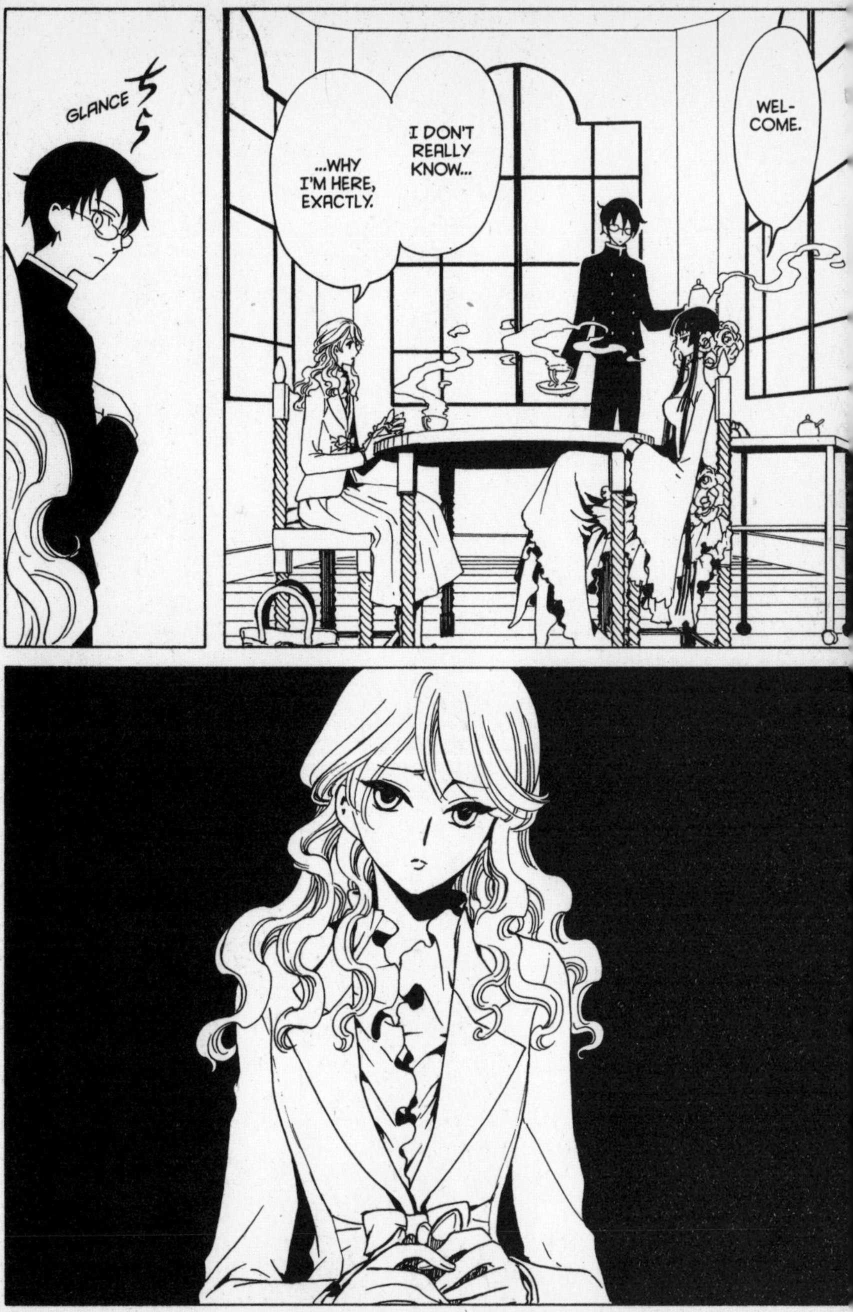
WEL-
COME.
I DON'T REALLY KNOW...
...WHY I'M HERE, EXACTLY.
ちら
GLANCE

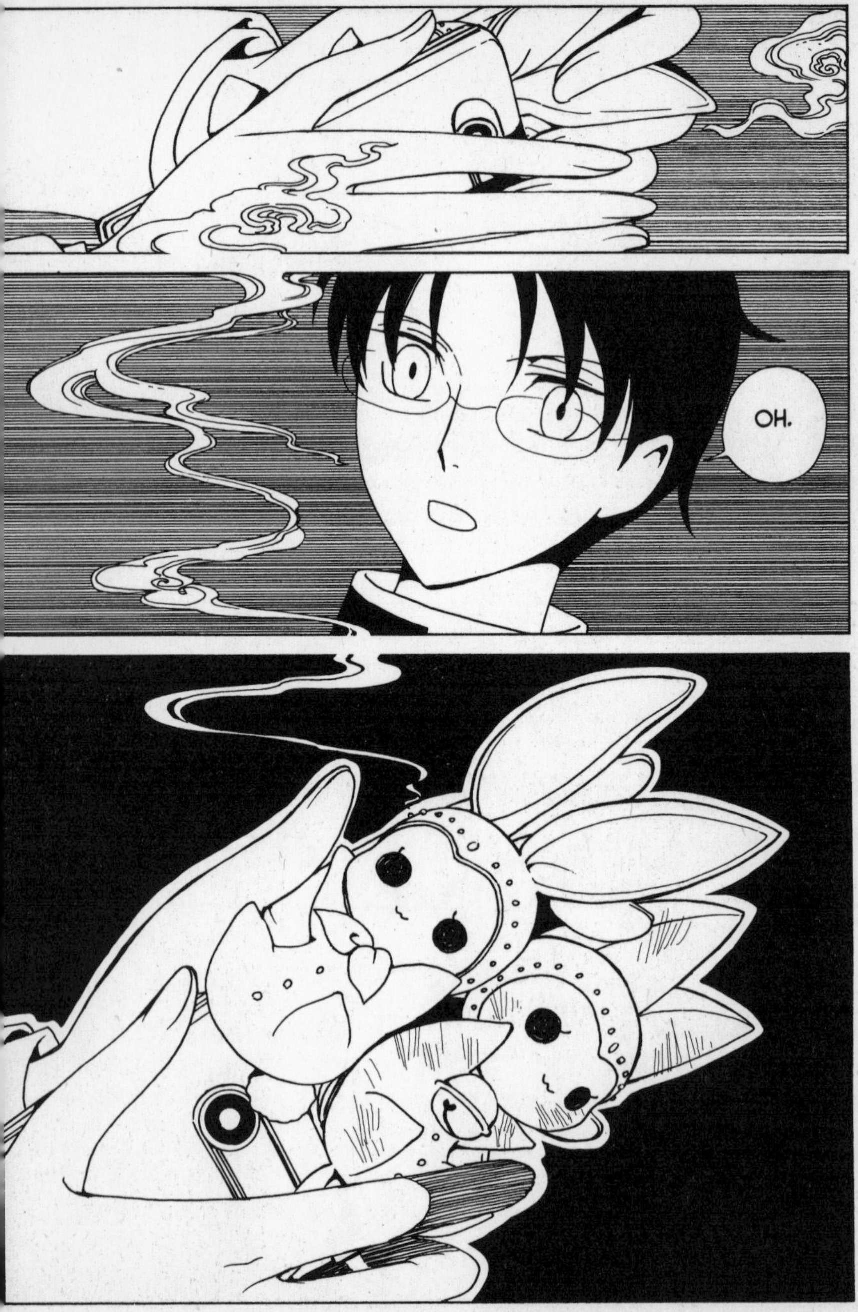
OH.

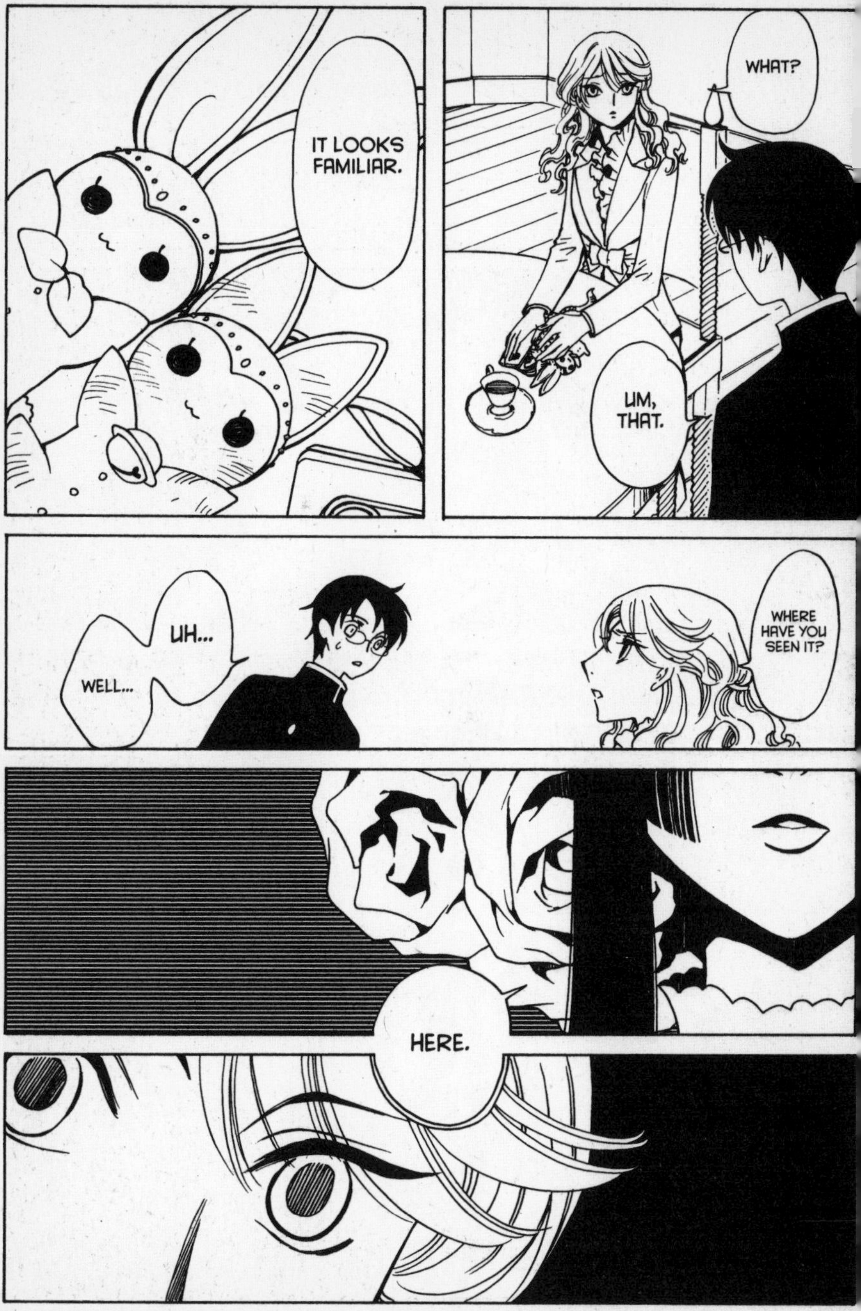
WHAT?
UM, THAT.
IT LOOKS FAMILIAR.
WHERE HAVE YOU SEEN IT?
UH...
WELL...
HERE.

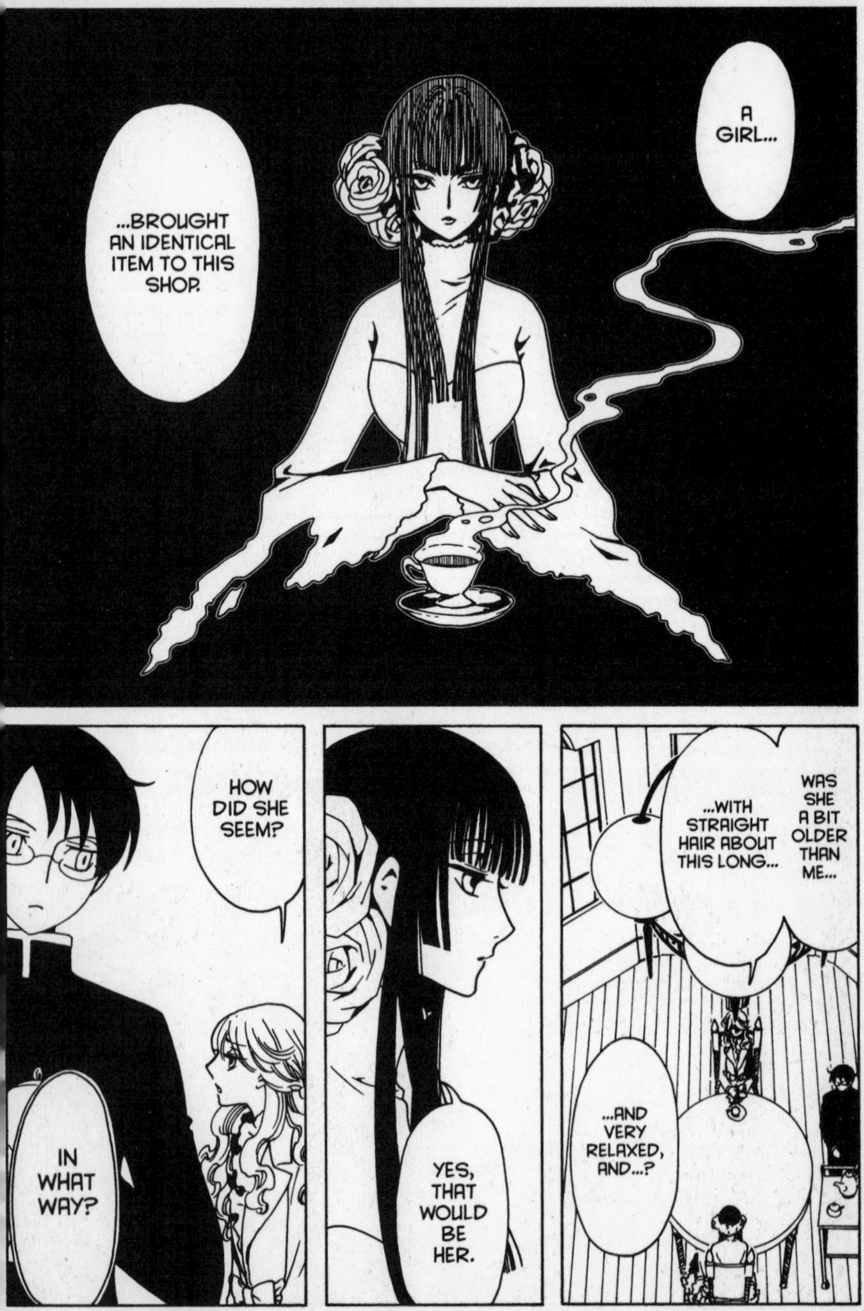
A GIRL...
...BROUGHT AN IDENTICAL ITEM TO THIS SHOP.
WAS SHE A BIT OLDER THAN ME...
...WITH STRAIGHT HAIR ABOUT THIS LONG...
...AND VERY RELAXED, AND...?
YES, THAT WOULD BE HER.
HOW DID SHE SEEM?
IN WHAT WAY?

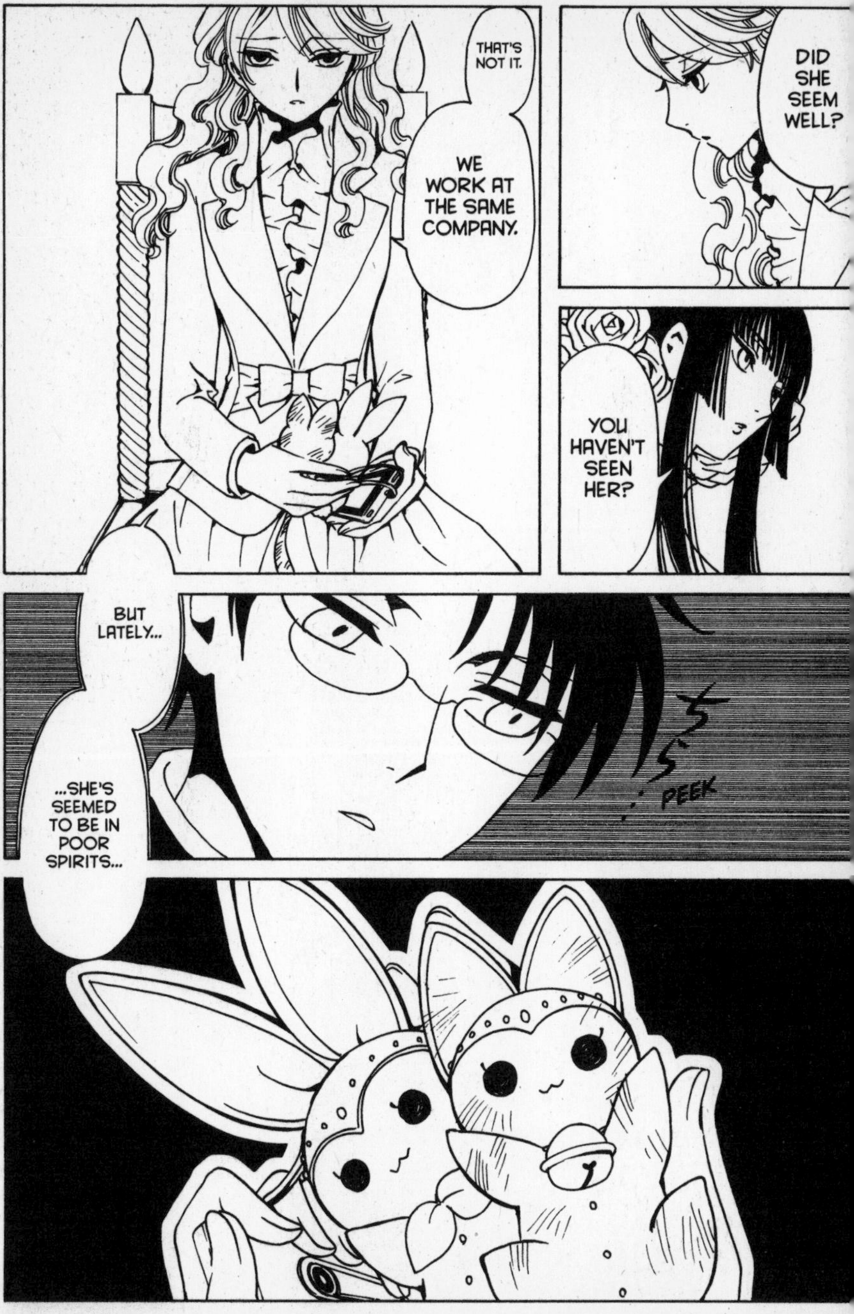
DID SHE SEEM WELL?
YOU HAVEN'T SEEN HER?
THAT'S NOT IT.
WE WORK AT THE SAME COMPANY.
BUT LATELY...
...SHE'S SEEMED TO BE IN POOR SPIRITS...
PEEK

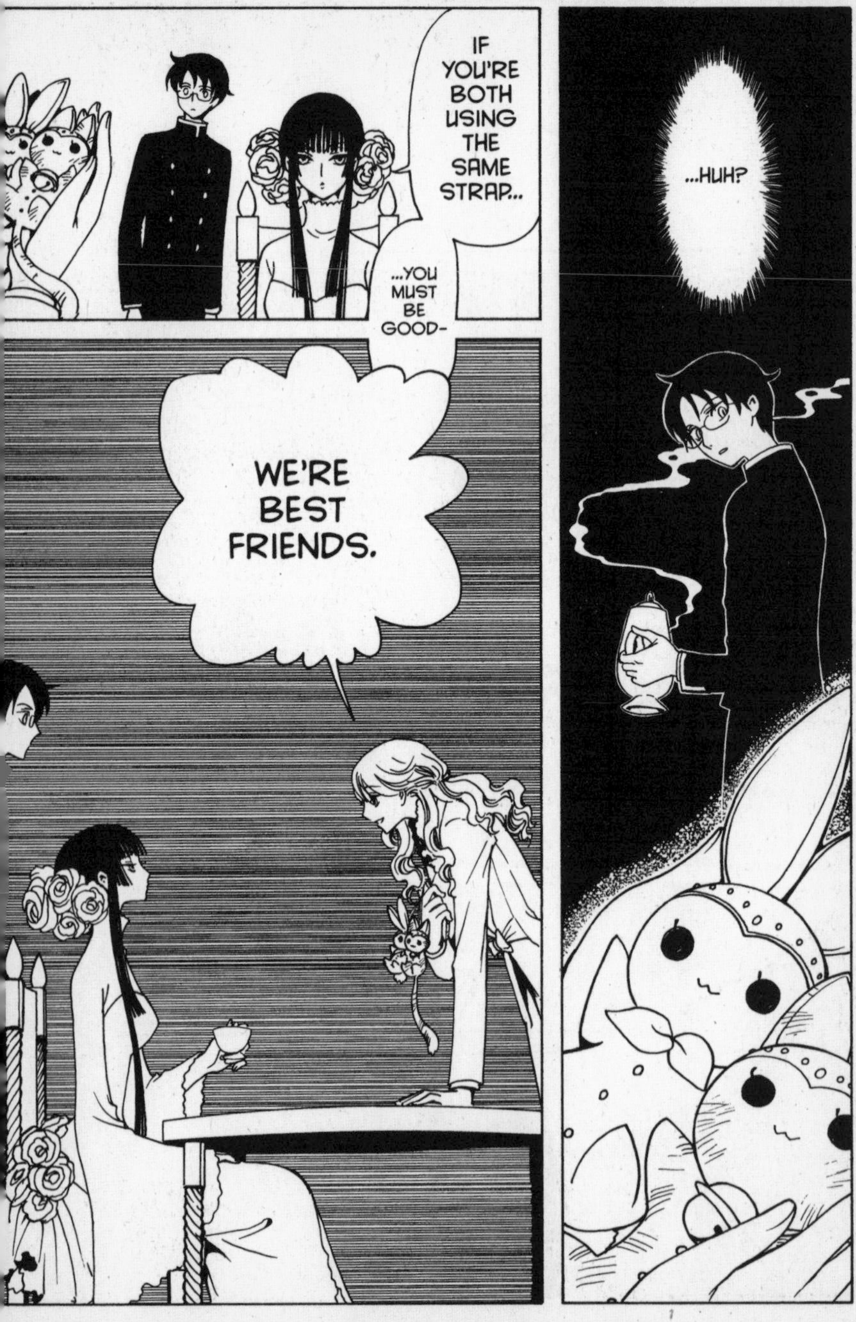
...HUH?
IF YOU'RE BOTH USING THE SAME STRAP...
...YOU MUST BE GOOD-
WE'RE BEST FRIENDS.

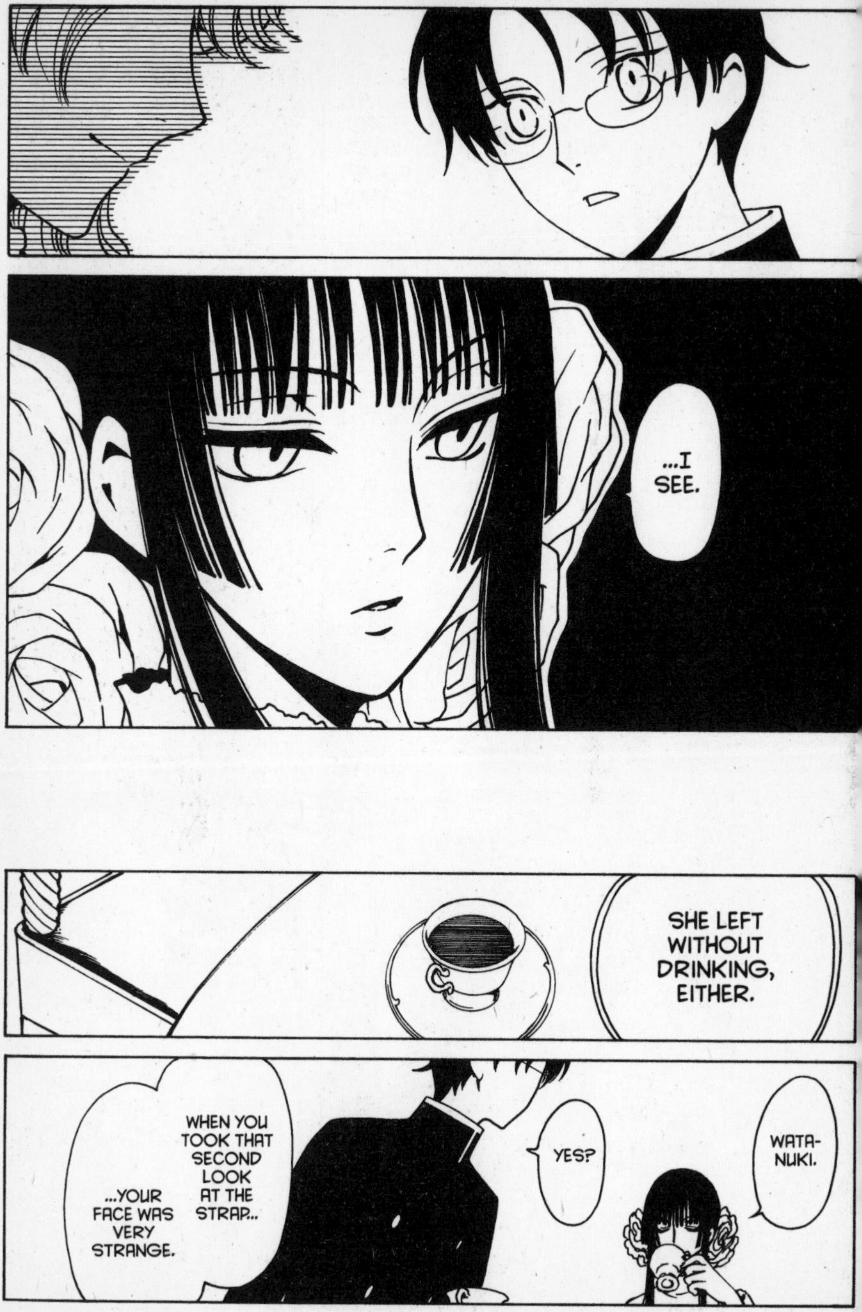
...I SEE.
SHE LEFT WITHOUT DRINKING, EITHER.
WATA-NUKI.
YES?
WHEN YOU TOOK THAT SECOND LOOK AT THE STRAP...
...YOUR FACE WAS VERY STRANGE.

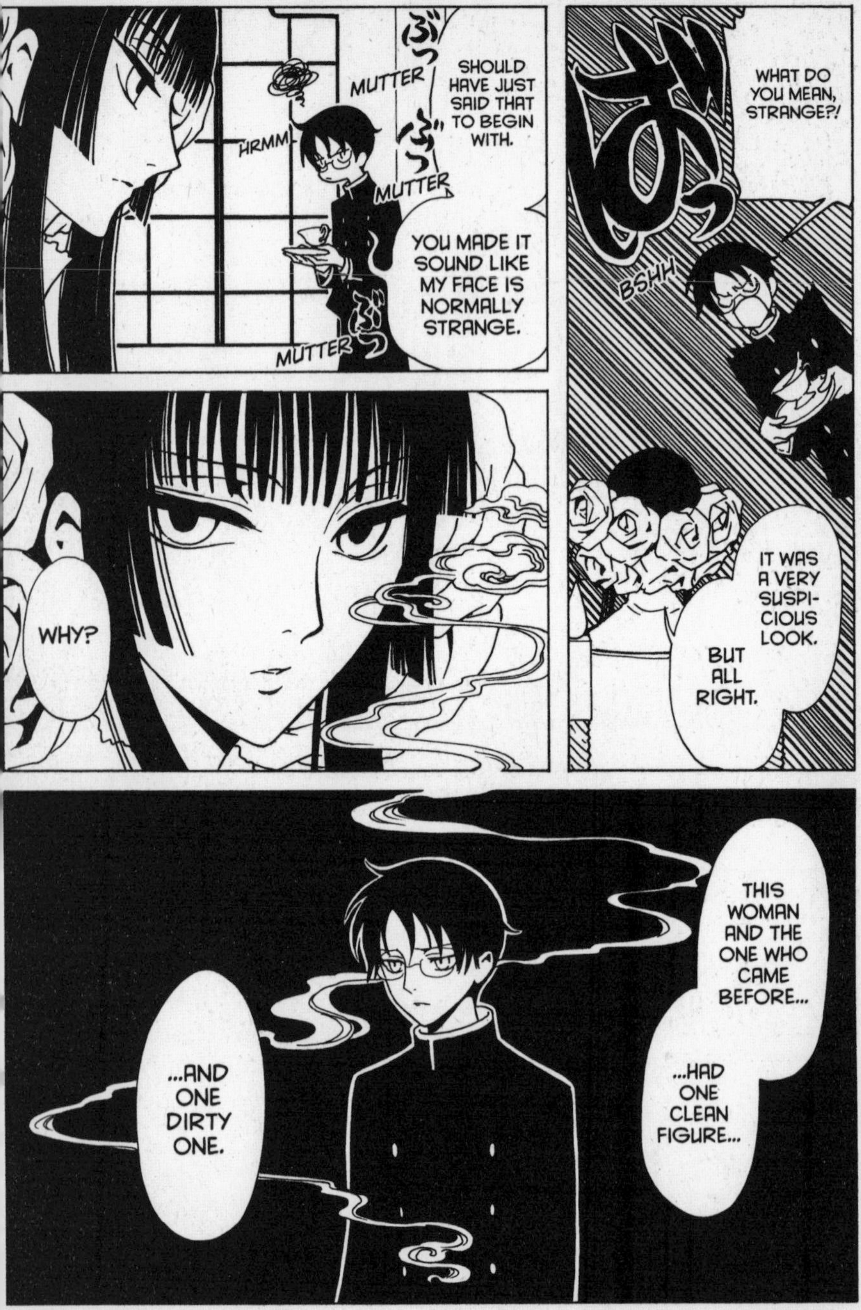
WHAT DO YOU MEAN, STRANGE?!
BSHH
IT WAS A VERY SUSPICIOUS LOOK.
BUT ALL RIGHT.
SHOULD HAVE JUST SAID THAT TO BEGIN WITH.
MUTTER
HRMM
MUTTER
YOU MADE IT SOUND LIKE MY FACE IS NORMALLY STRANGE.
MUTTER
WHY?
THIS WOMAN AND THE ONE WHO CAME BEFORE...
...HAD ONE CLEAN FIGURE...
...AND ONE DIRTY ONE.

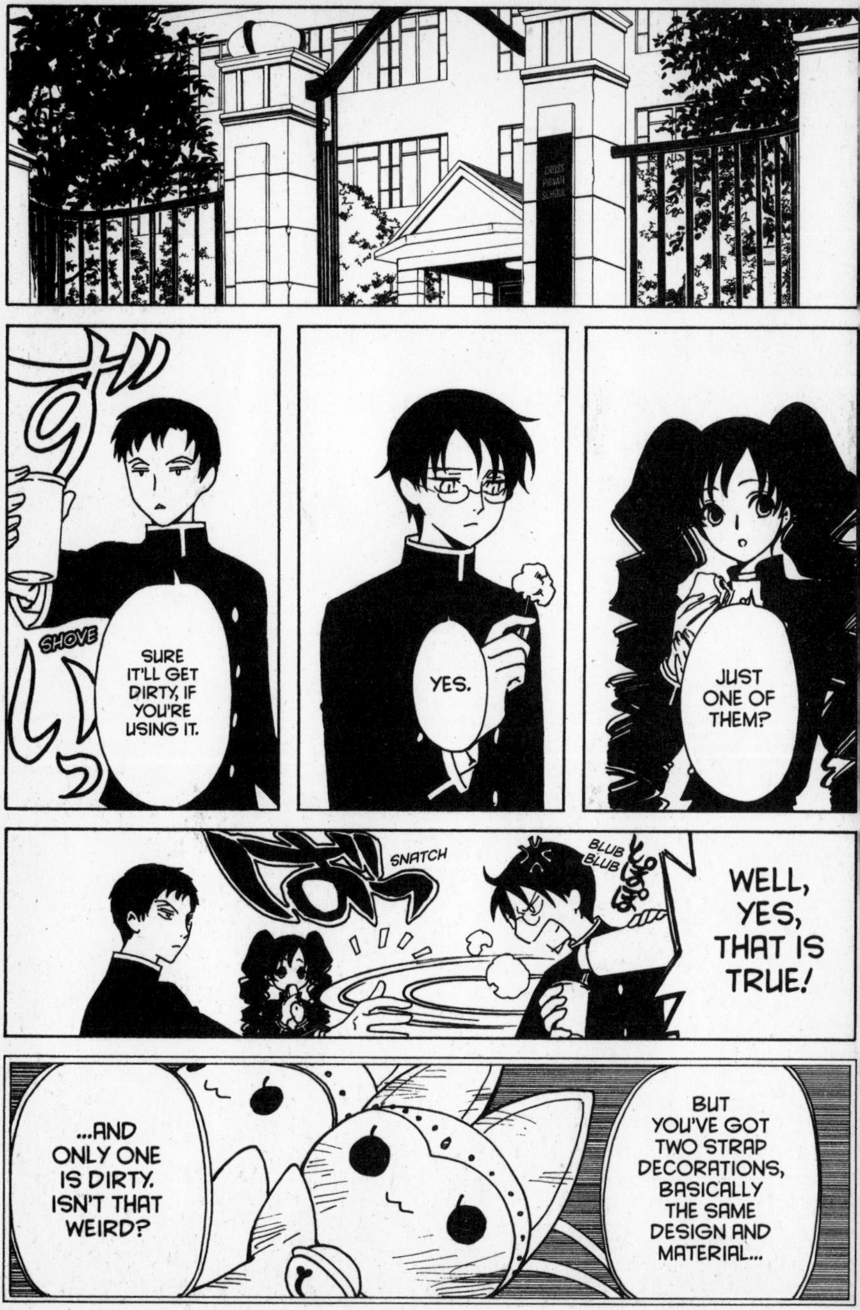
CROSS PRIVATE SCHOOL
JUST ONE OF THEM?
YES.
SURE IT'LL GET DIRTY, IF YOU'RE USING IT.
SHOVE
WELL, YES, THAT IS TRUE!
BLUB BLUB
SNATCH
BUT YOU'VE GOT TWO STRAP DECORATIONS, BASICALLY THE SAME DESIGN AND MATERIAL...
...AND ONLY ONE IS DIRTY. ISN'T THAT WEIRD?

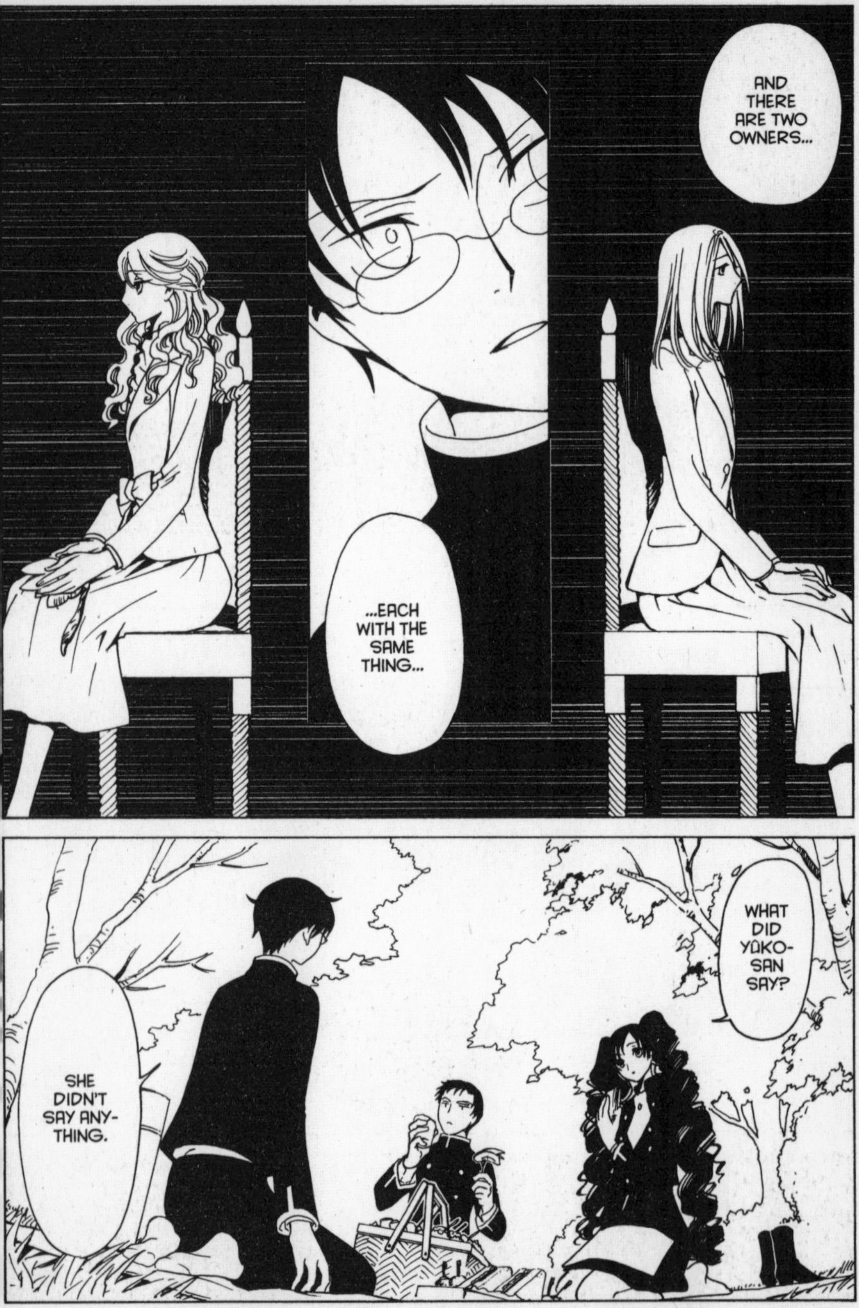
AND THERE ARE TWO OWNERS...
...EACH WITH THE SAME THING...
WHAT DID YŪKO-SAN SAY?
SHE DIDN'T SAY ANY-THING.

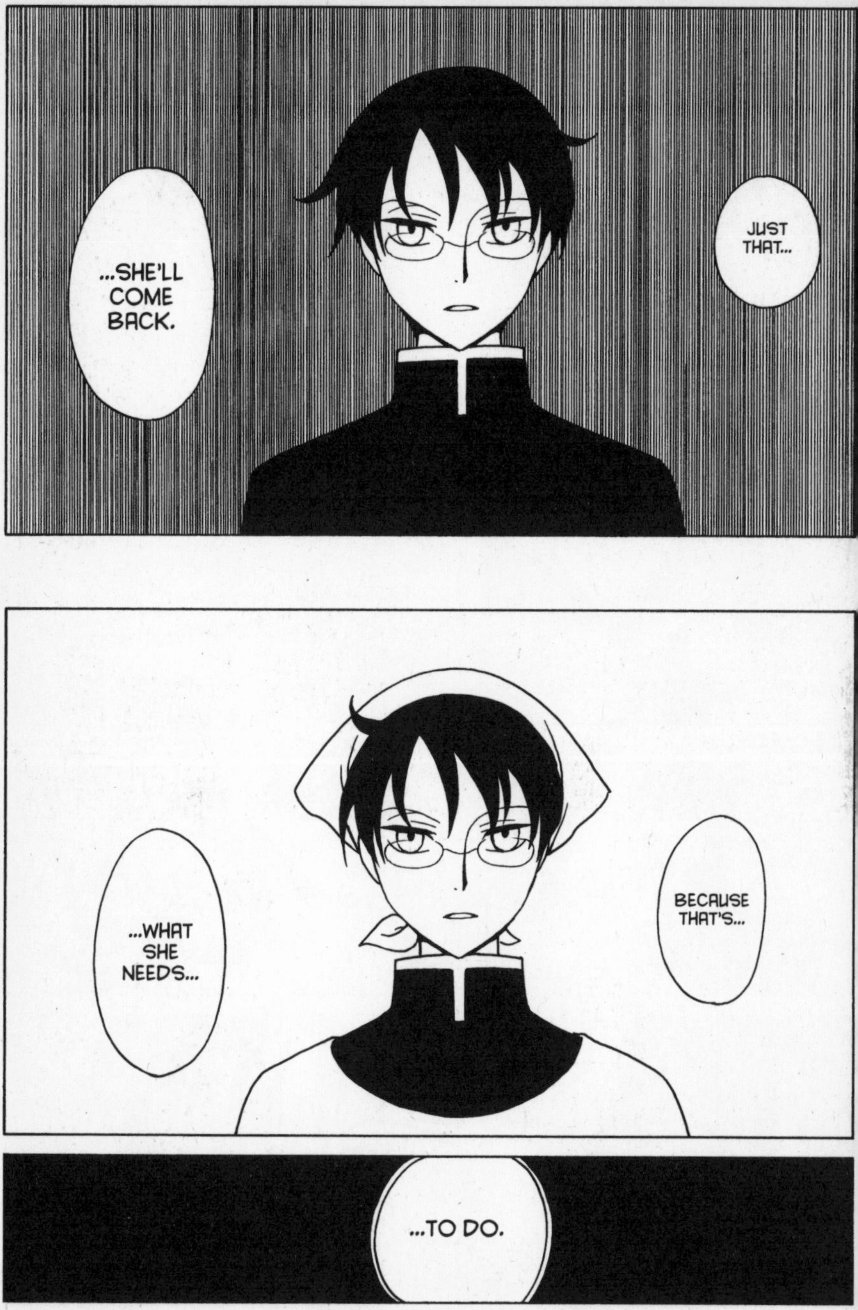
JUST THAT...
...SHE'LL COME BACK.
BECAUSE THAT'S...
...WHAT SHE NEEDS...
...TO DO.

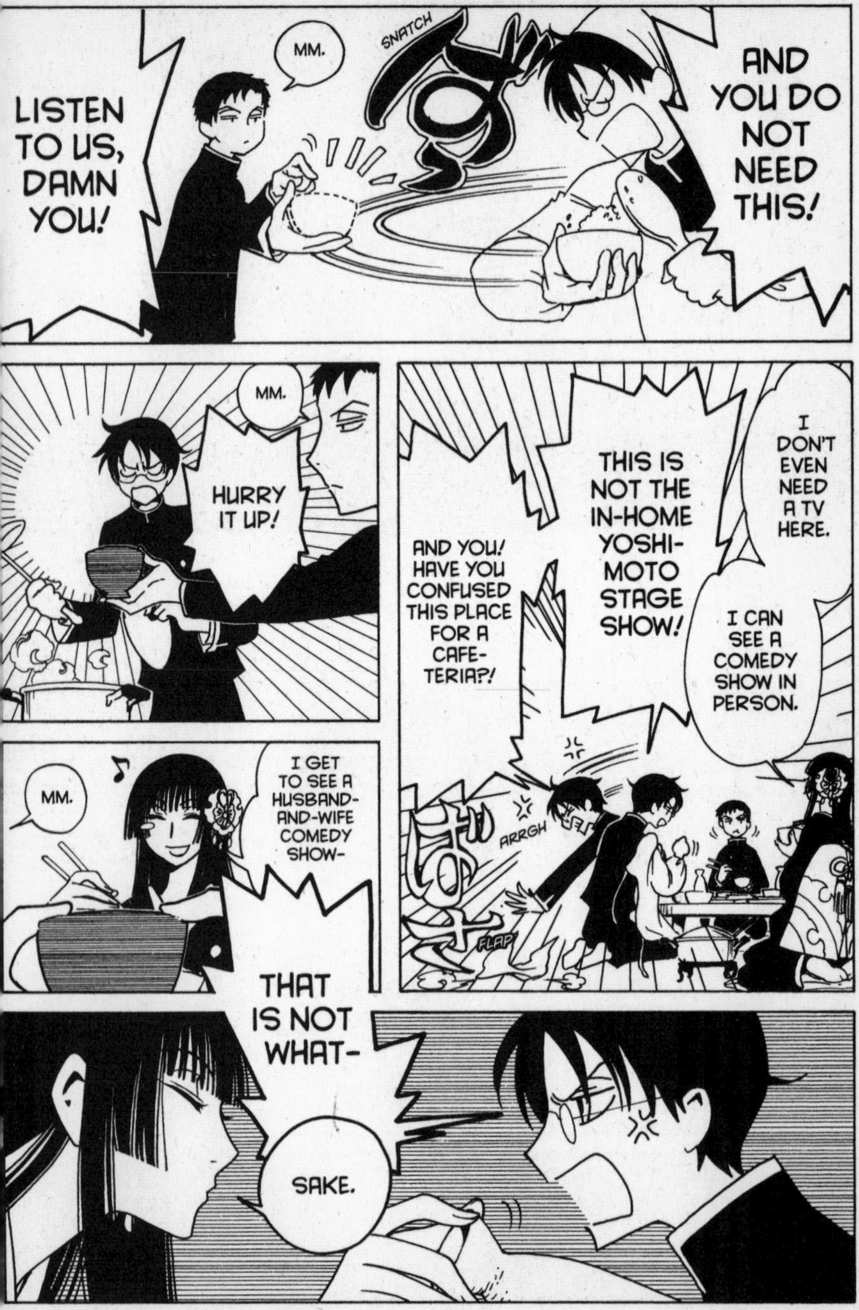
AND YOU DO NOT NEED THIS!
SNATCH
MM.
LISTEN TO US, DAMN YOU!
I DON'T EVEN NEED A TV HERE.
I CAN SEE A COMEDY SHOW IN PERSON.
THIS IS NOT THE IN-HOME YOSHI-MOTO STAGE SHOW!
AND YOU! HAVE YOU CONFUSED THIS PLACE FOR A CAFE-TERIA?!
ARRGH
FLAP
MM.
HURRY IT UP!
I GET TO SEE A HUSBAND-AND-WIFE COMEDY SHOW-
MM.
THAT IS NOT WHAT-
SAKE.

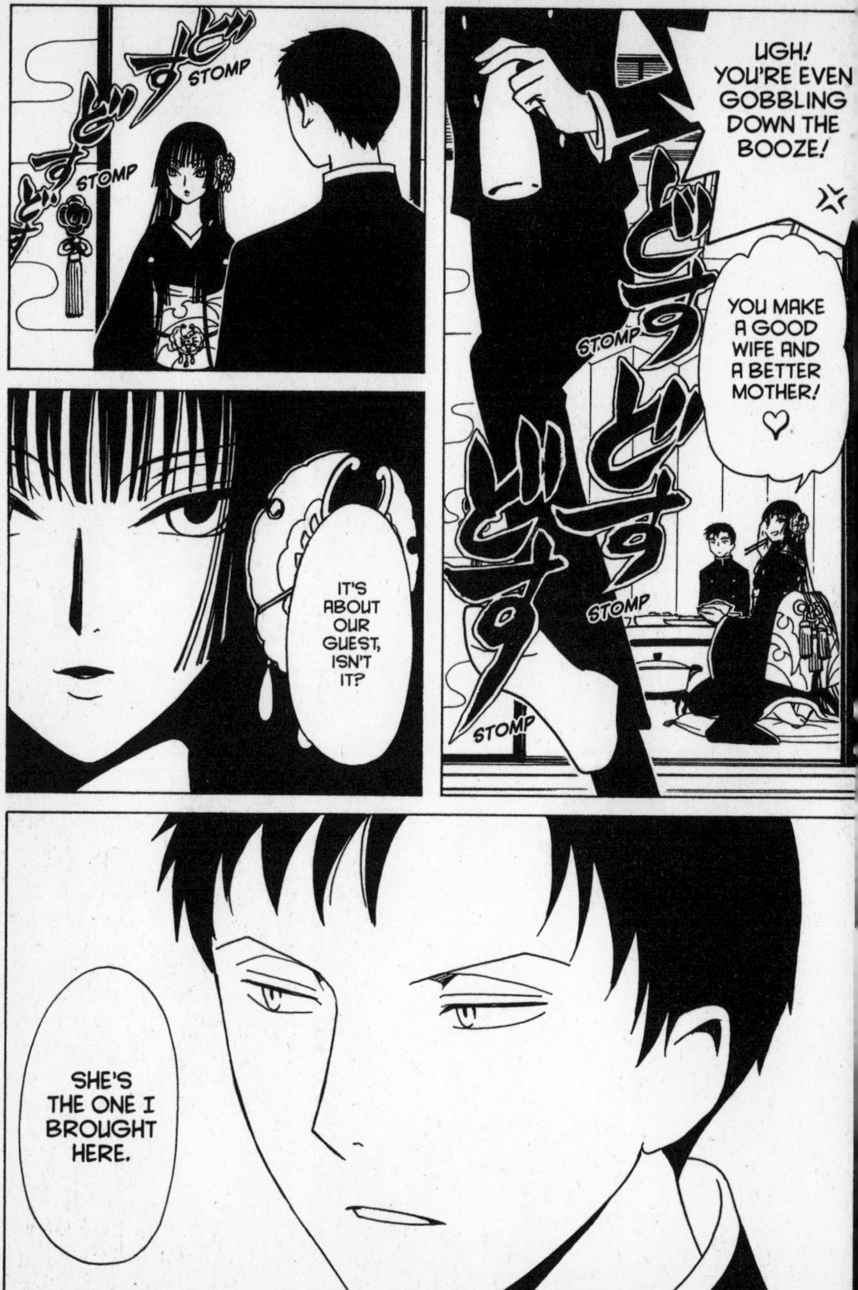
UGH! YOU'RE EVEN GOBBLING DOWN THE BOOZE!
YOU MAKE A GOOD WIFE AND A BETTER MOTHER! ♡
STOMP
STOMP
STOMP
STOMP
STOMP
IT'S ABOUT OUR GUEST, ISN'T IT?
SHE'S THE ONE I BROUGHT HERE.

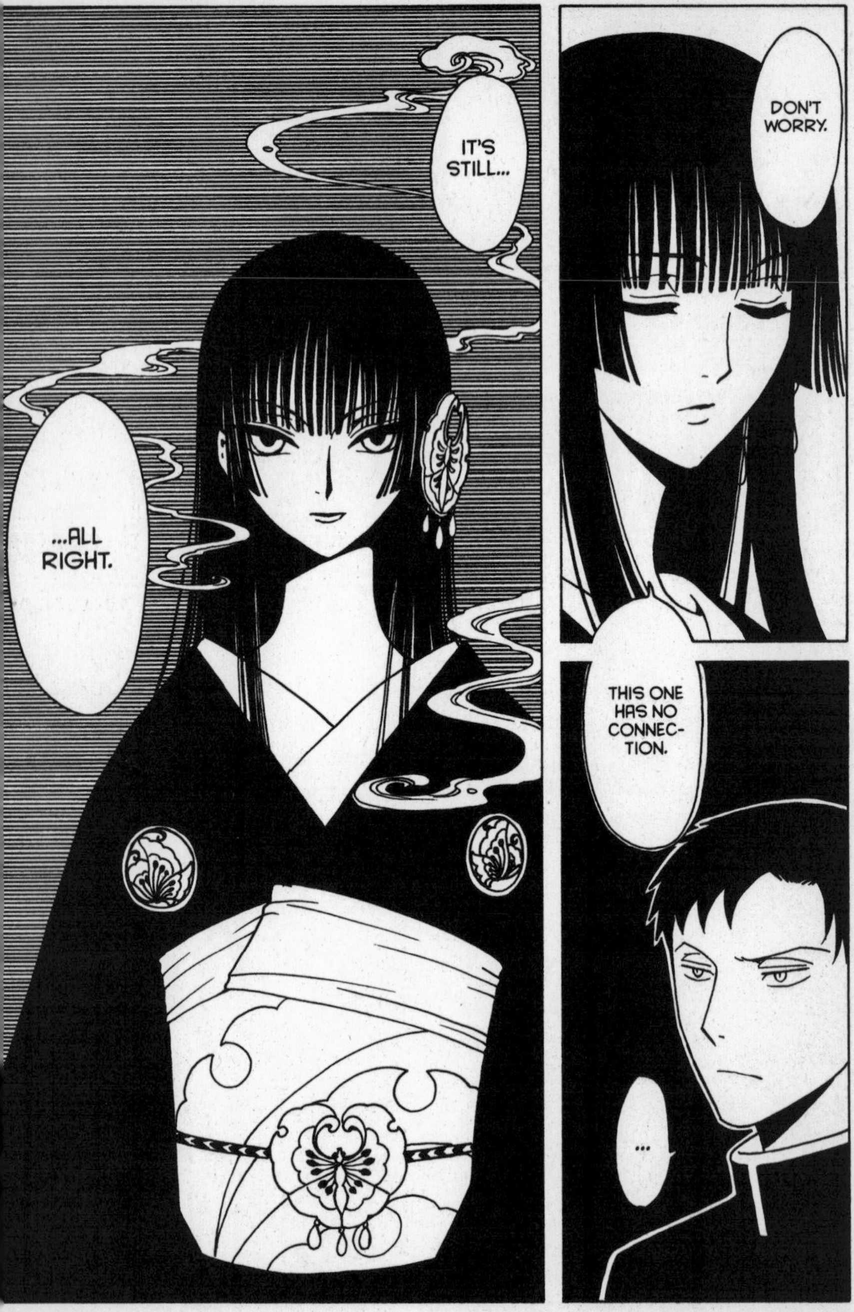
DON'T WORRY.
THIS ONE HAS NO CONNECTION.
...
IT'S STILL...
...ALL RIGHT.

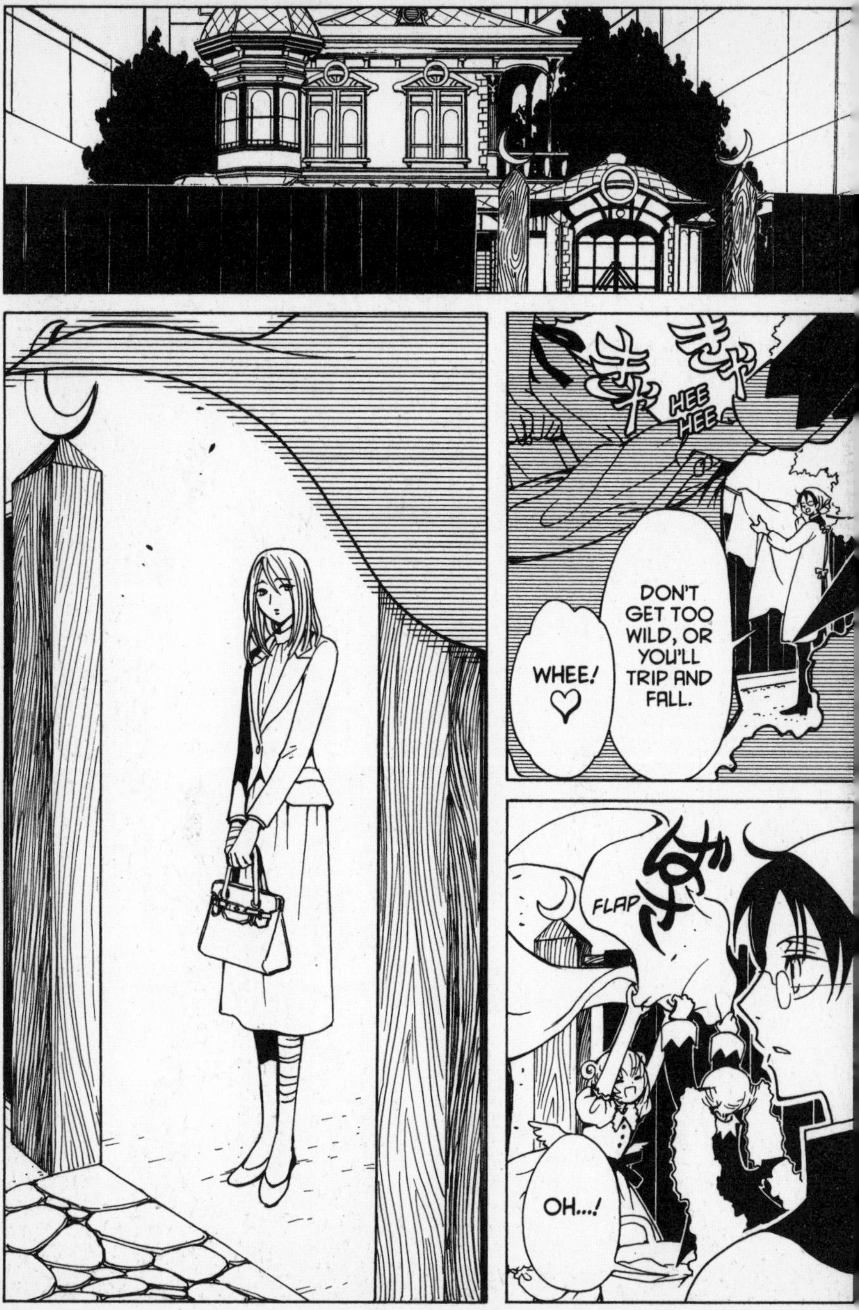
きゃ きゃ
HEE HEE
DON'T GET TOO WILD, OR YOU'LL TRIP AND FALL.
WHEE! ♥
FLAP
OH...!

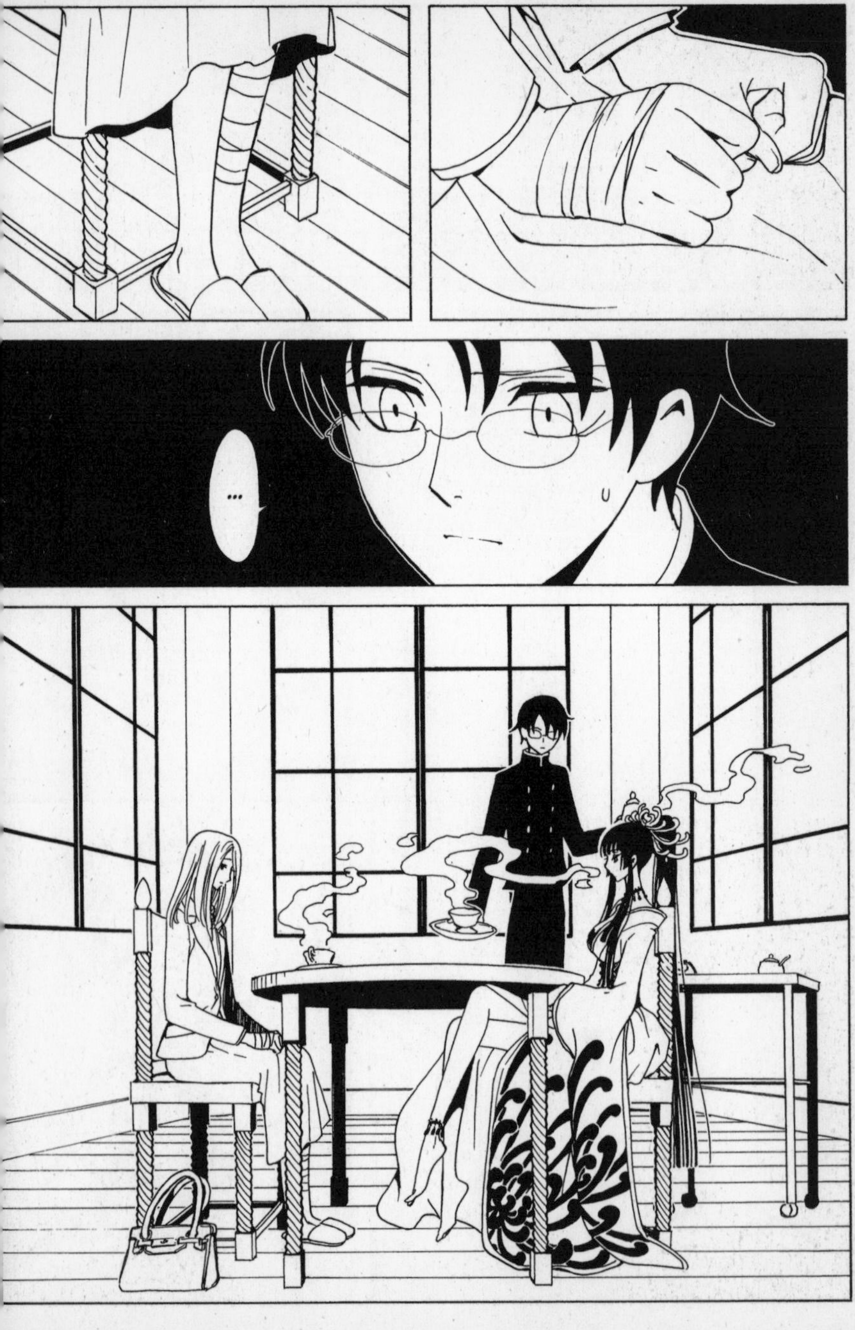
...

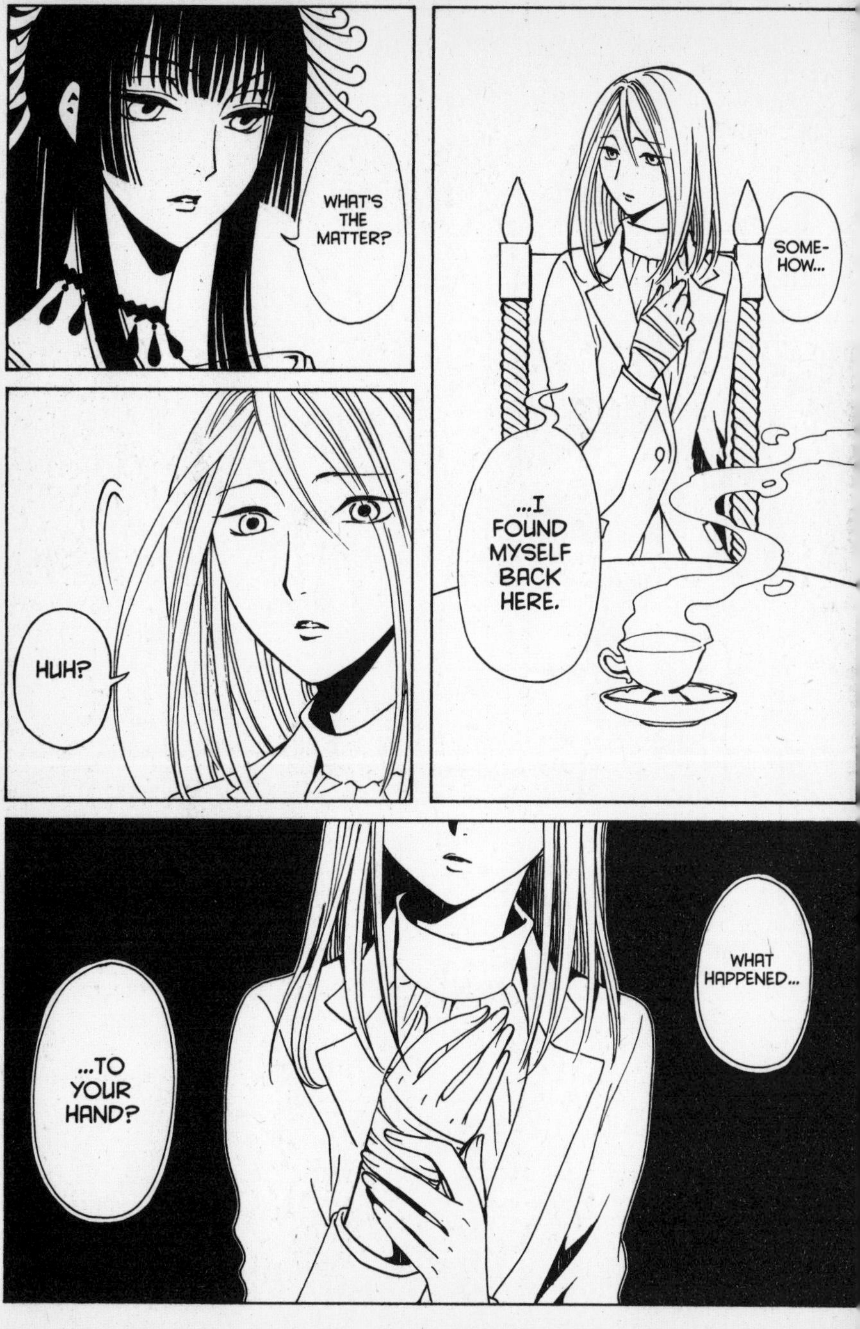
SOME-HOW...
...I FOUND MYSELF BACK HERE.
WHAT'S THE MATTER?
HUH?
WHAT HAPPENED...
...TO YOUR HAND?

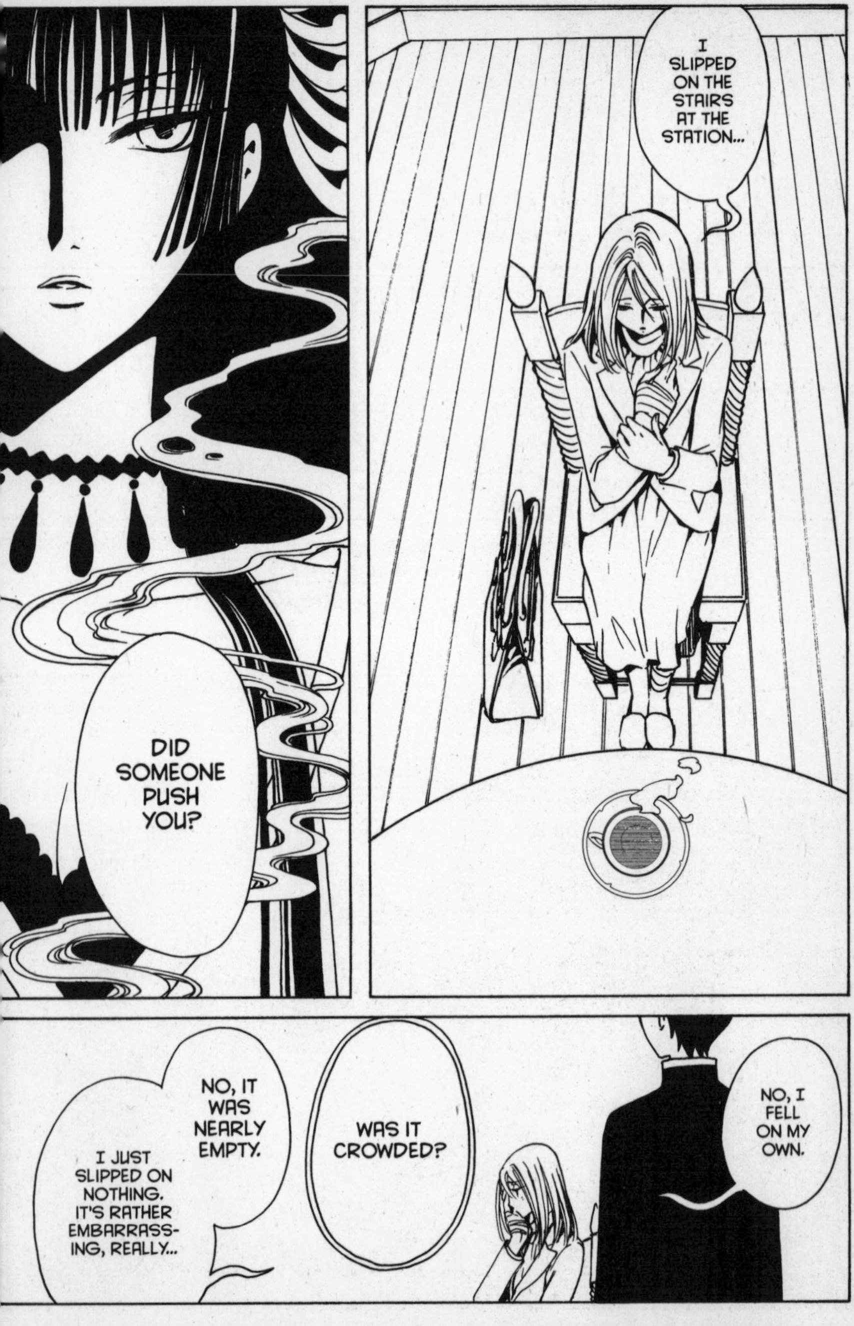
I SLIPPED ON THE STAIRS AT THE STATION...
DID SOMEONE PUSH YOU?
NO, I FELL ON MY OWN.
WAS IT CROWDED?
NO, IT WAS NEARLY EMPTY.
I JUST SLIPPED ON NOTHING. IT'S RATHER EMBARRASS-ING, REALLY...

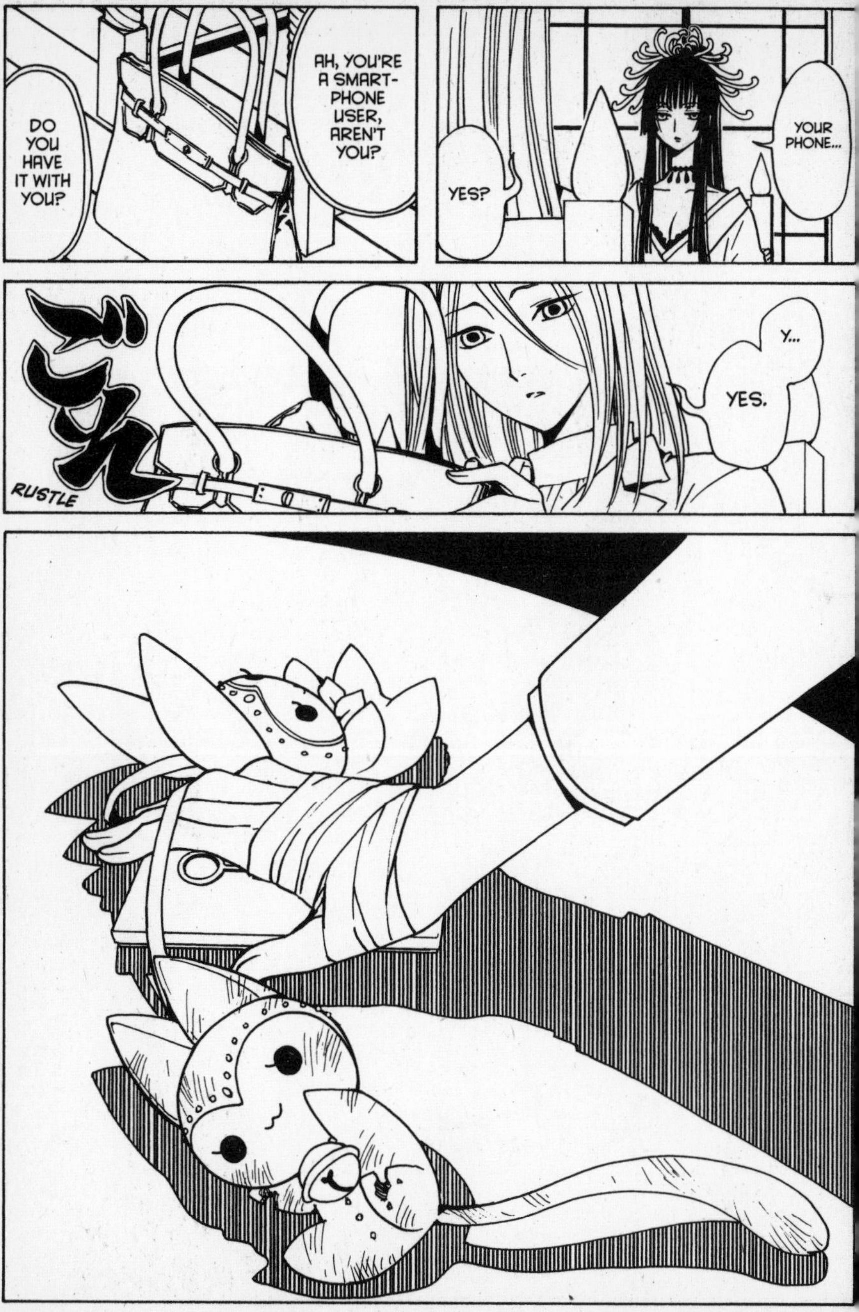
YOUR PHONE...
YES?
AH, YOU'RE A SMART-PHONE USER, AREN'T YOU?
DO YOU HAVE IT WITH YOU?
Y...
YES.
RUSTLE

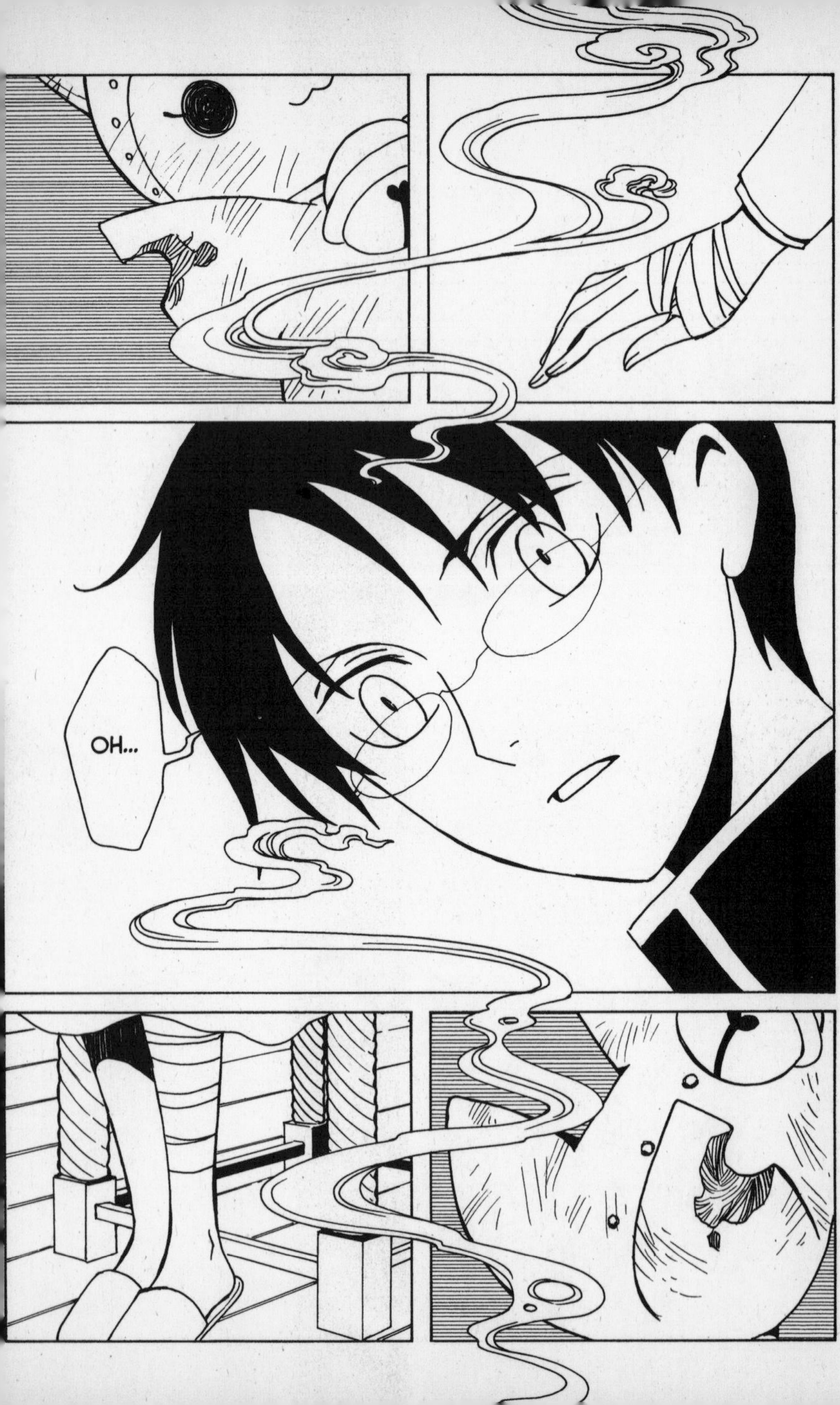
OH...

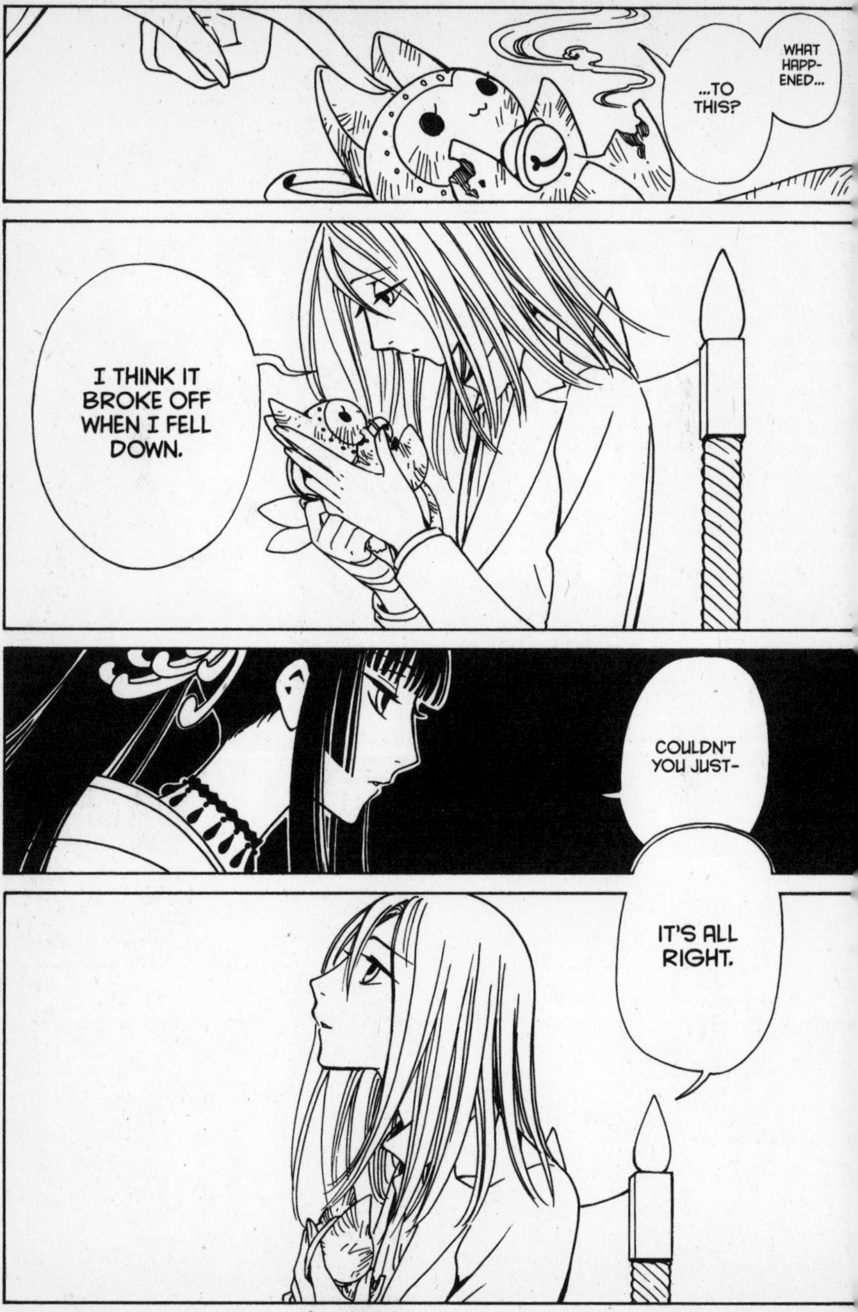
WHAT HAPP-ENED...
...TO THIS?
I THINK IT BROKE OFF WHEN I FELL DOWN.
COULDN'T YOU JUST-
IT'S ALL RIGHT.

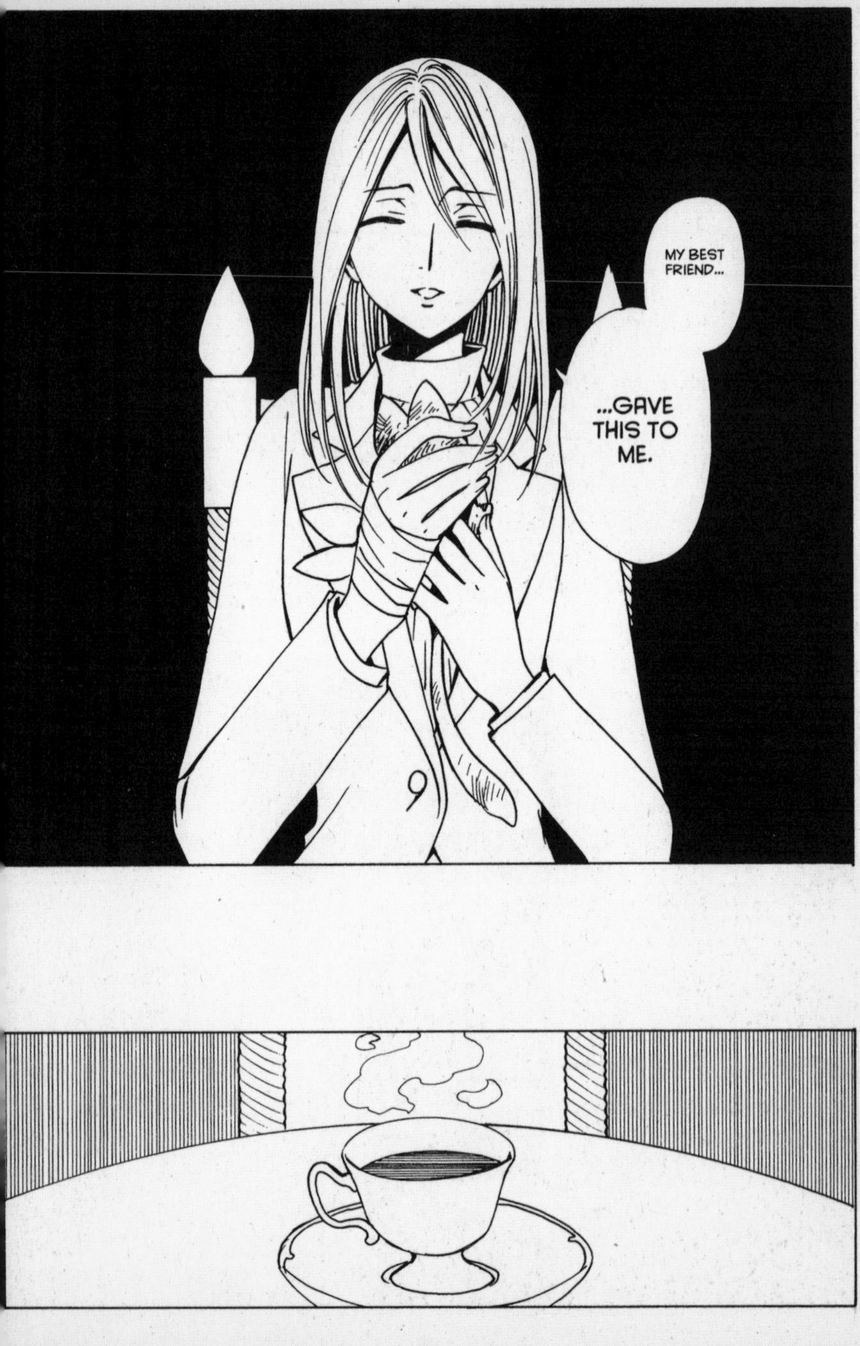
MY BEST FRIEND...
...GAVE THIS TO ME.

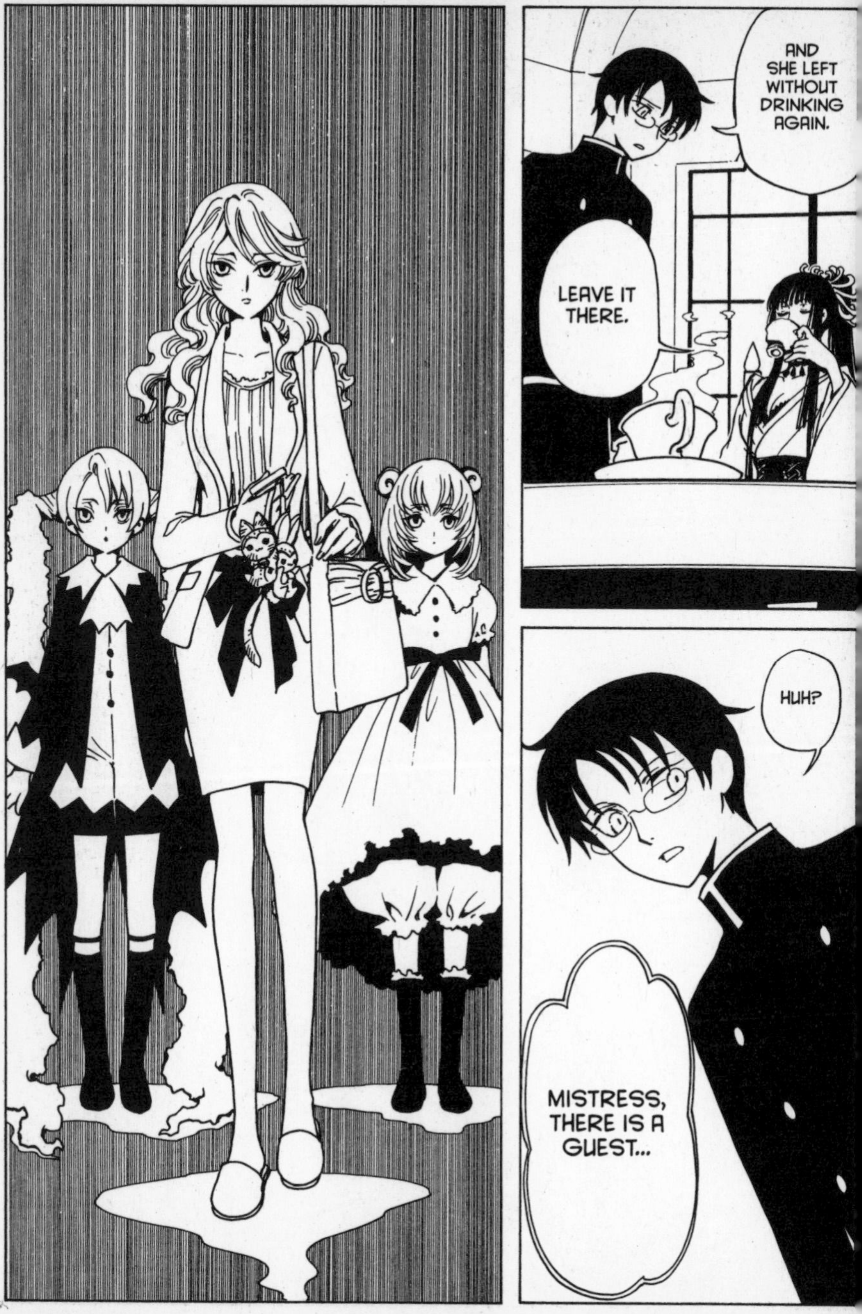
AND SHE LEFT WITHOUT DRINKING AGAIN.
LEAVE IT THERE.
HUH?
MISTRESS, THERE IS A GUEST...

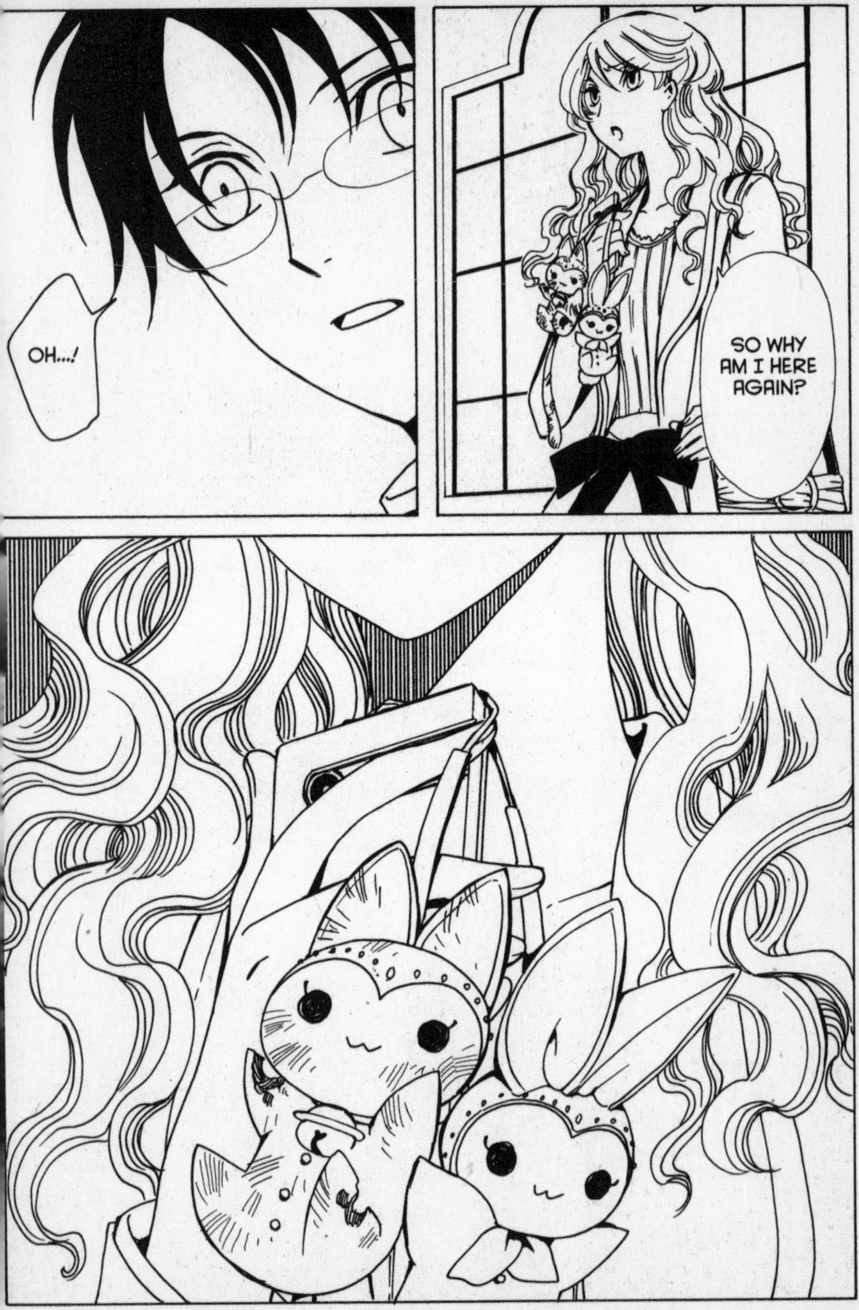
SO WHY AM I HERE AGAIN?
OH...!

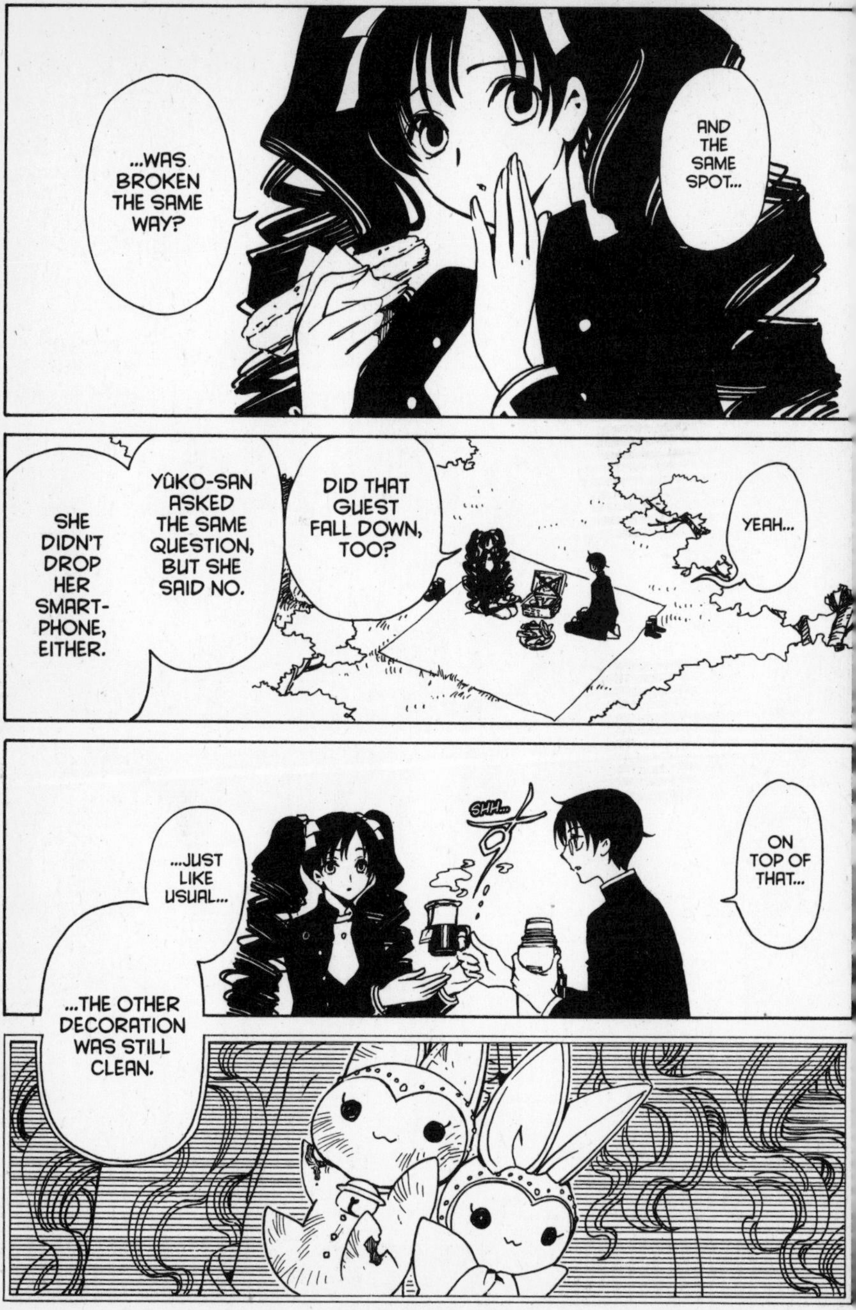
AND THE SAME SPOT...
...WAS BROKEN THE SAME WAY?
YEAH...
DID THAT GUEST FALL DOWN, TOO?
YŪKO-SAN ASKED THE SAME QUESTION, BUT SHE SAID NO.
SHE DIDN'T DROP HER SMART-PHONE, EITHER.
ON TOP OF THAT...
SHH...
...JUST LIKE USUAL...
...THE OTHER DECORATION WAS STILL CLEAN.

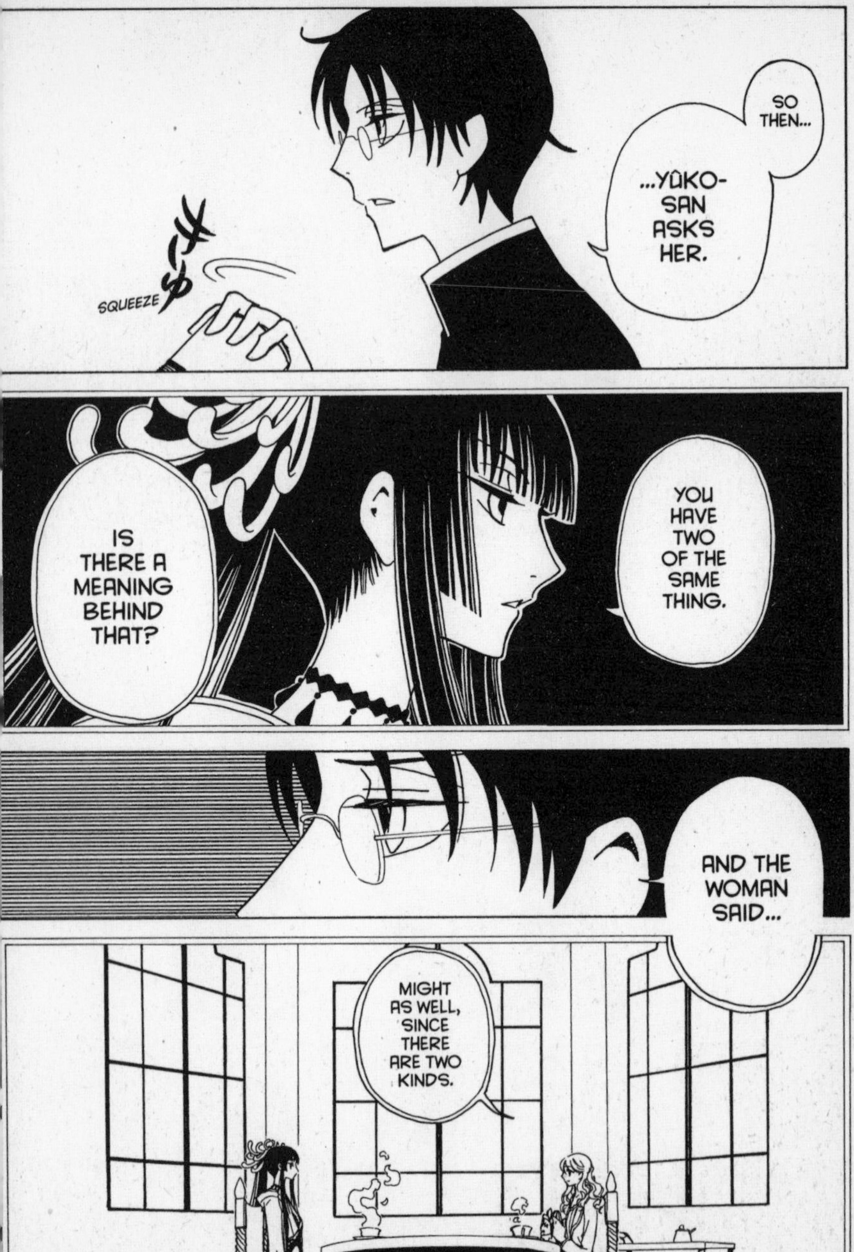
SO THEN...
...YÛKO-SAN ASKS HER.
きゅ
SQUEEZE
YOU HAVE TWO OF THE SAME THING.
IS THERE A MEANING BEHIND THAT?
AND THE WOMAN SAID...
MIGHT AS WELL, SINCE THERE ARE TWO KINDS.

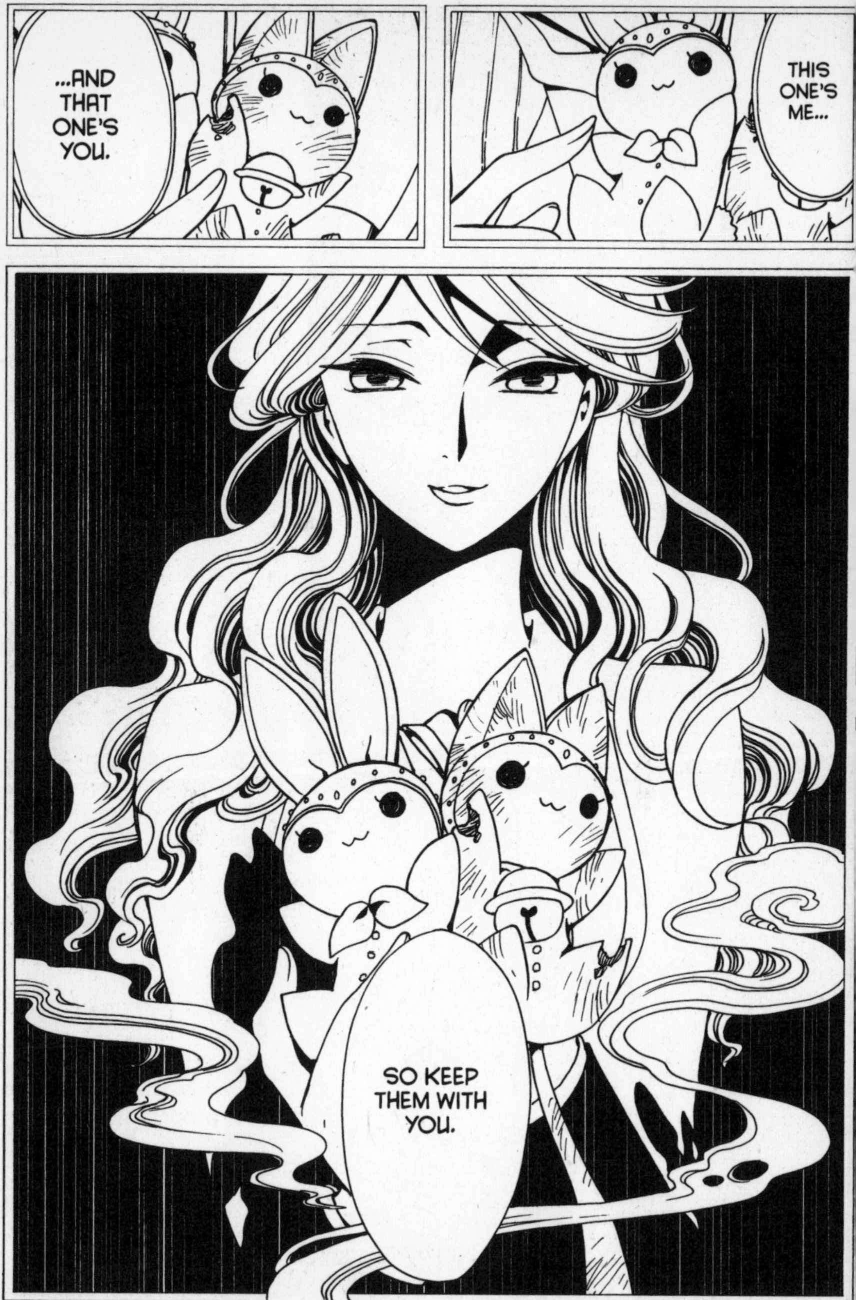
THIS ONE'S ME...
...AND THAT ONE'S YOU.
SO KEEP THEM WITH YOU.

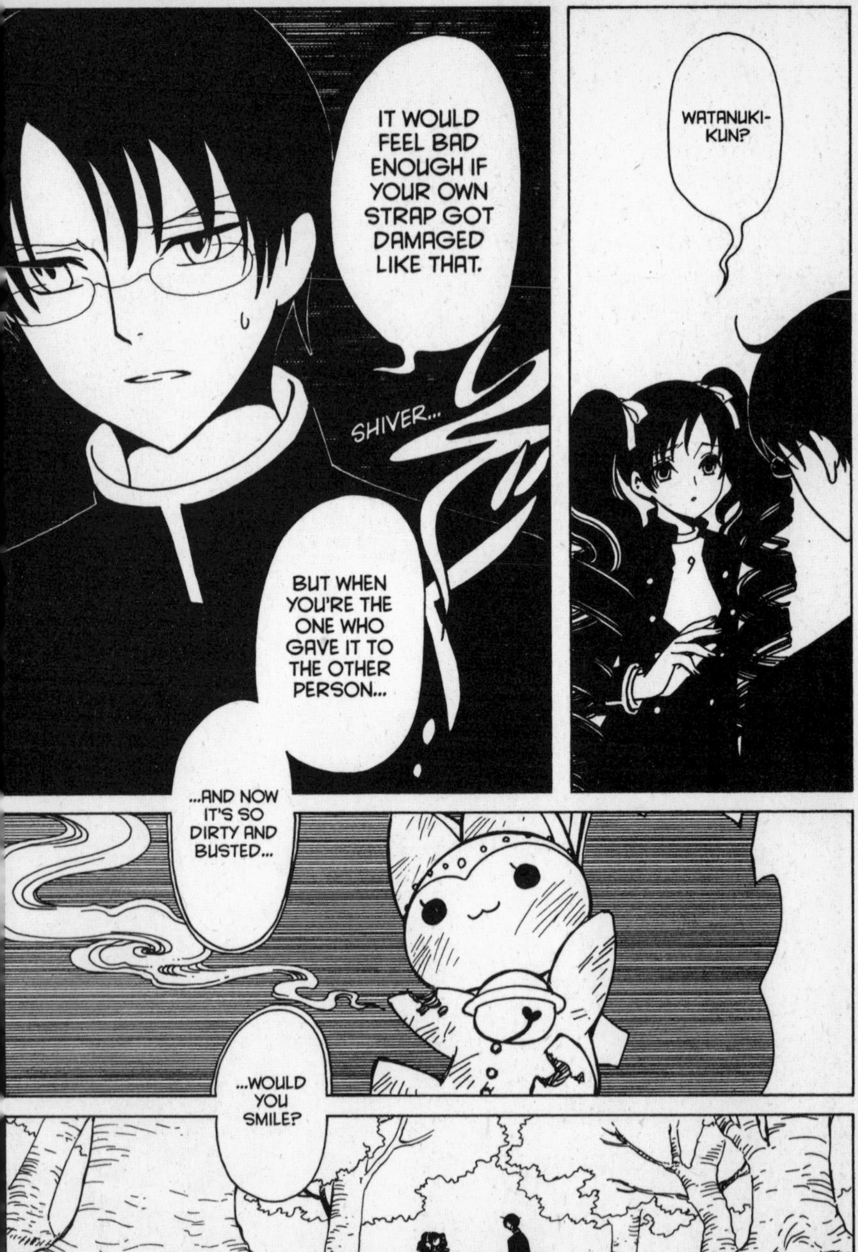
WATANUKI-KUN?
IT WOULD FEEL BAD ENOUGH IF YOUR OWN STRAP GOT DAMAGED LIKE THAT.
SHIVER...
BUT WHEN YOU'RE THE ONE WHO GAVE IT TO THE OTHER PERSON...
...AND NOW IT'S SO DIRTY AND BUSTED...
...WOULD YOU SMILE?

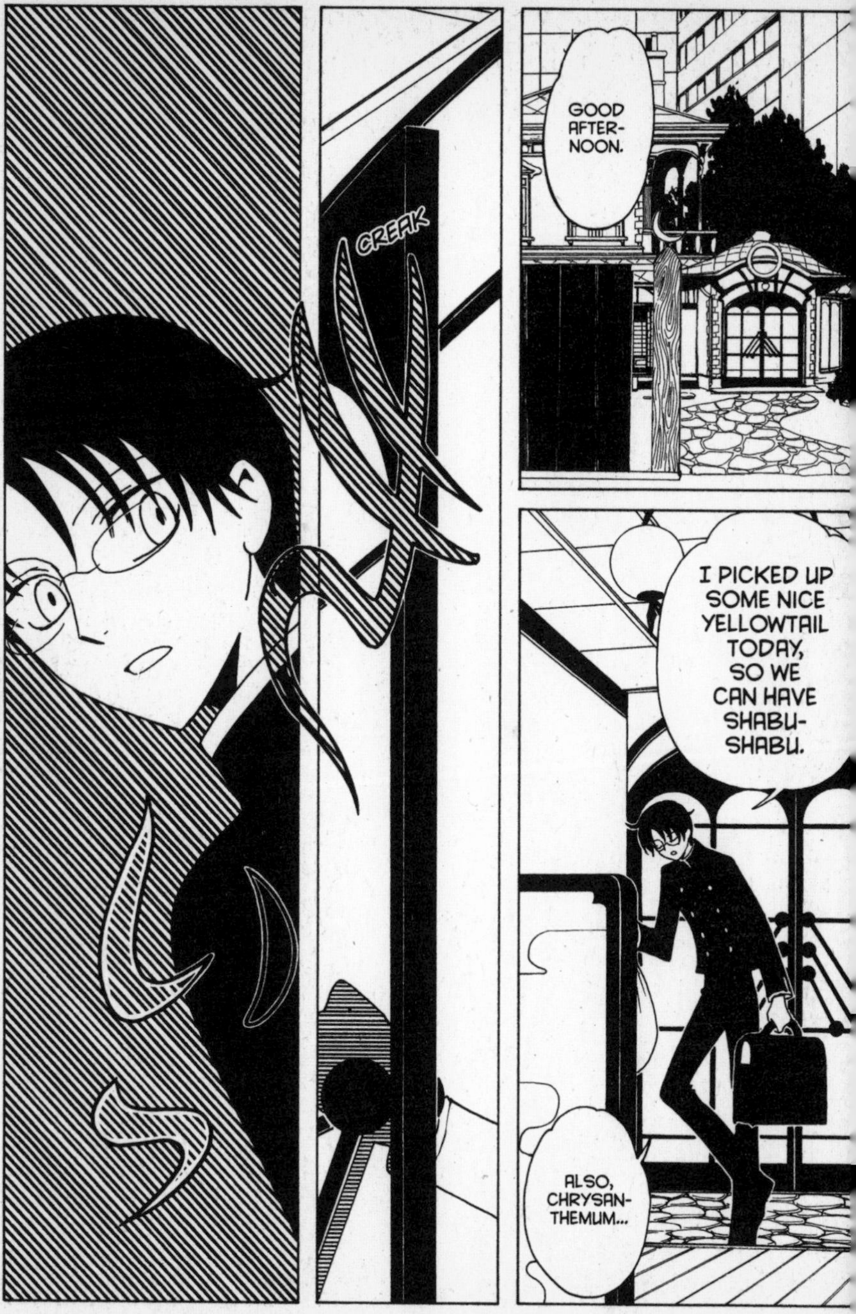
GOOD AFTER-NOON.
I PICKED UP SOME NICE YELLOWTAIL TODAY, SO WE CAN HAVE SHABU-SHABU.
ALSO, CHRYSAN-THEMUM...
CREAK

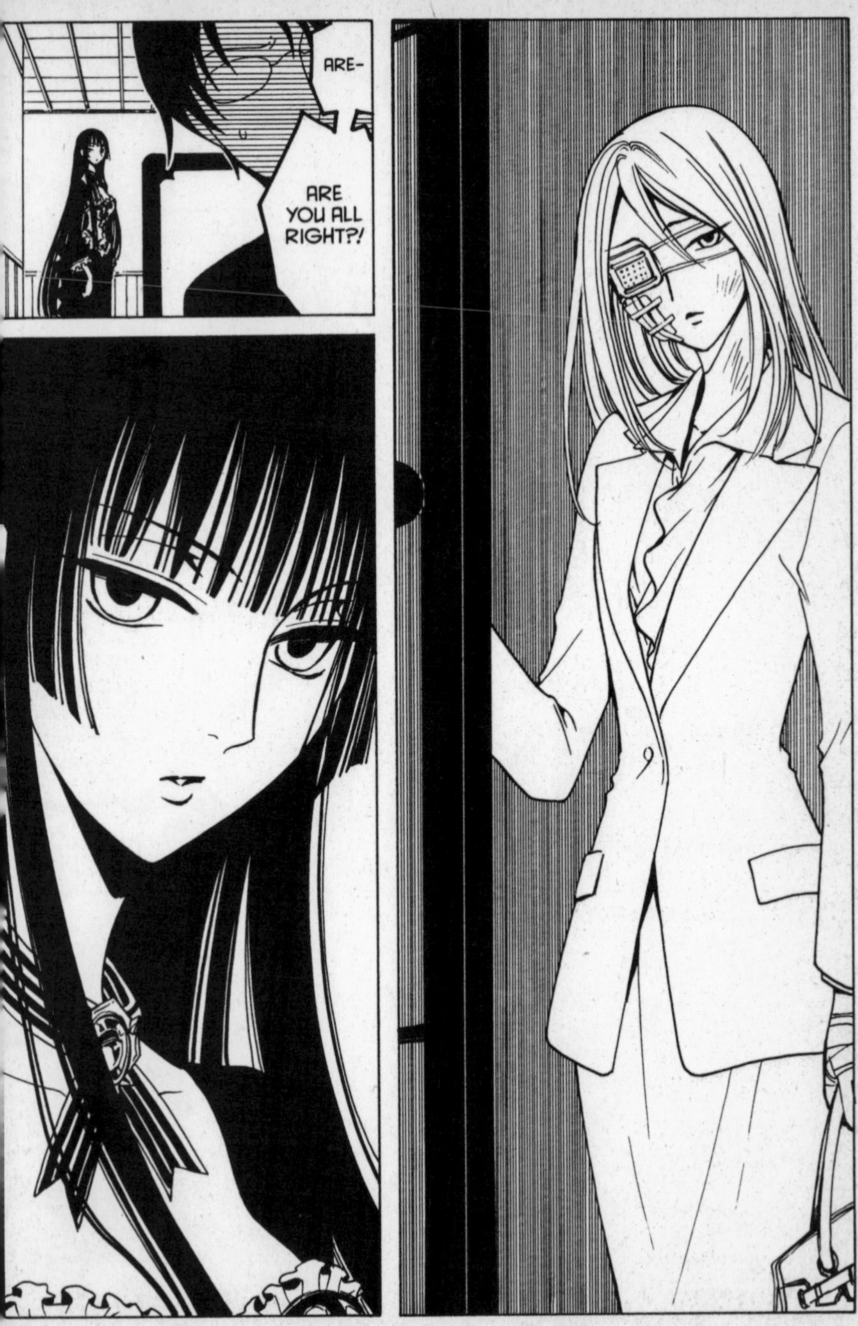
ARE-
ARE YOU ALL RIGHT?!

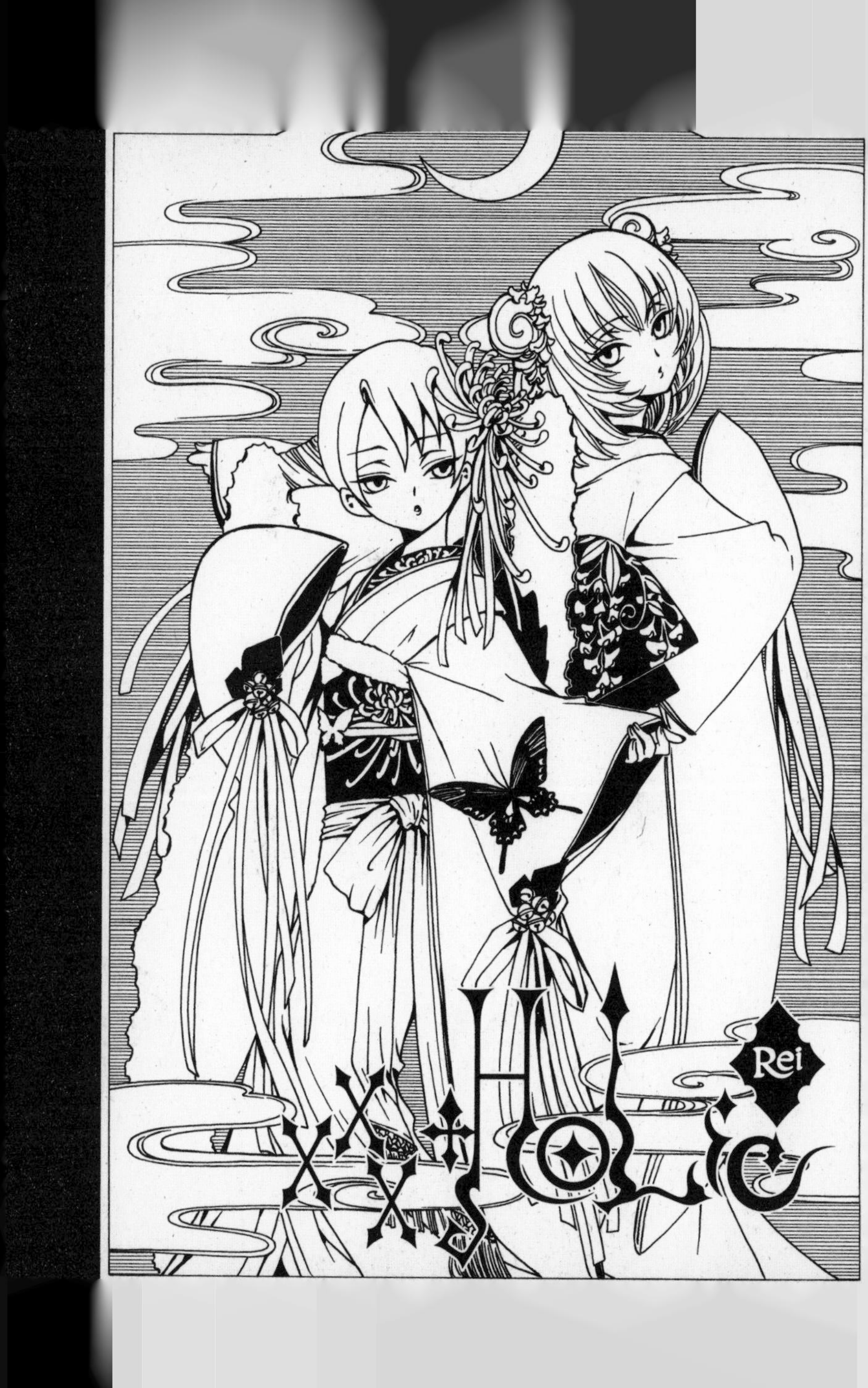
xxxHOLiC
Rei

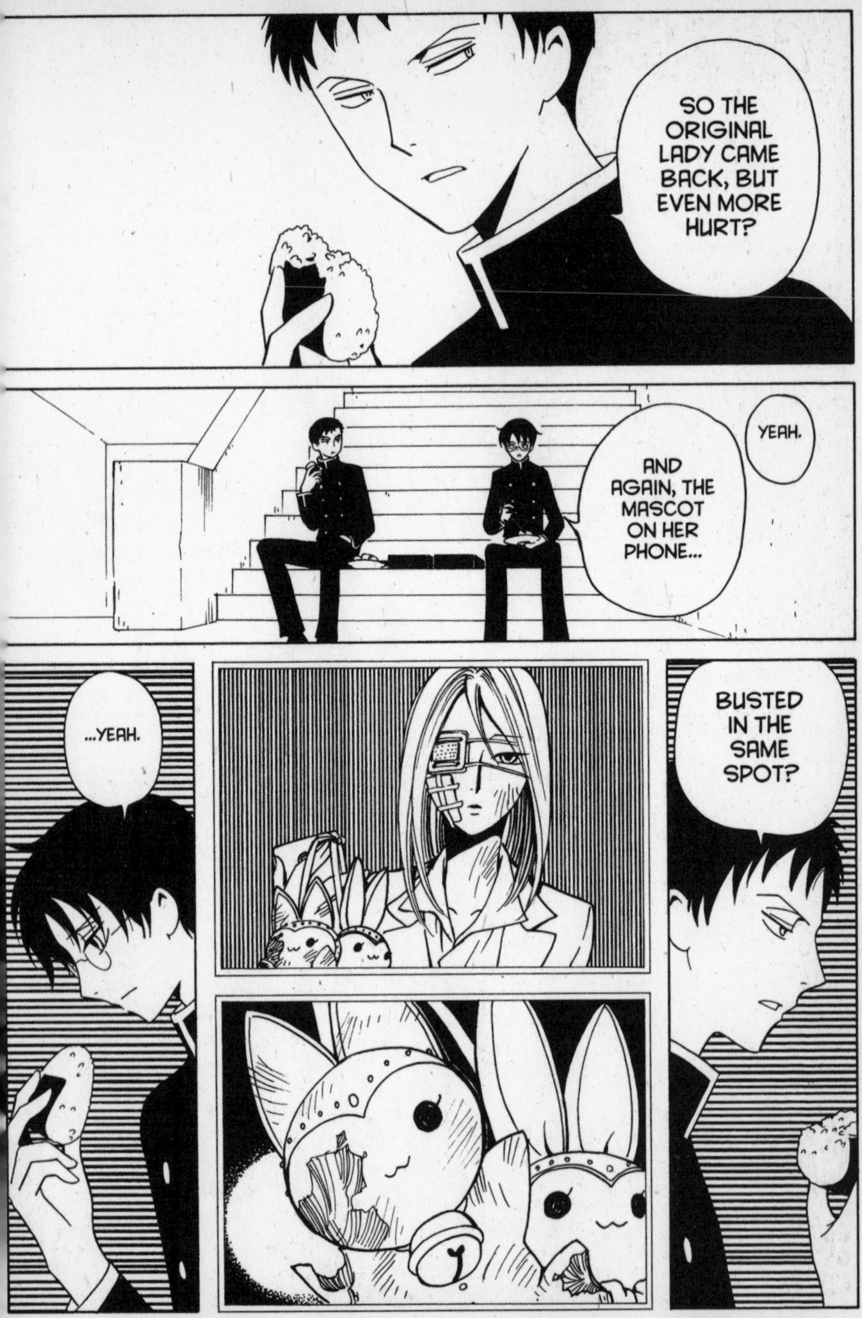
SO THE ORIGINAL LADY CAME BACK, BUT EVEN MORE HURT?
YEAH.
AND AGAIN, THE MASCOT ON HER PHONE...
BUSTED IN THE SAME SPOT?
...YEAH.

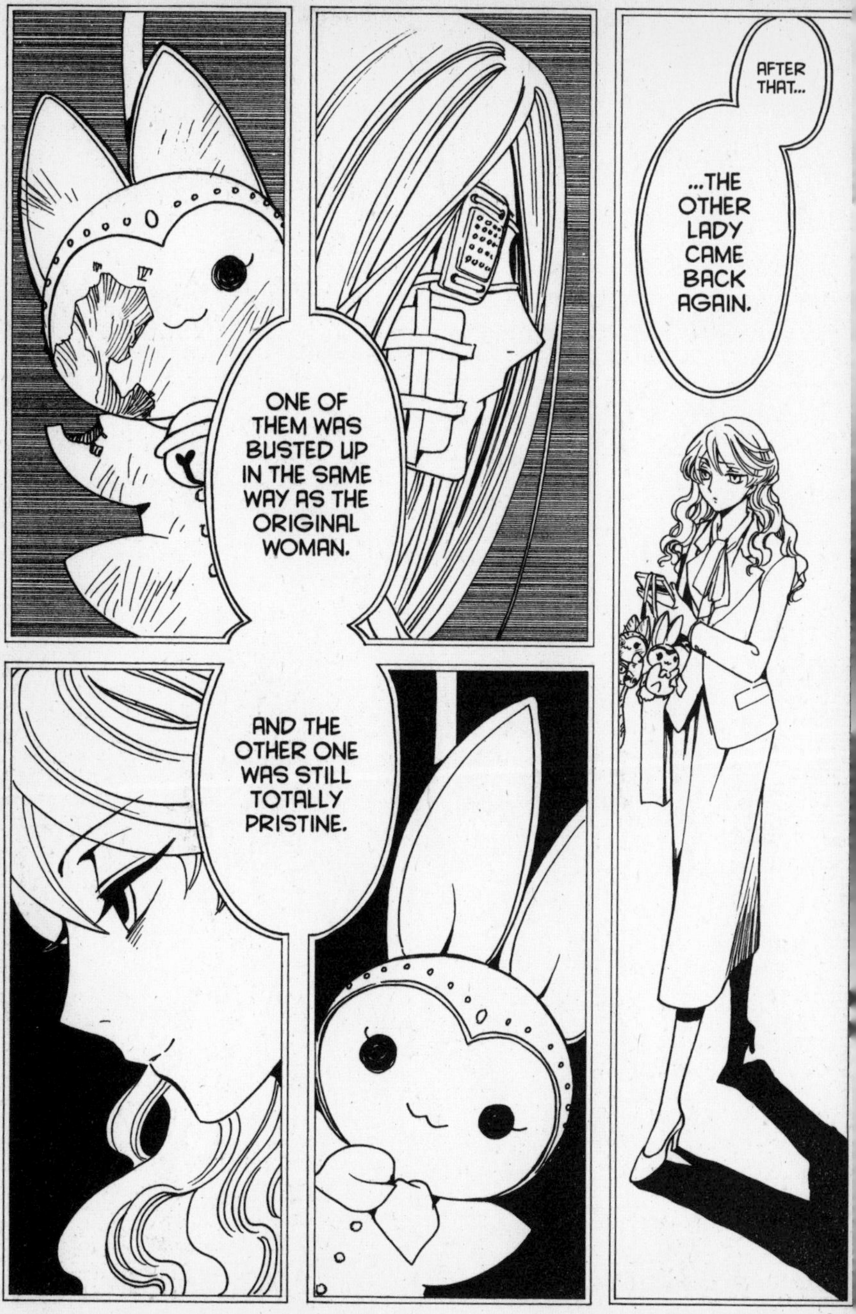
AFTER THAT...
...THE OTHER LADY CAME BACK AGAIN.
ONE OF THEM WAS BUSTED UP IN THE SAME WAY AS THE ORIGINAL WOMAN.
AND THE OTHER ONE WAS STILL TOTALLY PRISTINE.

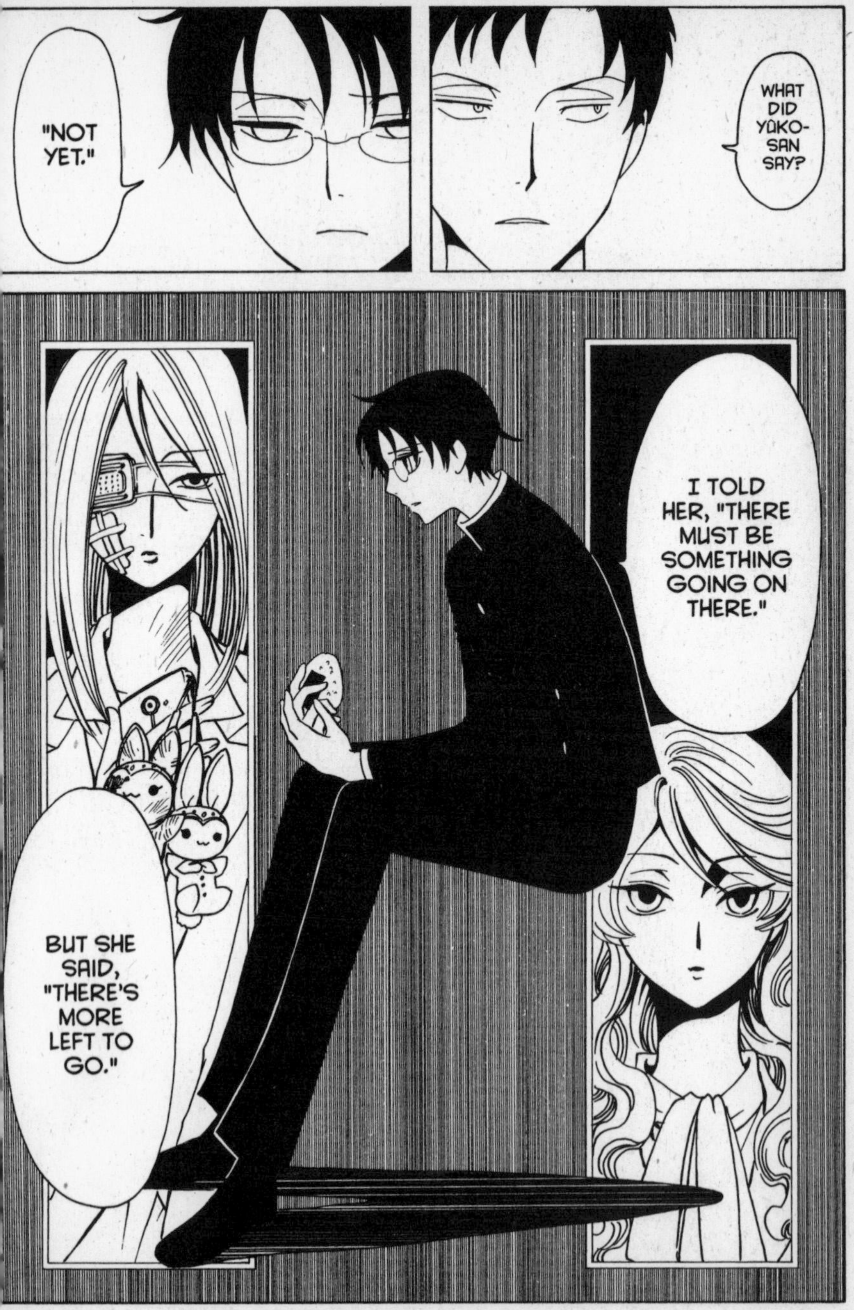
WHAT DID YÛKO-SAN SAY?
"NOT YET."
I TOLD HER, "THERE MUST BE SOMETHING GOING ON THERE."
BUT SHE SAID, "THERE'S MORE LEFT TO GO."

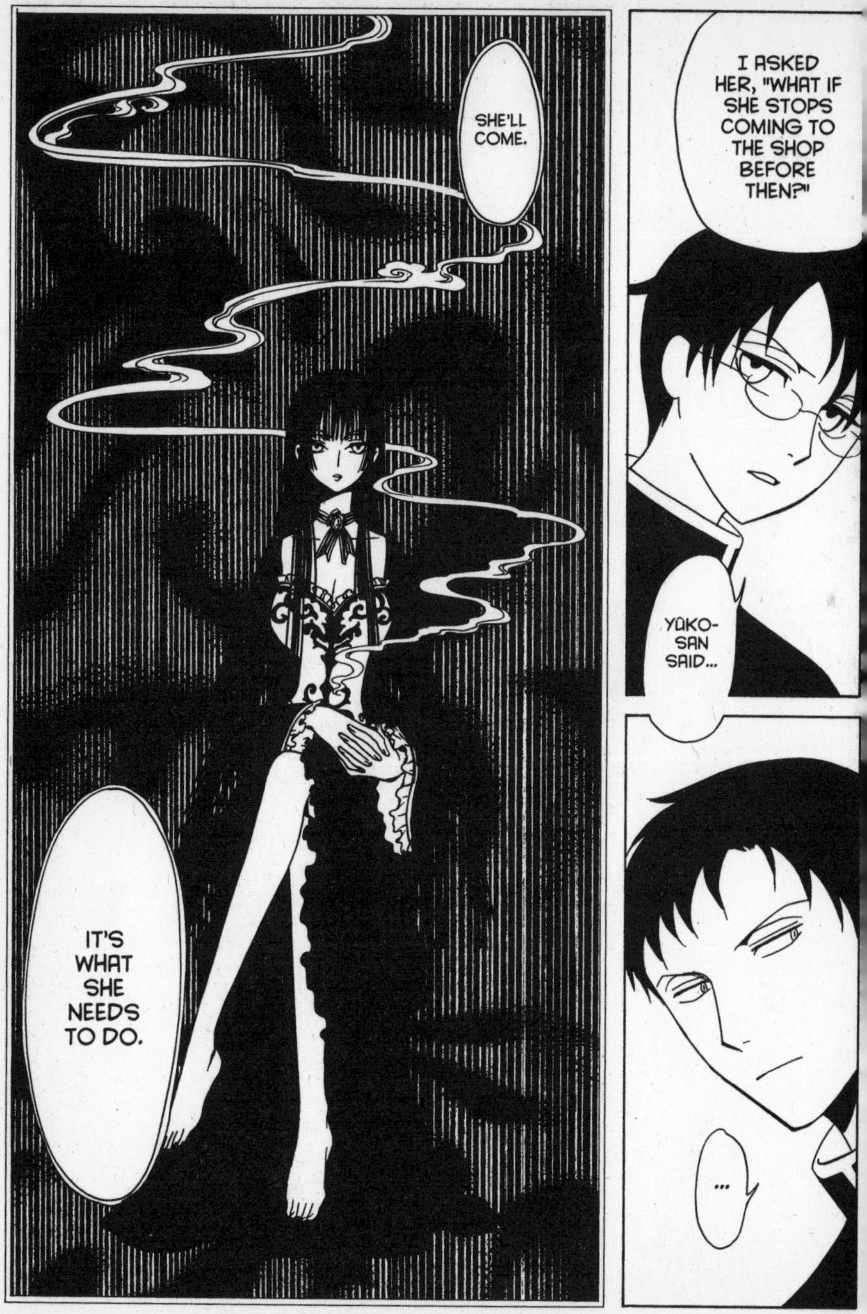
I ASKED HER, "WHAT IF SHE STOPS COMING TO THE SHOP BEFORE THEN?"
YÛKO-SAN SAID...
...
SHE'LL COME.
IT'S WHAT SHE NEEDS TO DO.

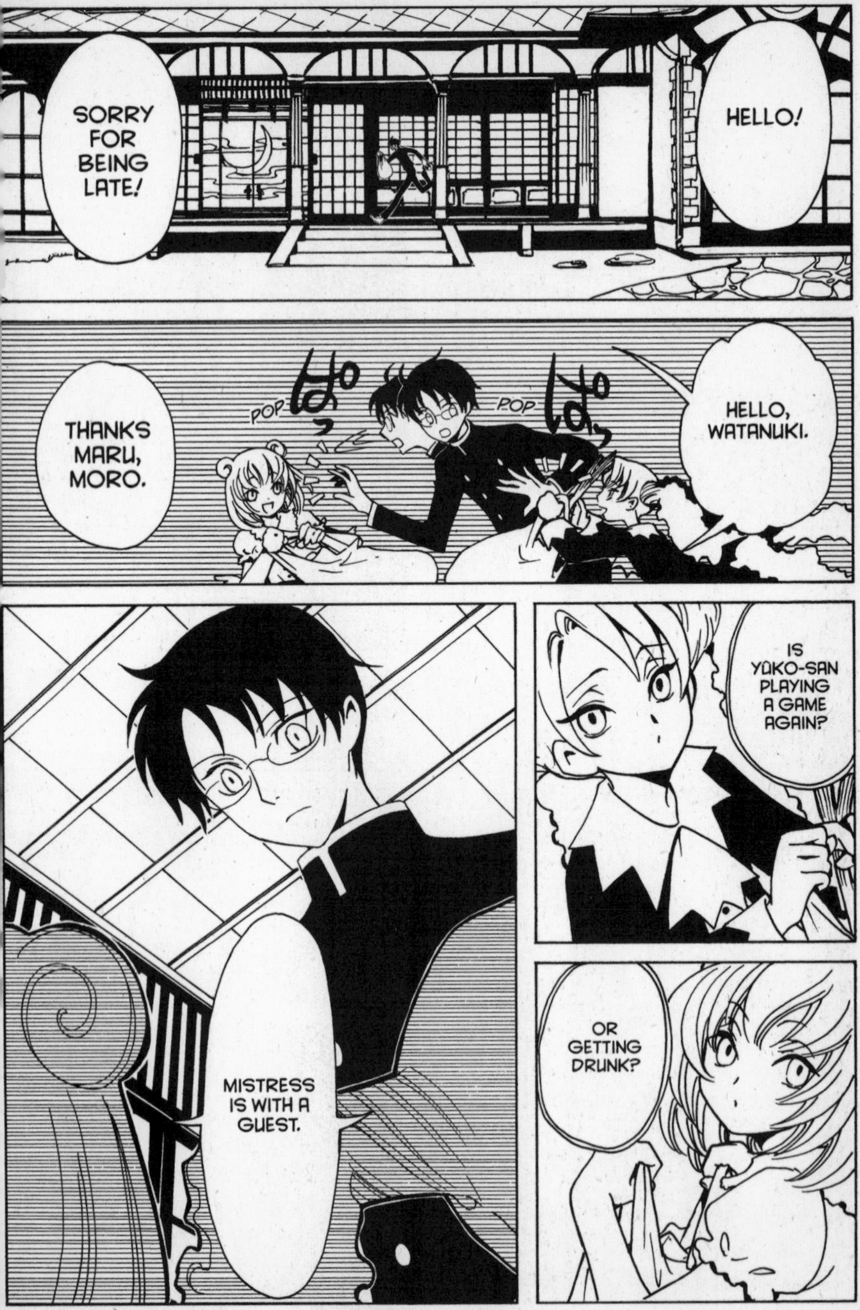
HELLO!
SORRY FOR BEING LATE!
HELLO, WATANUKI.
POP ぱっ
POP ぱっ
THANKS MARU, MORO.
IS YŪKO-SAN PLAYING A GAME AGAIN?
OR GETTING DRUNK?
MISTRESS IS WITH A GUEST.

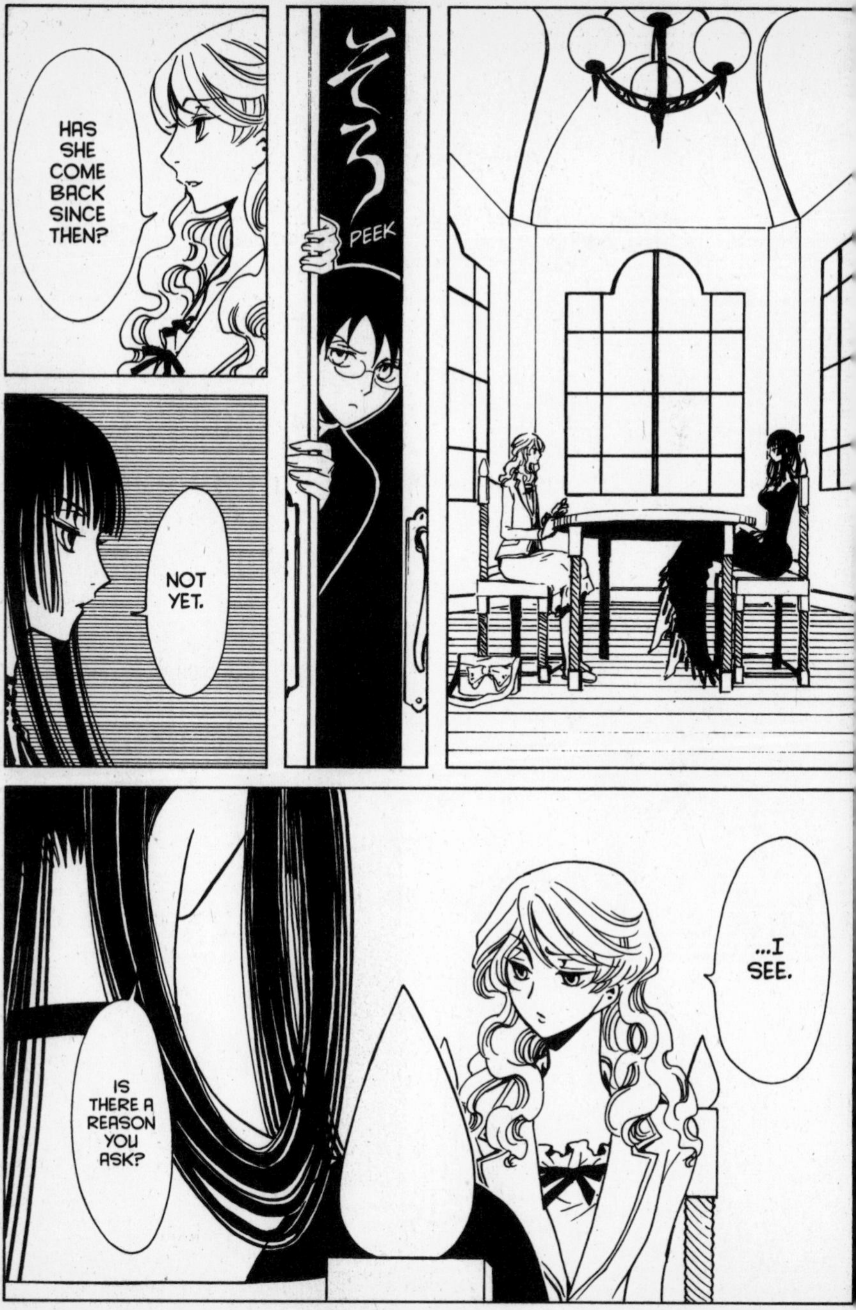
そろ
PEEK
HAS SHE COME BACK SINCE THEN?
NOT YET.
...I SEE.
IS THERE A REASON YOU ASK?

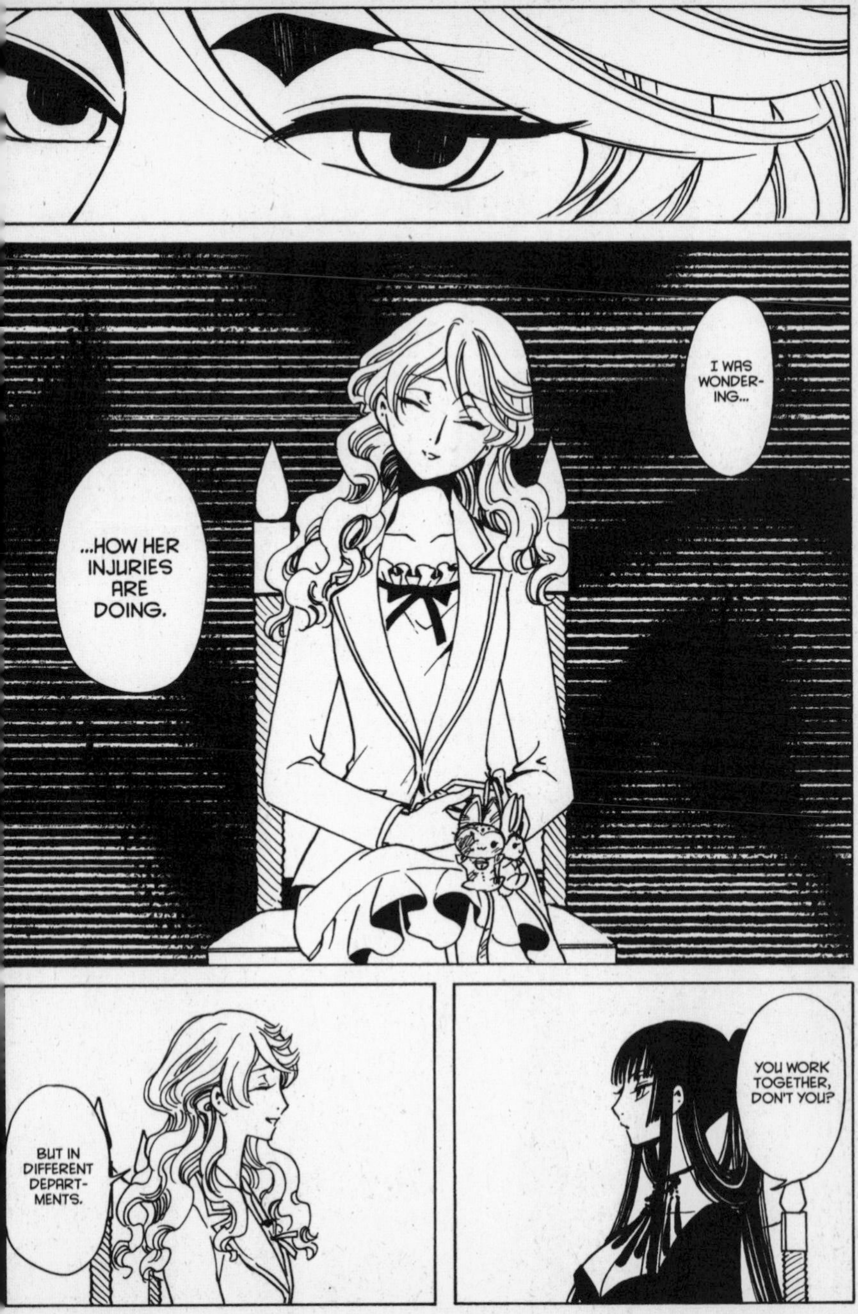
I WAS WONDER-ING...
...HOW HER INJURIES ARE DOING.
YOU WORK TOGETHER, DON'T YOU?
BUT IN DIFFERENT DEPART-MENTS.

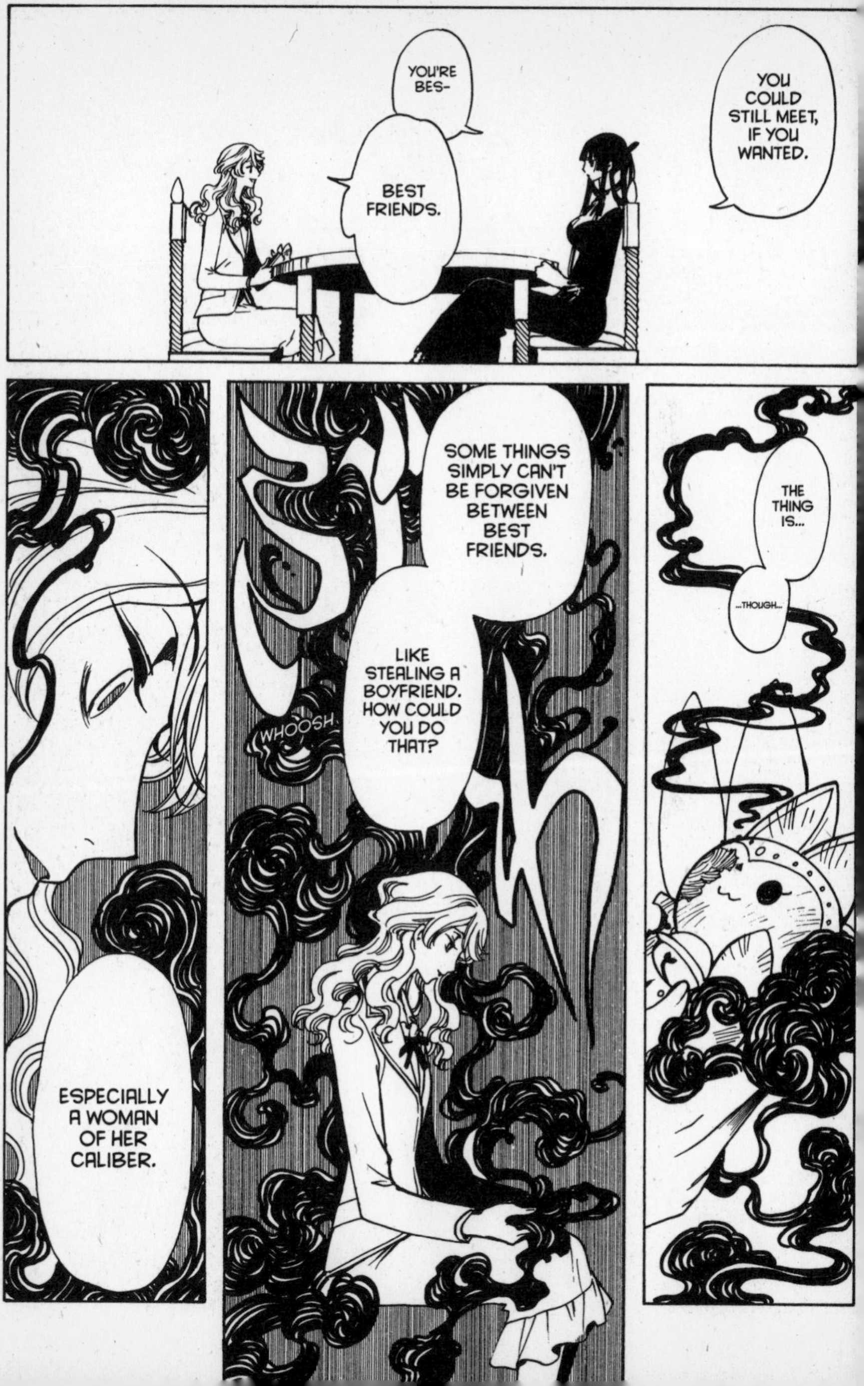
YOU COULD STILL MEET, IF YOU WANTED.
YOU'RE BES-
BEST FRIENDS.
THE THING IS...
...THOUGH...
SOME THINGS SIMPLY CAN'T BE FORGIVEN BETWEEN BEST FRIENDS.
LIKE STEALING A BOYFRIEND. HOW COULD YOU DO THAT?
WHOOSH
ESPECIALLY A WOMAN OF HER CALIBER.

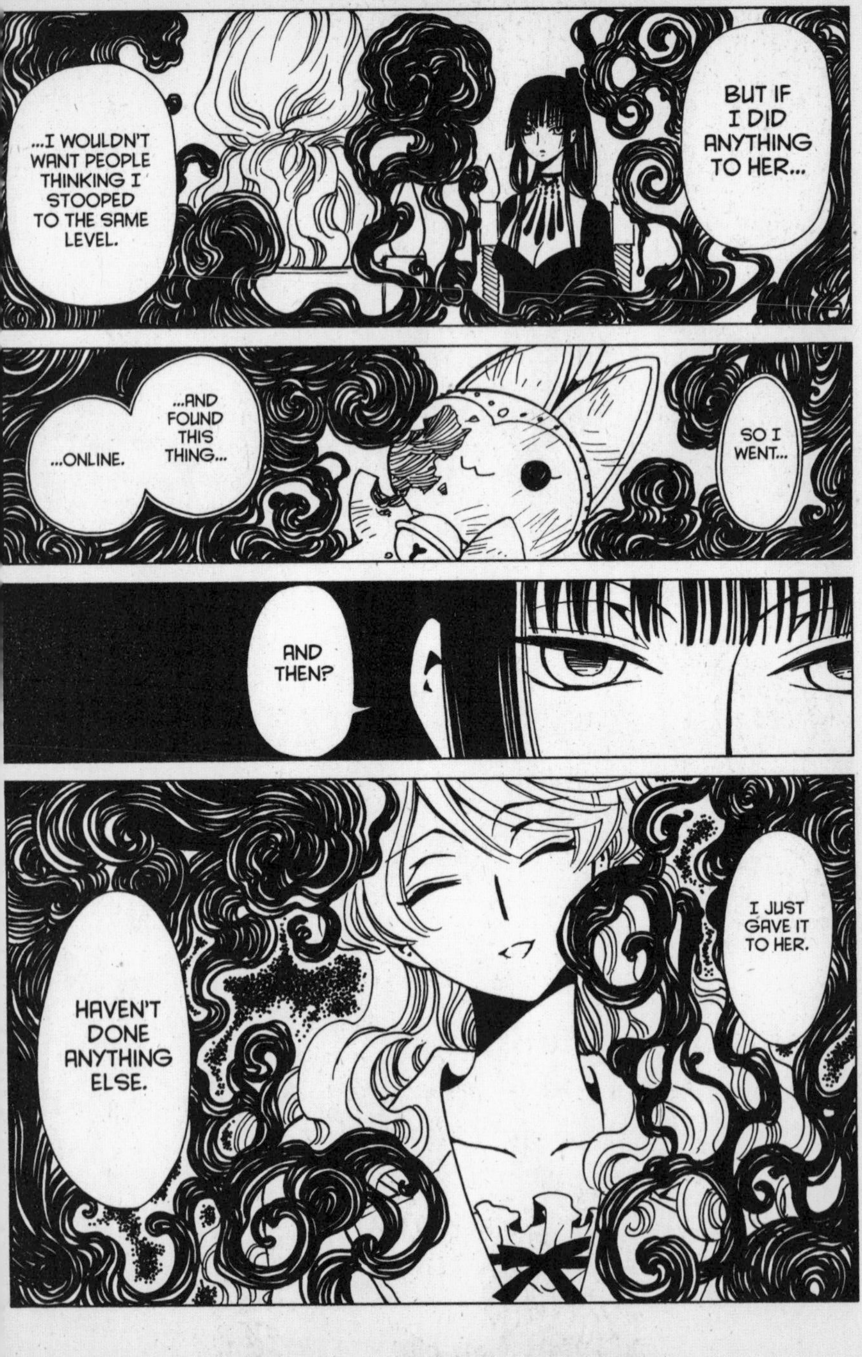
BUT IF I DID ANYTHING TO HER...
...I WOULDN'T WANT PEOPLE THINKING I STOOPED TO THE SAME LEVEL.
SO I WENT...
...AND FOUND THIS THING...
...ONLINE.
AND THEN?
I JUST GAVE IT TO HER.
HAVEN'T DONE ANYTHING ELSE.

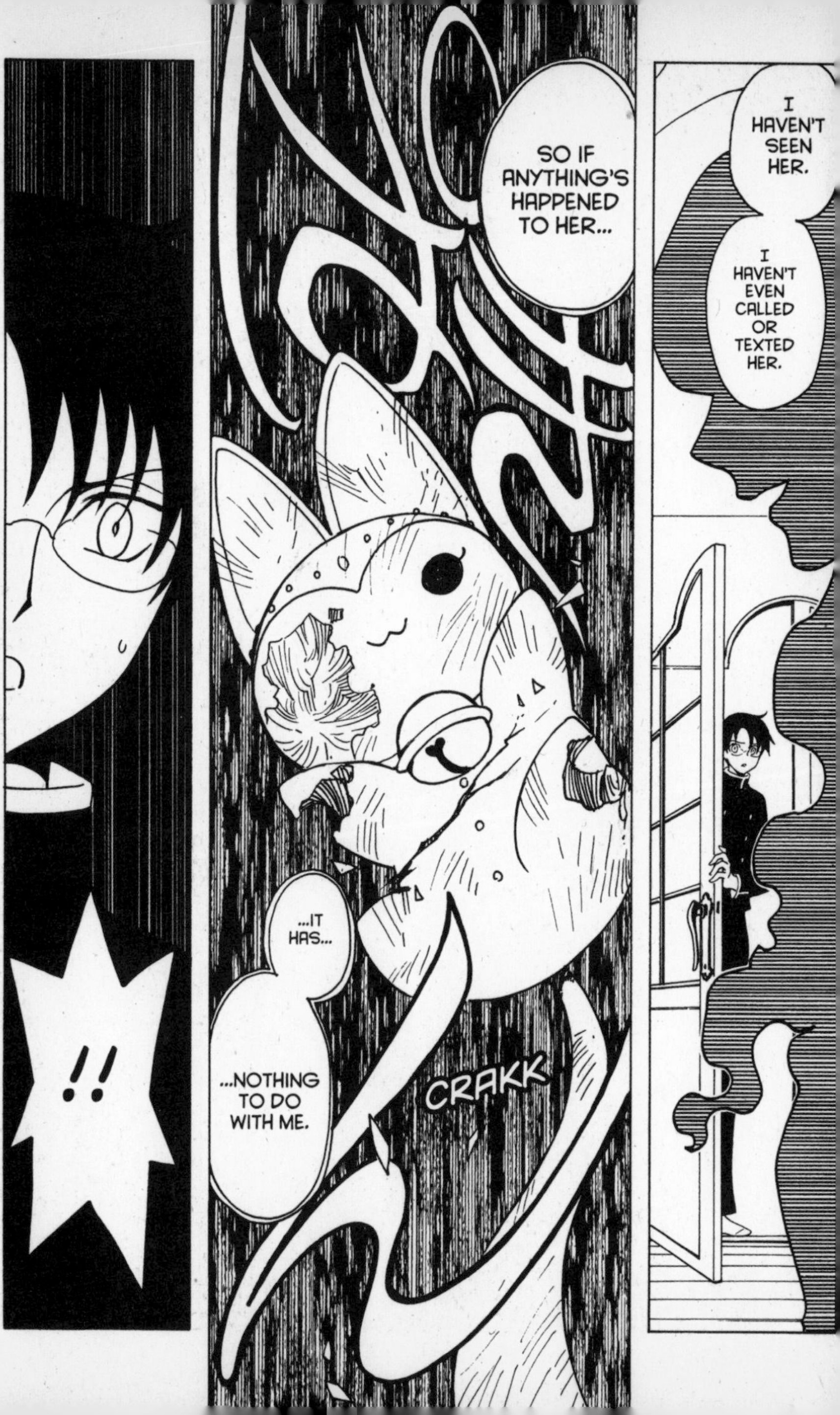
I HAVEN'T SEEN HER.
I HAVEN'T EVEN CALLED OR TEXTED HER.
SO IF ANYTHING'S HAPPENED TO HER...
...IT HAS...
...NOTHING TO DO WITH ME.
CRAKK
!!

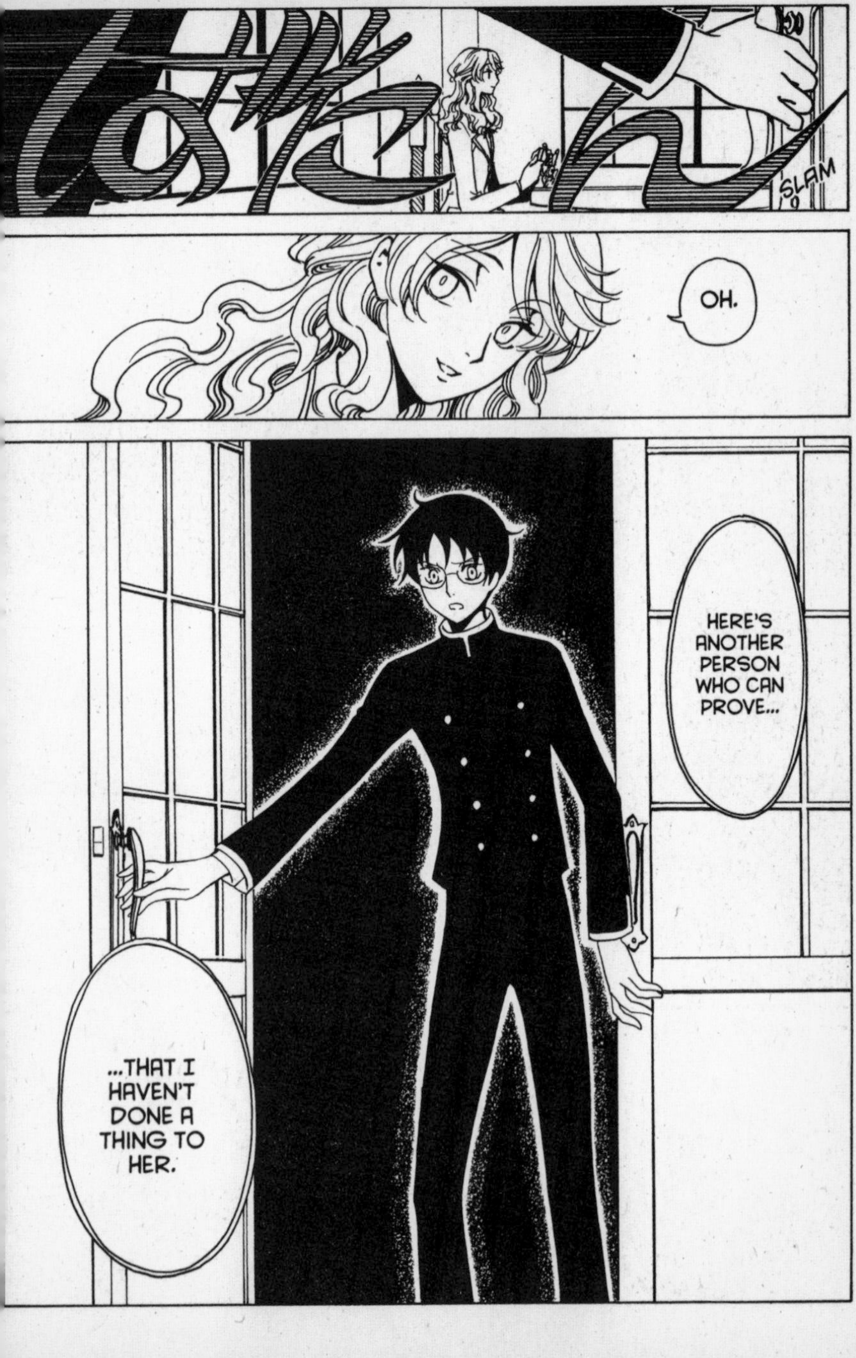
SLAM
OH.
HERE'S ANOTHER PERSON WHO CAN PROVE...
...THAT I HAVEN'T DONE A THING TO HER.

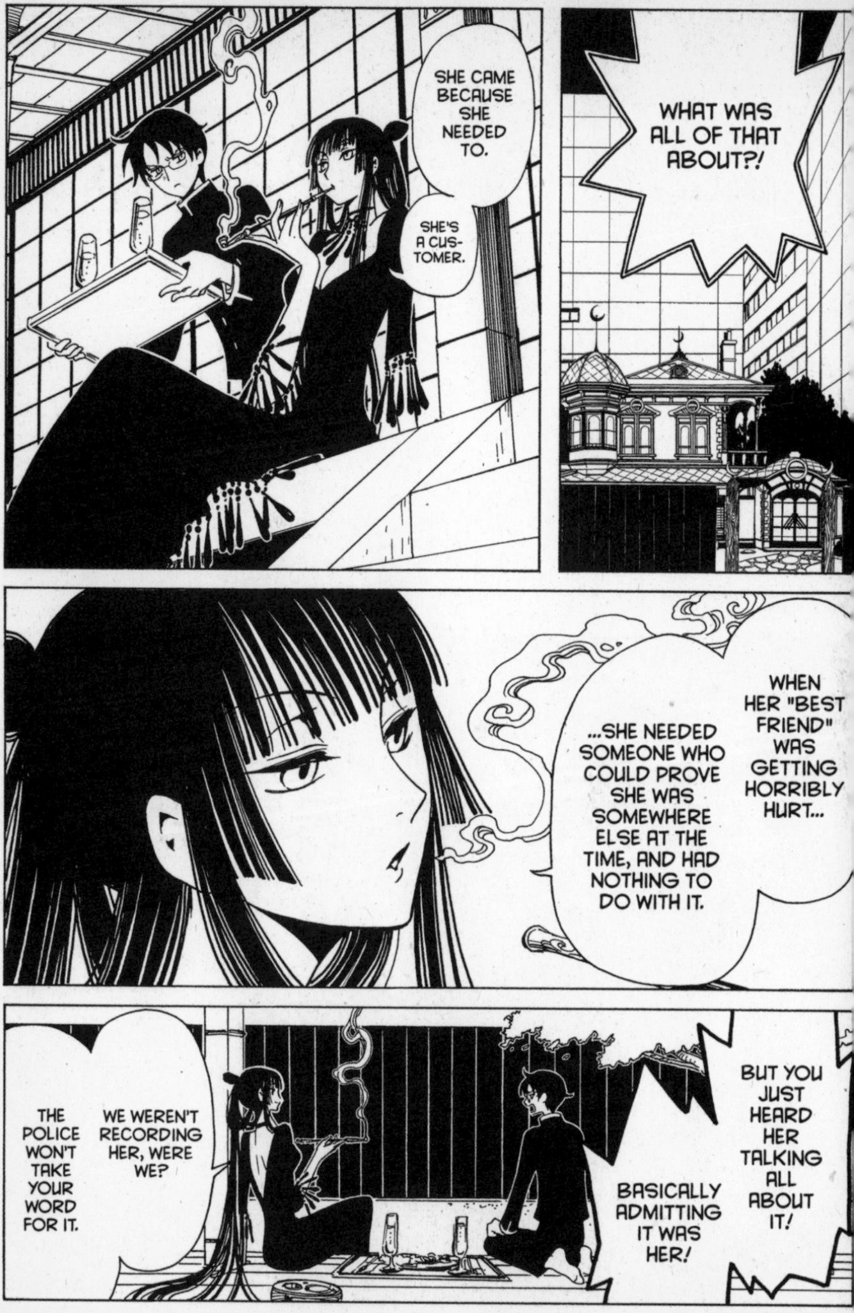
WHAT WAS ALL OF THAT ABOUT?!
SHE CAME BECAUSE SHE NEEDED TO.
SHE'S A CUS-TOMER.
WHEN HER "BEST FRIEND" WAS GETTING HORRIBLY HURT...
...SHE NEEDED SOMEONE WHO COULD PROVE SHE WAS SOMEWHERE ELSE AT THE TIME, AND HAD NOTHING TO DO WITH IT.
BUT YOU JUST HEARD HER TALKING ALL ABOUT IT!
BASICALLY ADMITTING IT WAS HER!
WE WEREN'T RECORDING HER, WERE WE?
THE POLICE WON'T TAKE YOUR WORD FOR IT.

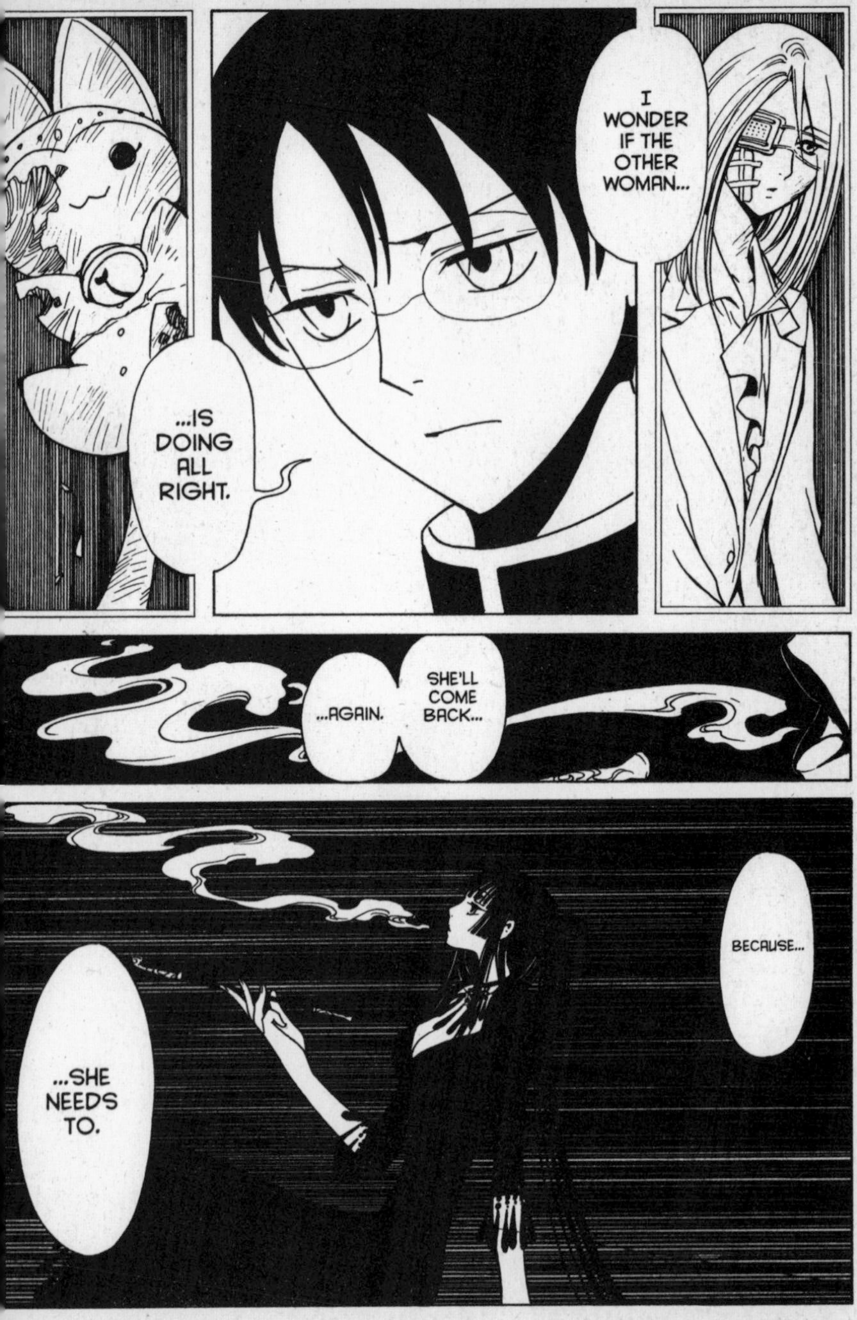
I WONDER IF THE OTHER WOMAN...
...IS DOING ALL RIGHT.
SHE'LL COME BACK...
...AGAIN.
BECAUSE...
...SHE NEEDS TO.

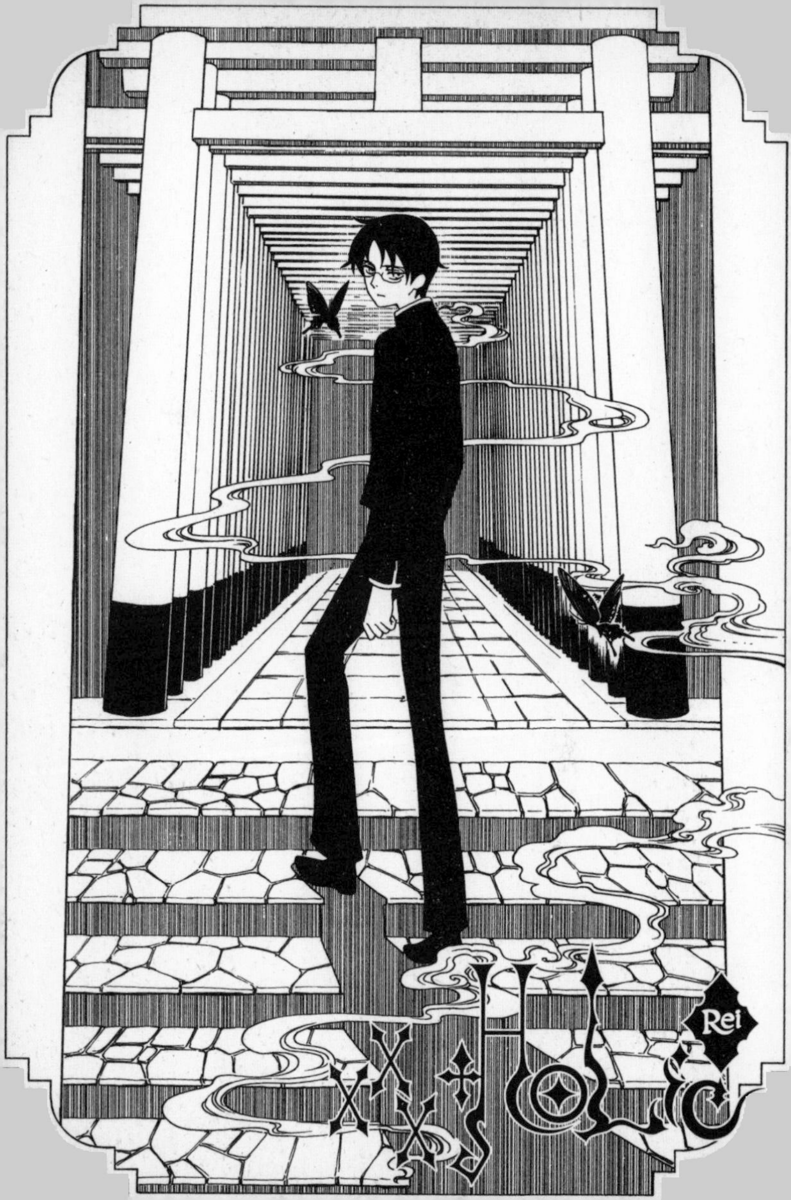
xxxHOLiC
Rei

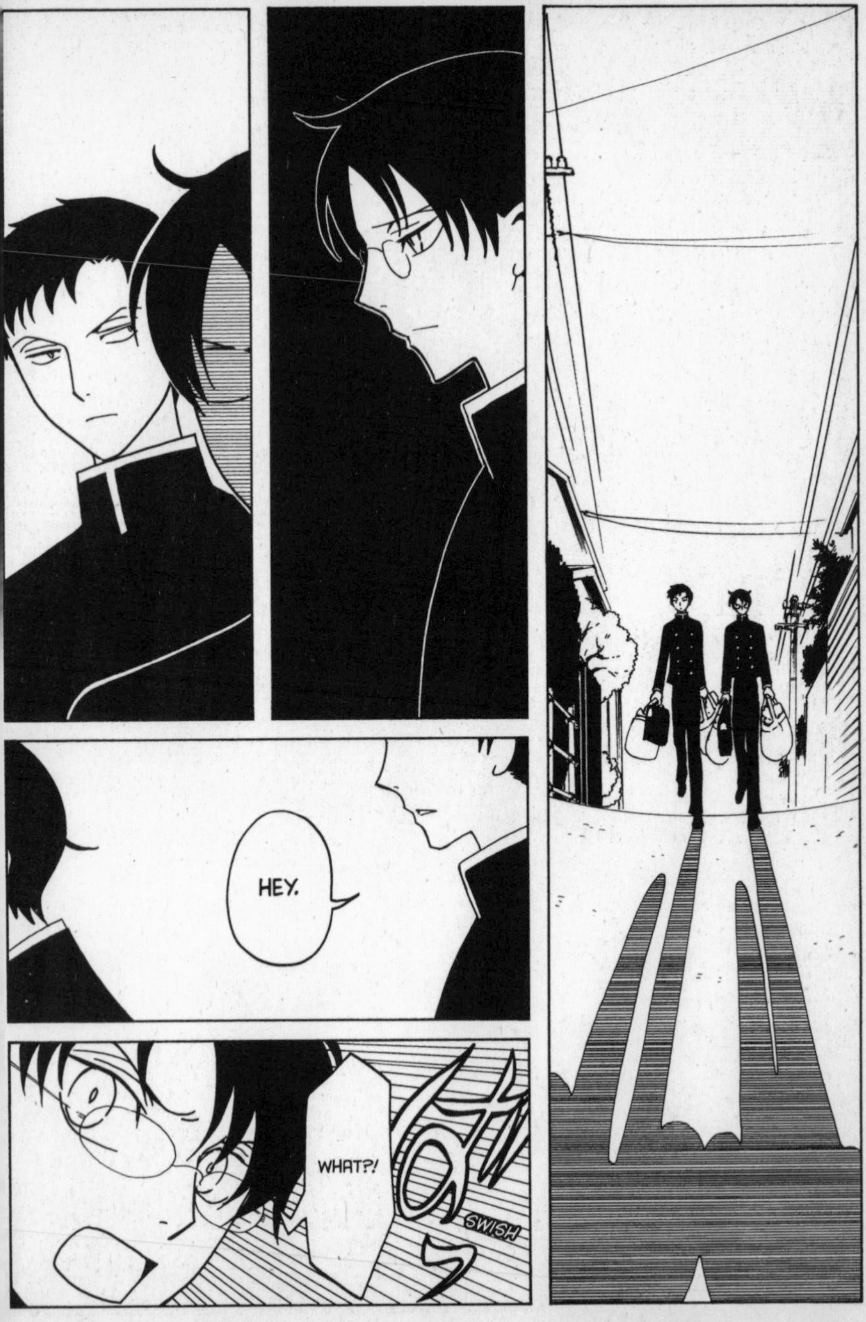
HEY.
WHAT?!
SWISH

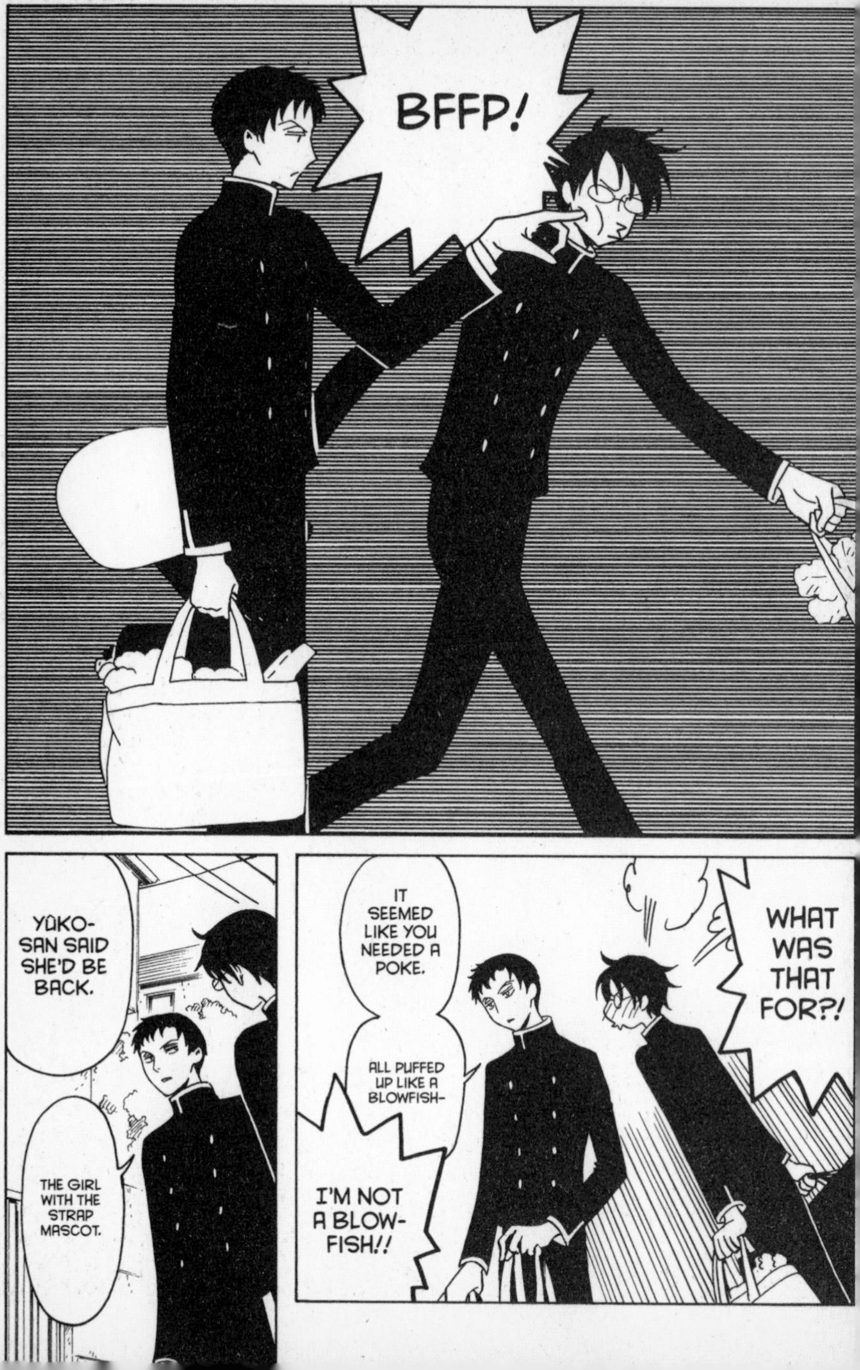
BFFP!
WHAT WAS THAT FOR?!
IT SEEMED LIKE YOU NEEDED A POKE.
ALL PUFFED UP LIKE A BLOWFISH-
I'M NOT A BLOW-FISH!!
YÛKO-SAN SAID SHE'D BE BACK.
THE GIRL WITH THE STRAP MASCOT.

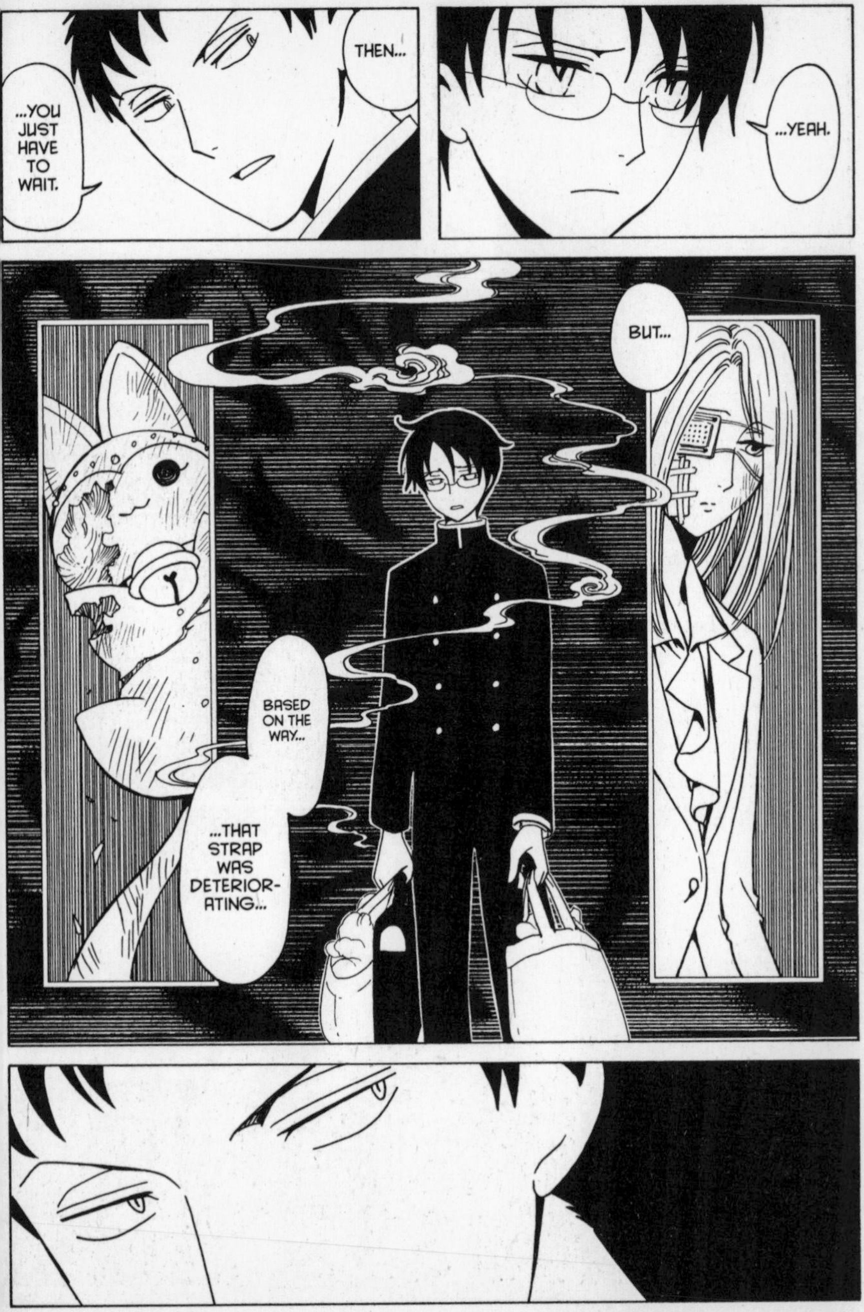
...YEAH.
THEN...
...YOU JUST HAVE TO WAIT.
BUT...
BASED ON THE WAY...
...THAT STRAP WAS DETERIOR-ATING...

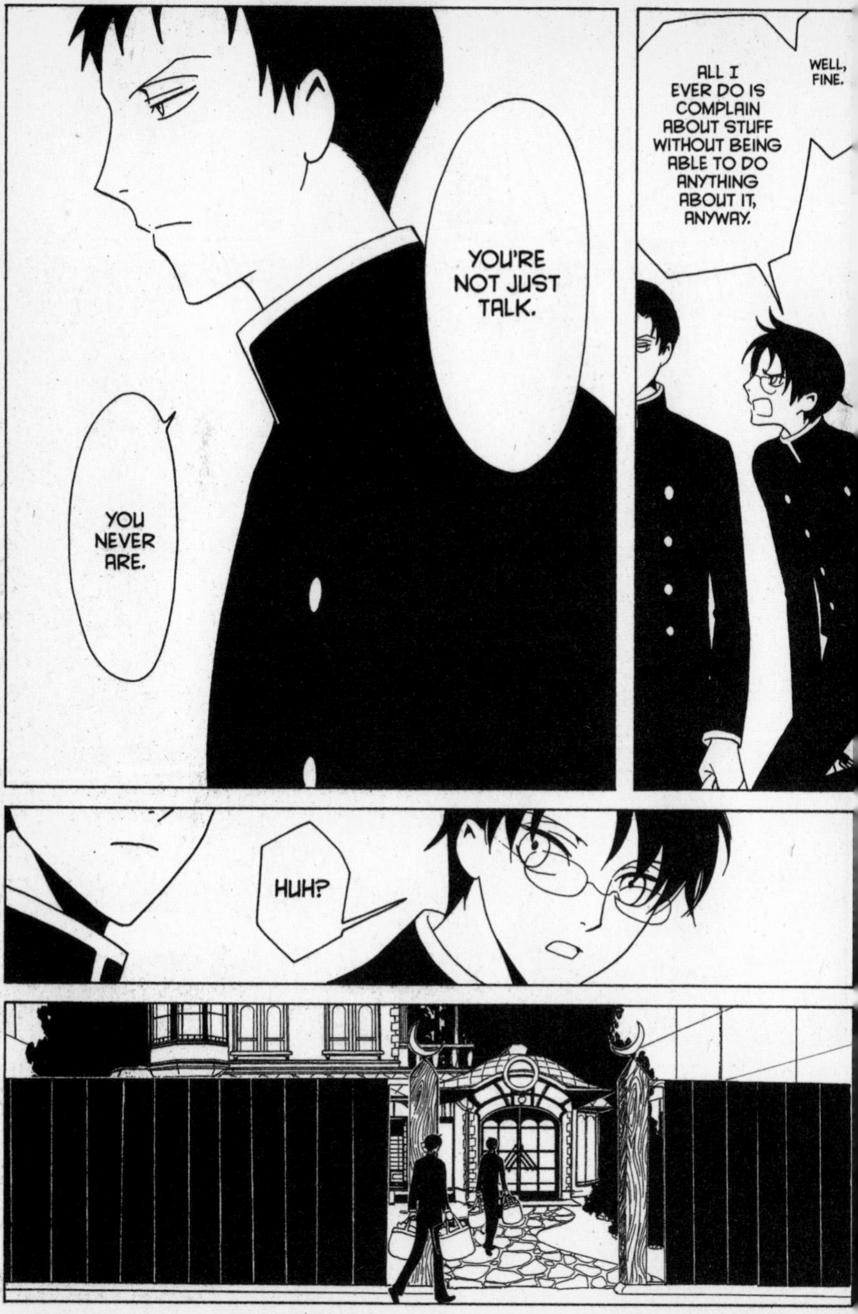
WELL, FINE.
ALL I EVER DO IS COMPLAIN ABOUT STUFF WITHOUT BEING ABLE TO DO ANYTHING ABOUT IT, ANYWAY.
YOU'RE NOT JUST TALK.
YOU NEVER ARE.
HUH?

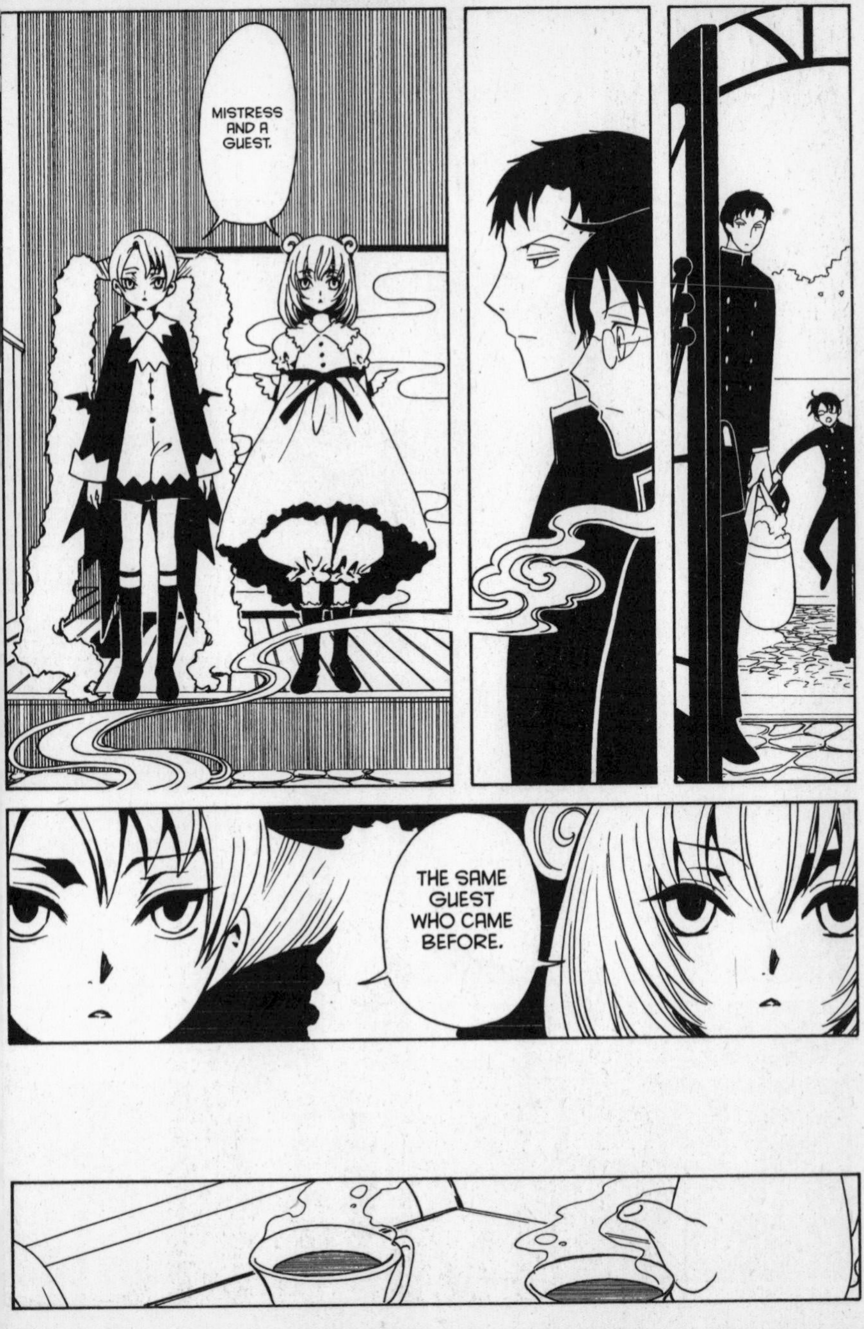
MISTRESS AND A GUEST.
THE SAME GUEST WHO CAME BEFORE.

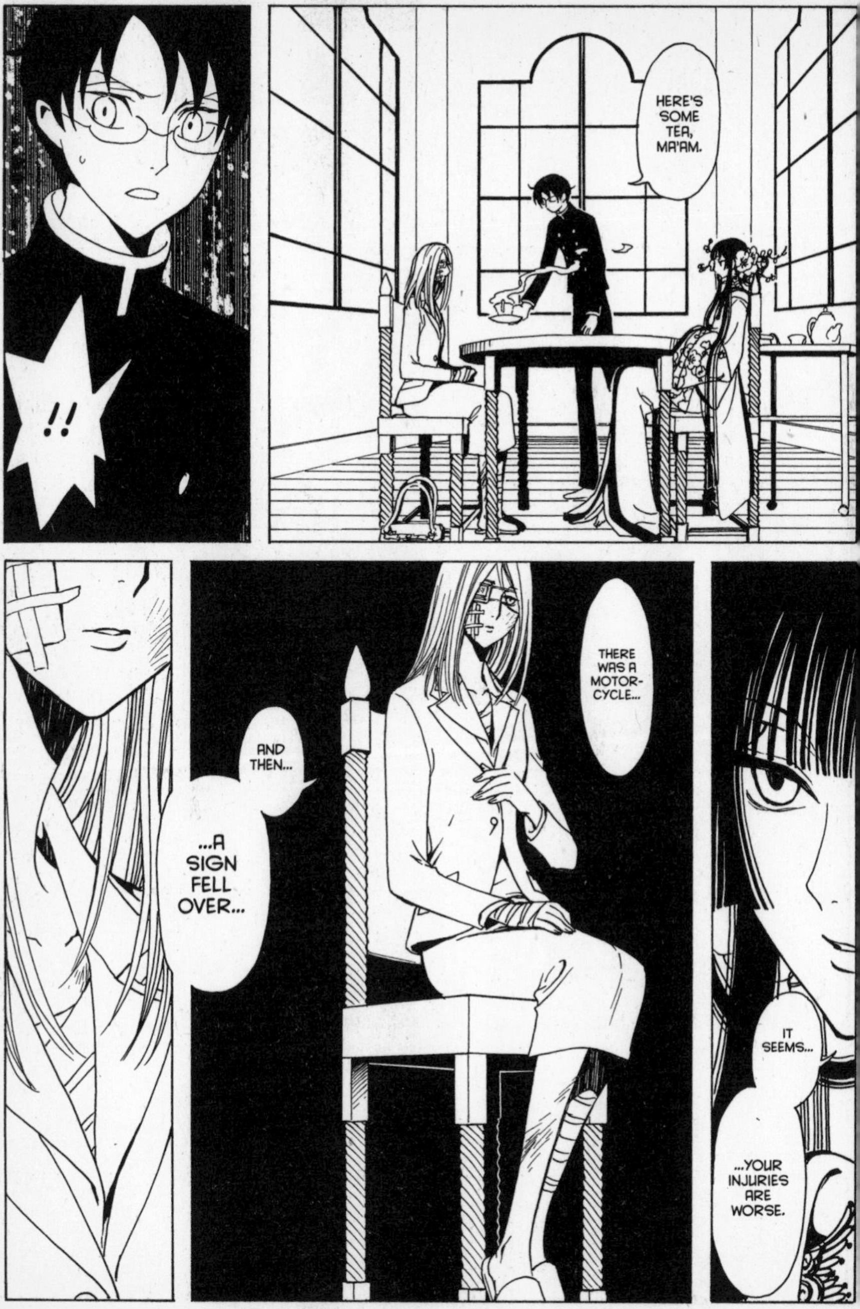
HERE'S SOME TEA, MA'AM.
!!
IT SEEMS...
...YOUR INJURIES ARE WORSE.
THERE WAS A MOTORCYCLE...
AND THEN...
...A SIGN FELL OVER...

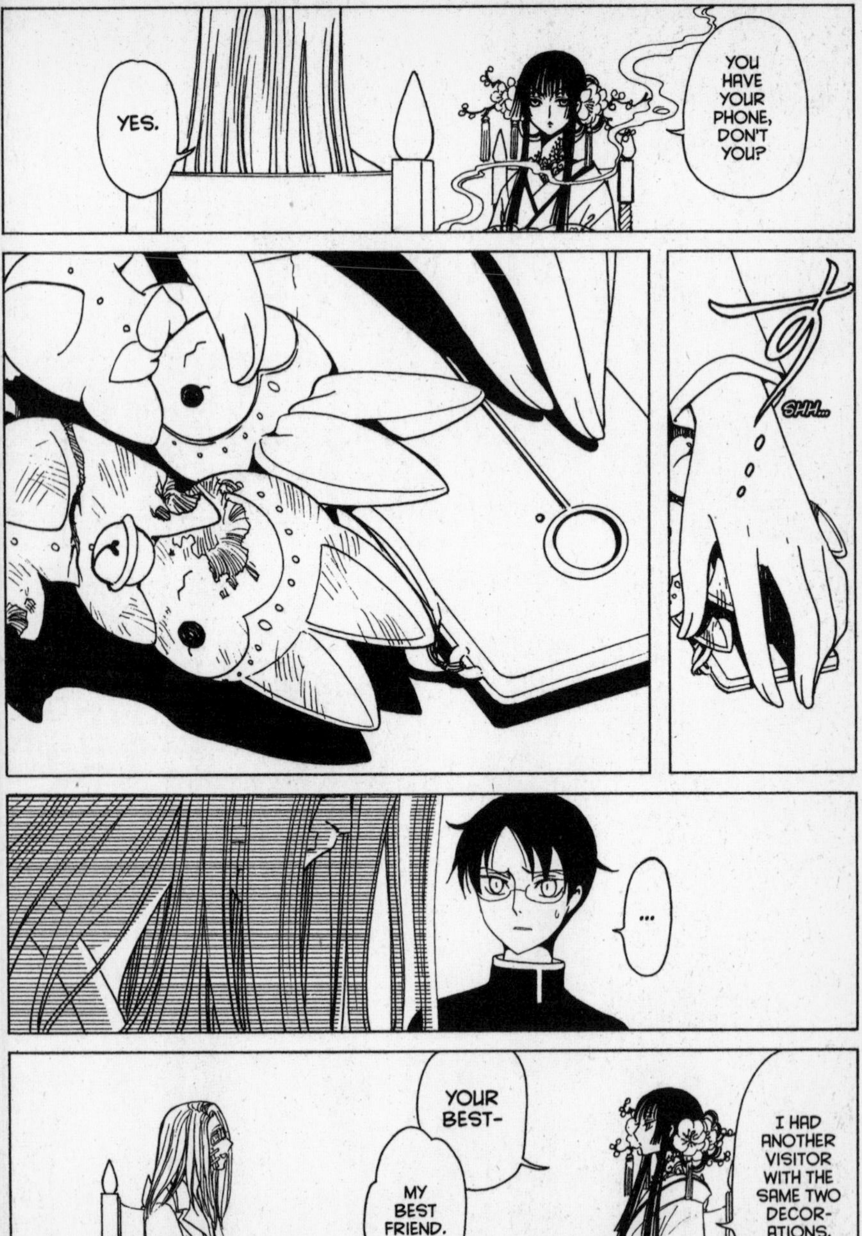
YOU HAVE YOUR PHONE, DON'T YOU?
YES.
SHH...
...
I HAD ANOTHER VISITOR WITH THE SAME TWO DECOR-ATIONS.
YOUR BEST-
MY BEST FRIEND.

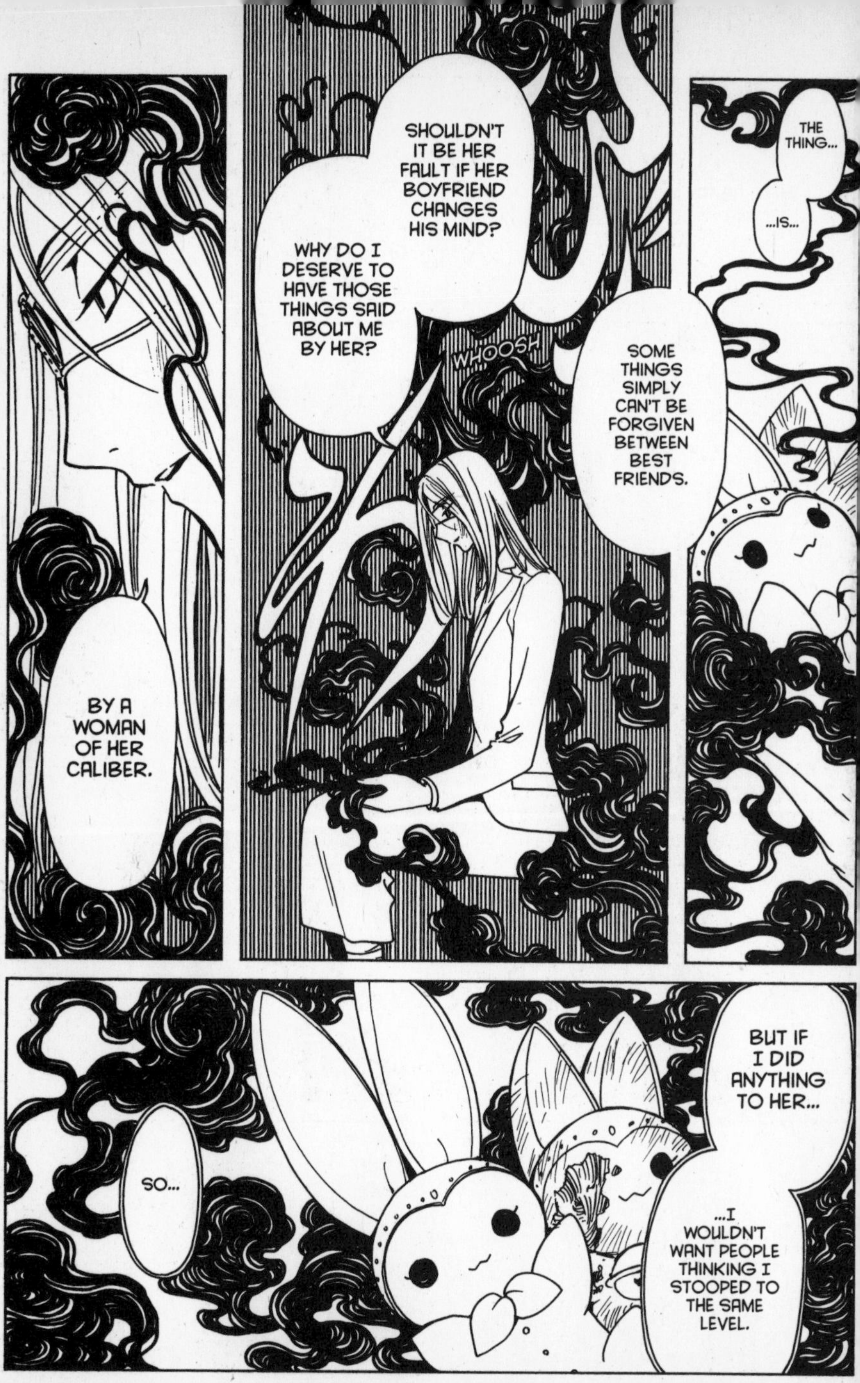
THE THING...
...IS...
SOME THINGS SIMPLY CAN'T BE FORGIVEN BETWEEN BEST FRIENDS.
SHOULDN'T IT BE HER FAULT IF HER BOYFRIEND CHANGES HIS MIND?
WHY DO I DESERVE TO HAVE THOSE THINGS SAID ABOUT ME BY HER?
WHOOSH
BY A WOMAN OF HER CALIBER.
BUT IF I DID ANYTHING TO HER...
...I WOULDN'T WANT PEOPLE THINKING I STOOPED TO THE SAME LEVEL.
SO...

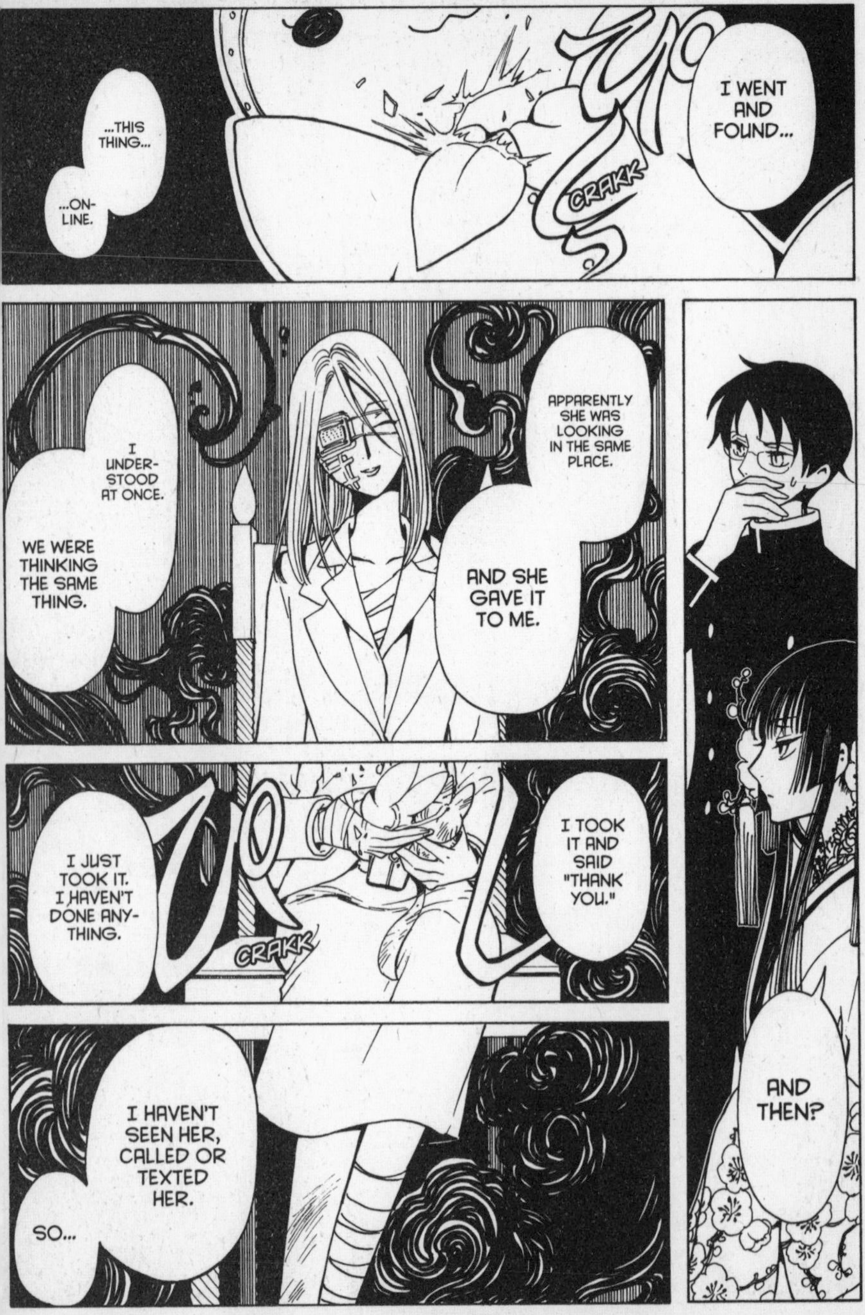
I WENT AND FOUND...
CRAKK
...THIS THING...
...ON-LINE.
AND THEN?
APPARENTLY SHE WAS LOOKING IN THE SAME PLACE.
AND SHE GAVE IT TO ME.
I UNDERSTOOD AT ONCE.
WE WERE THINKING THE SAME THING.
I TOOK IT AND SAID "THANK YOU."
CRAKK
I JUST TOOK IT. I HAVEN'T DONE ANYTHING.
I HAVEN'T SEEN HER, CALLED OR TEXTED HER.
SO...

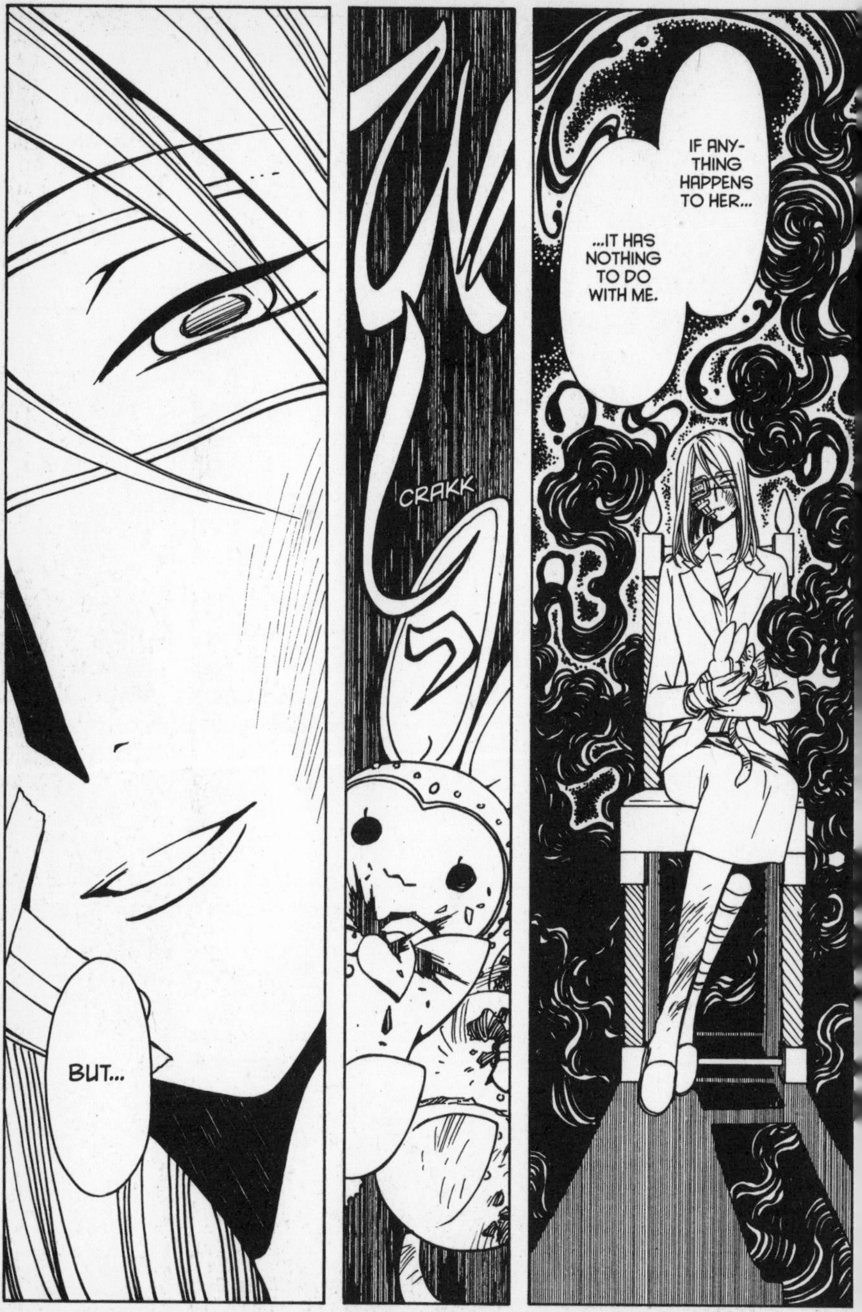
IF ANY-THING HAPPENS TO HER...
...IT HAS NOTHING TO DO WITH ME.
CRAKK
BUT...

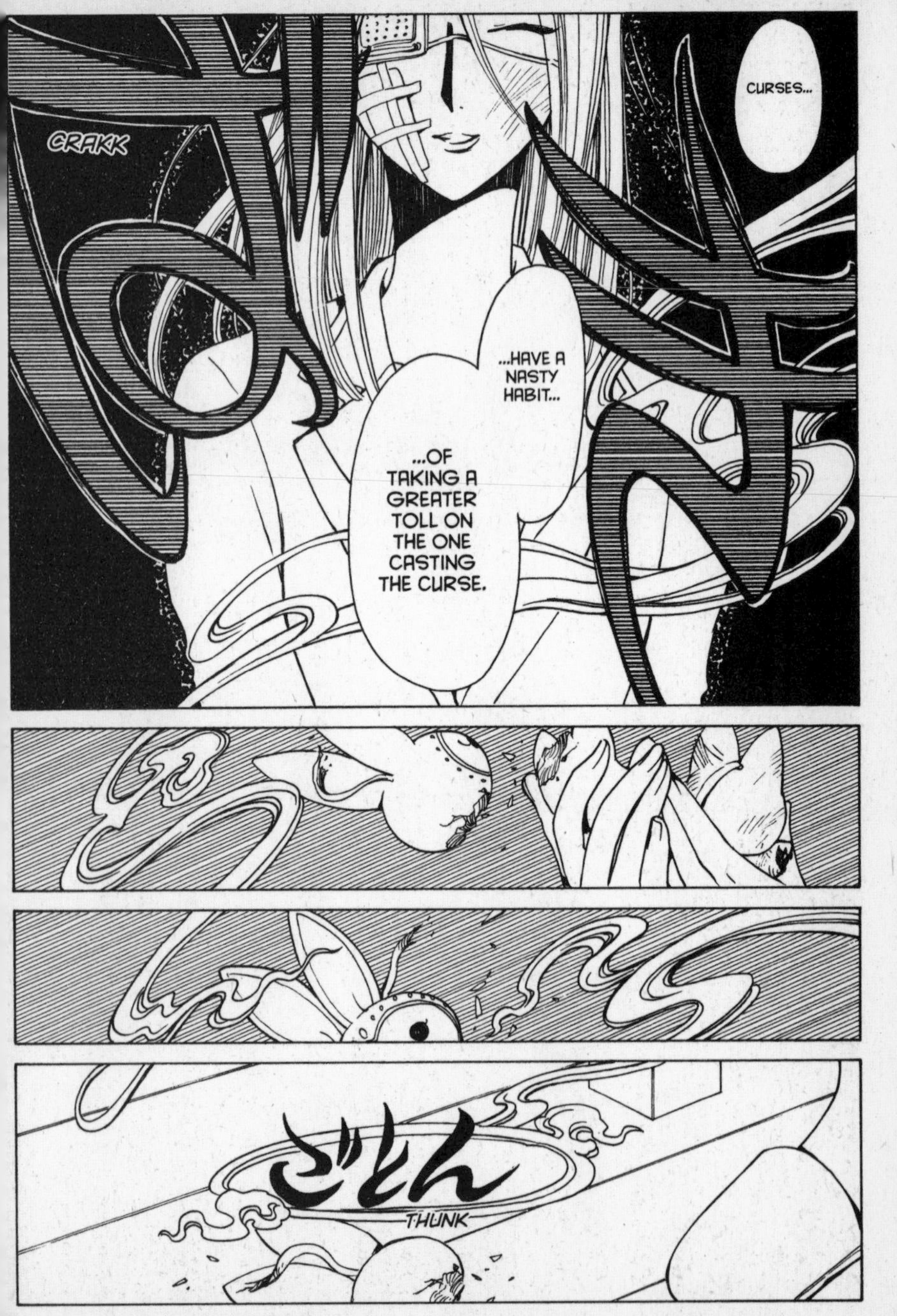
CURSES...
...HAVE A NASTY HABIT...
...OF TAKING A GREATER TOLL ON THE ONE CASTING THE CURSE.
CRAKK
ごとん
THUNK

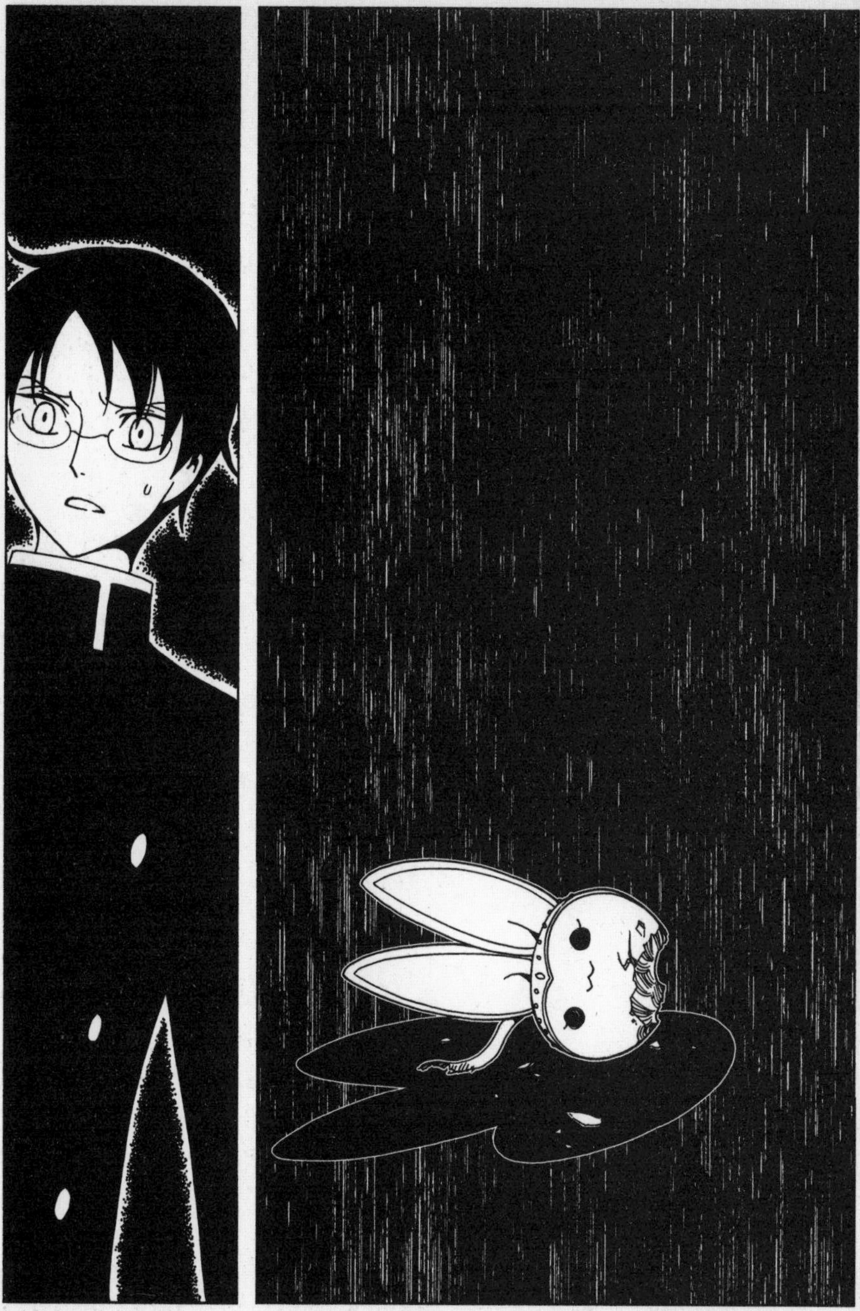

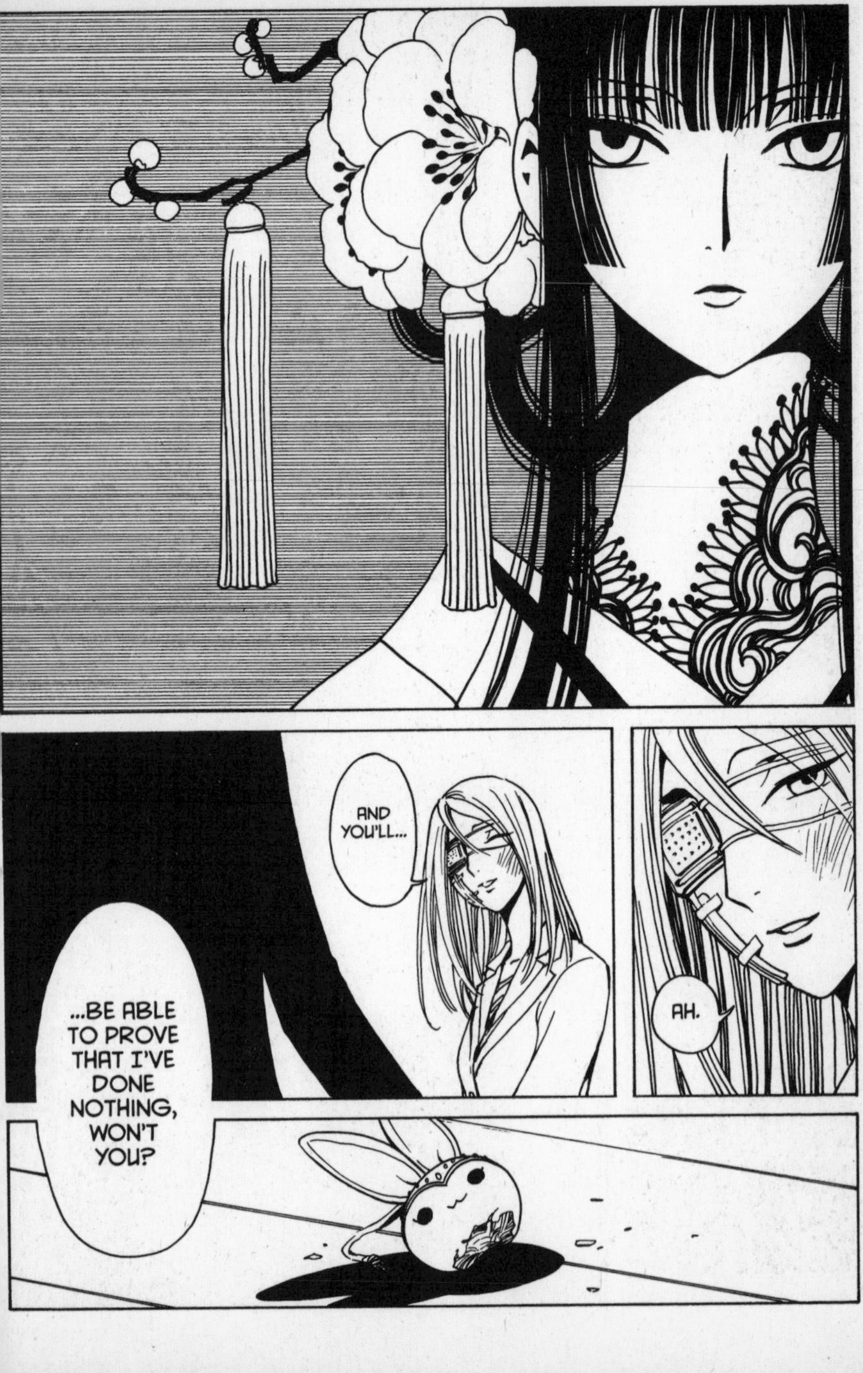
AH.
AND YOU'LL...
...BE ABLE TO PROVE THAT I'VE DONE NOTHING, WON'T YOU?

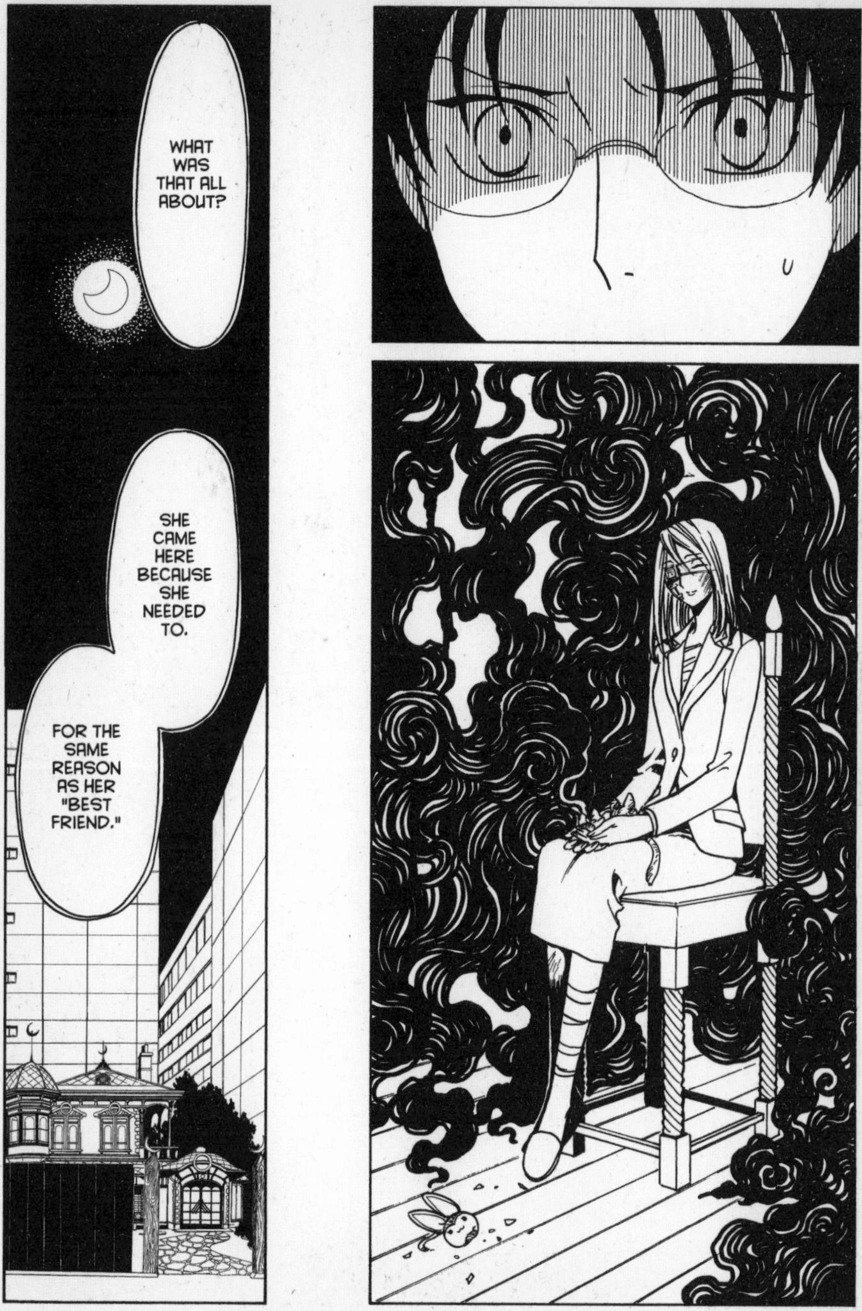
WHAT WAS THAT ALL ABOUT?
SHE CAME HERE BECAUSE SHE NEEDED TO.
FOR THE SAME REASON AS HER "BEST FRIEND."

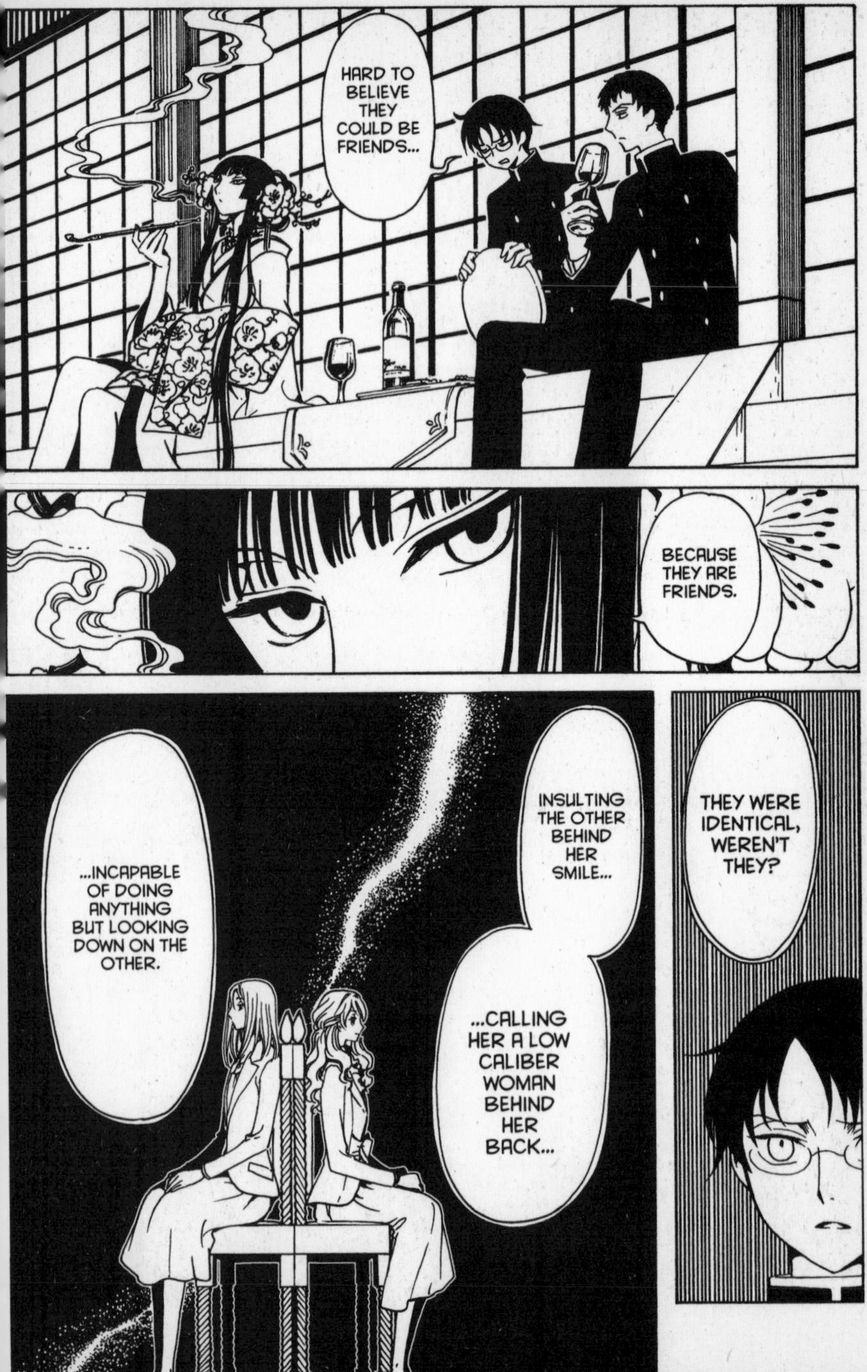
HARD TO BELIEVE THEY COULD BE FRIENDS...
BECAUSE THEY ARE FRIENDS.
...
THEY WERE IDENTICAL, WEREN'T THEY?
INSULTING THE OTHER BEHIND HER SMILE...
...CALLING HER A LOW CALIBER WOMAN BEHIND HER BACK...
...INCAPABLE OF DOING ANYTHING BUT LOOKING DOWN ON THE OTHER.

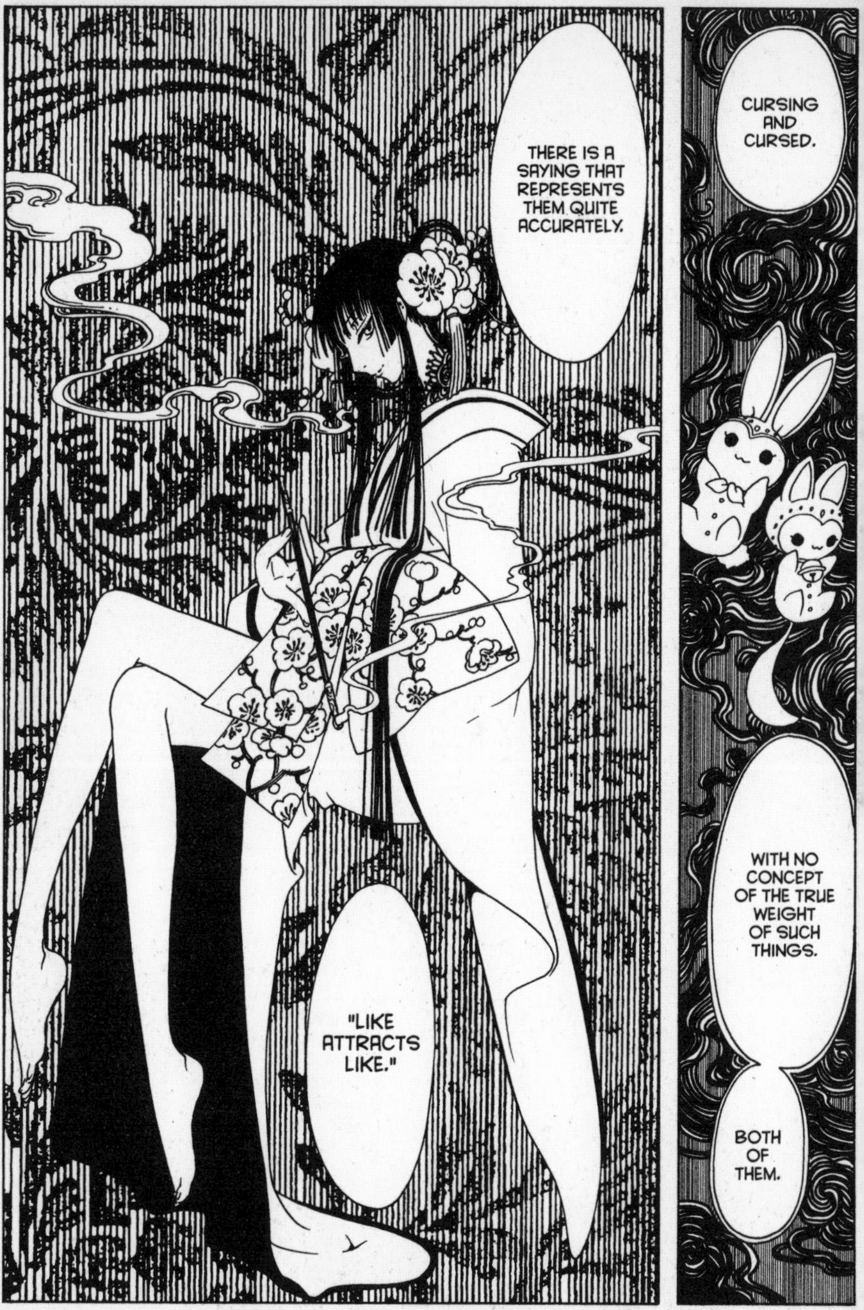
CURSING AND CURSED.
WITH NO CONCEPT OF THE TRUE WEIGHT OF SUCH THINGS.
BOTH OF THEM.
THERE IS A SAYING THAT REPRESENTS THEM QUITE ACCURATELY.
"LIKE ATTRACTS LIKE."

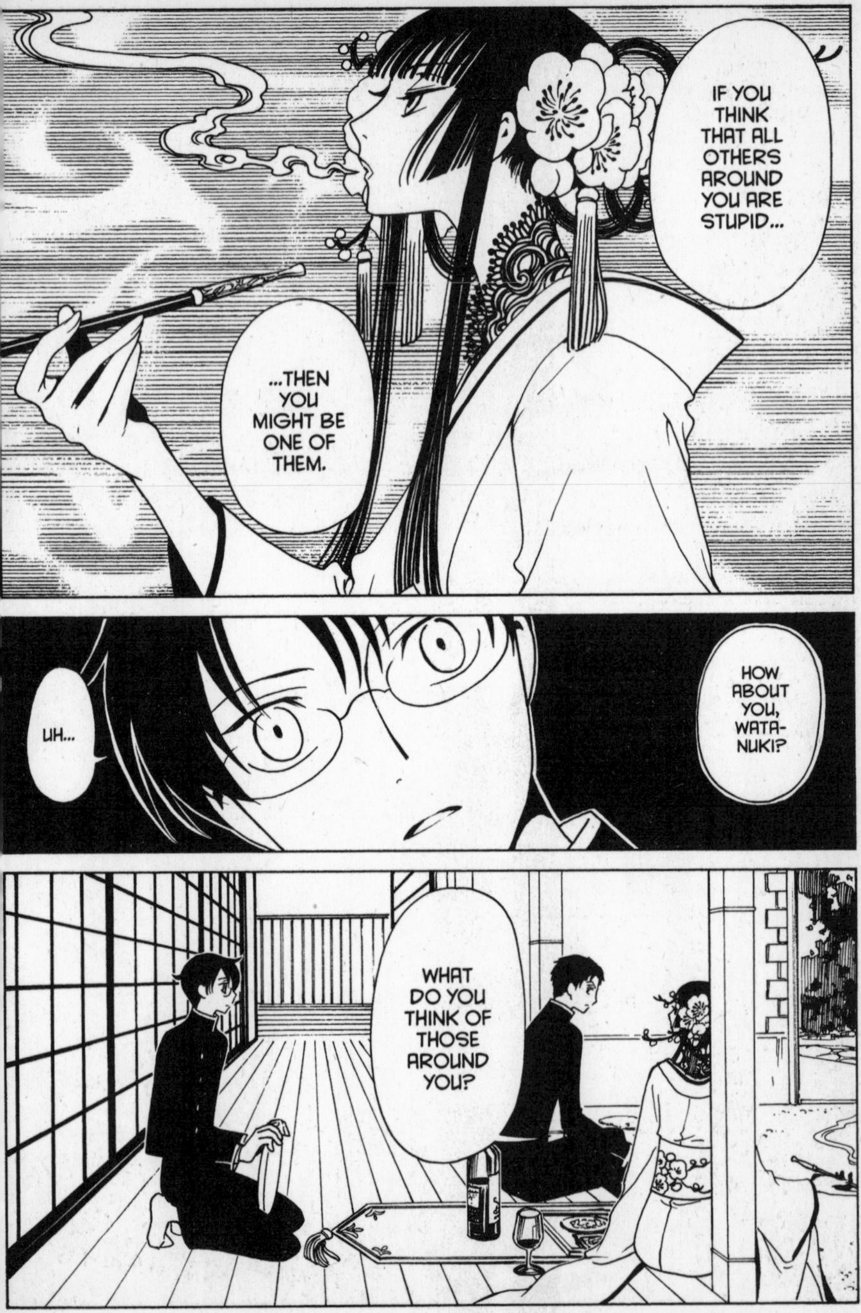
IF YOU THINK THAT ALL OTHERS AROUND YOU ARE STUPID...
...THEN YOU MIGHT BE ONE OF THEM.
HOW ABOUT YOU, WATA-NUKI?
UH...
WHAT DO YOU THINK OF THOSE AROUND YOU?

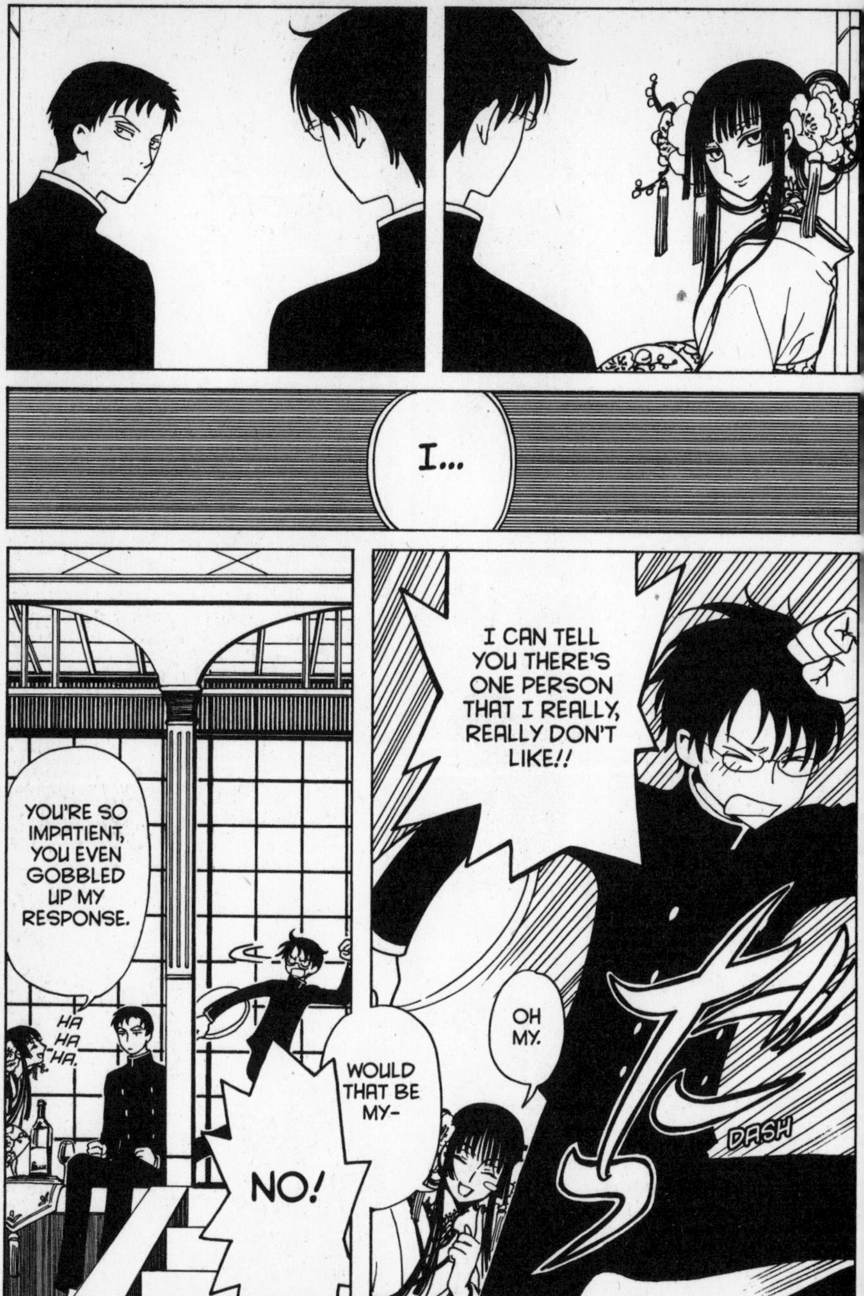
I...
I CAN TELL YOU THERE'S ONE PERSON THAT I REALLY, REALLY DON'T LIKE!!
OH MY.
WOULD THAT BE MY-
NO!
DASH
YOU'RE SO IMPATIENT, YOU EVEN GOBBLED UP MY RESPONSE.
HA HA HA.

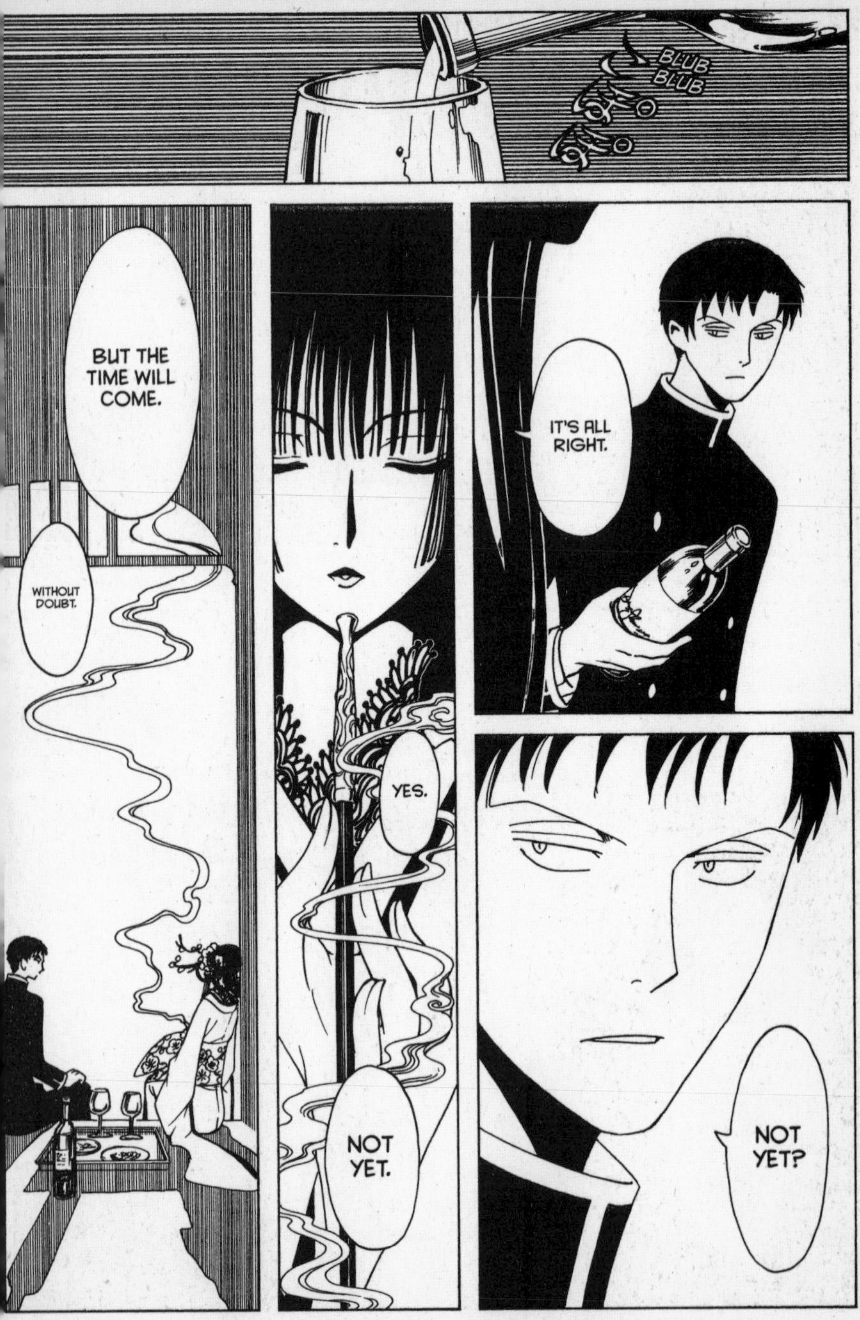
BLUB BLUB
IT'S ALL RIGHT.
NOT YET?
YES.
NOT YET.
BUT THE TIME WILL COME.
WITHOUT DOUBT.

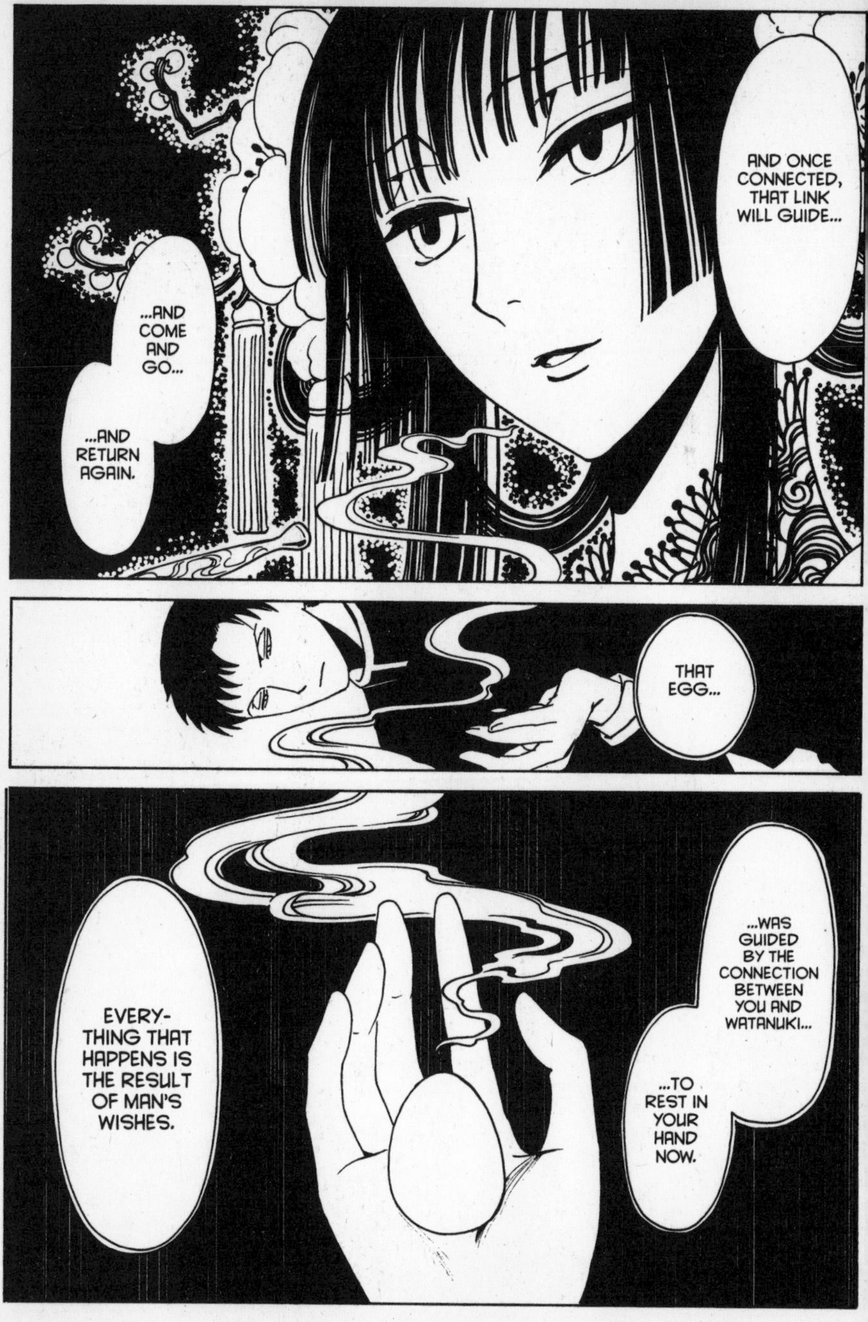
AND ONCE CONNECTED, THAT LINK WILL GUIDE...
...AND COME AND GO...
...AND RETURN AGAIN.
THAT EGG...
...WAS GUIDED BY THE CONNECTION BETWEEN YOU AND WATANUKI...
...TO REST IN YOUR HAND NOW.
EVERY-THING THAT HAPPENS IS THE RESULT OF MAN'S WISHES.

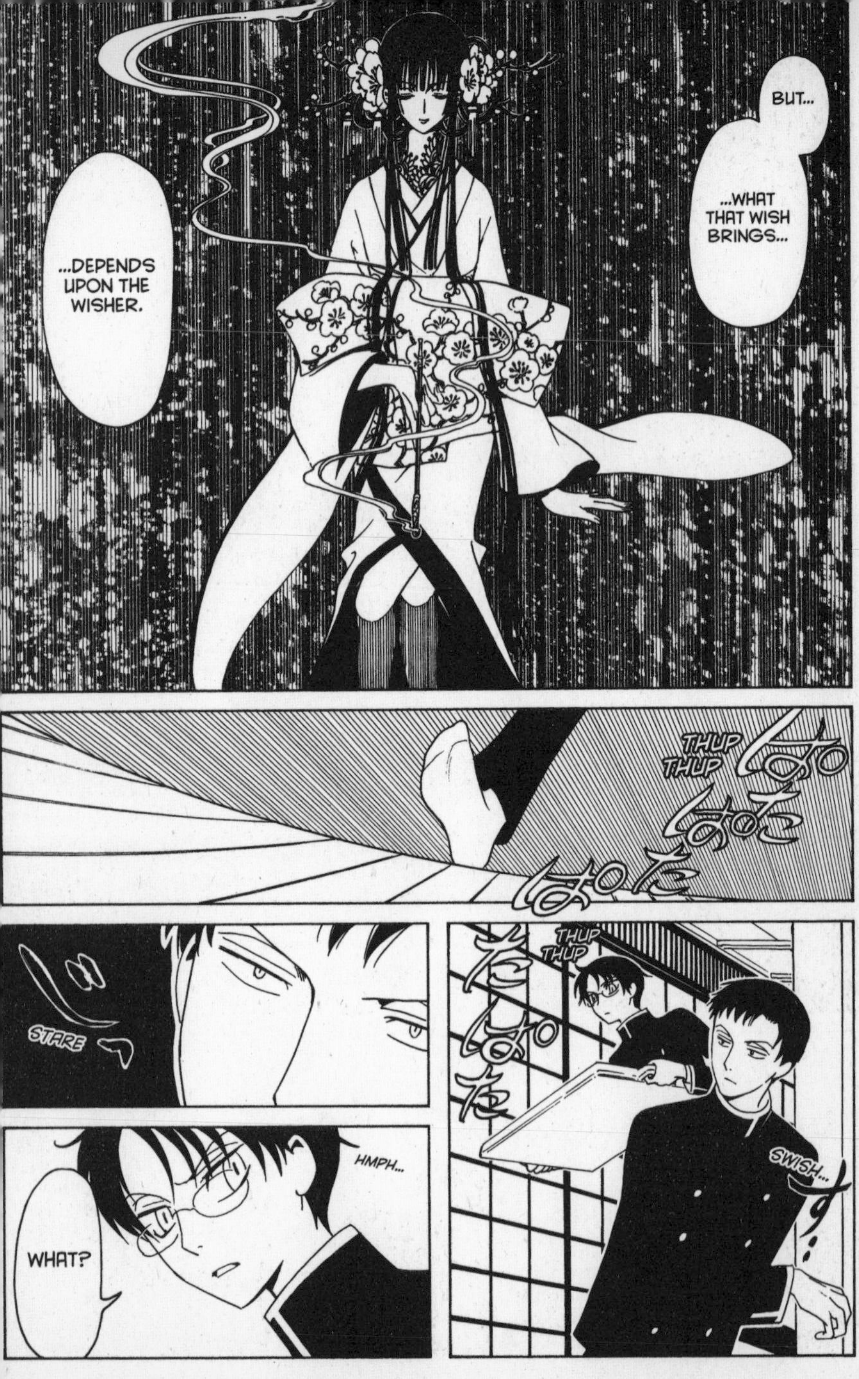
BUT...
...WHAT THAT WISH BRINGS...
...DEPENDS UPON THE WISHER.
THUP THUP
THUP THUP
SWISH...
STARE
HMPH...
WHAT?

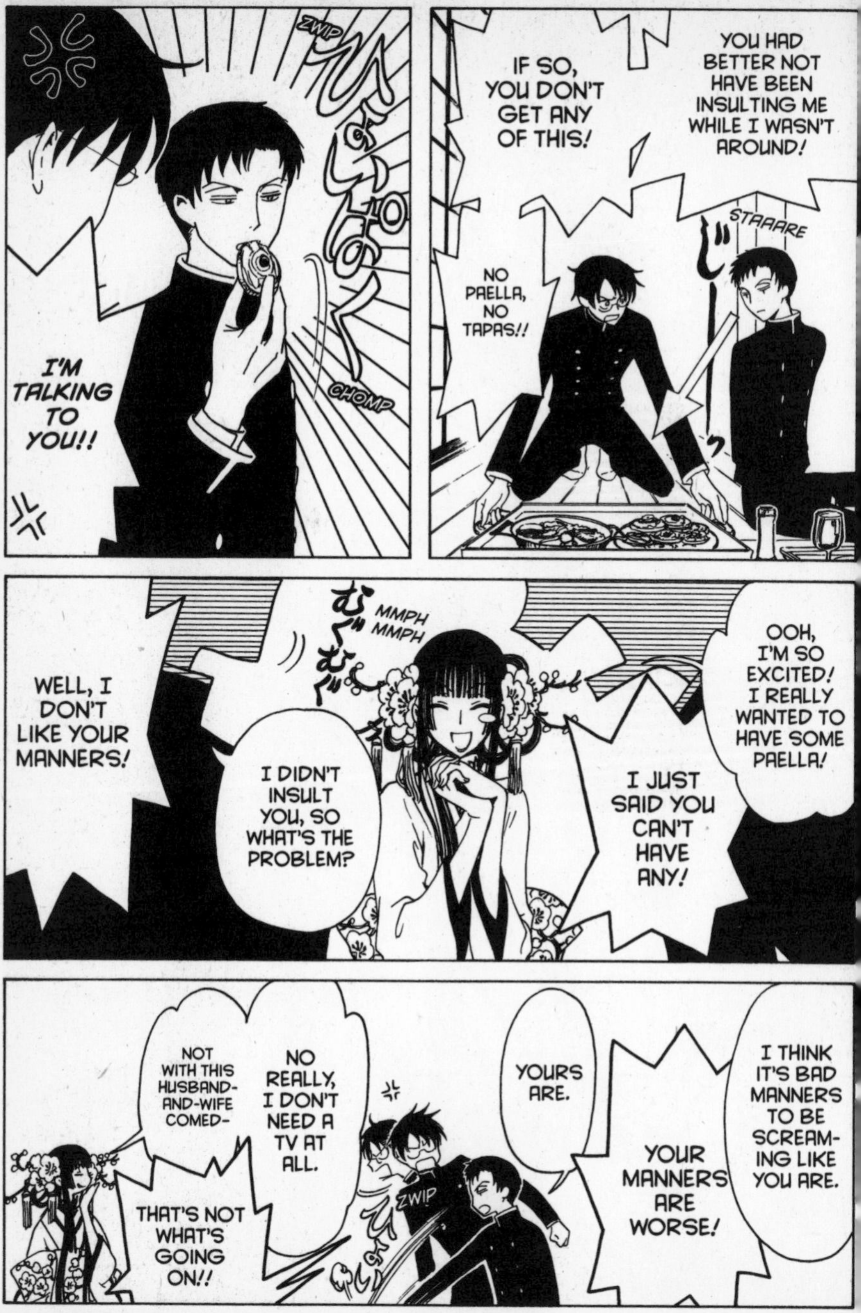
YOU HAD BETTER NOT HAVE BEEN INSULTING ME WHILE I WASN'T AROUND!
IF SO, YOU DON'T GET ANY OF THIS!
STAAARE
NO PAELLA, NO TAPAS!!
ZWIP
CHOMP
I'M TALKING TO YOU!!
OOH, I'M SO EXCITED! I REALLY WANTED TO HAVE SOME PAELLA!
MMPH MMPH
I JUST SAID YOU CAN'T HAVE ANY!
I DIDN'T INSULT YOU, SO WHAT'S THE PROBLEM?
WELL, I DON'T LIKE YOUR MANNERS!
I THINK IT'S BAD MANNERS TO BE SCREAMING LIKE YOU ARE.
YOUR MANNERS ARE WORSE!
YOURS ARE.
ZWIP
NO REALLY, I DON'T NEED A TV AT ALL.
NOT WITH THIS HUSBAND-AND-WIFE COMED-
THAT'S NOT WHAT'S GOING ON!!

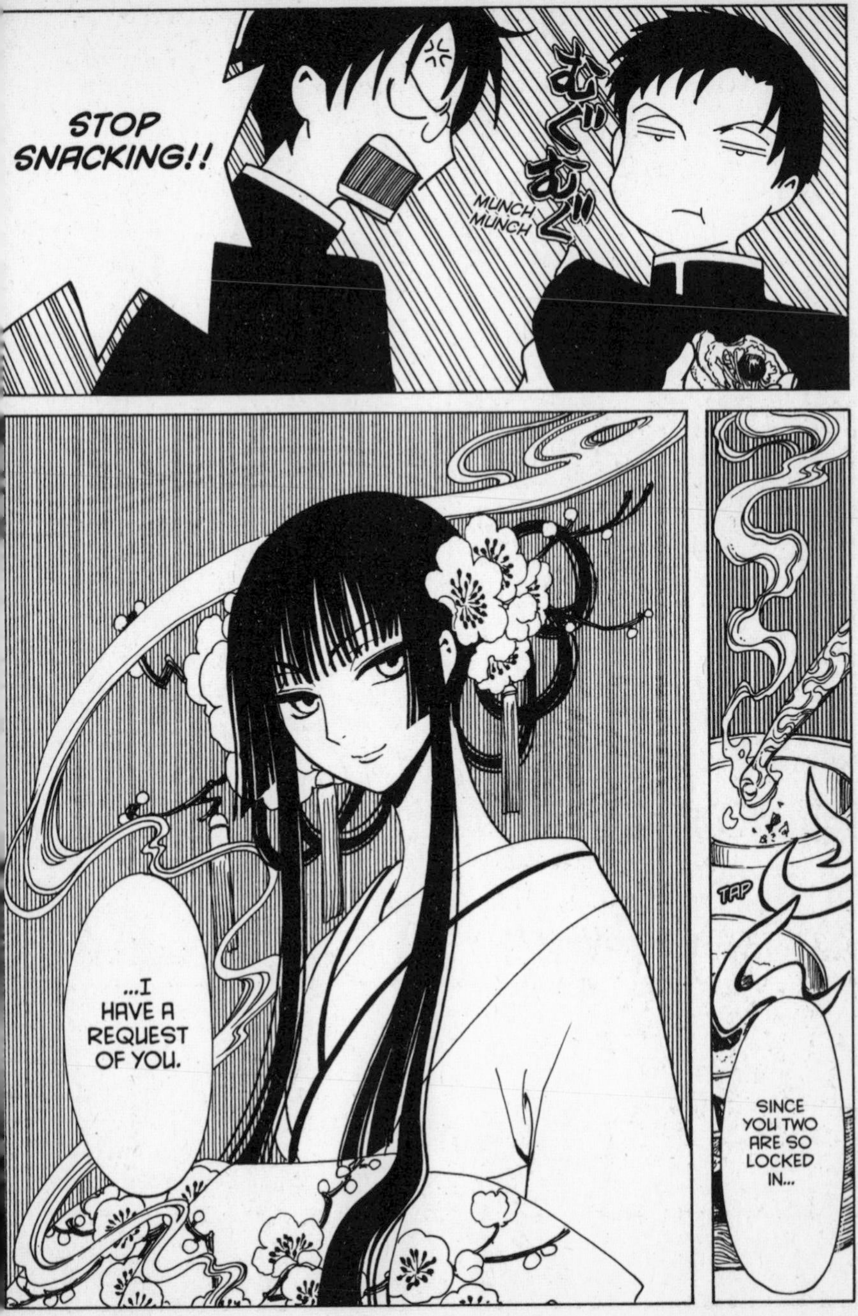
むぐむぐ
MUNCH MUNCH
STOP SNACKING!!
TAP
SINCE YOU TWO ARE SO LOCKED IN...
...I HAVE A REQUEST OF YOU.

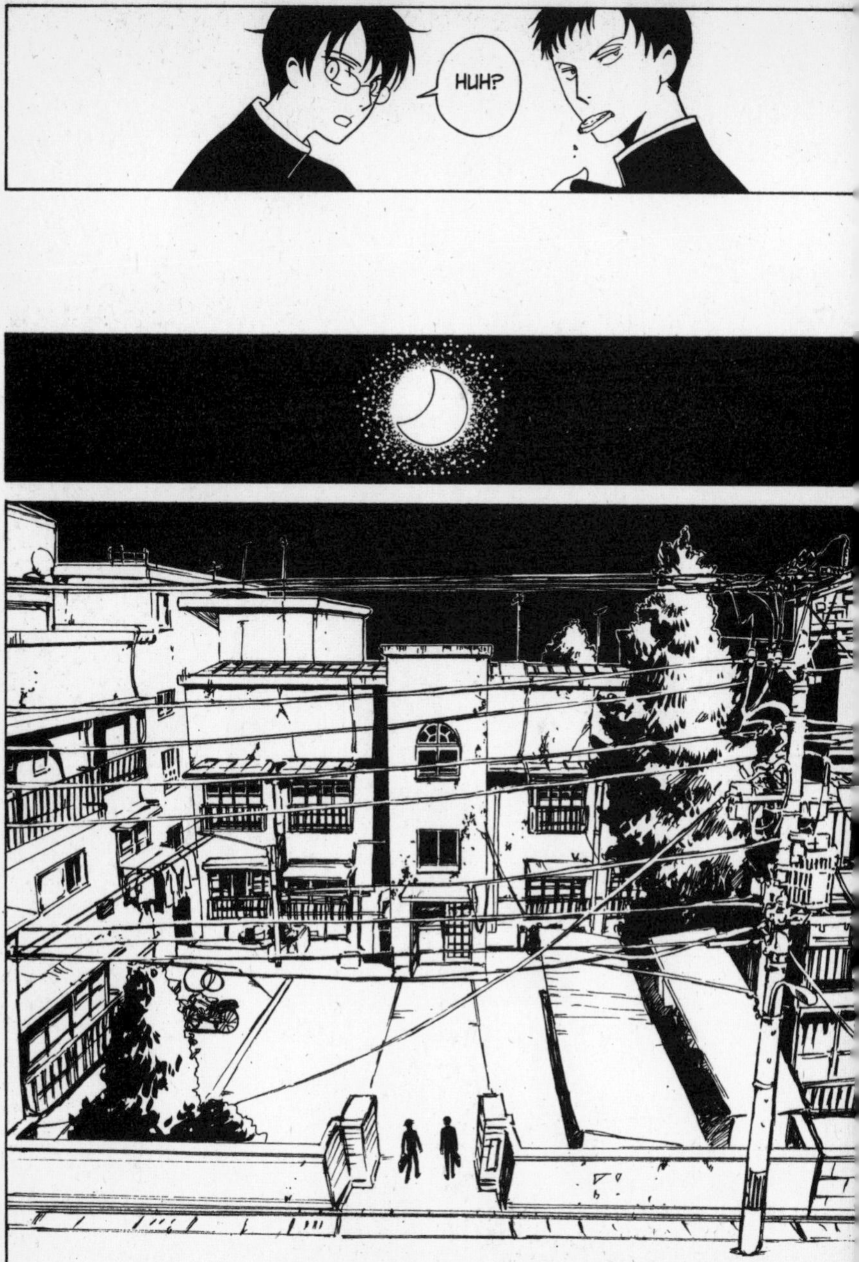
HUH?

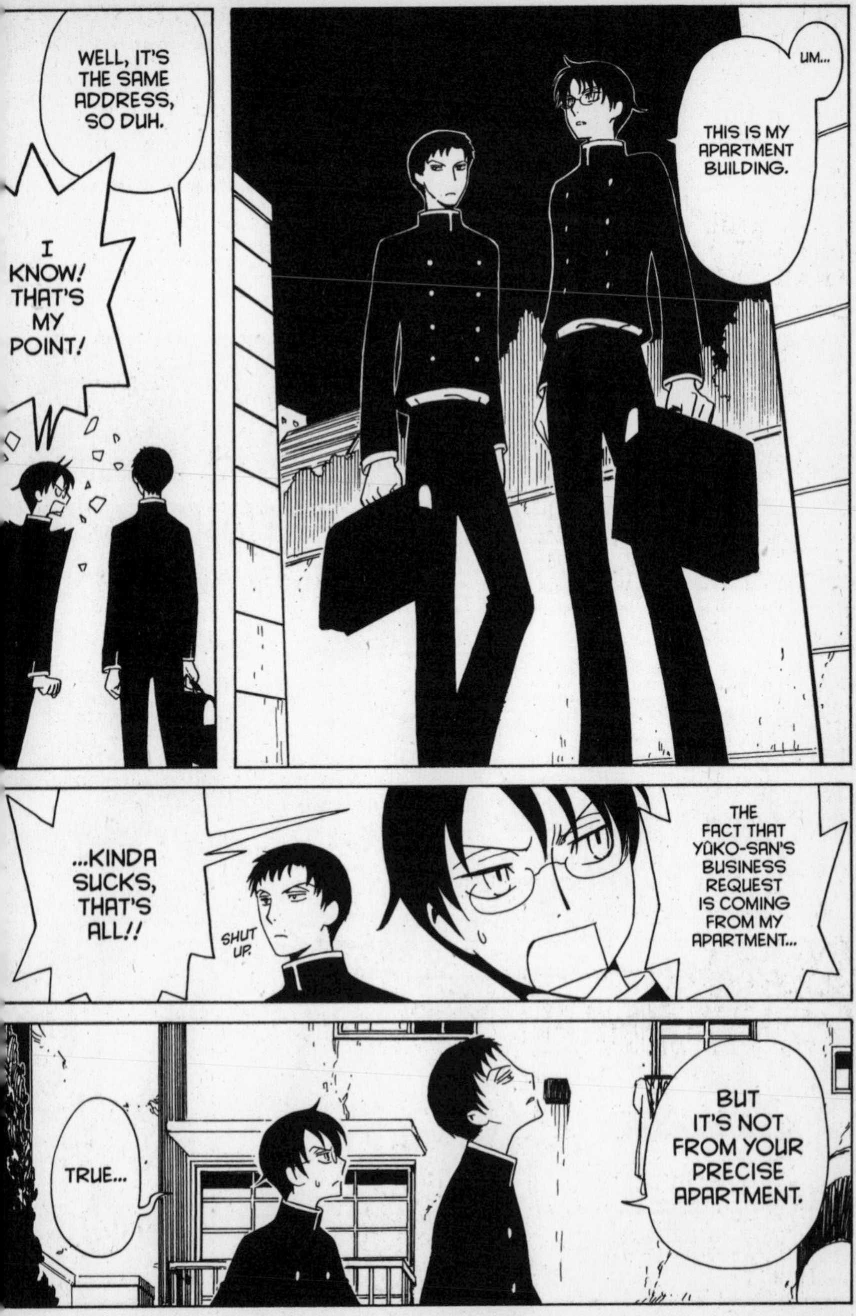
UM...
THIS IS MY APARTMENT BUILDING.
WELL, IT'S THE SAME ADDRESS, SO DUH.
I KNOW! THAT'S MY POINT!
THE FACT THAT YŪKO-SAN'S BUSINESS REQUEST IS COMING FROM MY APARTMENT...
...KINDA SUCKS, THAT'S ALL!!
SHUT UP.
BUT IT'S NOT FROM YOUR PRECISE APARTMENT.
TRUE...

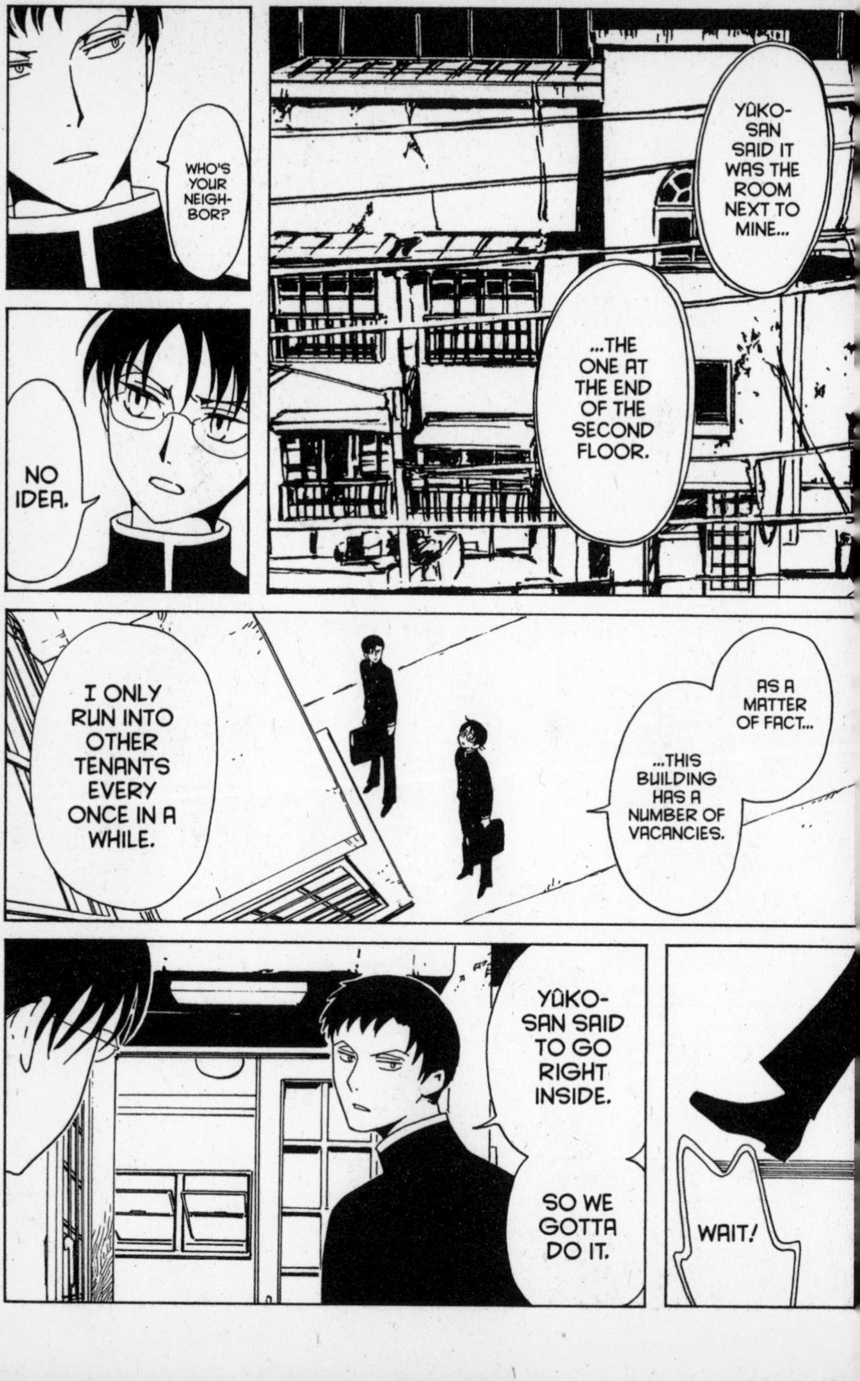
YÛKO-SAN SAID IT WAS THE ROOM NEXT TO MINE...
...THE ONE AT THE END OF THE SECOND FLOOR.
WHO'S YOUR NEIGH-BOR?
NO IDEA.
AS A MATTER OF FACT...
...THIS BUILDING HAS A NUMBER OF VACANCIES.
I ONLY RUN INTO OTHER TENANTS EVERY ONCE IN A WHILE.
WAIT!
YÛKO-SAN SAID TO GO RIGHT INSIDE.
SO WE GOTTA DO IT.

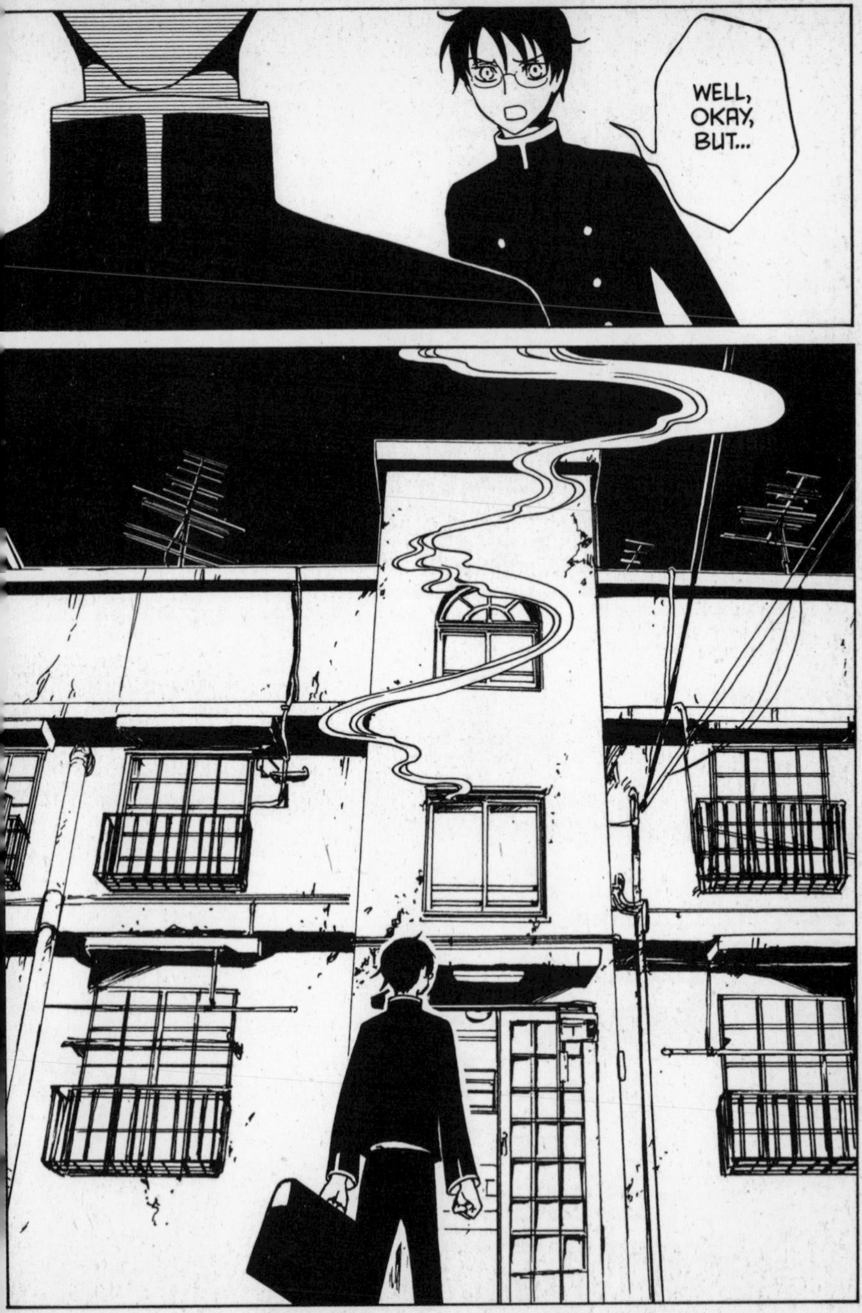
WELL, OKAY, BUT...

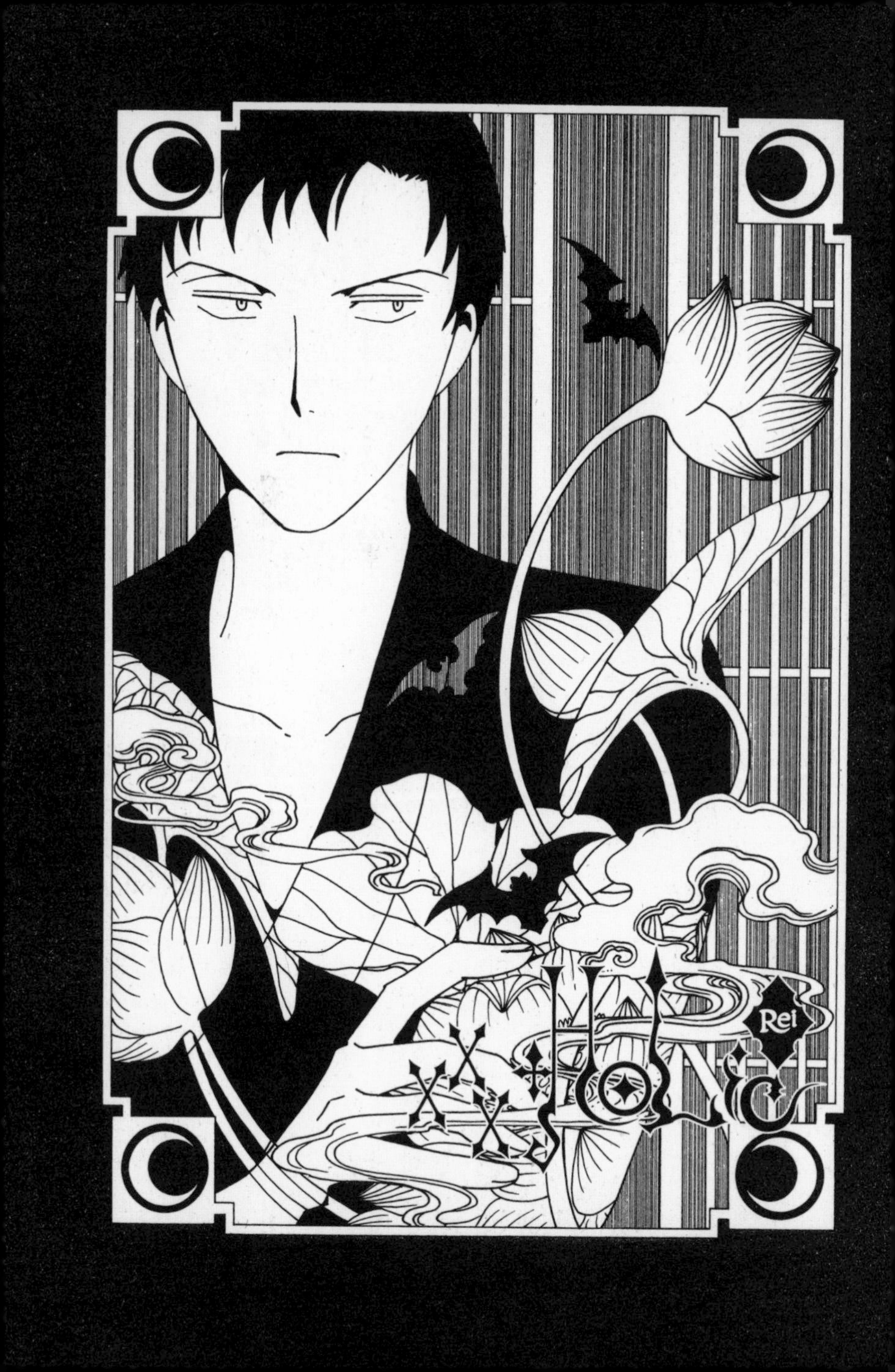
xxxHOLiC
Rei

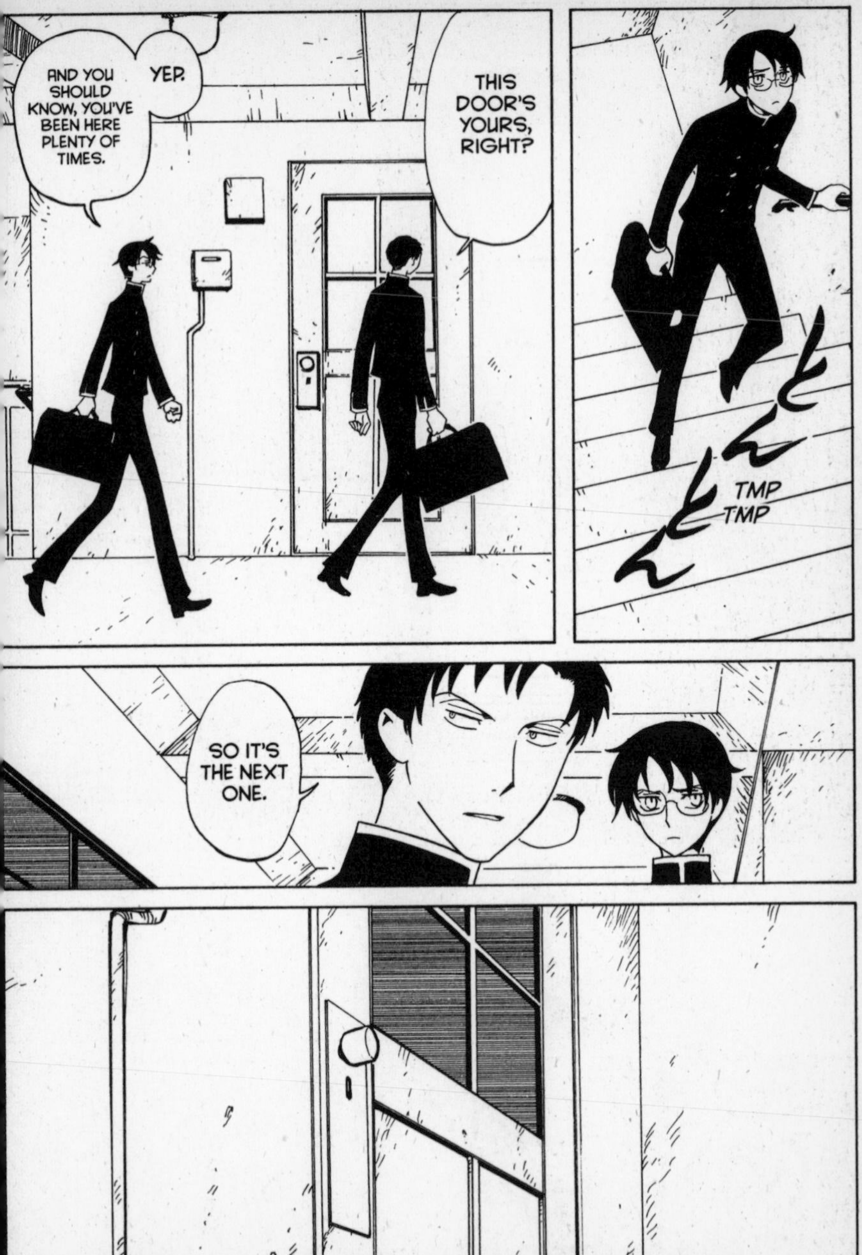
とん とん
TMP TMP
THIS DOOR'S YOURS, RIGHT?
YEP.
AND YOU SHOULD KNOW, YOU'VE BEEN HERE PLENTY OF TIMES.
SO IT'S THE NEXT ONE.

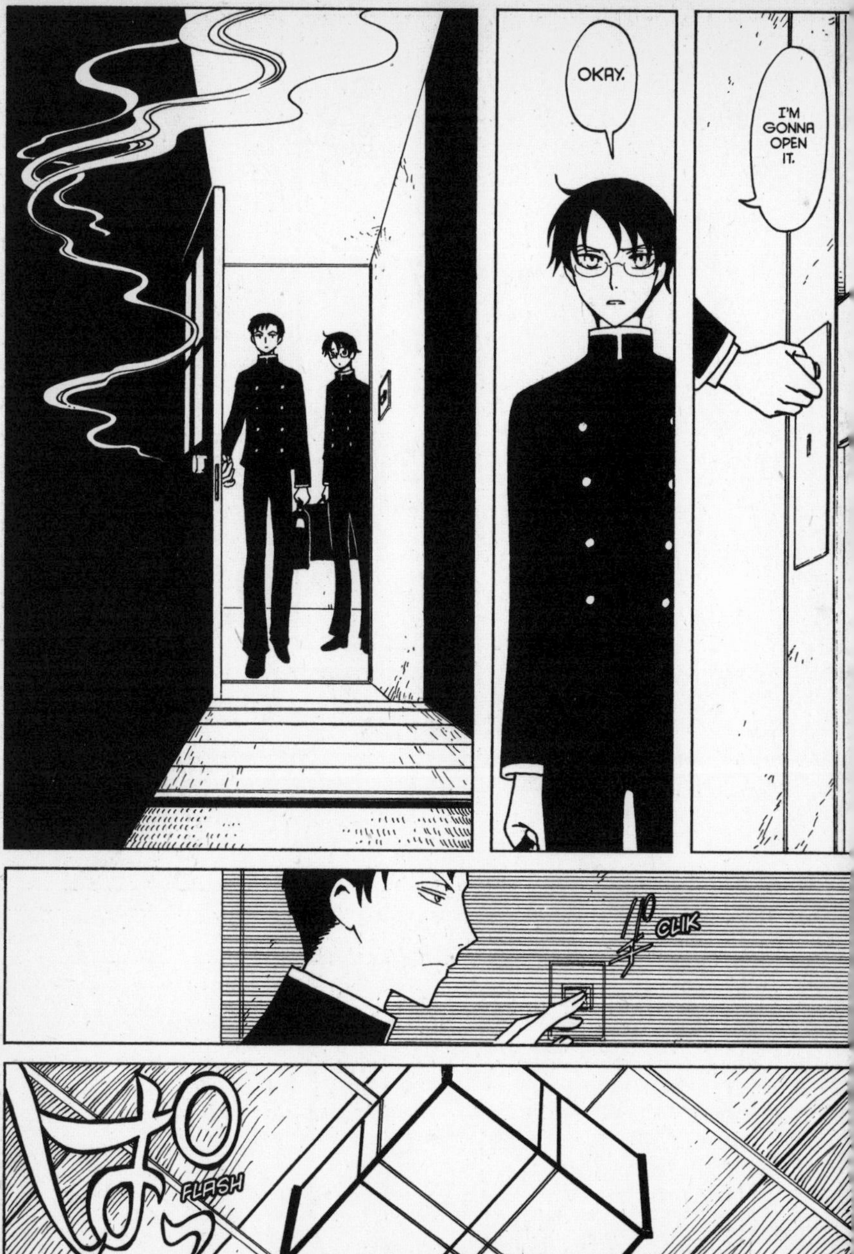
I'M GONNA OPEN IT.
OKAY.
CLIK
FLASH

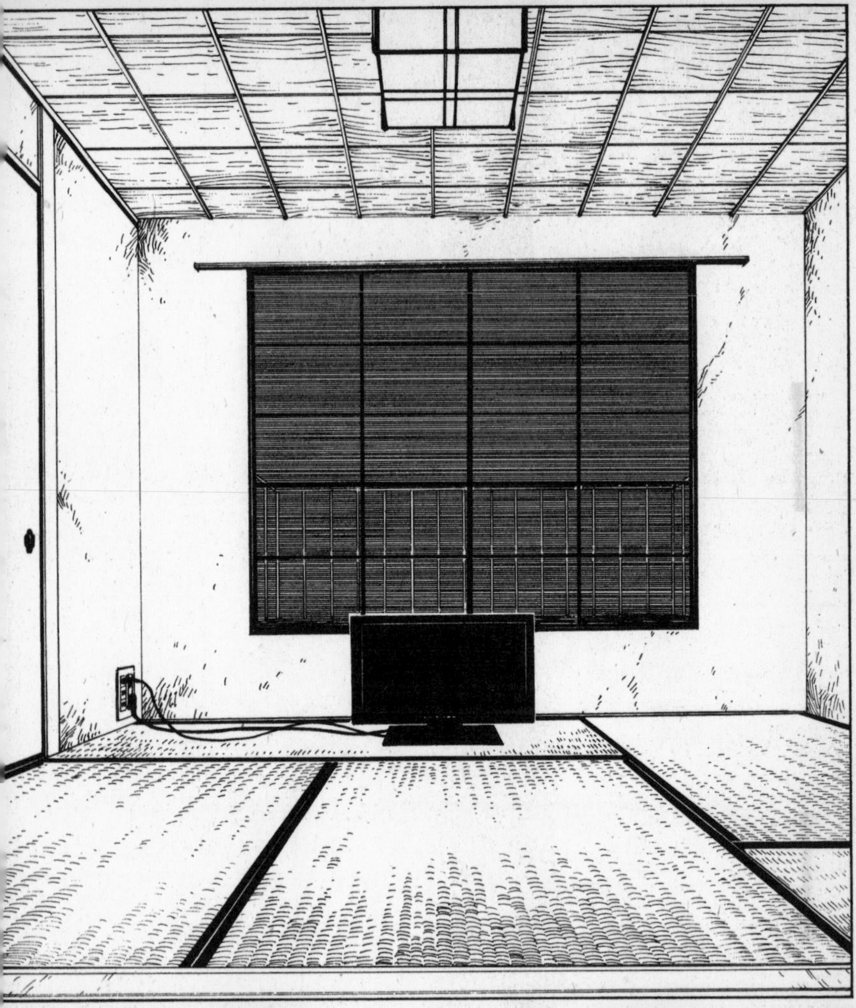

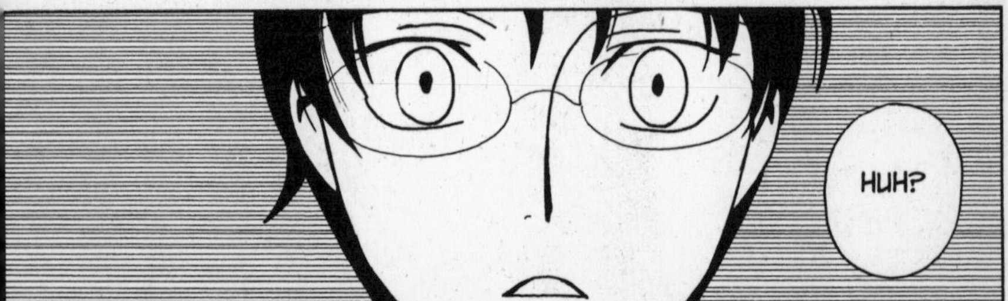
HUH?

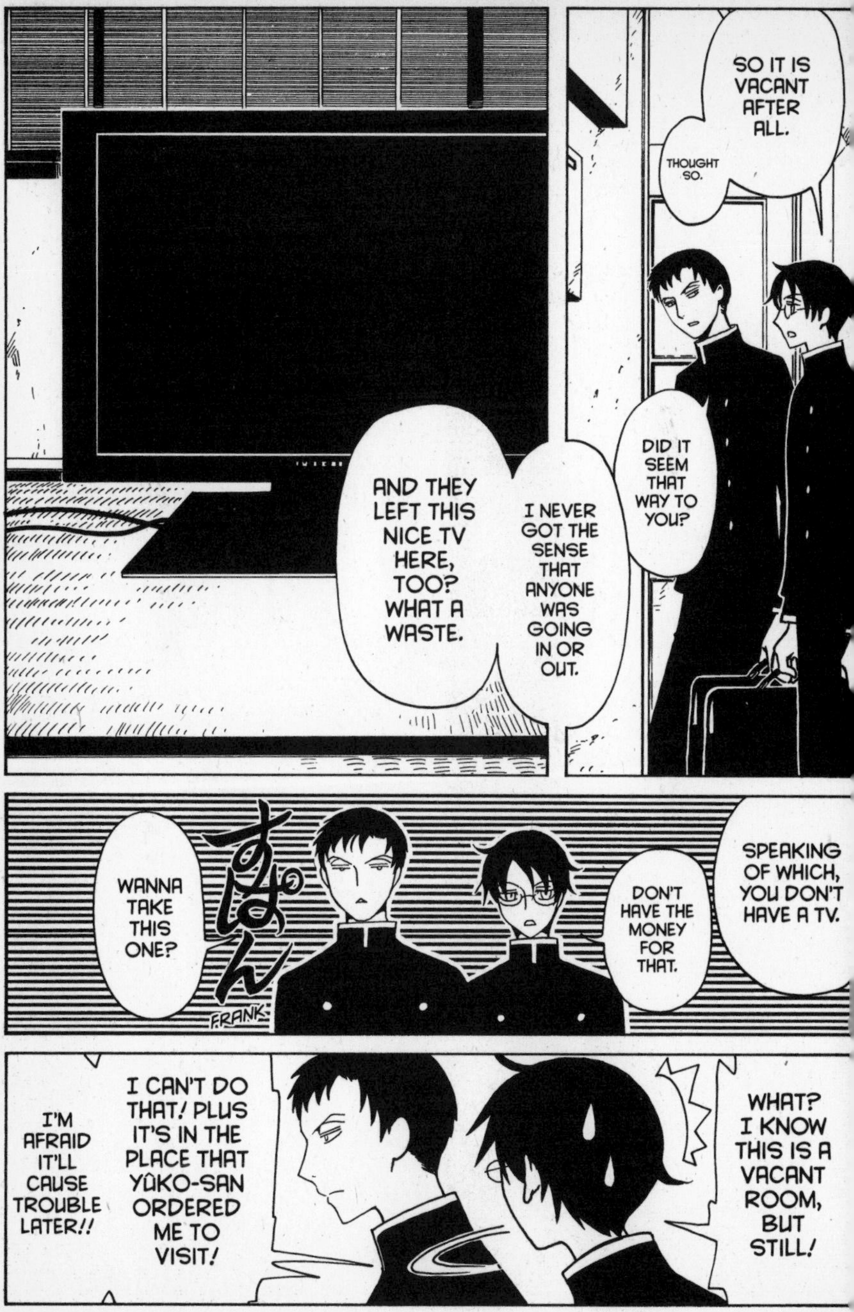
SO IT IS VACANT AFTER ALL.
THOUGHT SO.
DID IT SEEM THAT WAY TO YOU?
I NEVER GOT THE SENSE THAT ANYONE WAS GOING IN OR OUT.
AND THEY LEFT THIS NICE TV HERE, TOO? WHAT A WASTE.
SPEAKING OF WHICH, YOU DON'T HAVE A TV.
DON'T HAVE THE MONEY FOR THAT.
すぱん
FRANK
WANNA TAKE THIS ONE?
WHAT? I KNOW THIS IS A VACANT ROOM, BUT STILL!
I CAN'T DO THAT! PLUS IT'S IN THE PLACE THAT YÛKO-SAN ORDERED ME TO VISIT!
I'M AFRAID IT'LL CAUSE TROUBLE LATER!!

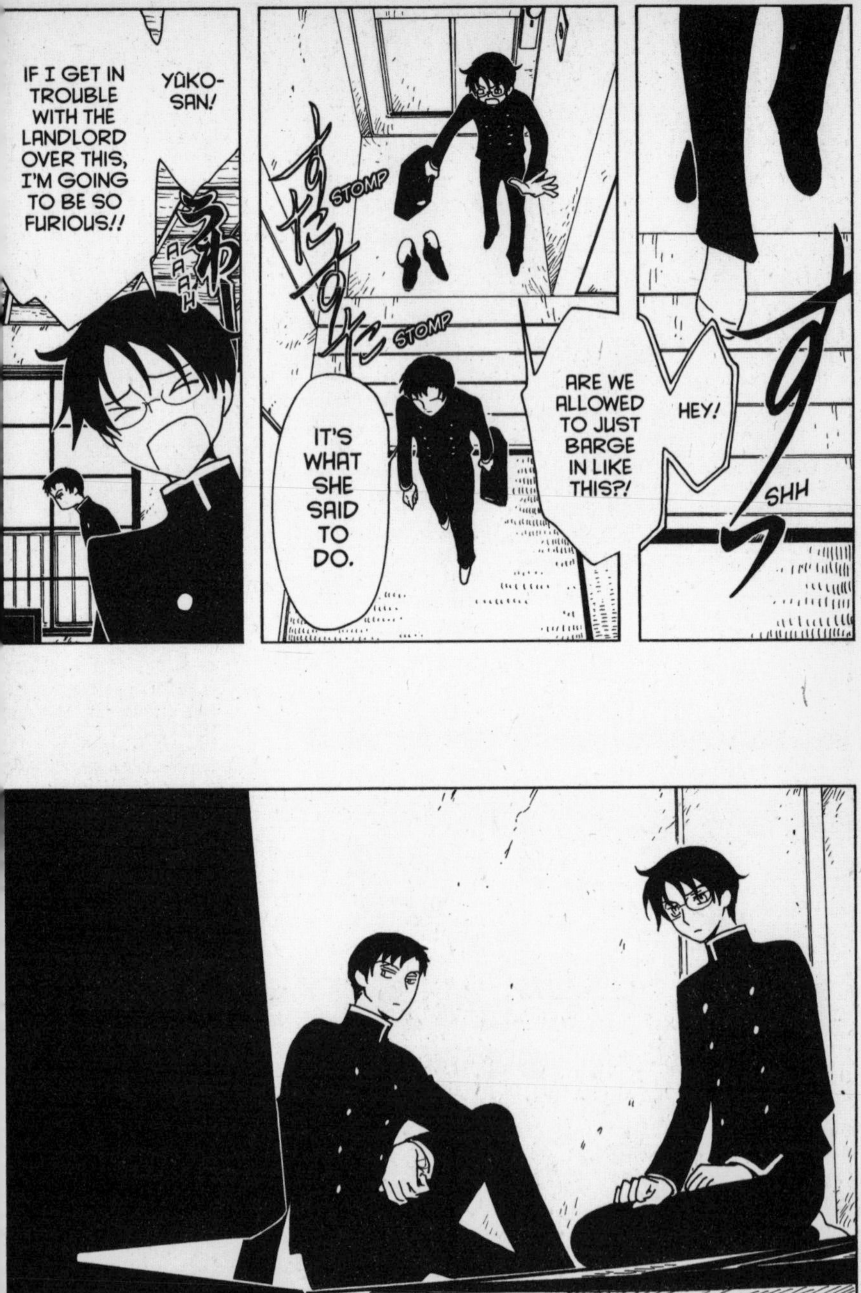
HEY!
SHH
ARE WE ALLOWED TO JUST BARGE IN LIKE THIS?!
STOMP
STOMP
IT'S WHAT SHE SAID TO DO.
YÛKO-SAN!
AAAH
IF I GET IN TROUBLE WITH THE LANDLORD OVER THIS, I'M GOING TO BE SO FURIOUS!!

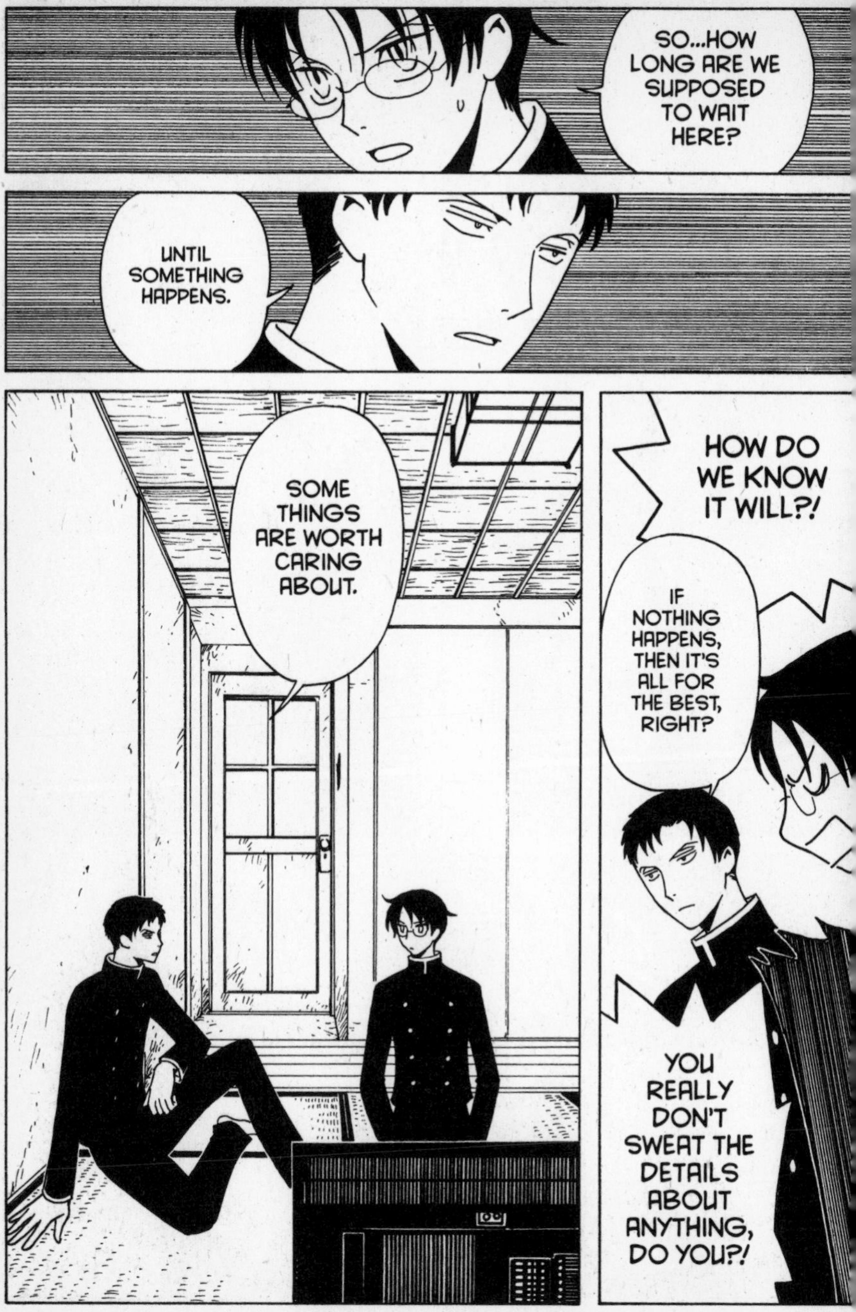
SO...HOW LONG ARE WE SUPPOSED TO WAIT HERE?
UNTIL SOMETHING HAPPENS.
HOW DO WE KNOW IT WILL?!
IF NOTHING HAPPENS, THEN IT'S ALL FOR THE BEST, RIGHT?
YOU REALLY DON'T SWEAT THE DETAILS ABOUT ANYTHING, DO YOU?!
SOME THINGS ARE WORTH CARING ABOUT.

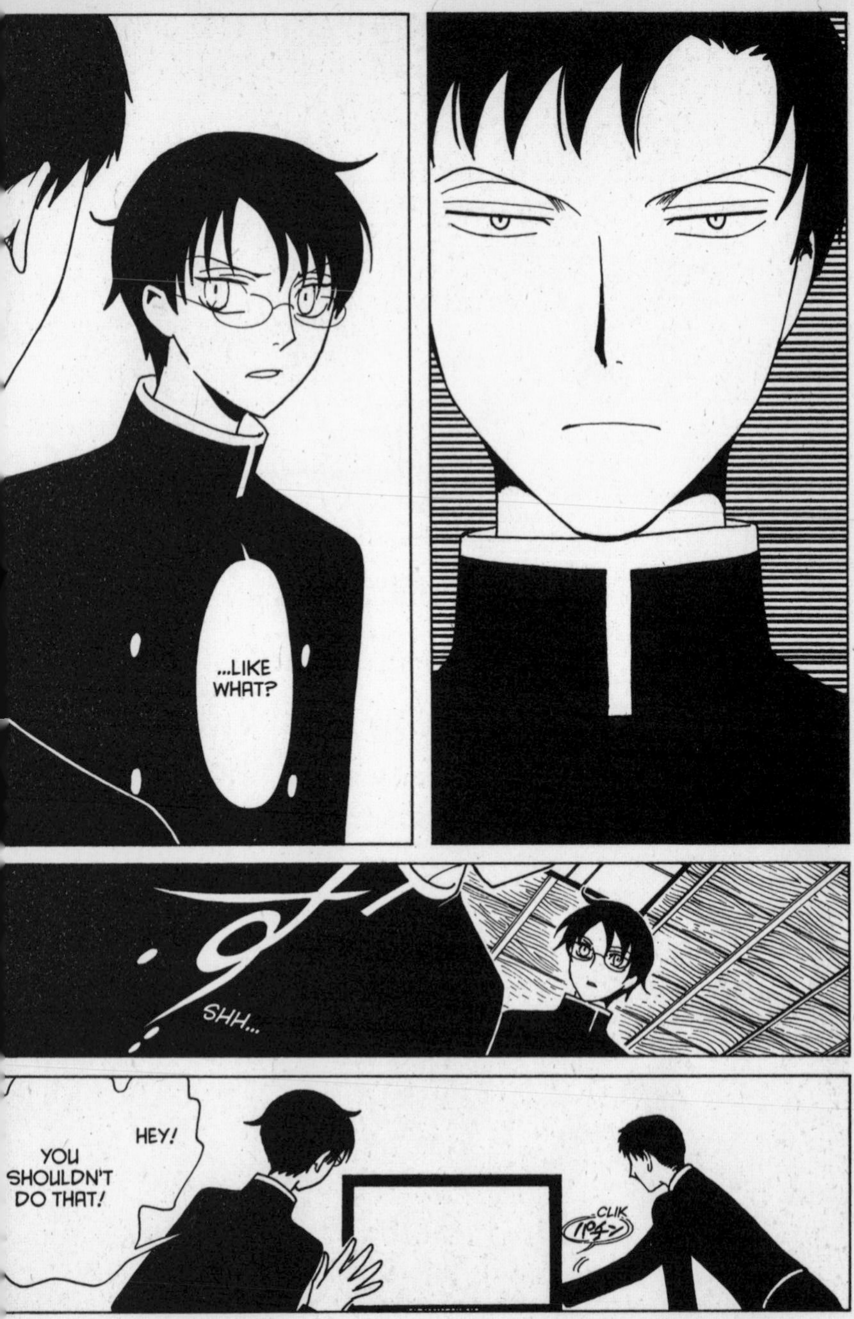
...LIKE WHAT?
SHH...
HEY!
YOU SHOULDN'T DO THAT!
CLIK

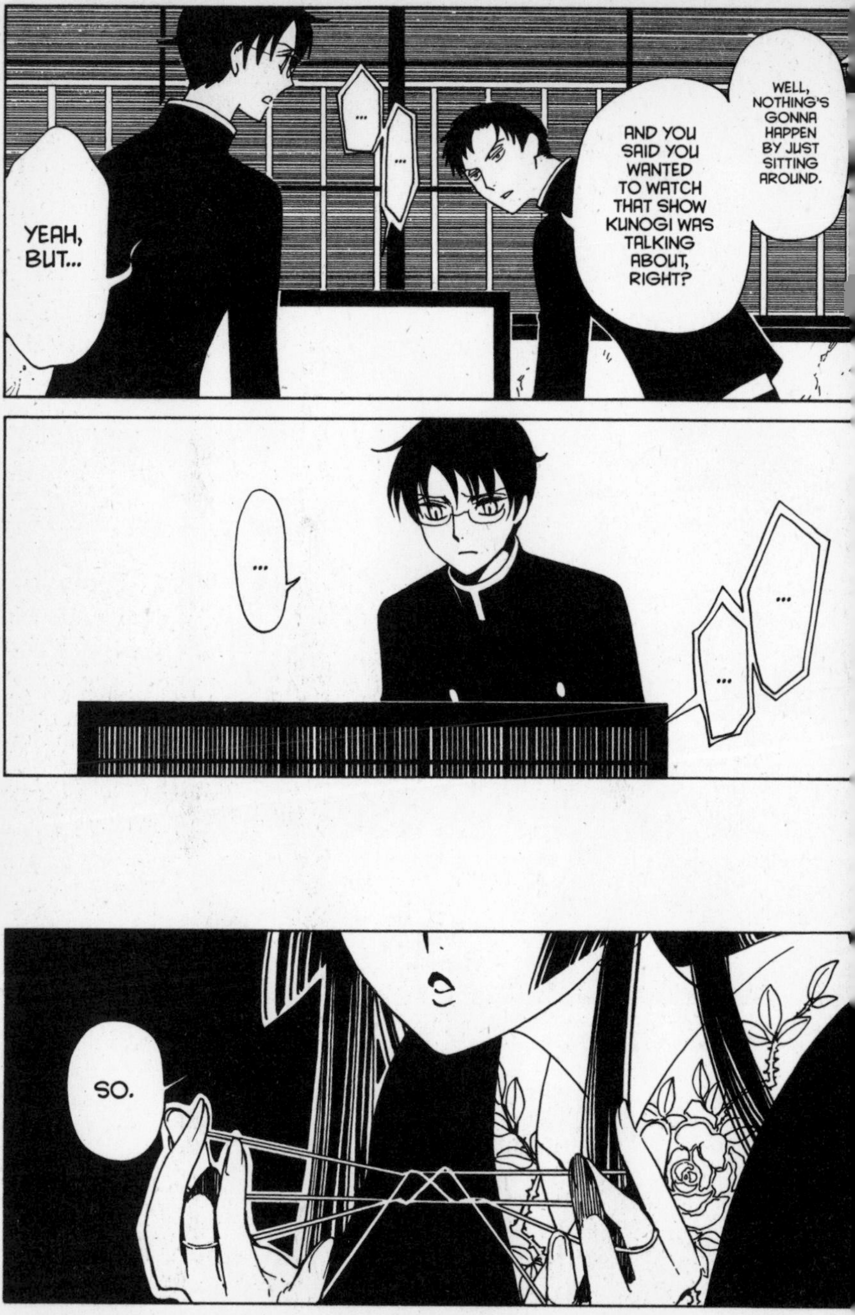
WELL, NOTHING'S GONNA HAPPEN BY JUST SITTING AROUND.
AND YOU SAID YOU WANTED TO WATCH THAT SHOW KUNOGI WAS TALKING ABOUT, RIGHT?
...
...
YEAH, BUT...
...
...
...
SO.

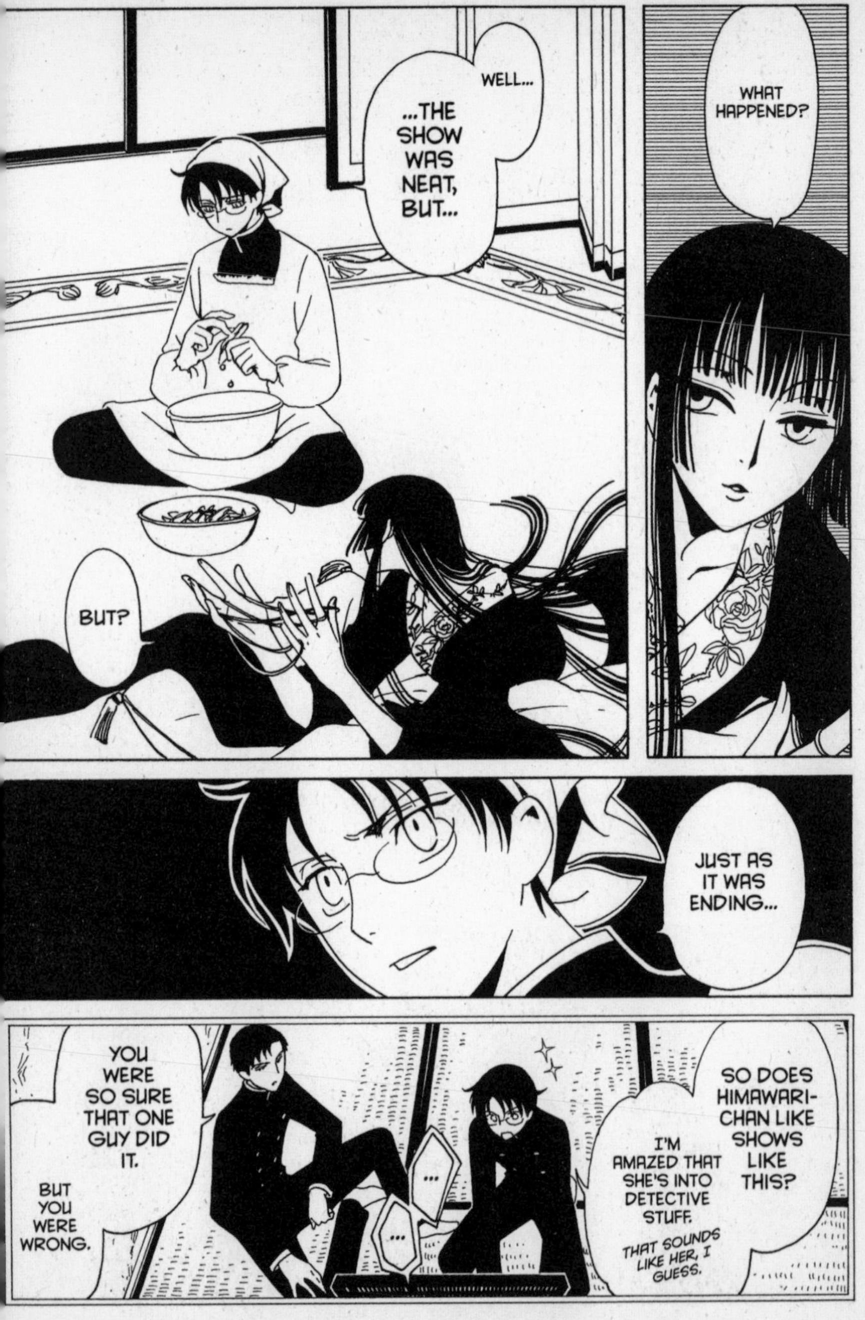
WHAT HAPPENED?
WELL...
...THE SHOW WAS NEAT, BUT...
BUT?
JUST AS IT WAS ENDING...
SO DOES HIMAWARI-CHAN LIKE SHOWS LIKE THIS?
I'M AMAZED THAT SHE'S INTO DETECTIVE STUFF.
THAT SOUNDS LIKE HER, I GUESS.
...
...
YOU WERE SO SURE THAT ONE GUY DID IT.
BUT YOU WERE WRONG.

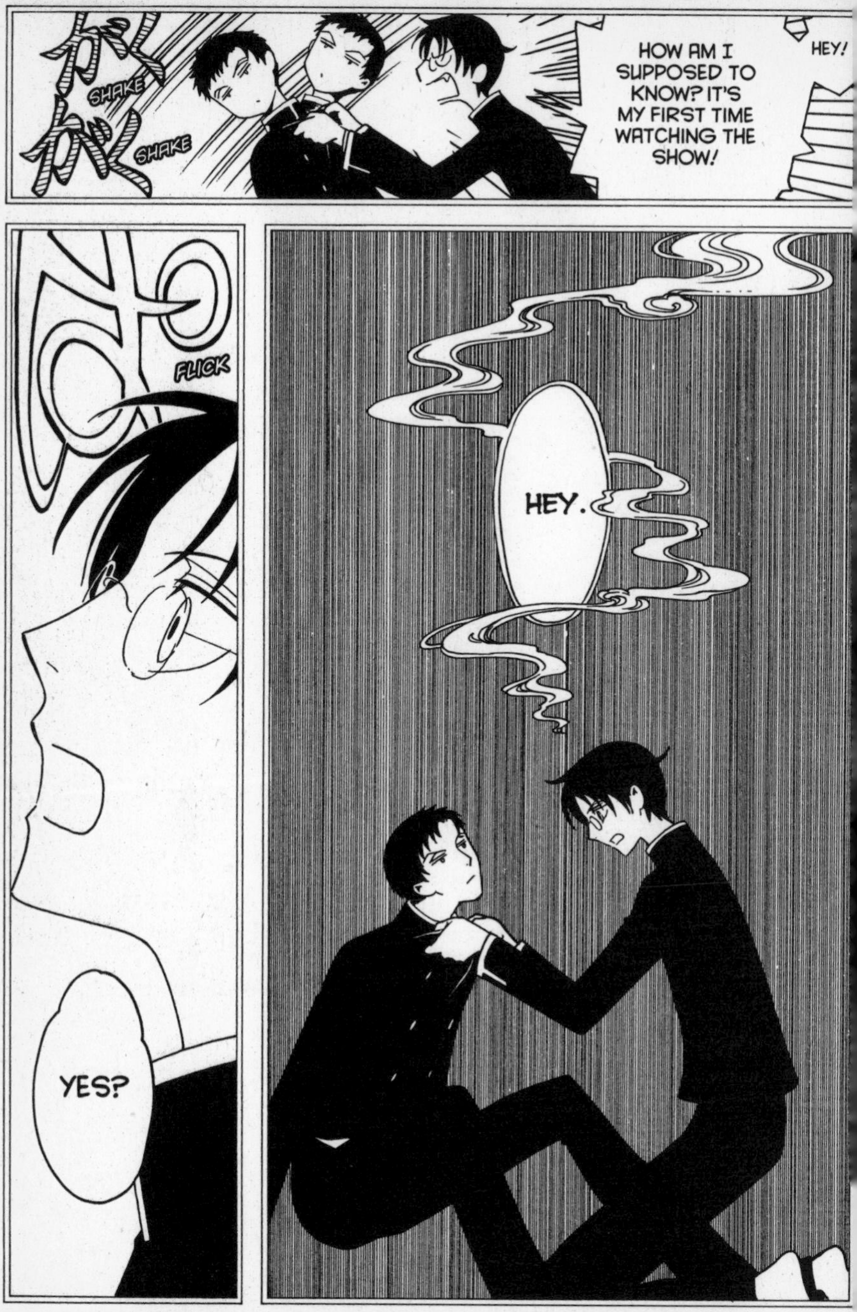
HEY!
HOW AM I SUPPOSED TO KNOW? IT'S MY FIRST TIME WATCHING THE SHOW!
SHAKE
SHAKE
HEY.
FLICK
YES?

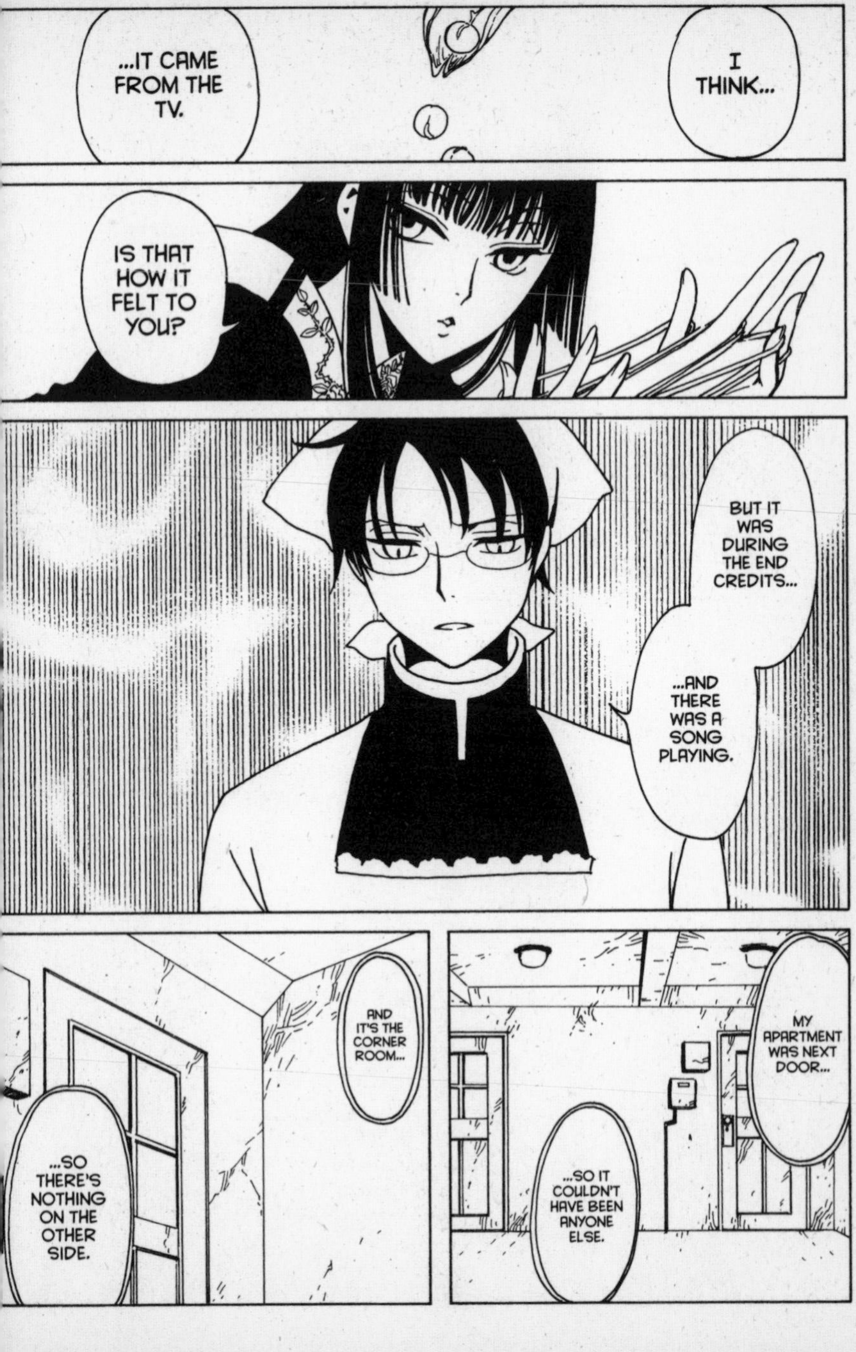
I THINK...
...IT CAME FROM THE TV.
IS THAT HOW IT FELT TO YOU?
BUT IT WAS DURING THE END CREDITS...
...AND THERE WAS A SONG PLAYING.
MY APARTMENT WAS NEXT DOOR...
...SO IT COULDN'T HAVE BEEN ANYONE ELSE.
AND IT'S THE CORNER ROOM...
...SO THERE'S NOTHING ON THE OTHER SIDE.

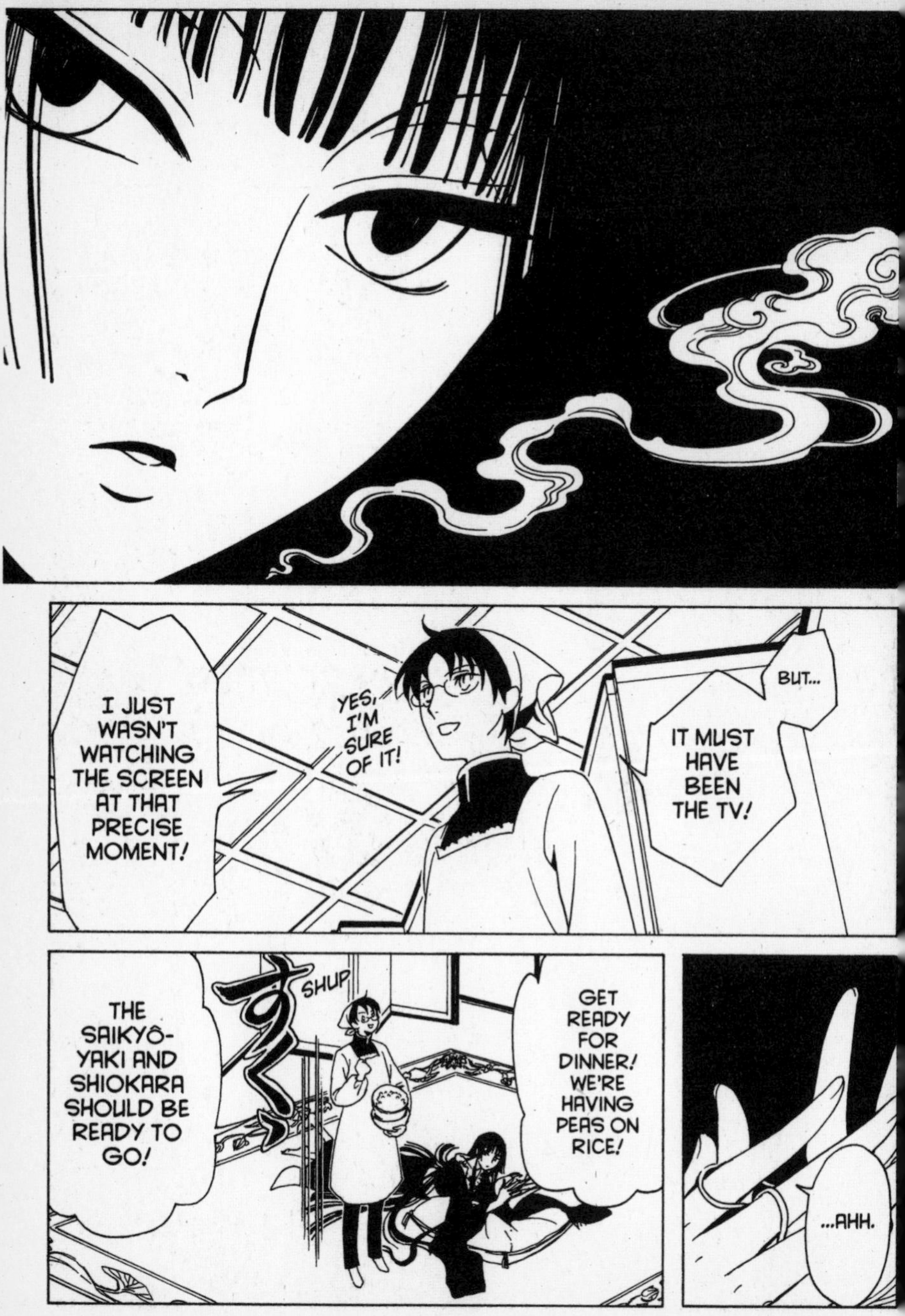
BUT...
IT MUST HAVE BEEN THE TV!
YES, I'M SURE OF IT!
I JUST WASN'T WATCHING THE SCREEN AT THAT PRECISE MOMENT!
...AHH.
GET READY FOR DINNER! WE'RE HAVING PEAS ON RICE!
SHUP
THE SAIKYÔ-YAKI AND SHIOKARA SHOULD BE READY TO GO!

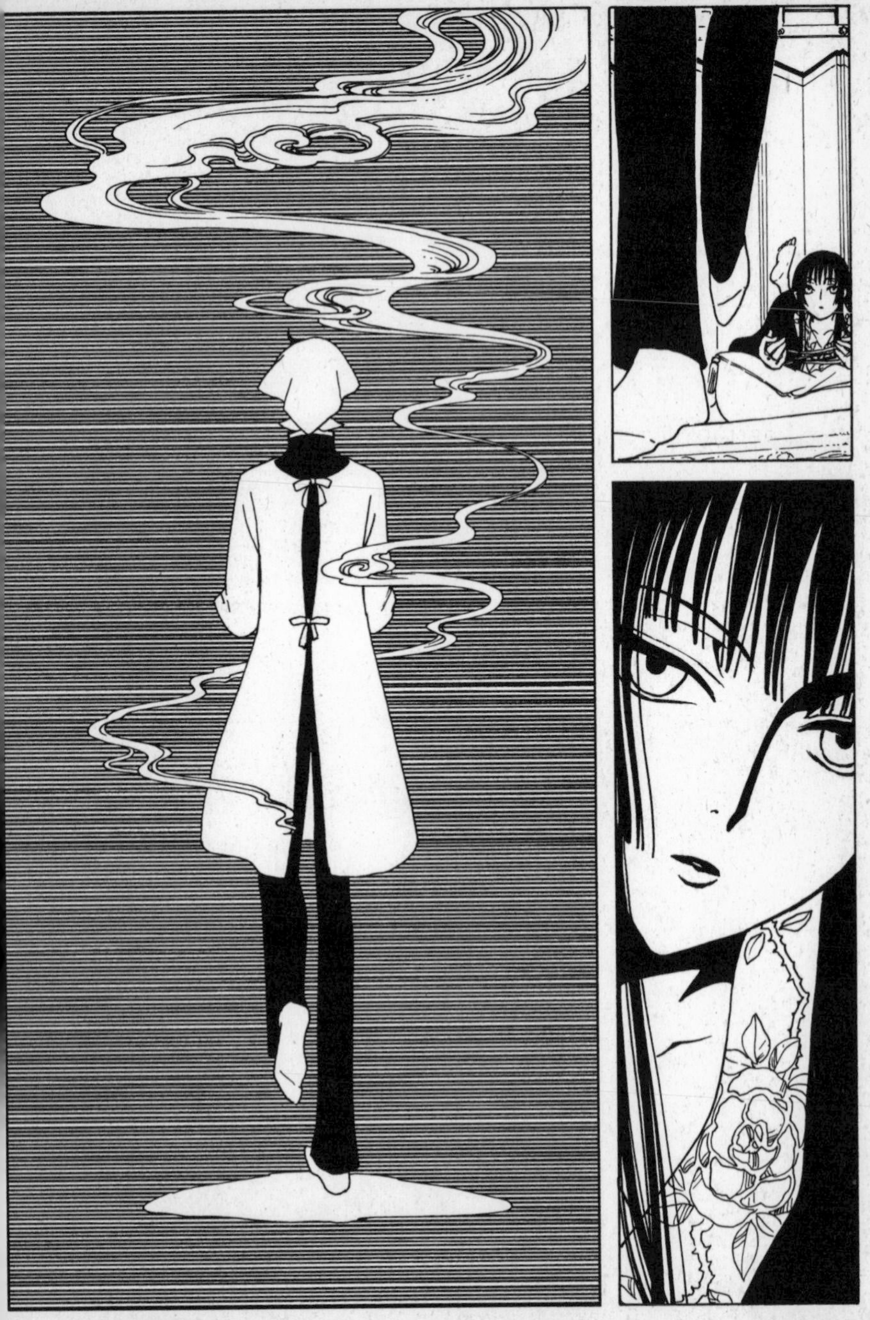

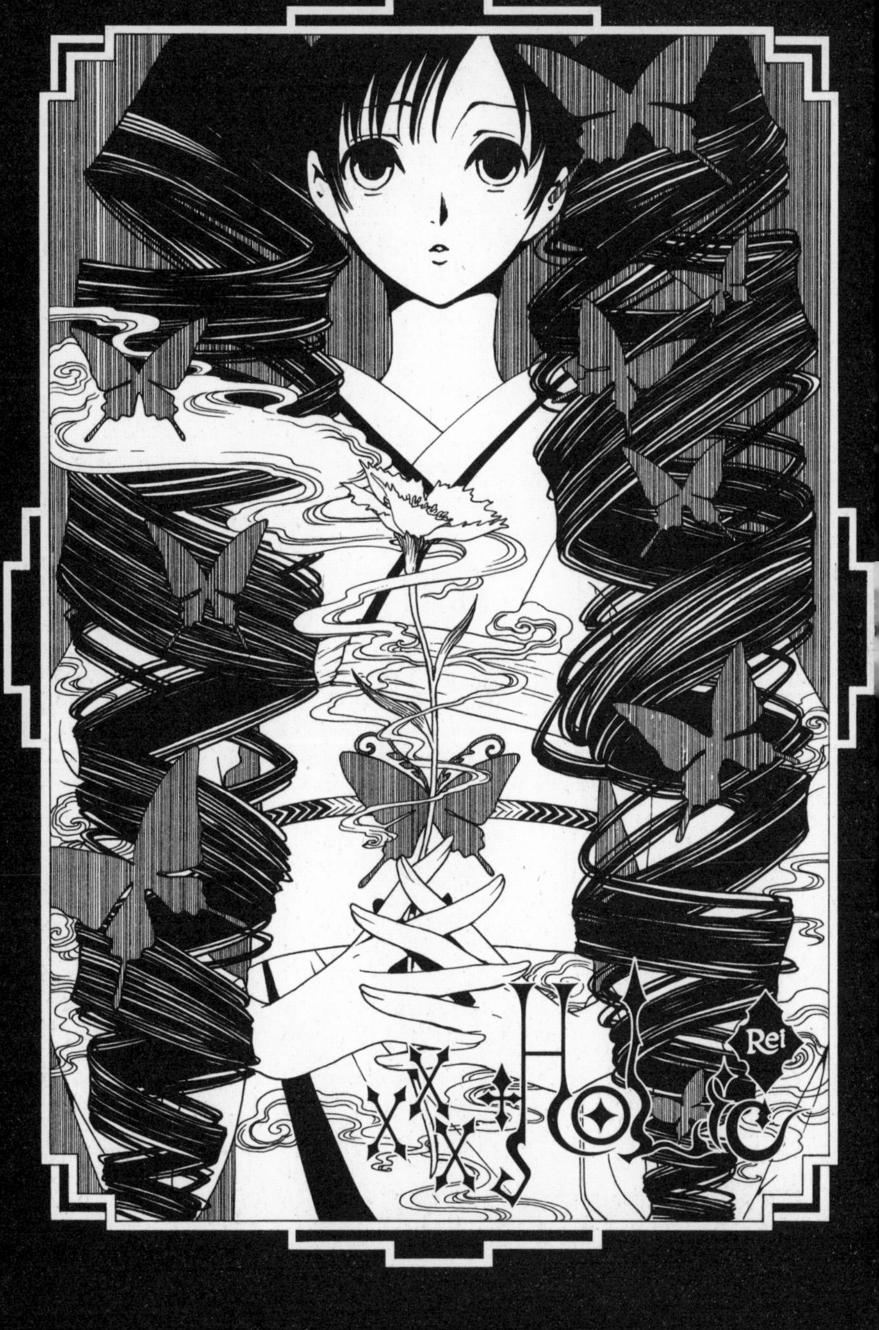
xxxHOLiC
Rei

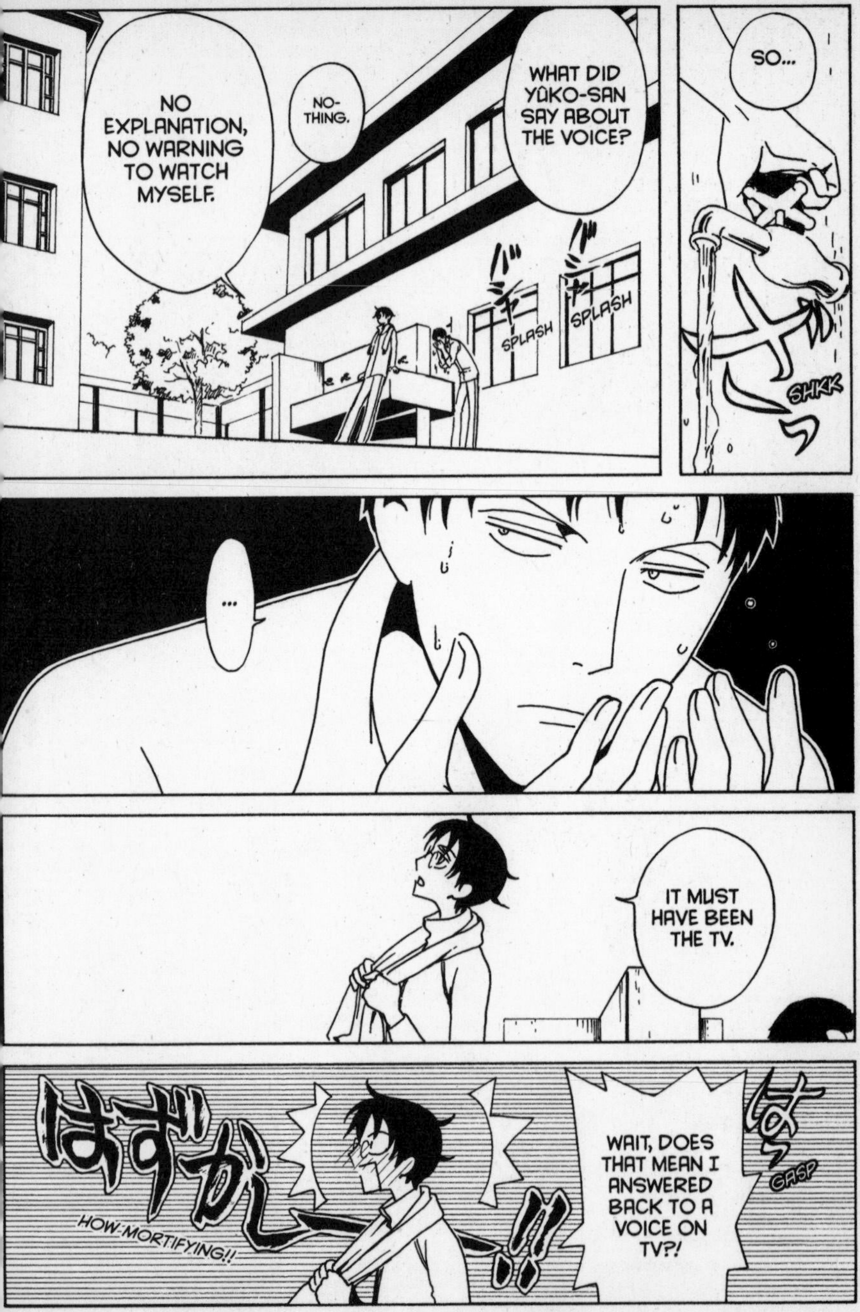
SO...
SHKK
WHAT DID YÛKO-SAN SAY ABOUT THE VOICE?
SPLASH
SPLASH
NO-THING.
NO EXPLANATION, NO WARNING TO WATCH MYSELF.
...
IT MUST HAVE BEEN THE TV.
GASP
WAIT, DOES THAT MEAN I ANSWERED BACK TO A VOICE ON TV?!
HOW MORTIFYING!!

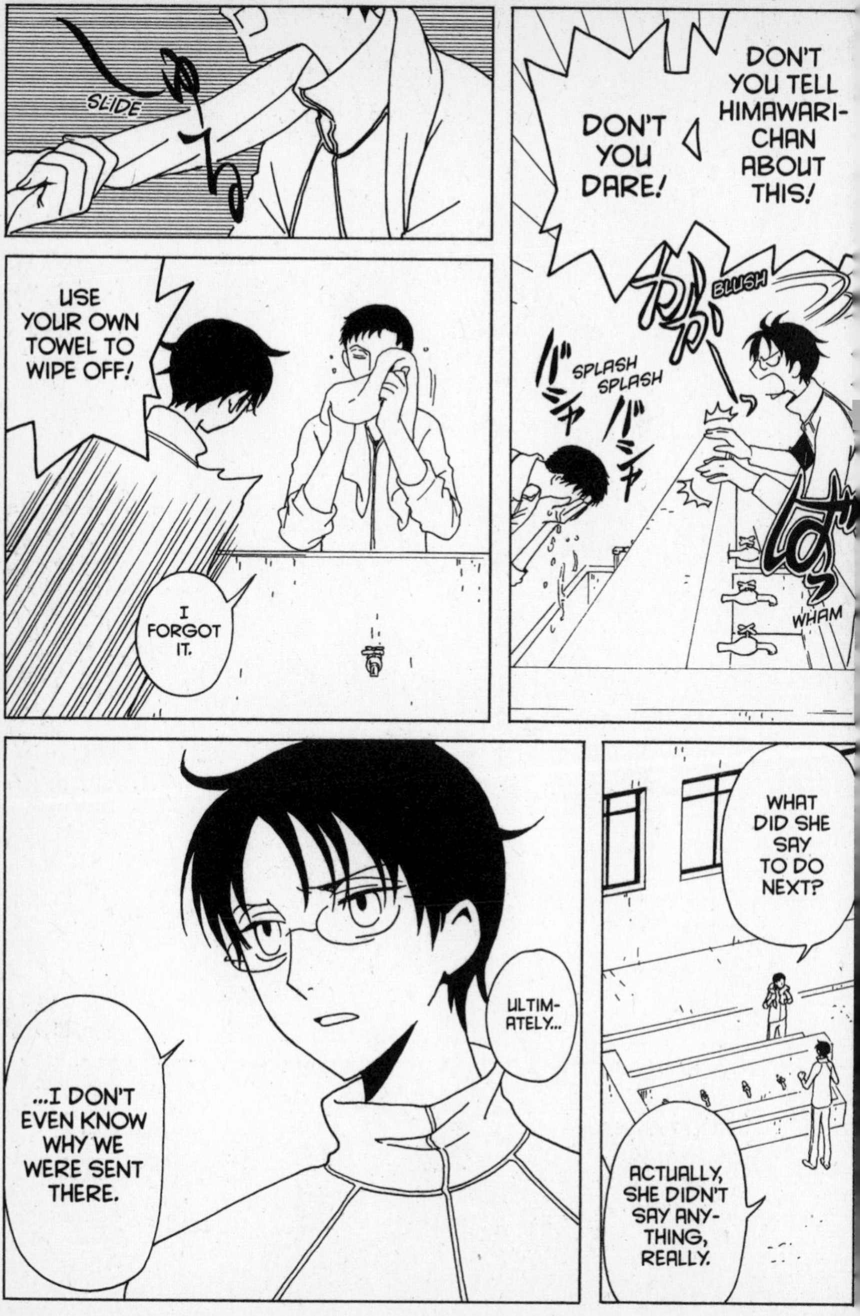
DON'T YOU TELL HIMAWARI-CHAN ABOUT THIS!
DON'T YOU DARE!
BLUSH
SPLASH SPLASH
WHAM
SLIDE
USE YOUR OWN TOWEL TO WIPE OFF!
I FORGOT IT.
WHAT DID SHE SAY TO DO NEXT?
ACTUALLY, SHE DIDN'T SAY ANY-THING, REALLY.
ULTIM-ATELY...
...I DON'T EVEN KNOW WHY WE WERE SENT THERE.

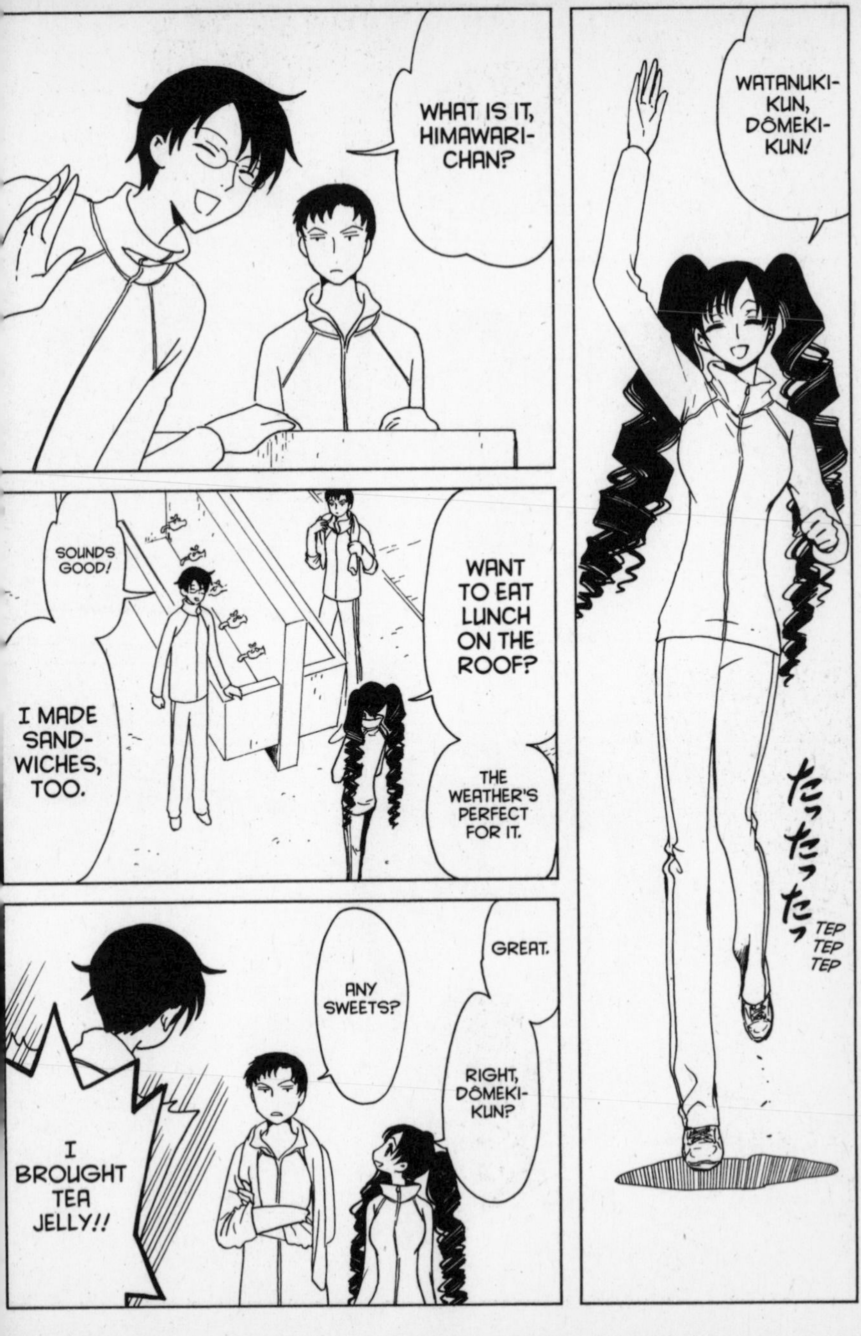
WATANUKI-KUN, DÔMEKI-KUN!
たったった
TEP TEP TEP
WHAT IS IT, HIMAWARI-CHAN?
WANT TO EAT LUNCH ON THE ROOF?
THE WEATHER'S PERFECT FOR IT.
SOUND'S GOOD!
I MADE SANDWICHES, TOO.
GREAT.
ANY SWEETS?
RIGHT, DÔMEKI-KUN?
I BROUGHT TEA JELLY!!

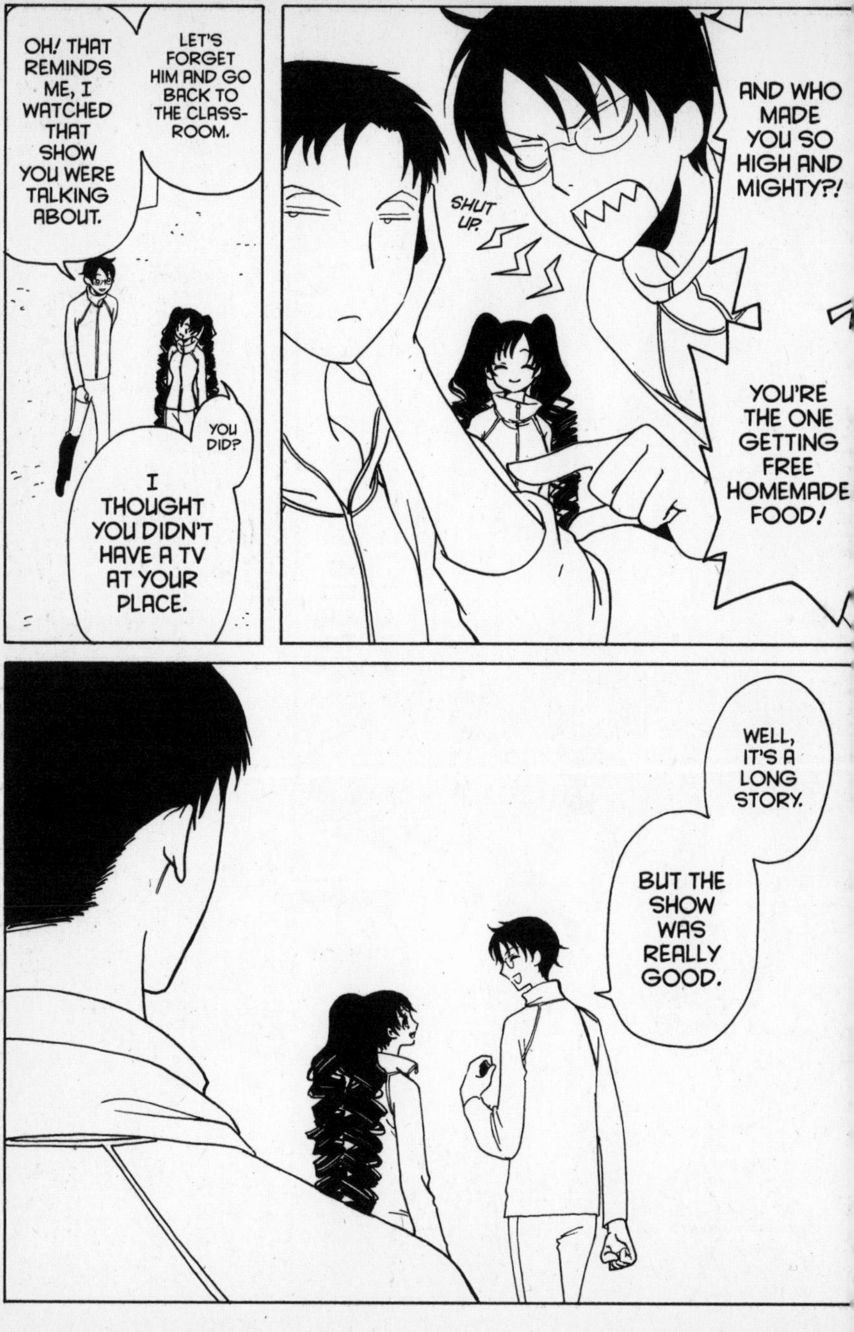
AND WHO MADE YOU SO HIGH AND MIGHTY?!
SHUT UP.
YOU'RE THE ONE GETTING FREE HOMEMADE FOOD!
LET'S FORGET HIM AND GO BACK TO THE CLASS-ROOM.
OH! THAT REMINDS ME, I WATCHED THAT SHOW YOU WERE TALKING ABOUT.
YOU DID?
I THOUGHT YOU DIDN'T HAVE A TV AT YOUR PLACE.
WELL, IT'S A LONG STORY.
BUT THE SHOW WAS REALLY GOOD.

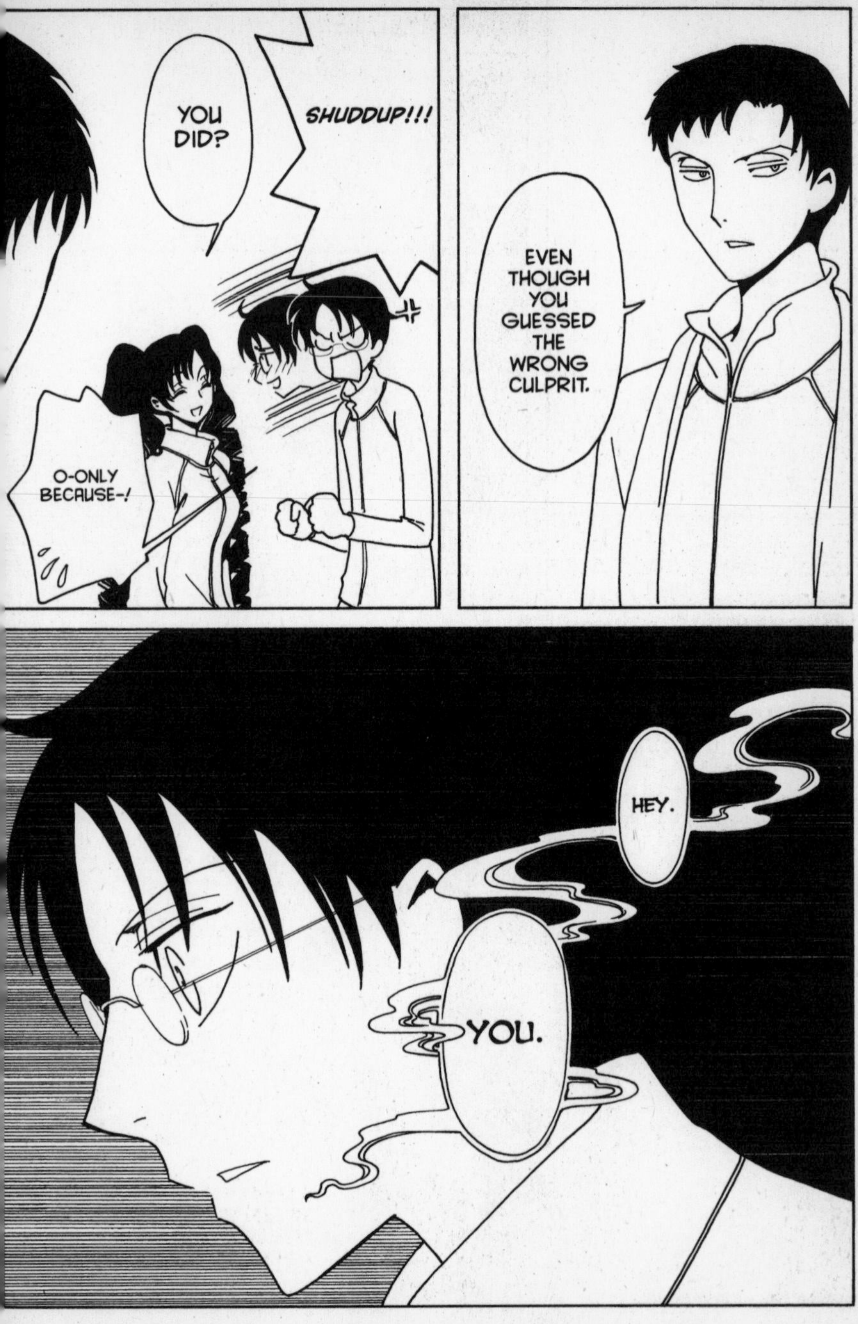
EVEN THOUGH YOU GUESSED THE WRONG CULPRIT.
SHUDDUP!!!
YOU DID?
O-ONLY BECAUSE-!
HEY.
YOU.

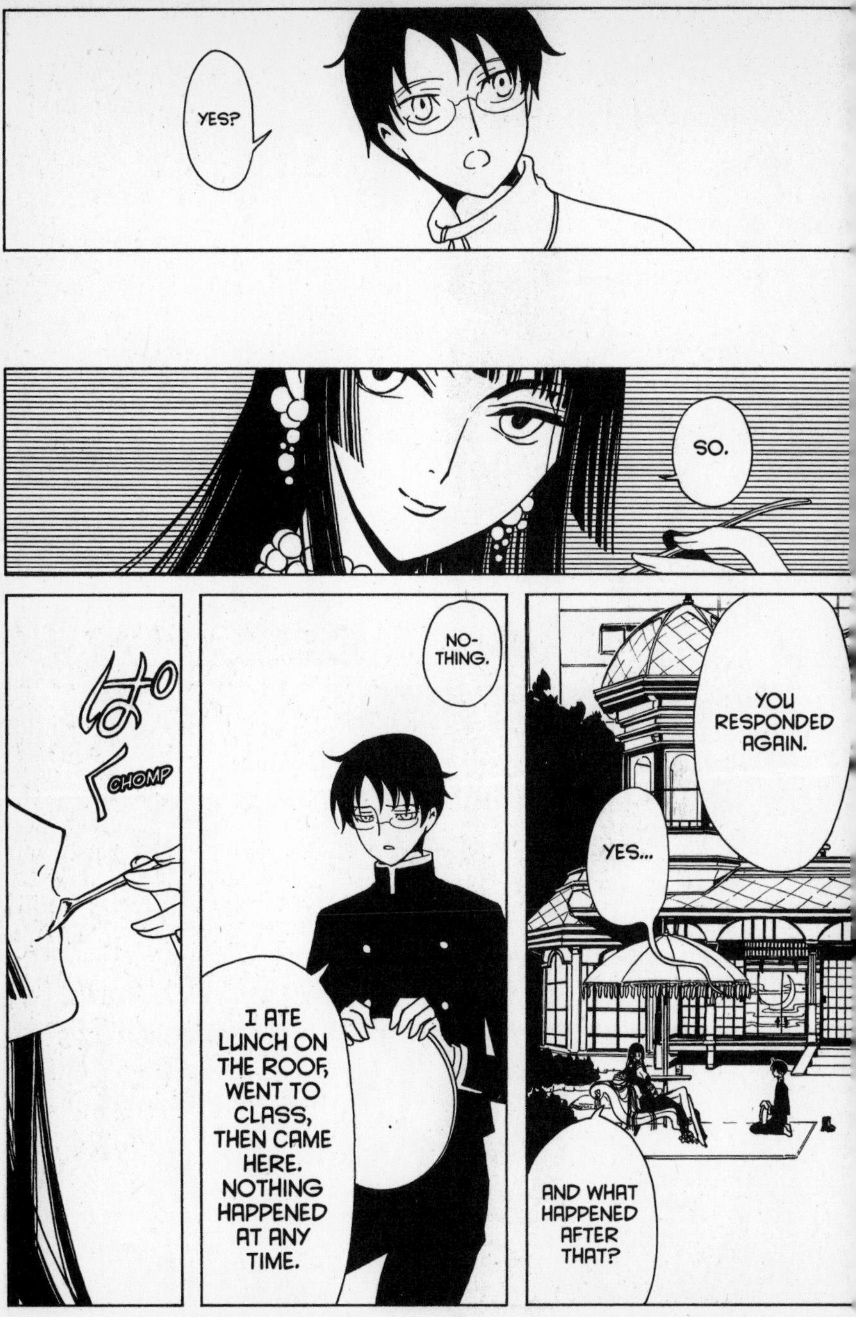
YES?
SO.
YOU RESPONDED AGAIN.
YES...
AND WHAT HAPPENED AFTER THAT?
NO-THING.
I ATE LUNCH ON THE ROOF, WENT TO CLASS, THEN CAME HERE. NOTHING HAPPENED AT ANY TIME.
CHOMP

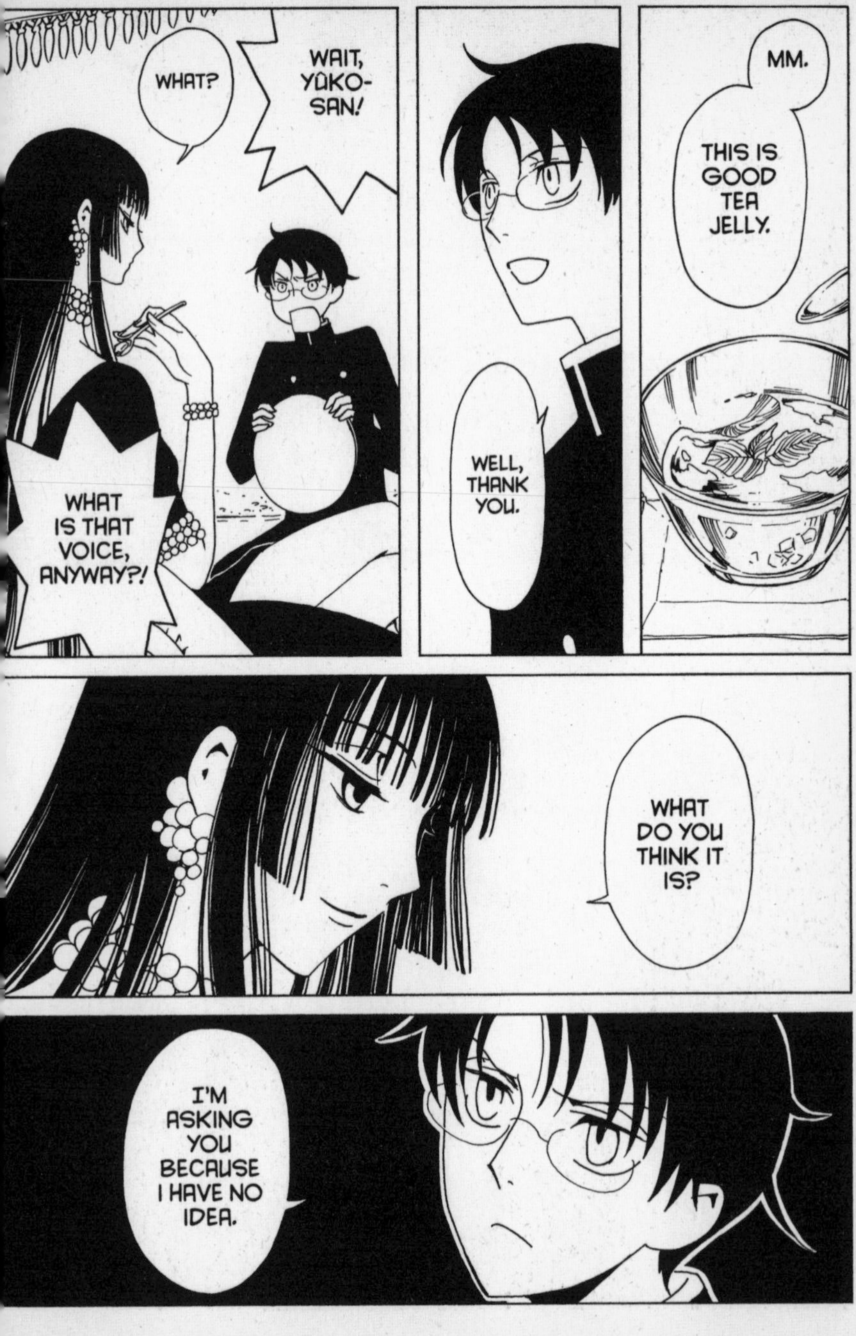
MM.
THIS IS GOOD TEA JELLY.
WELL, THANK YOU.
WAIT, YŪKO-SAN!
WHAT?
WHAT IS THAT VOICE, ANYWAY?!
WHAT DO YOU THINK IT IS?
I'M ASKING YOU BECAUSE I HAVE NO IDEA.

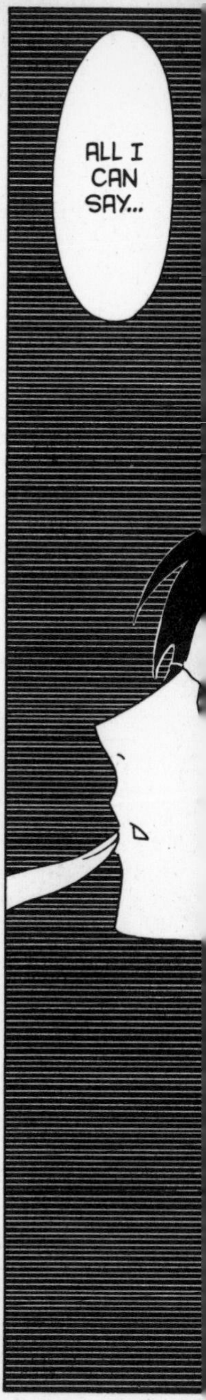
ALL I CAN SAY...
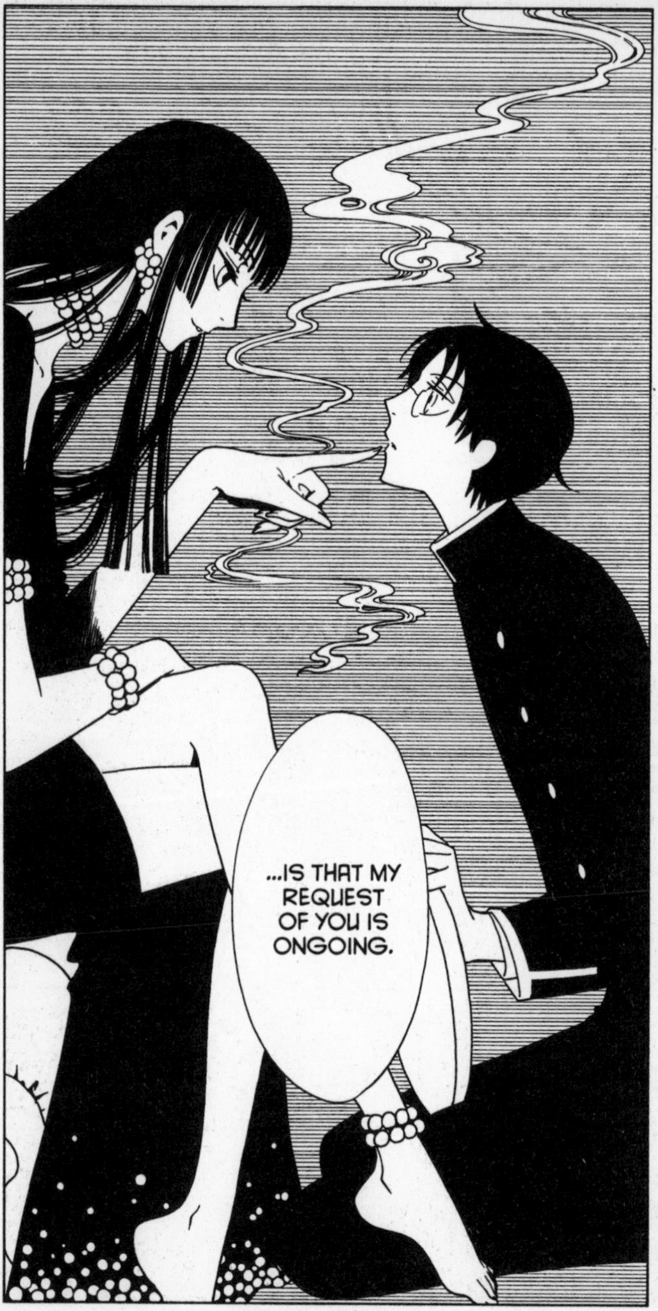
...IS THAT MY REQUEST OF YOU IS ONGOING.

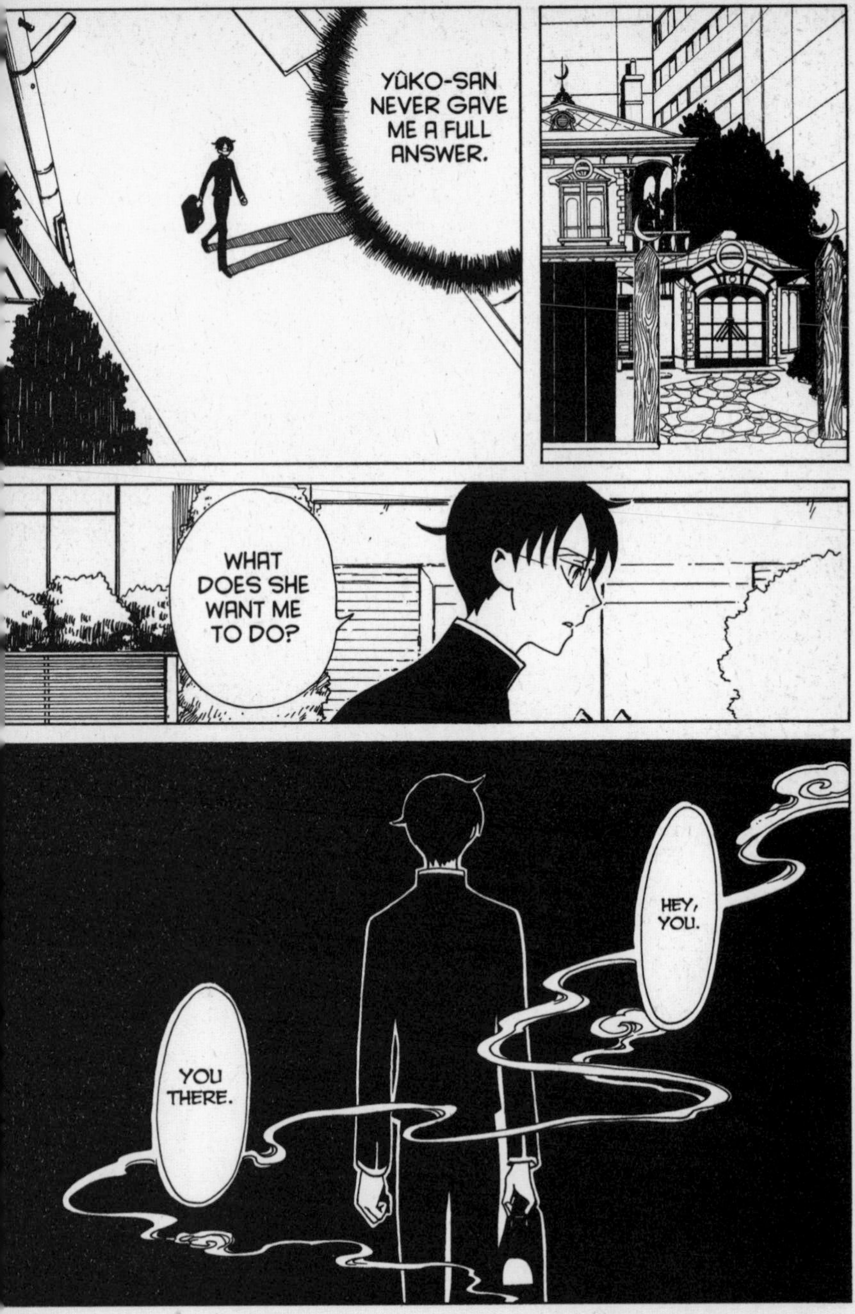
YÛKO-SAN NEVER GAVE ME A FULL ANSWER.
WHAT DOES SHE WANT ME TO DO?
HEY, YOU.
YOU THERE.

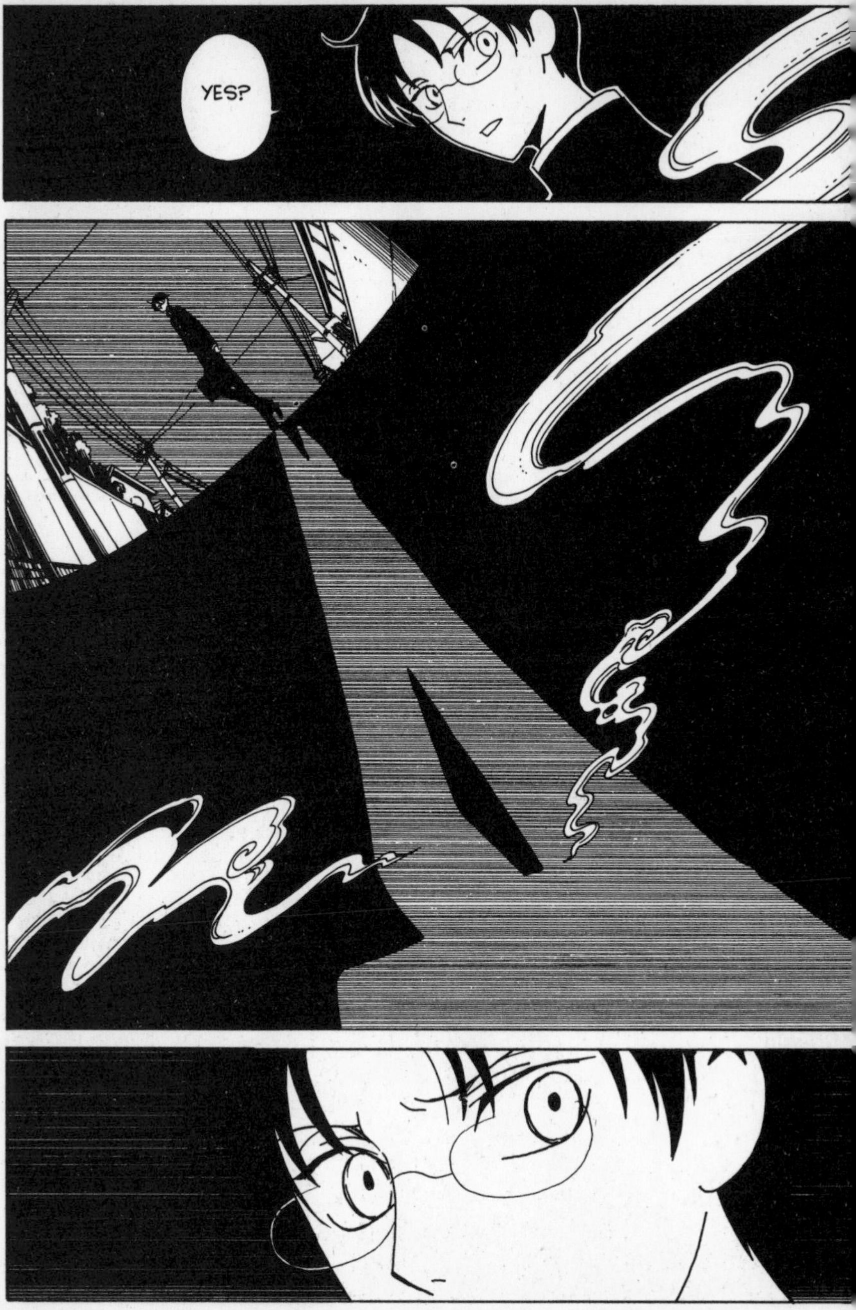
YES?

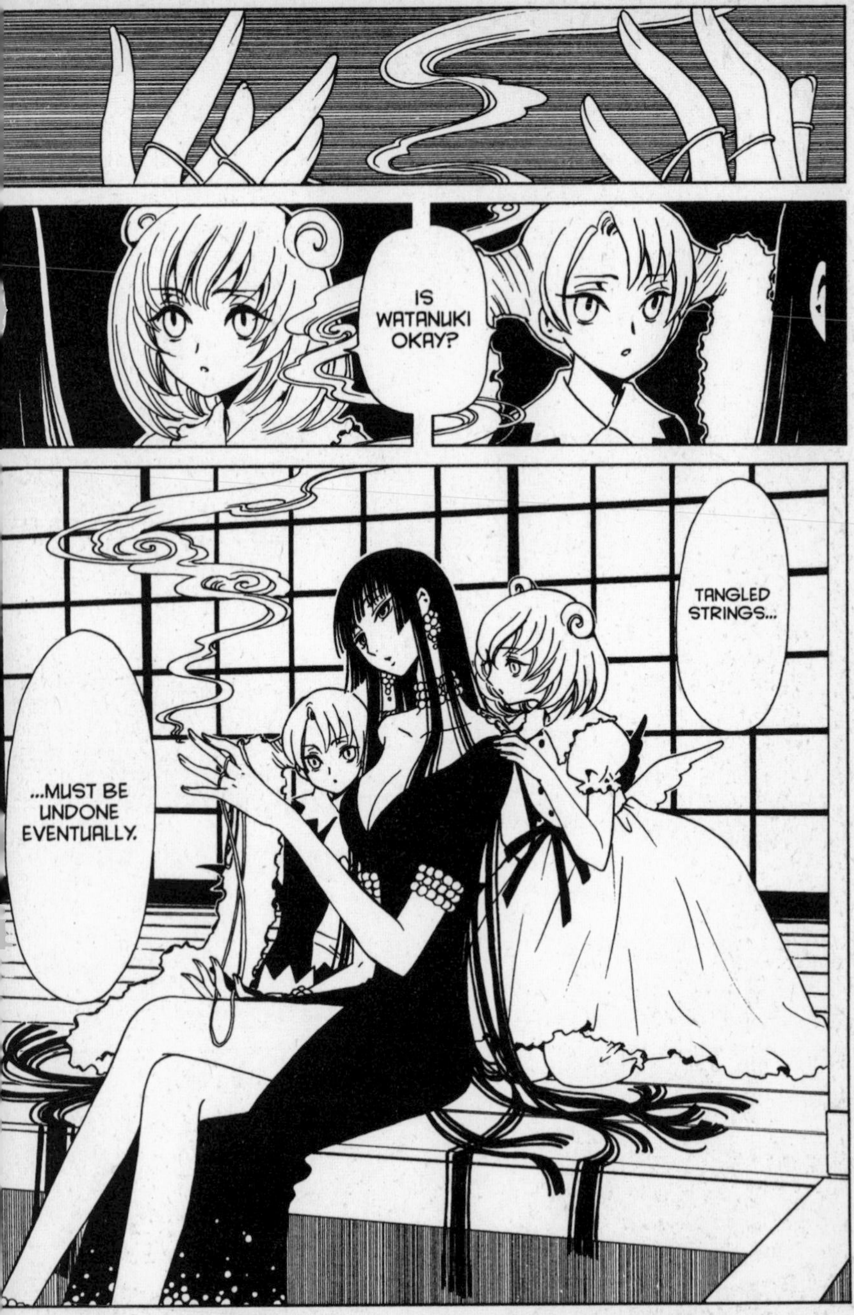
IS WATANUKI OKAY?
TANGLED STRINGS...
...MUST BE UNDONE EVENTUALLY.

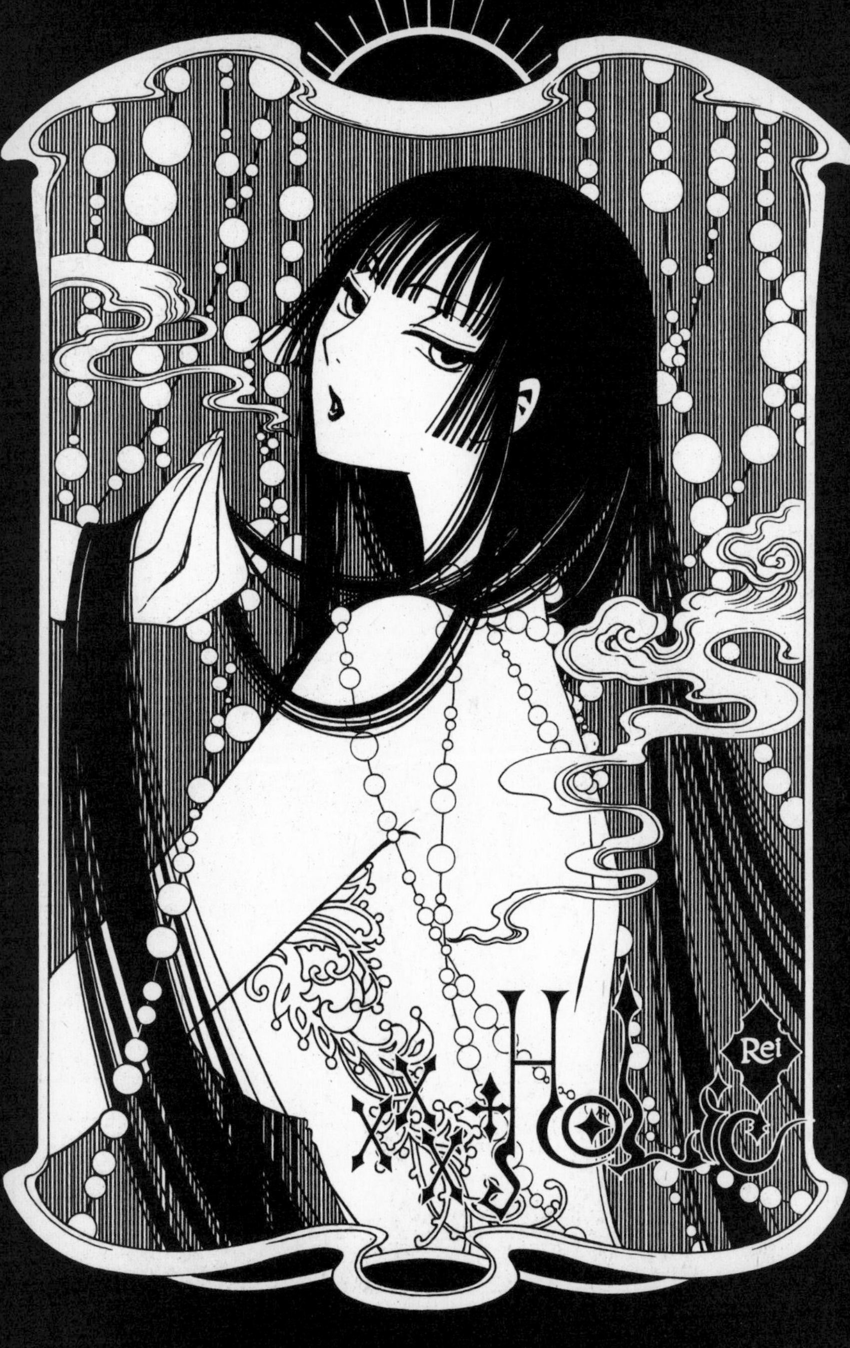
xxxHOLiC
Rei

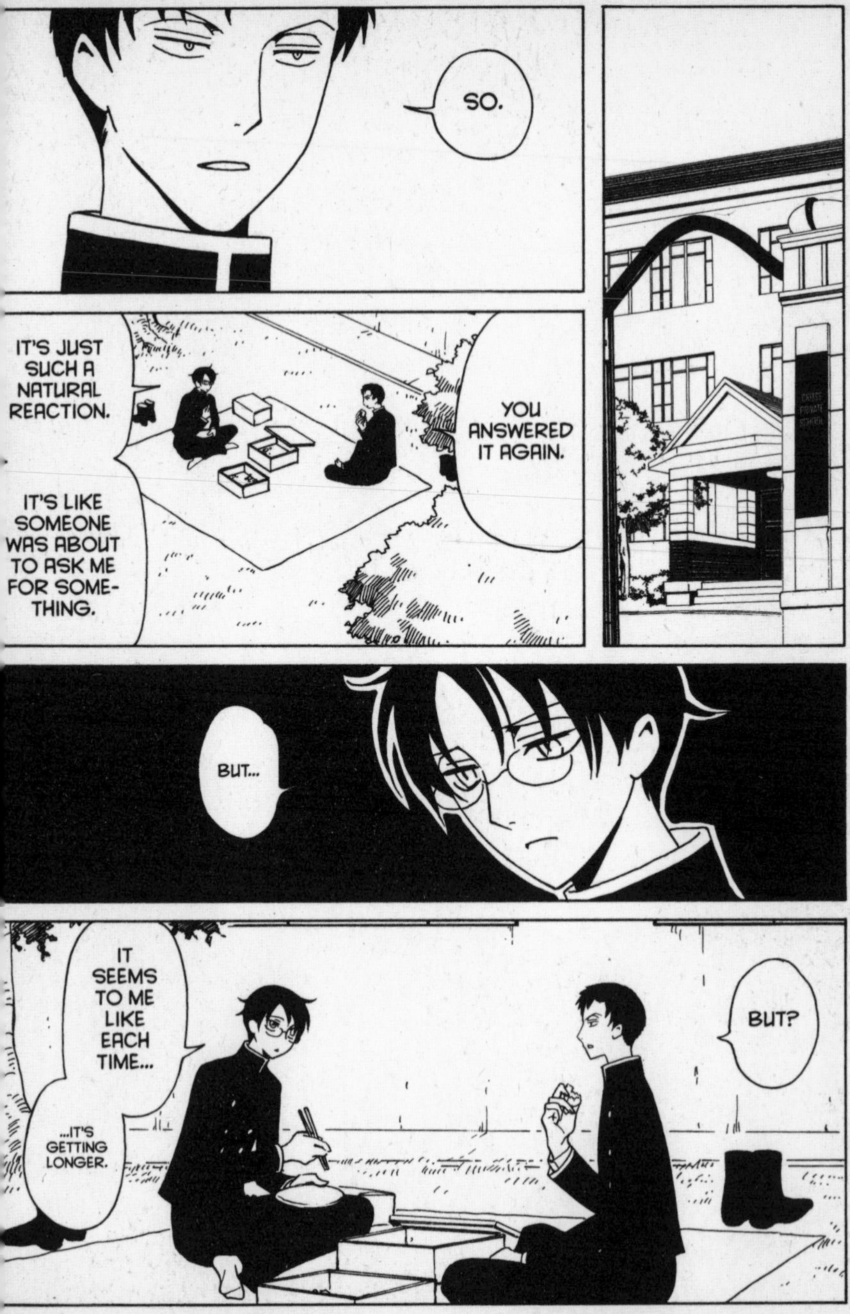
CROSS PRIVATE SCHOOL
SO.
YOU ANSWERED IT AGAIN.
IT'S JUST SUCH A NATURAL REACTION.
IT'S LIKE SOMEONE WAS ABOUT TO ASK ME FOR SOME-THING.
BUT...
BUT?
IT SEEMS TO ME LIKE EACH TIME...
...IT'S GETTING LONGER.

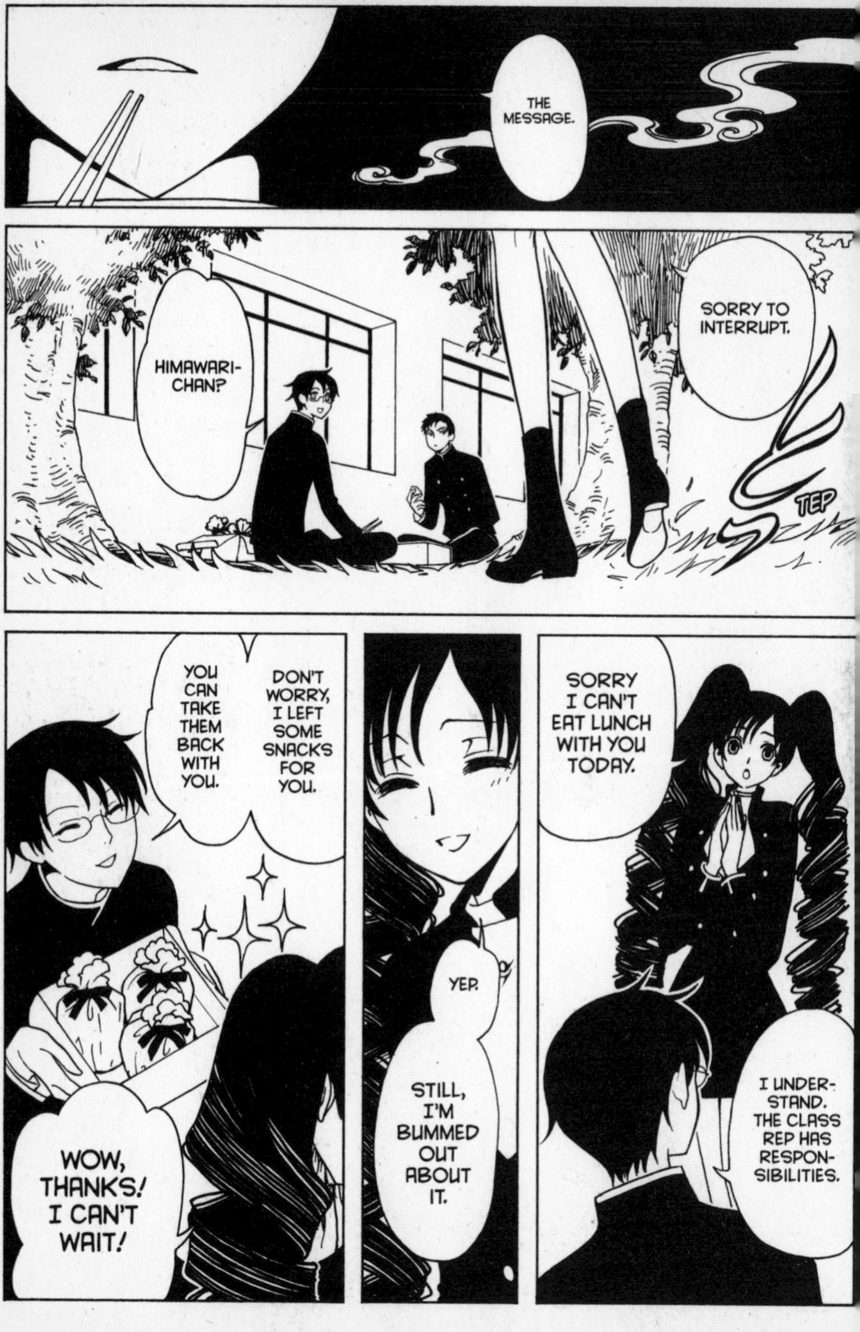
THE MESSAGE.
SORRY TO INTERRUPT.
TEP
HIMAWARI-CHAN?
SORRY I CAN'T EAT LUNCH WITH YOU TODAY.
I UNDER-STAND. THE CLASS REP HAS RESPON-SIBILITIES.
YEP.
STILL, I'M BUMMED OUT ABOUT IT.
DON'T WORRY, I LEFT SOME SNACKS FOR YOU.
YOU CAN TAKE THEM BACK WITH YOU.
WOW, THANKS! I CAN'T WAIT!

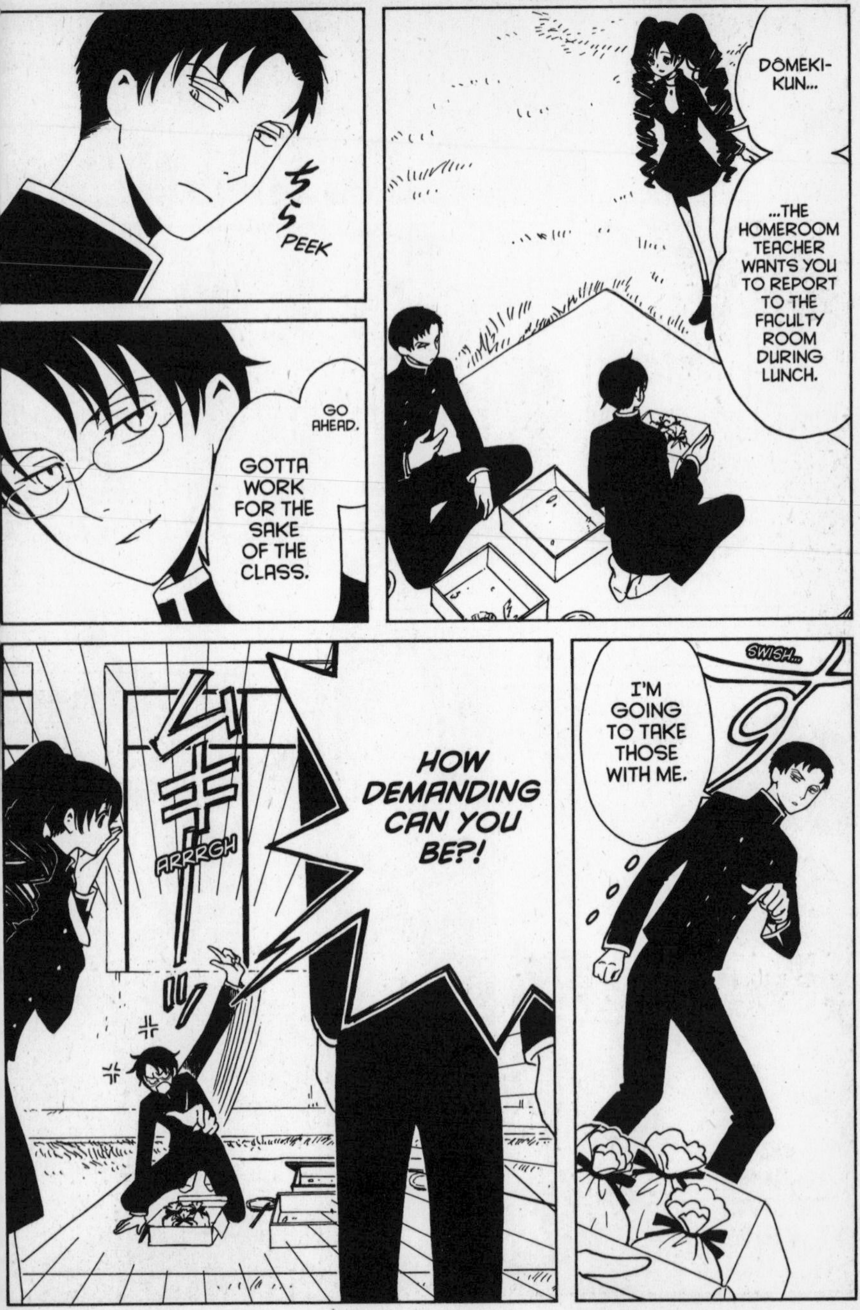
DÔMEKI-KUN...
...THE HOMEROOM TEACHER WANTS YOU TO REPORT TO THE FACULTY ROOM DURING LUNCH.
ちら
PEEK
GO AHEAD.
GOTTA WORK FOR THE SAKE OF THE CLASS.
SWISH...
I'M GOING TO TAKE THOSE WITH ME.
ARRRGH
HOW DEMANDING CAN YOU BE?!

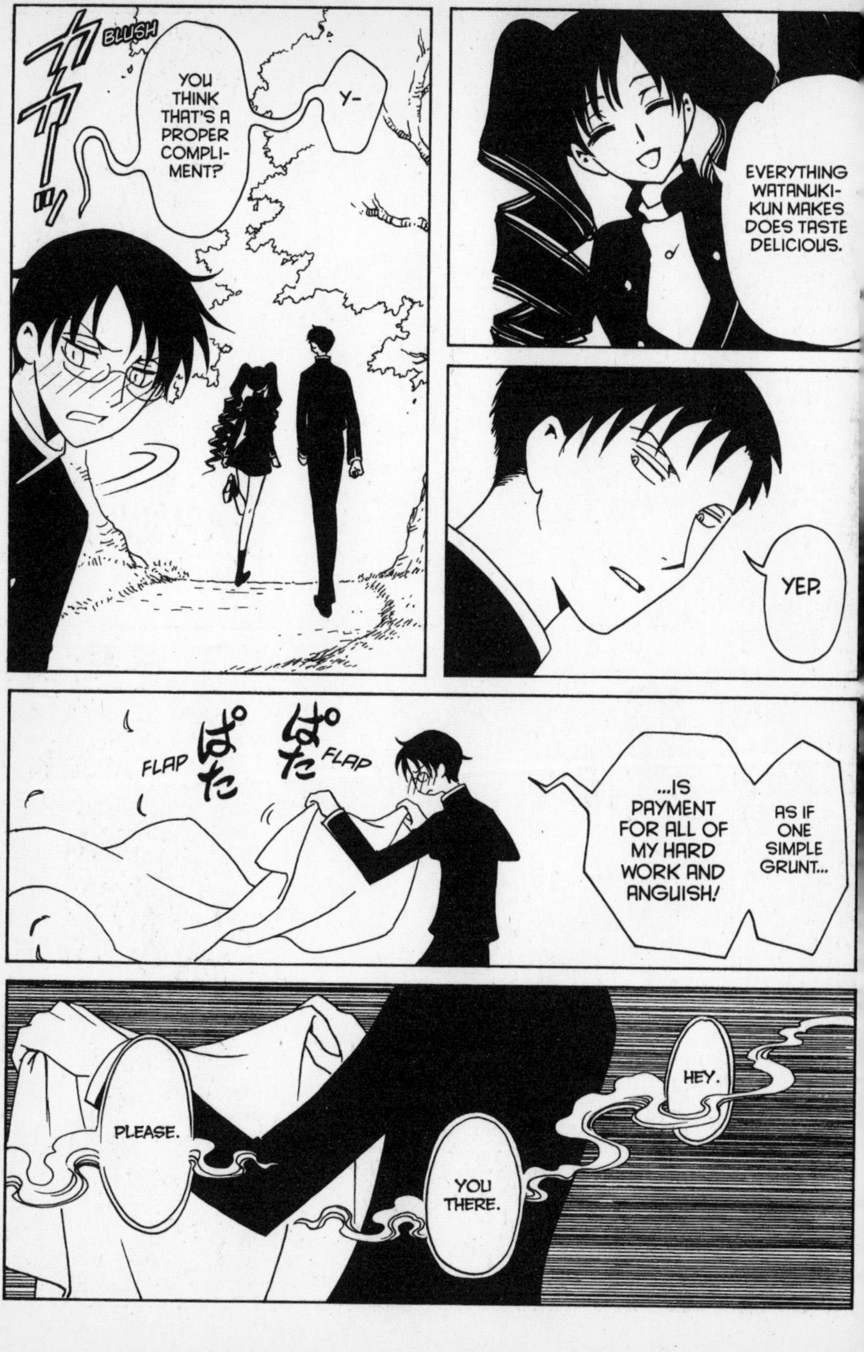
EVERYTHING WATANUKI-KUN MAKES DOES TASTE DELICIOUS.
YEP.
Y-
YOU THINK THAT'S A PROPER COMPLIMENT?
BLUSH
AS IF ONE SIMPLE GRUNT...
...IS PAYMENT FOR ALL OF MY HARD WORK AND ANGUISH!
ぱた
FLAP
ぱた
FLAP
HEY.
YOU THERE.
PLEASE.

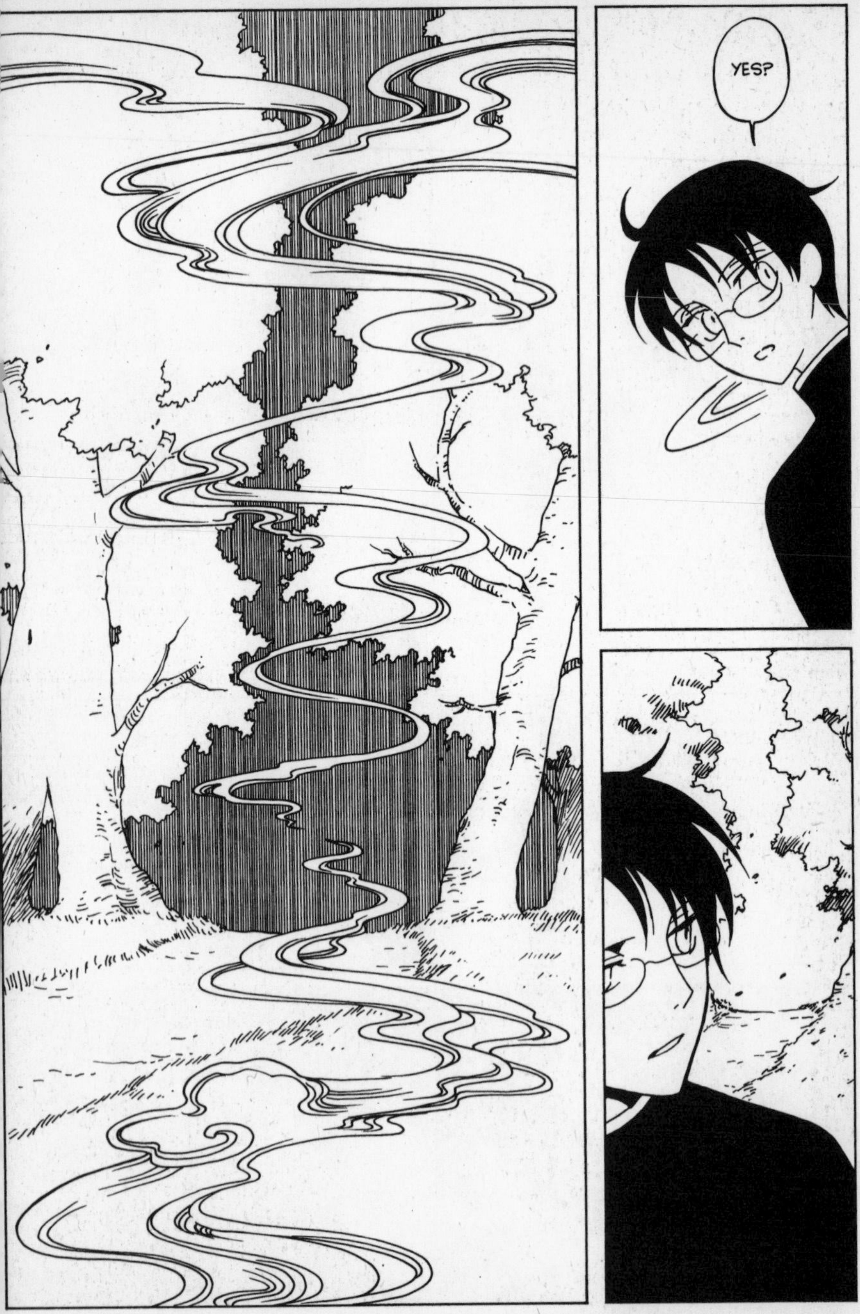
YES?

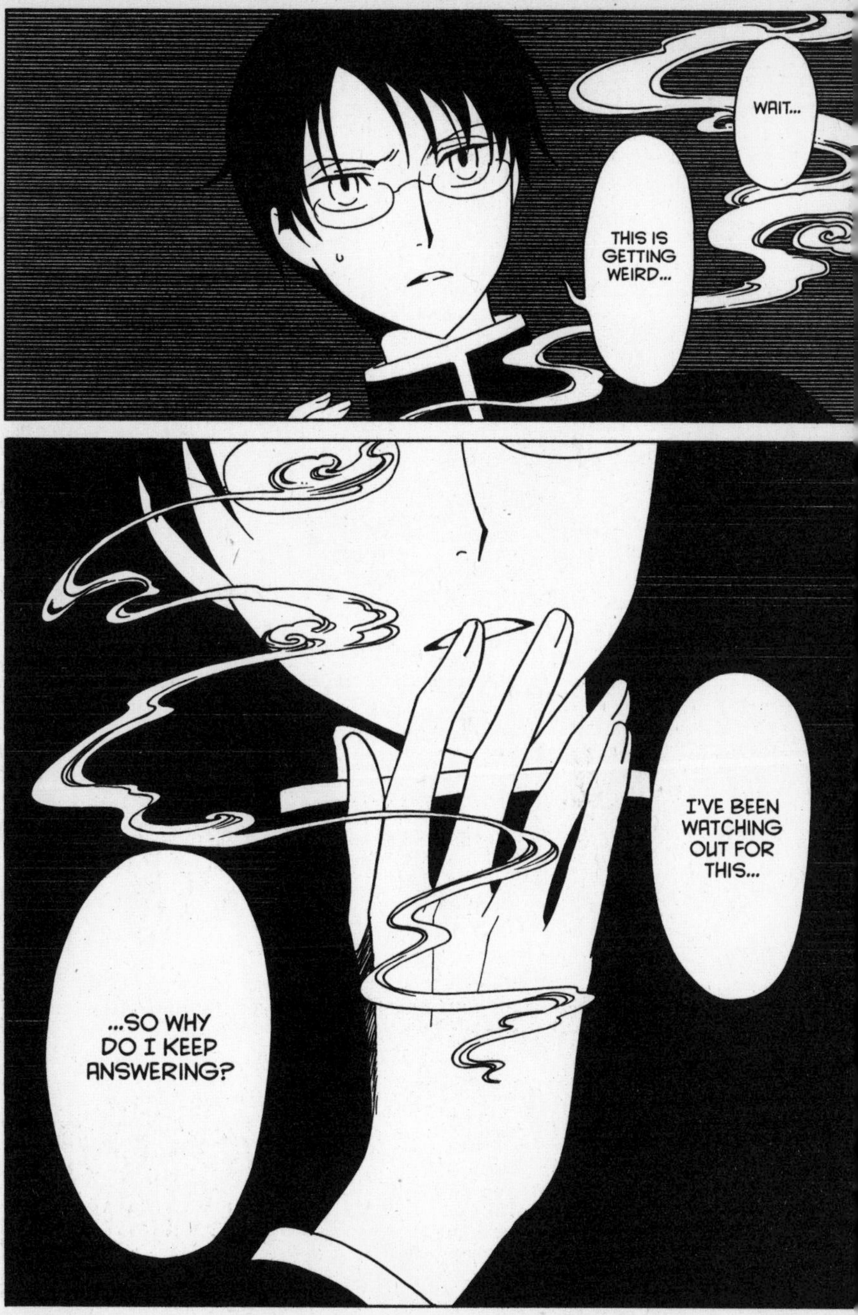
WAIT...
THIS IS GETTING WEIRD...
I'VE BEEN WATCHING OUT FOR THIS...
...SO WHY DO I KEEP ANSWERING?

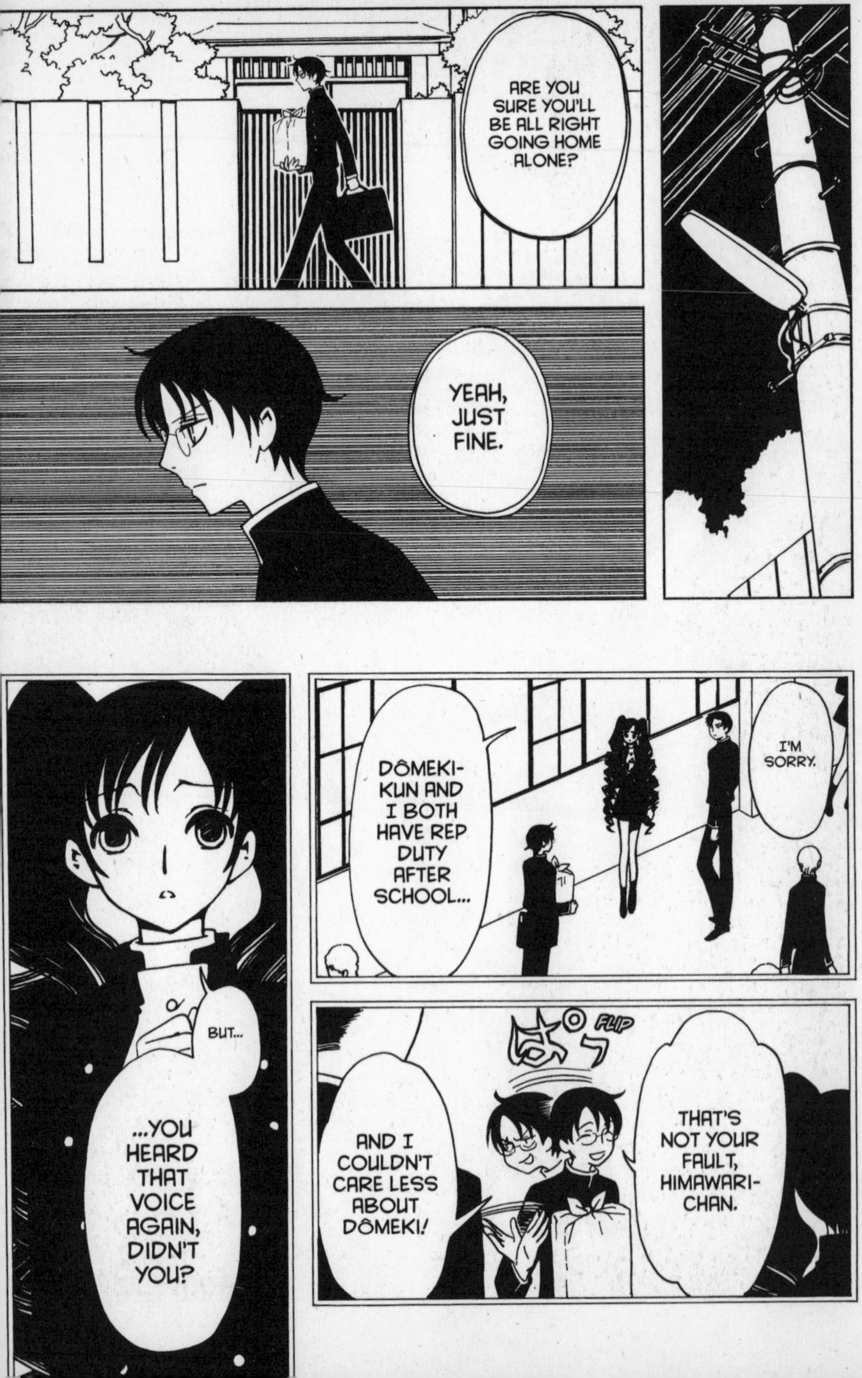
ARE YOU SURE YOU'LL BE ALL RIGHT GOING HOME ALONE?
YEAH, JUST FINE.
I'M SORRY.
DÔMEKI-KUN AND I BOTH HAVE REP DUTY AFTER SCHOOL...
FLIP
THAT'S NOT YOUR FAULT, HIMAWARI-CHAN.
AND I COULDN'T CARE LESS ABOUT DÔMEKI!
BUT...
...YOU HEARD THAT VOICE AGAIN, DIDN'T YOU?

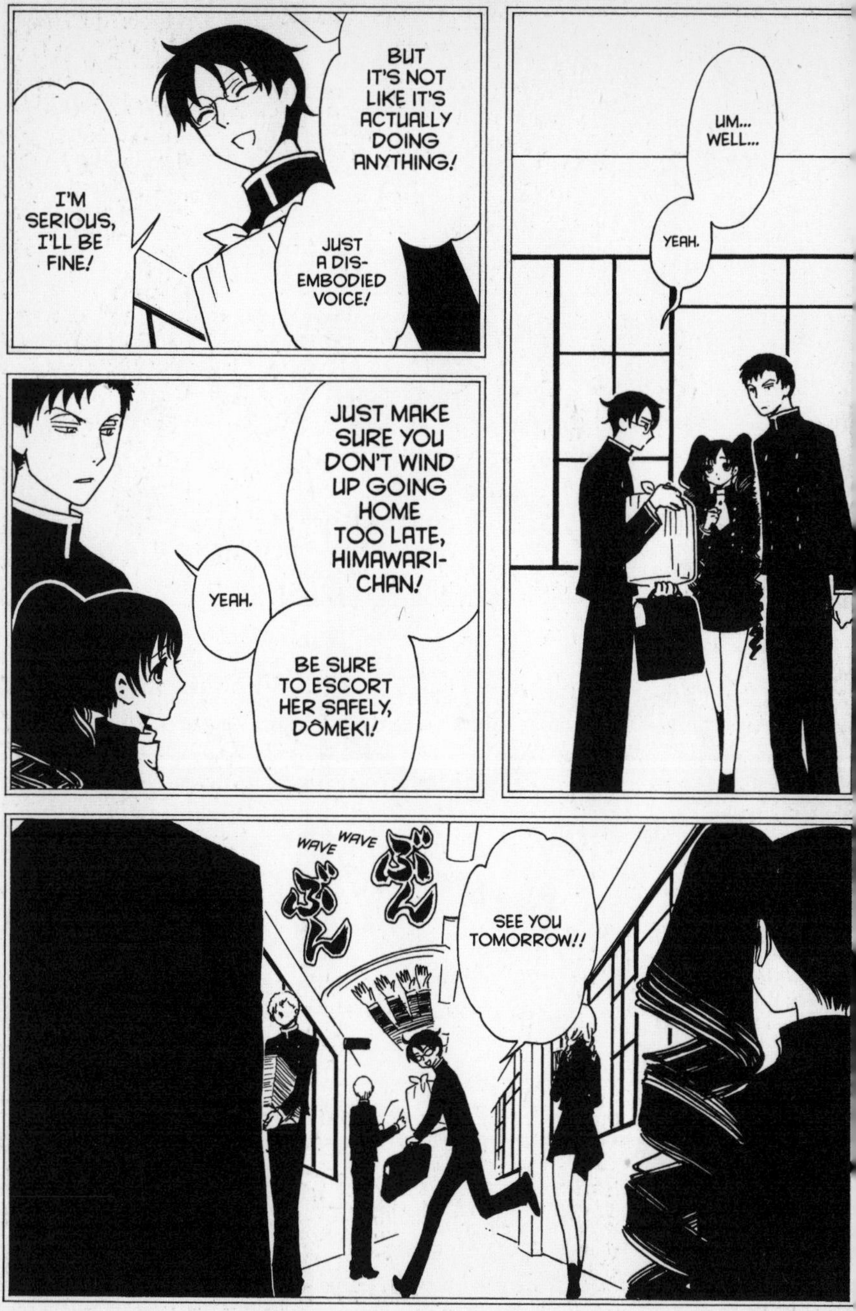
UM... WELL...
YEAH.
BUT IT'S NOT LIKE IT'S ACTUALLY DOING ANYTHING!
JUST A DIS-EMBODIED VOICE!
I'M SERIOUS, I'LL BE FINE!
JUST MAKE SURE YOU DON'T WIND UP GOING HOME TOO LATE, HIMAWARI-CHAN!
YEAH.
BE SURE TO ESCORT HER SAFELY, DÔMEKI!
WAVE WAVE
SEE YOU TOMORROW!!

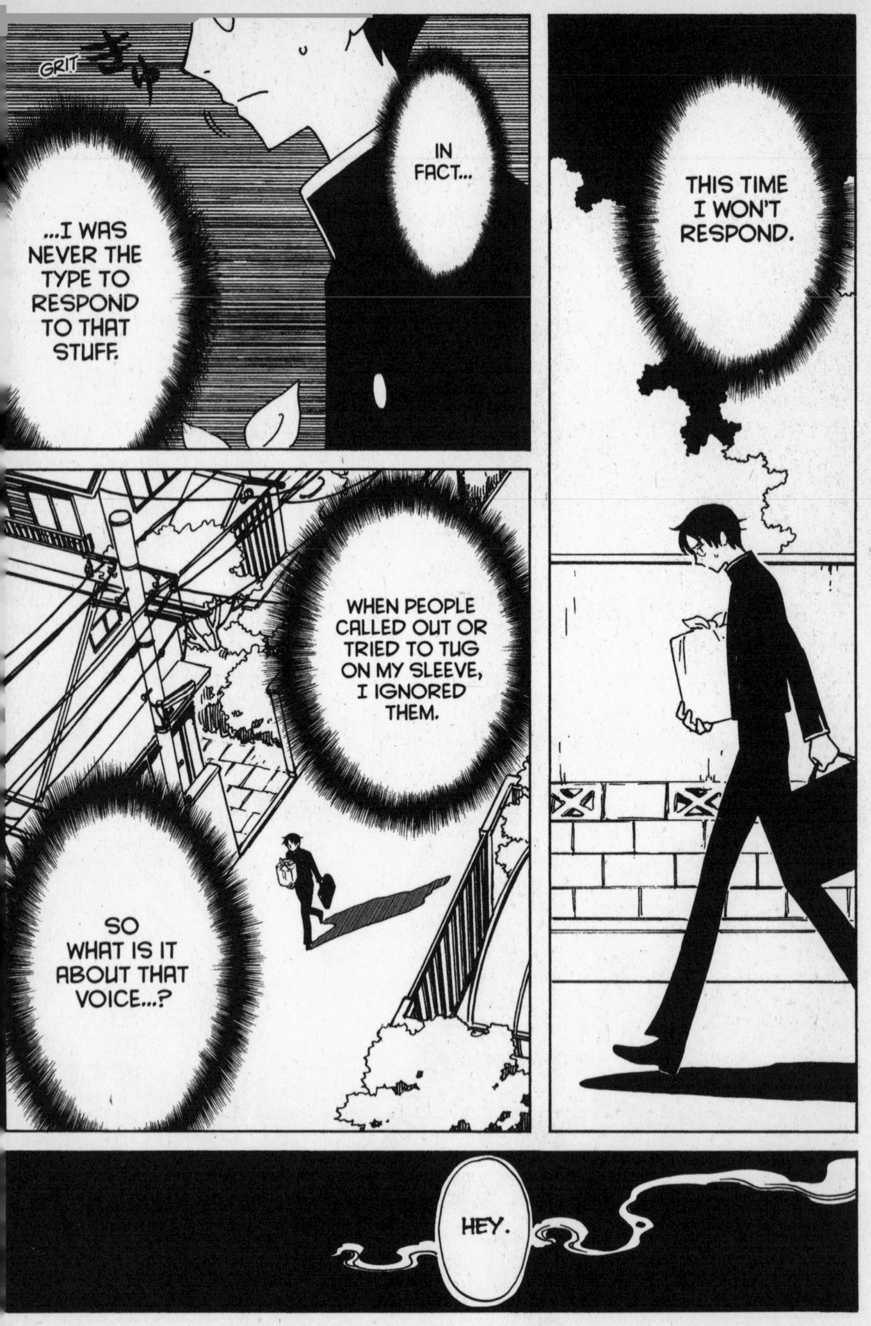
THIS TIME I WON'T RESPOND.
GRIT
IN FACT...
...I WAS NEVER THE TYPE TO RESPOND TO THAT STUFF.
WHEN PEOPLE CALLED OUT OR TRIED TO TUG ON MY SLEEVE, I IGNORED THEM.
SO WHAT IS IT ABOUT THAT VOICE...?
HEY.

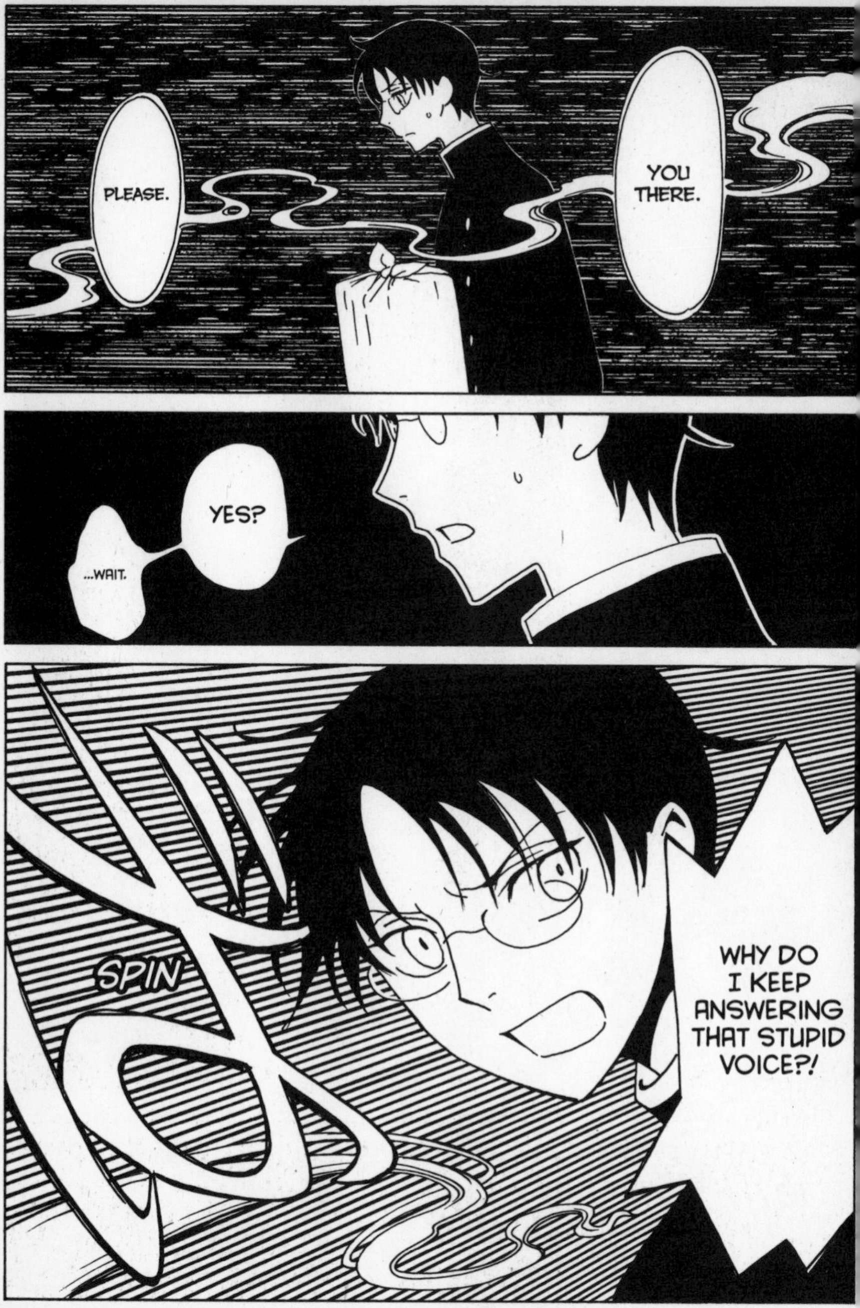
YOU THERE.
PLEASE.
YES?
...WAIT.
WHY DO I KEEP ANSWERING THAT STUPID VOICE?!
SPIN

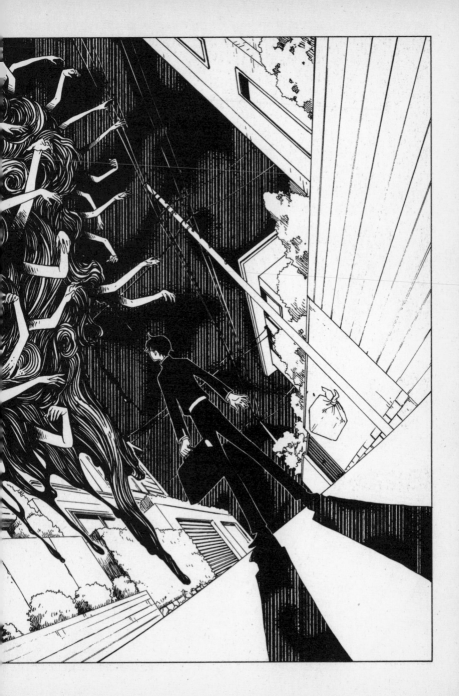

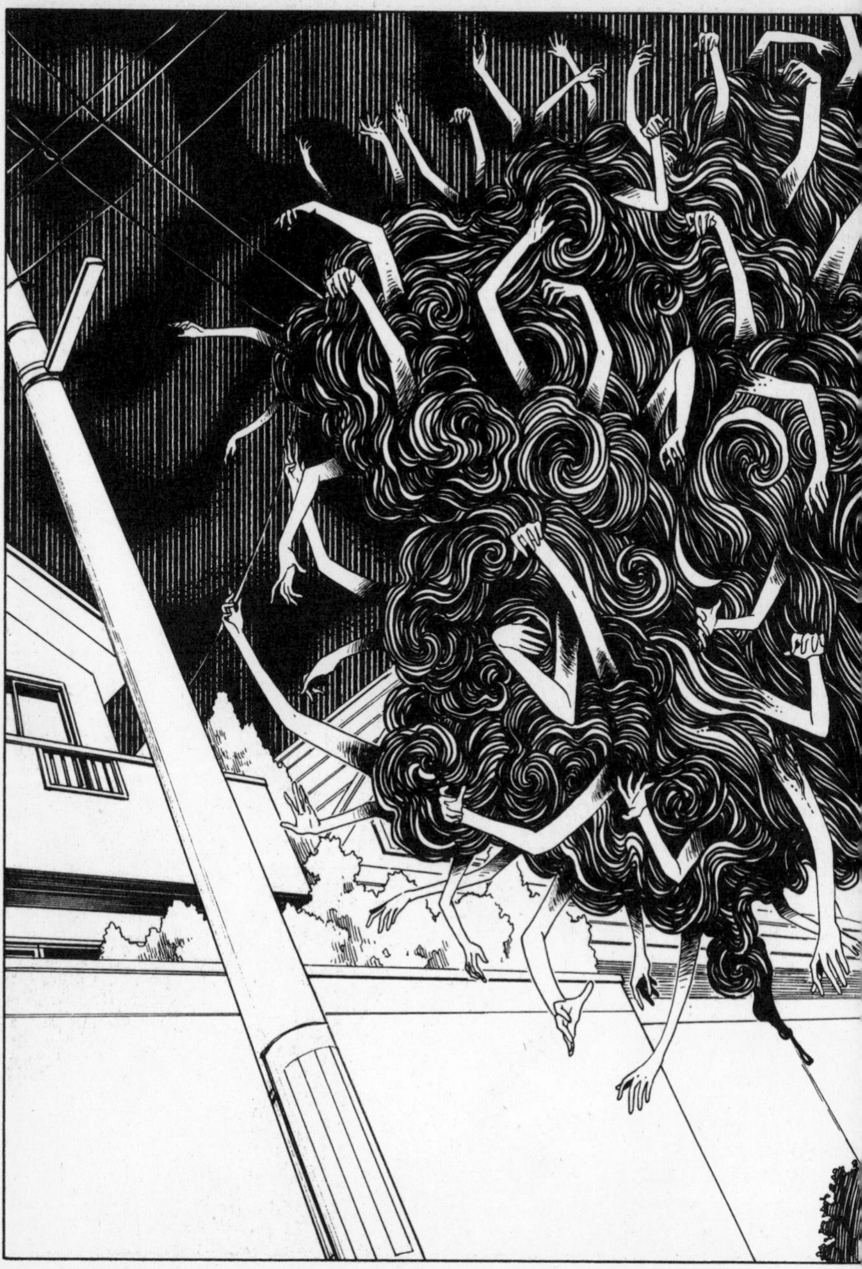

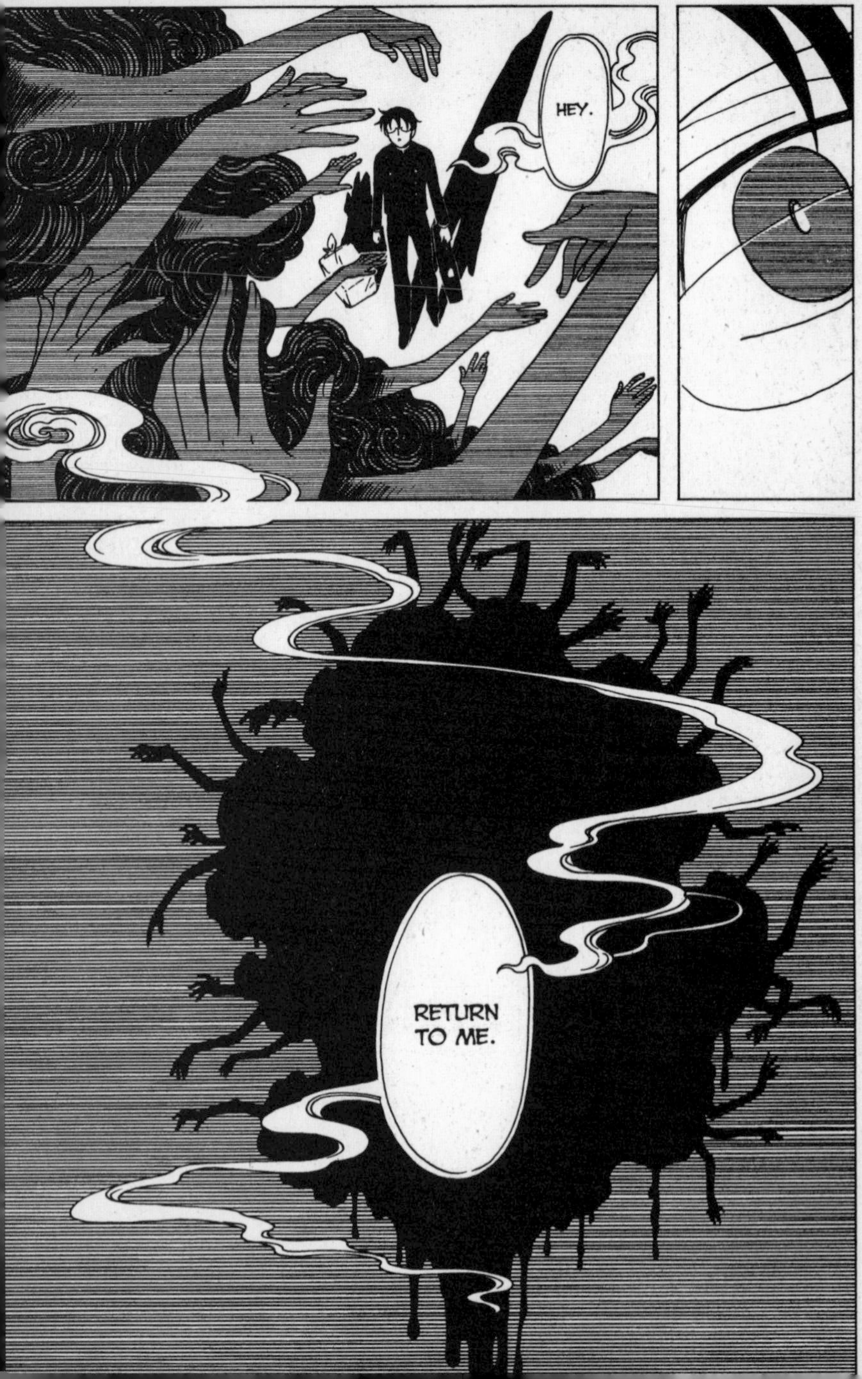
HEY.
RETURN TO ME.

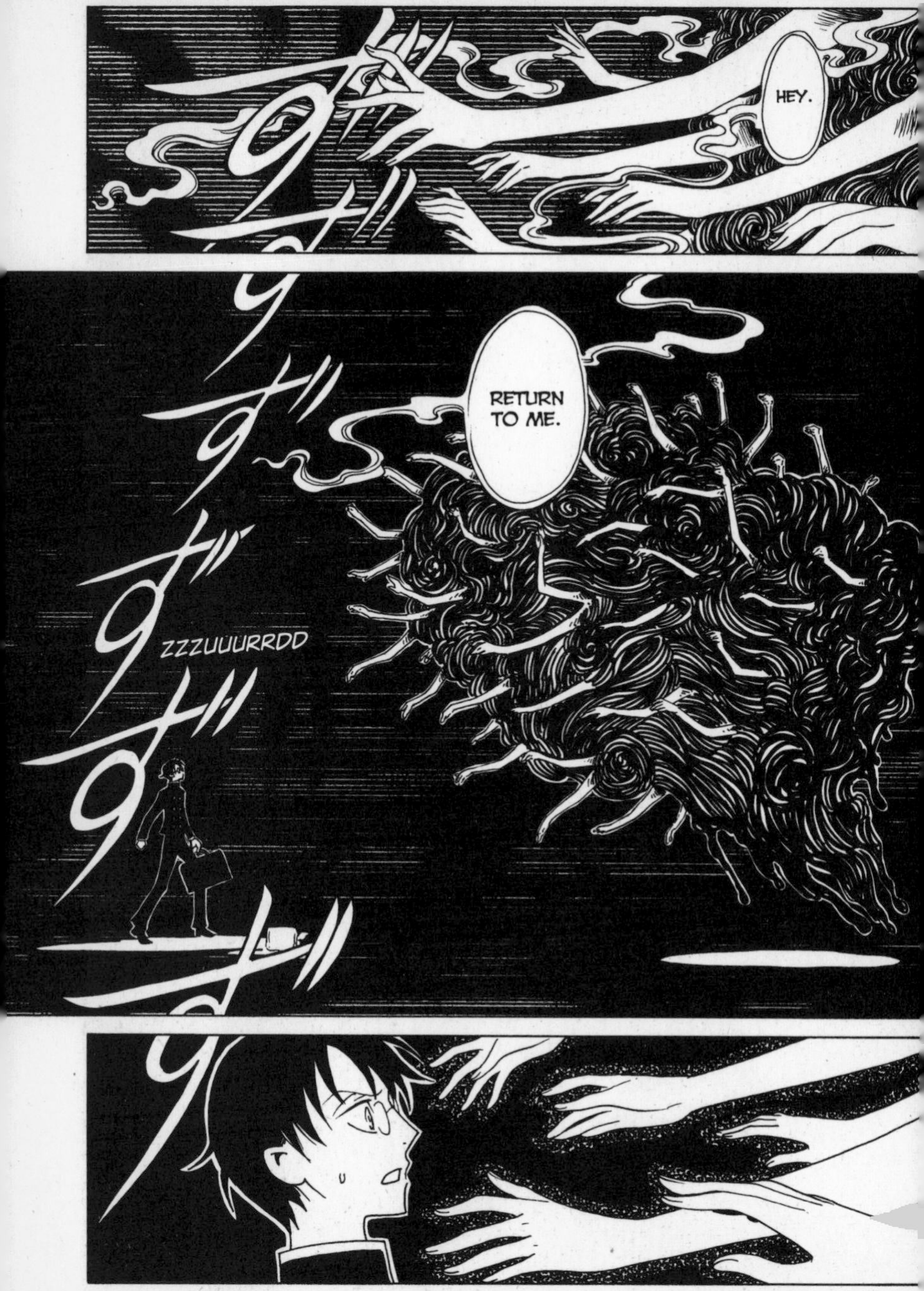
HEY.
RETURN TO ME.
ZZZUUURRDD

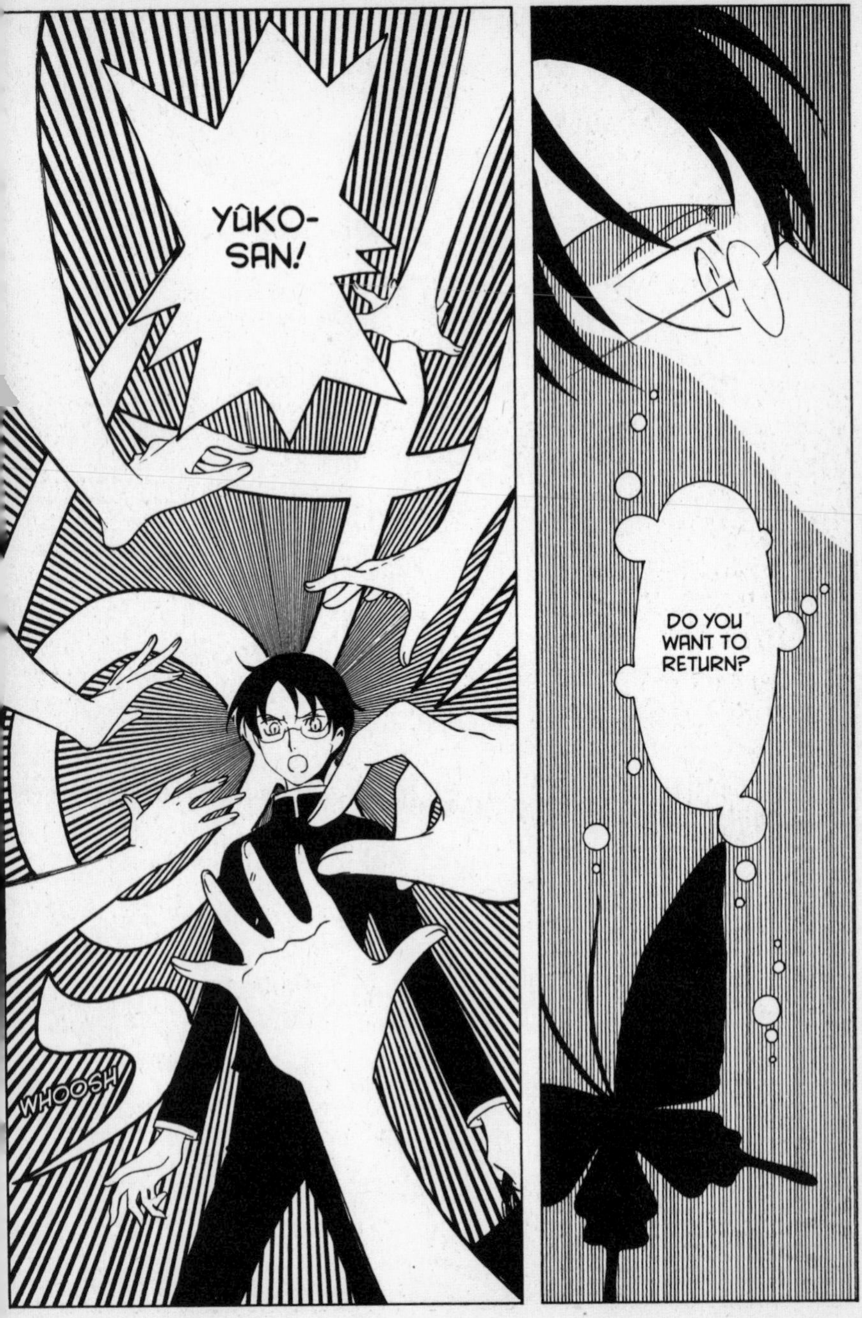
DO YOU WANT TO RETURN?
YÛKO-SAN!
WHOOSH

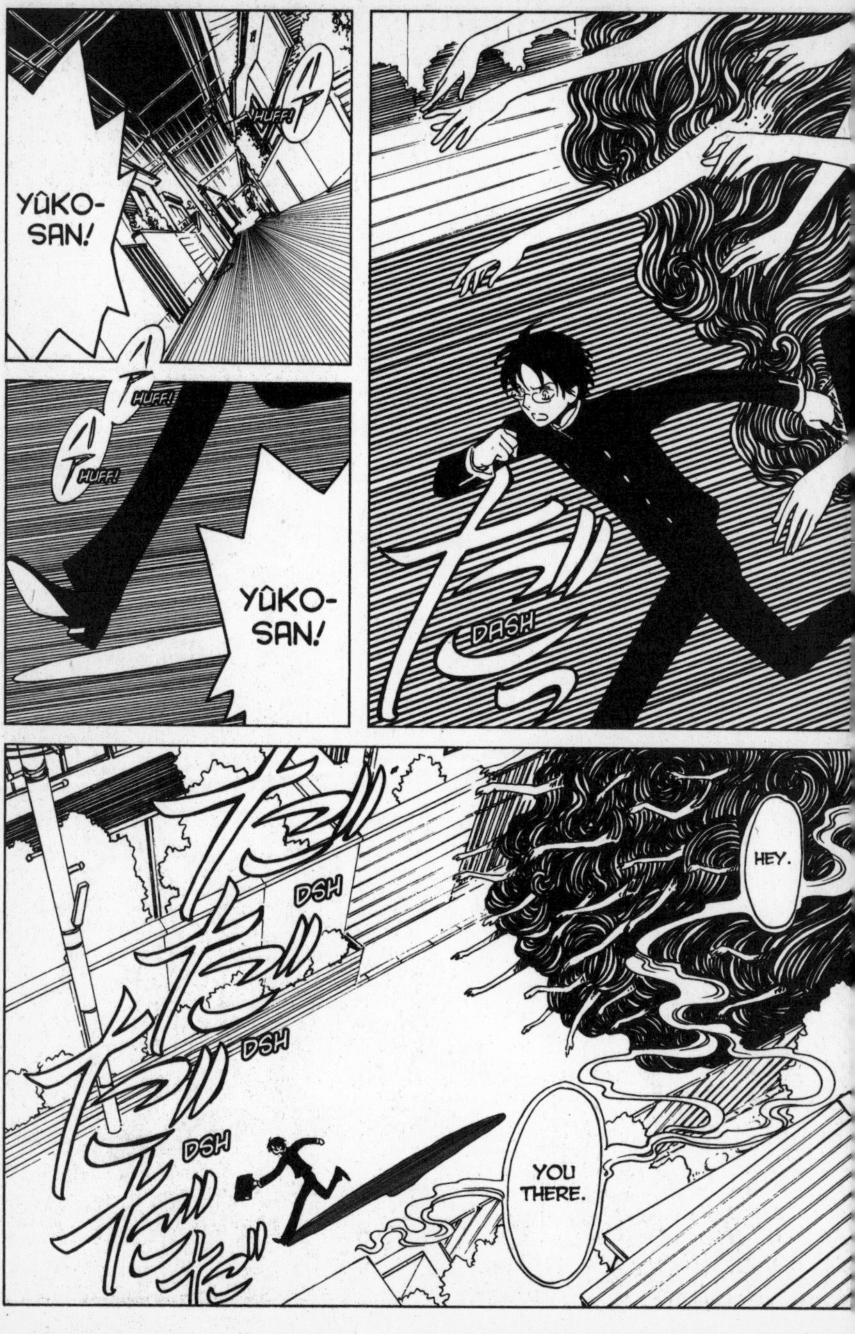
DASH
HUFF!
YÛKO-SAN!
HUFF!
HUFF!
YÛKO-SAN!
HEY.
YOU THERE.
DSH
DSH
DSH

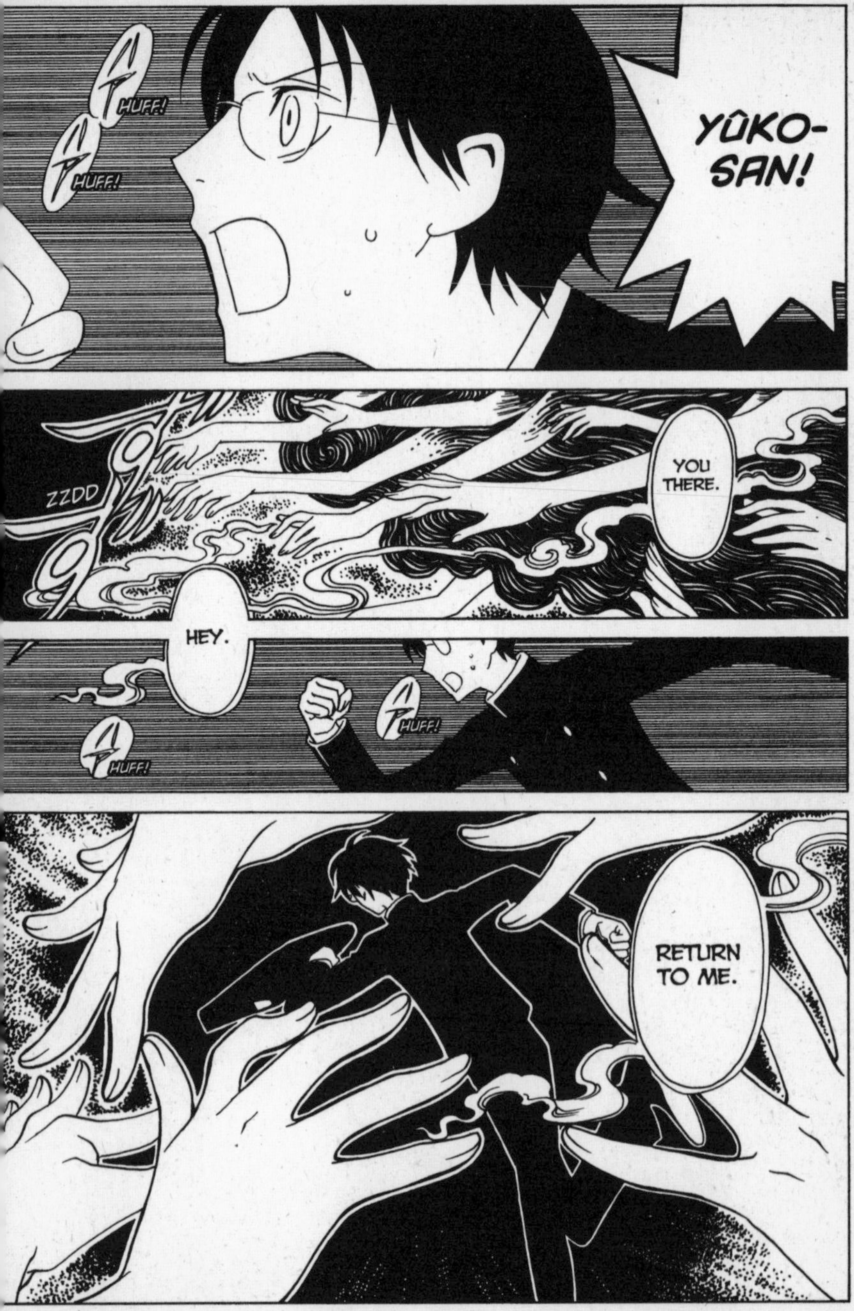
YÛKO-SAN!
HUFF!
HUFF!
YOU THERE.
ZZDD
HEY.
HUFF!
HUFF!
RETURN TO ME.

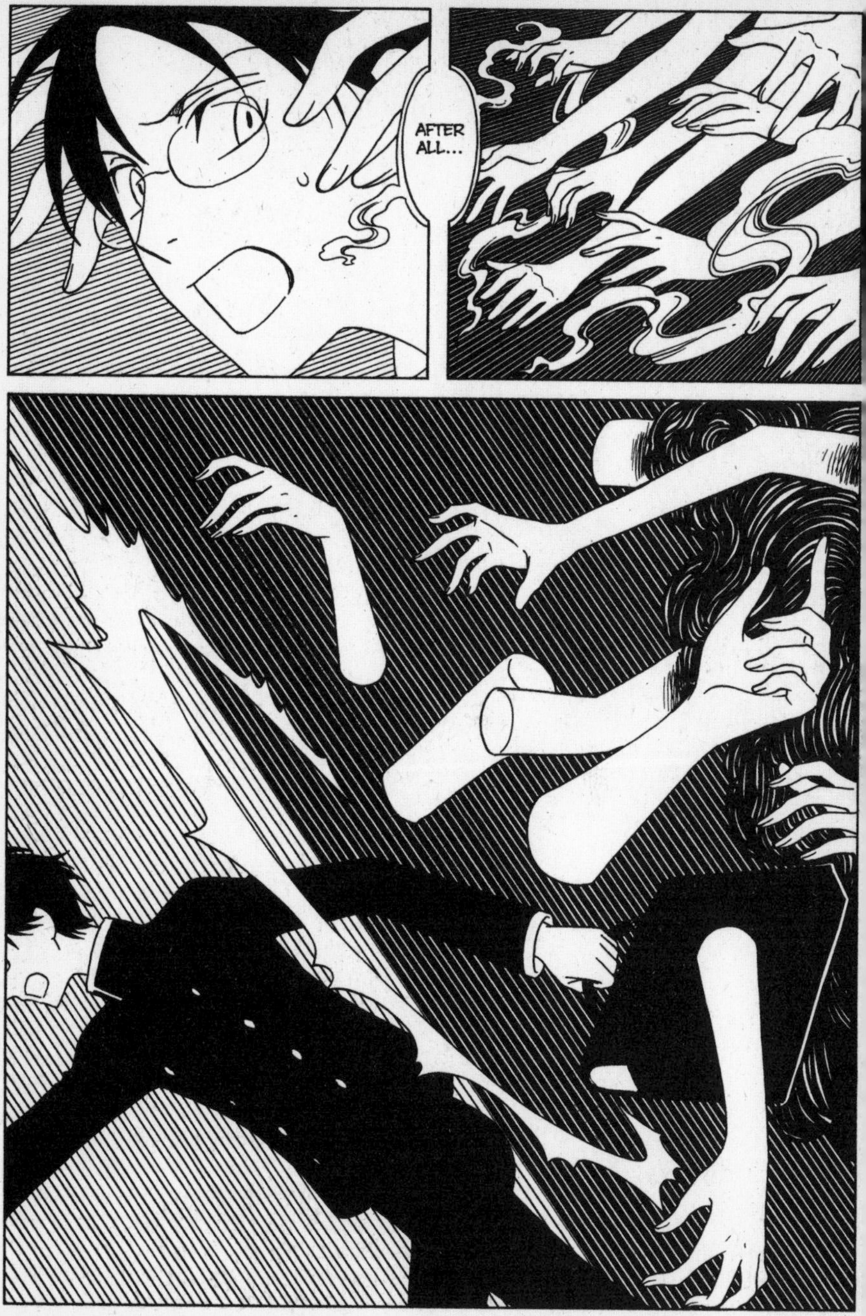
AFTER ALL...

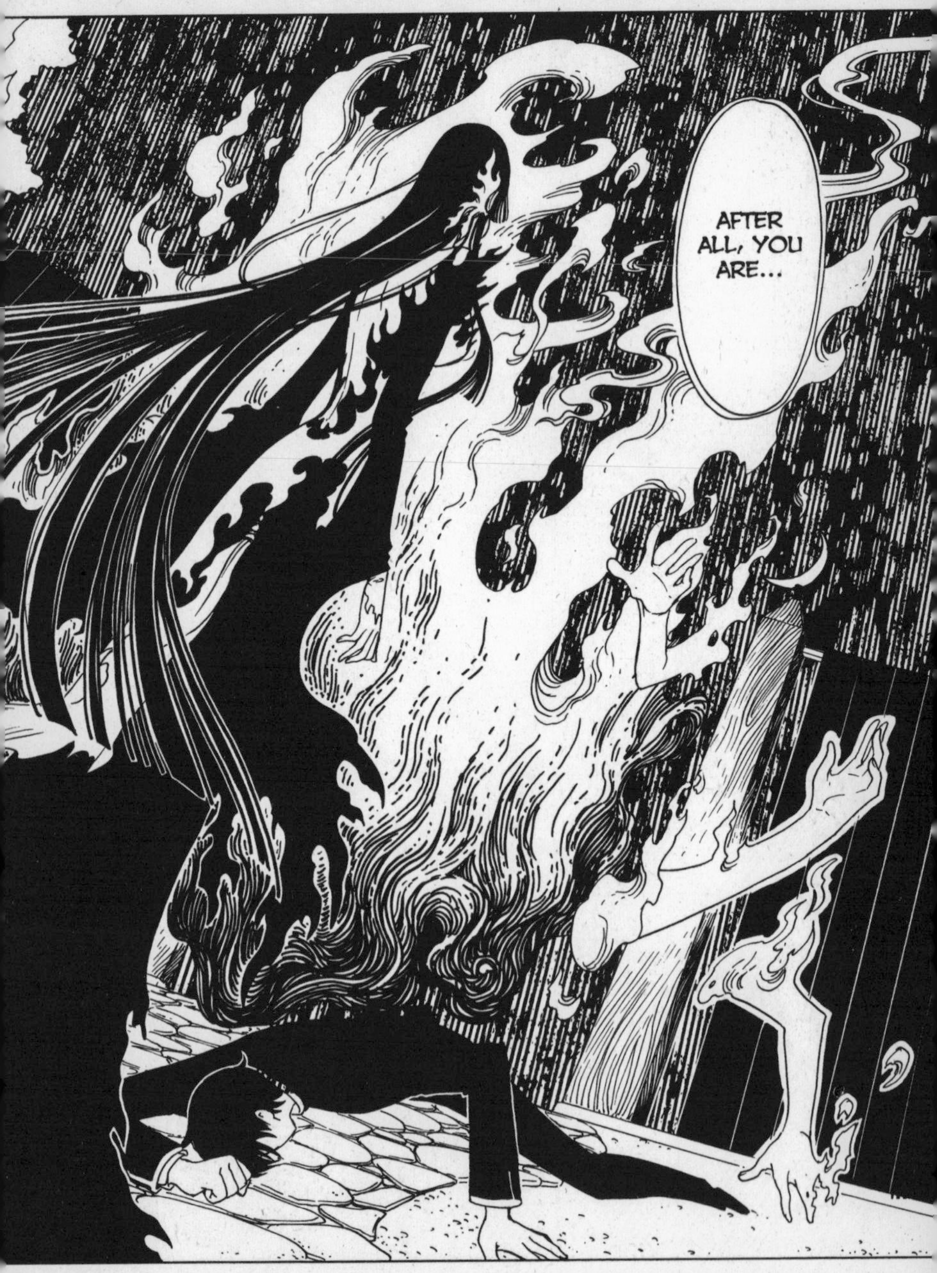
AFTER ALL, YOU ARE...

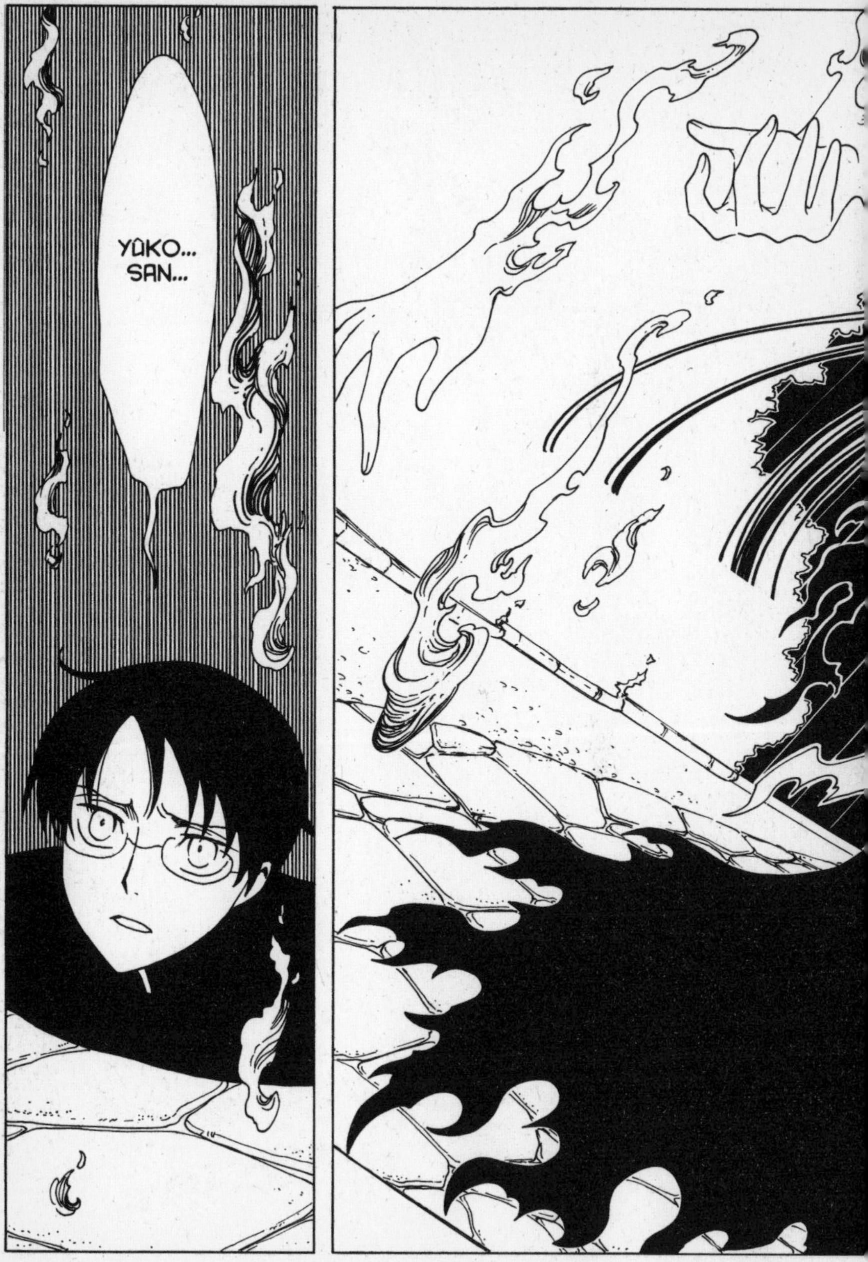
YÛKO... SAN...

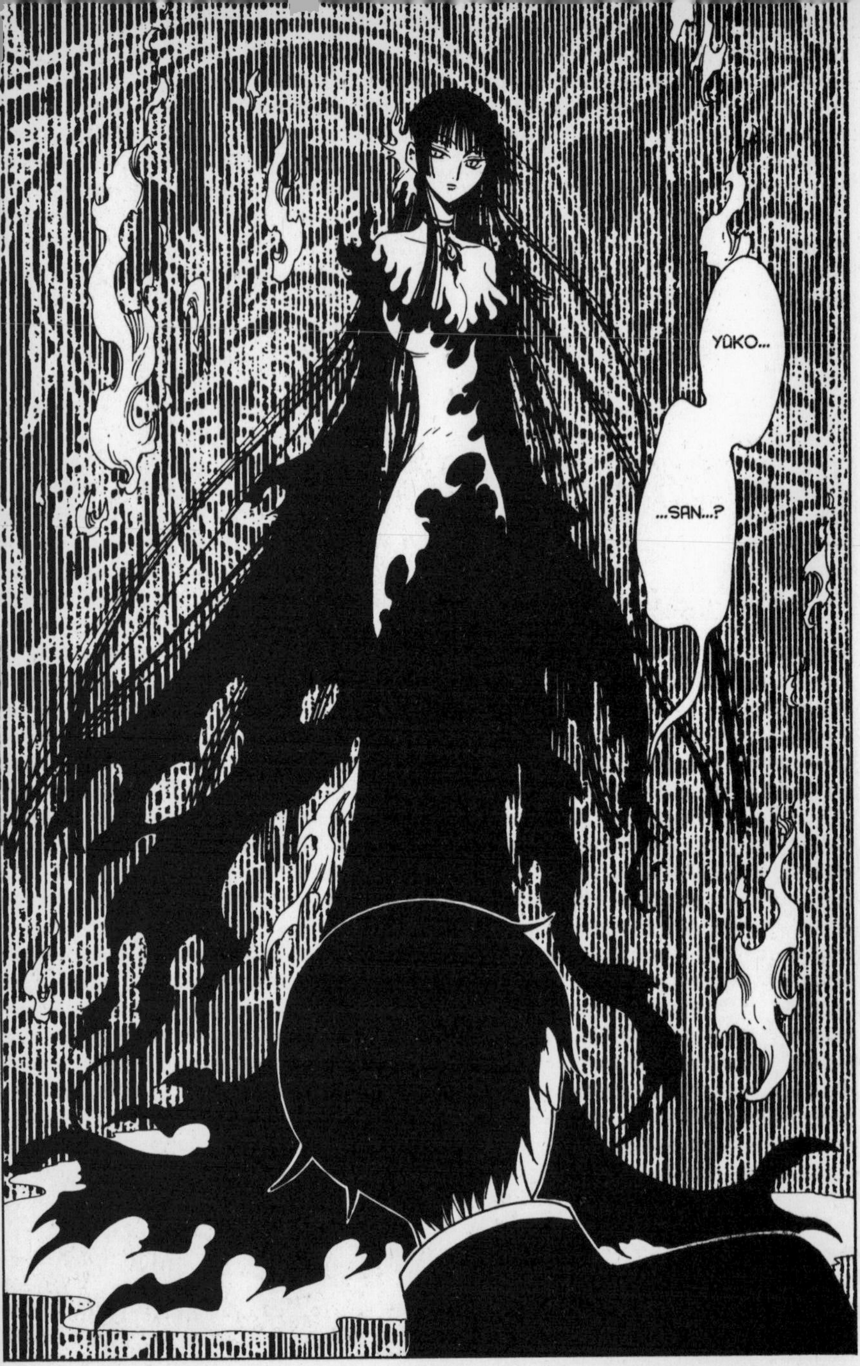
YŪKO...
...SAN...?

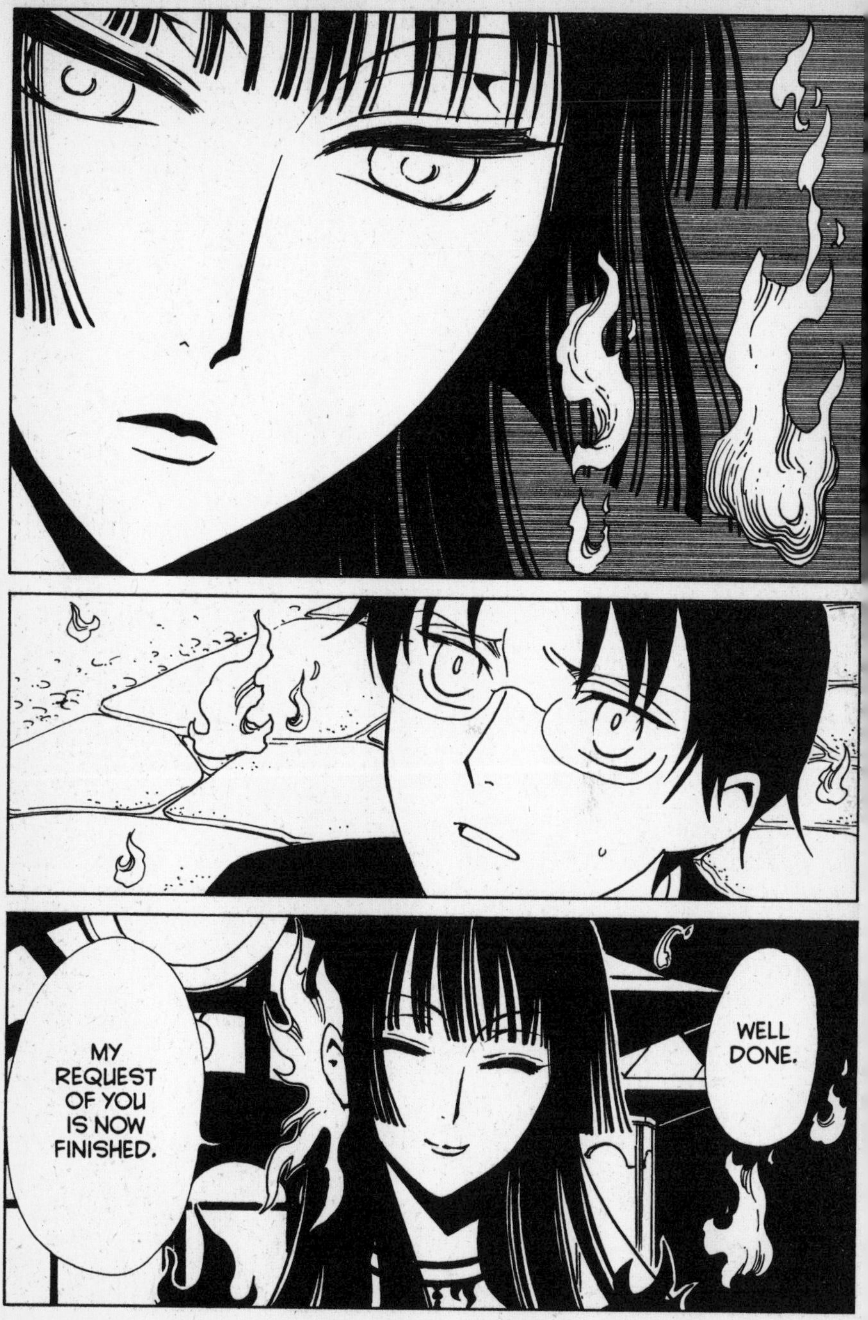
WELL DONE.
MY REQUEST OF YOU IS NOW FINISHED.

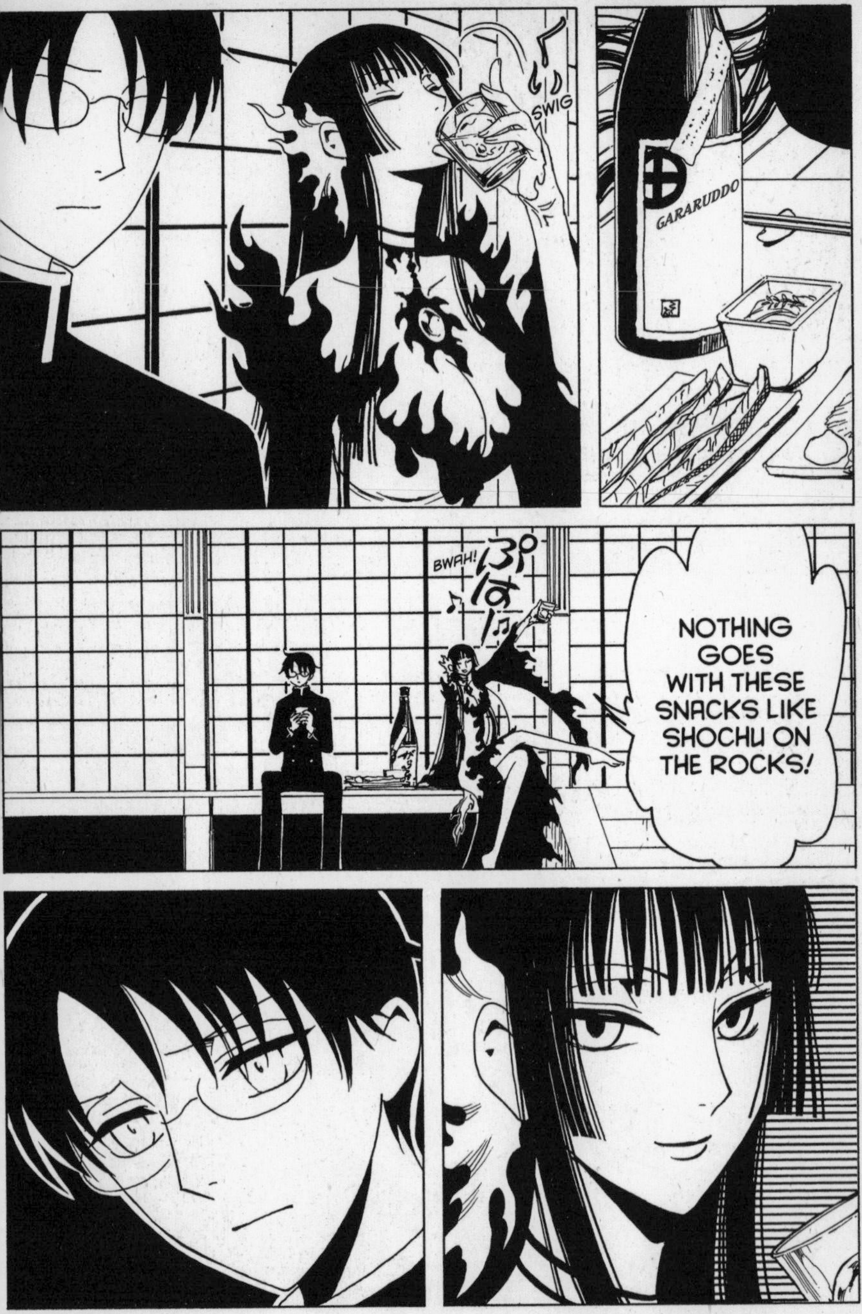
GARARUDDO
SWIG
NOTHING GOES WITH THESE SNACKS LIKE SHOCHU ON THE ROCKS!
BWAH!
ぷは!

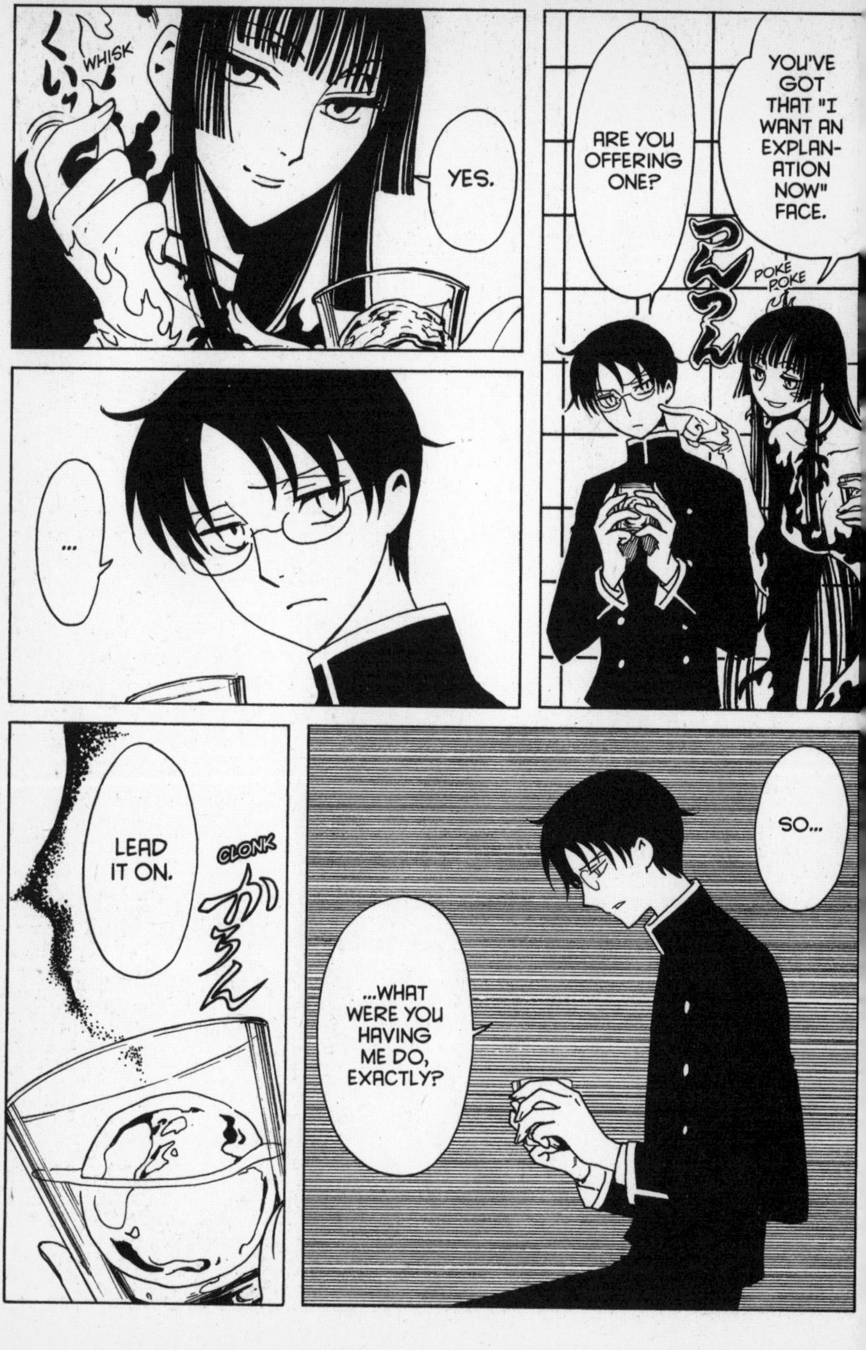
YOU'VE GOT THAT "I WANT AN EXPLANATION NOW" FACE.
ARE YOU OFFERING ONE?
POKE POKE
WHISK
YES.
...
SO...
...WHAT WERE YOU HAVING ME DO, EXACTLY?
LEAD IT ON.
CLONK

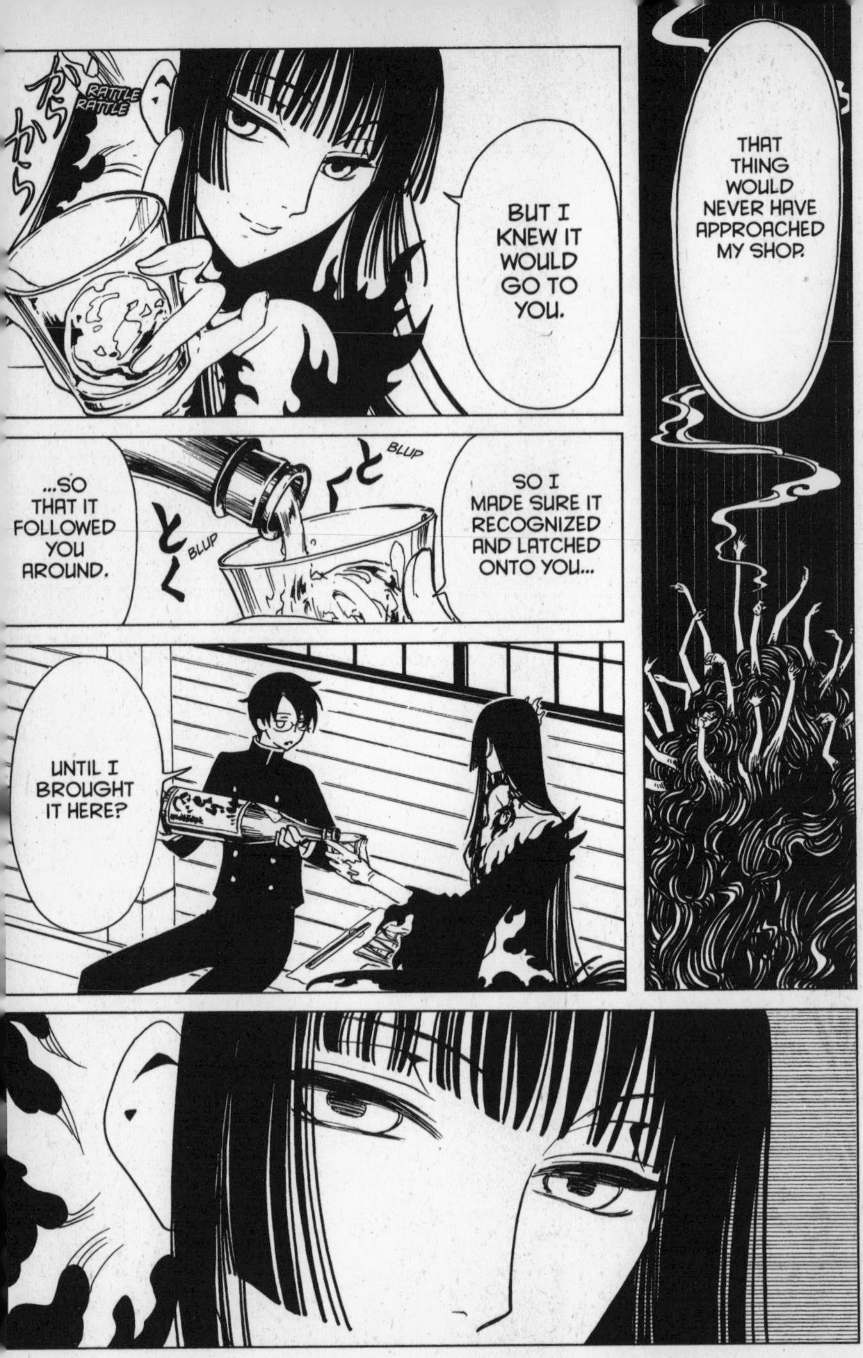
THAT THING WOULD NEVER HAVE APPROACHED MY SHOP.
BUT I KNEW IT WOULD GO TO YOU.
からから
RATTLE RATTLE
SO I MADE SURE IT RECOGNIZED AND LATCHED ONTO YOU...
とく
BLUP
とく
BLUP
...SO THAT IT FOLLOWED YOU AROUND.
UNTIL I BROUGHT IT HERE?

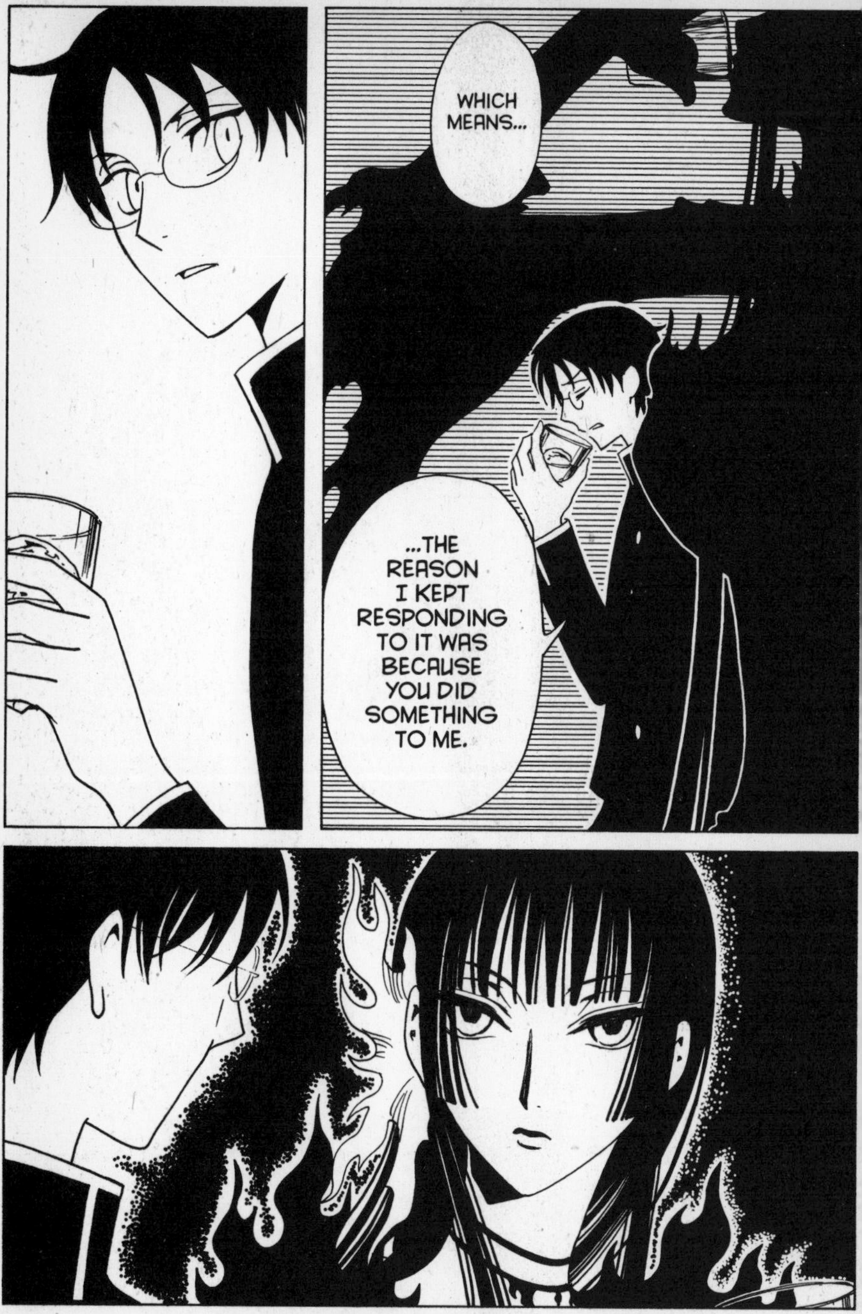
WHICH MEANS...
...THE REASON I KEPT RESPONDING TO IT WAS BECAUSE YOU DID SOMETHING TO ME.

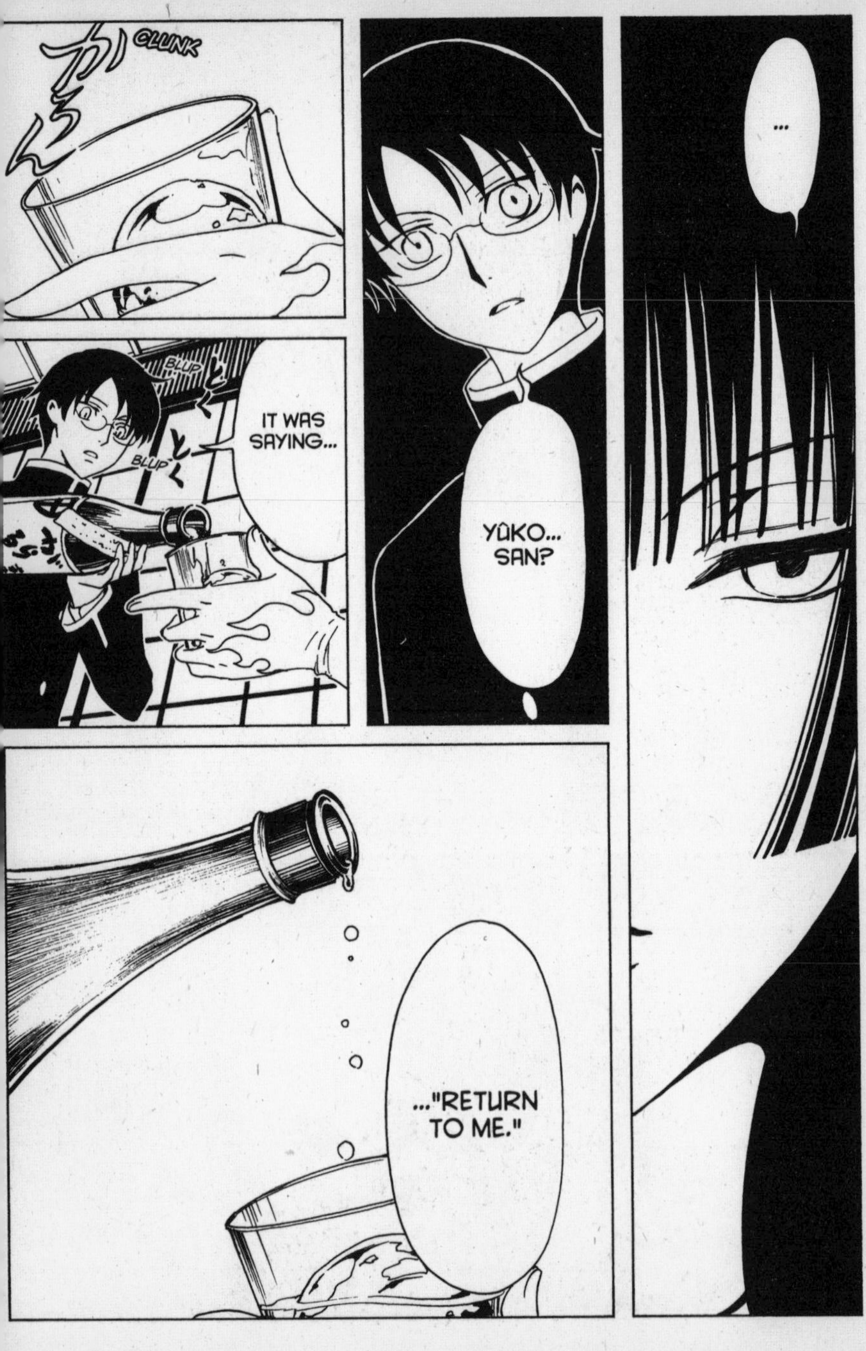
...
YÛKO... SAN?
CLUNK
BLUP
BLUP
IT WAS SAYING...
..."RETURN TO ME."

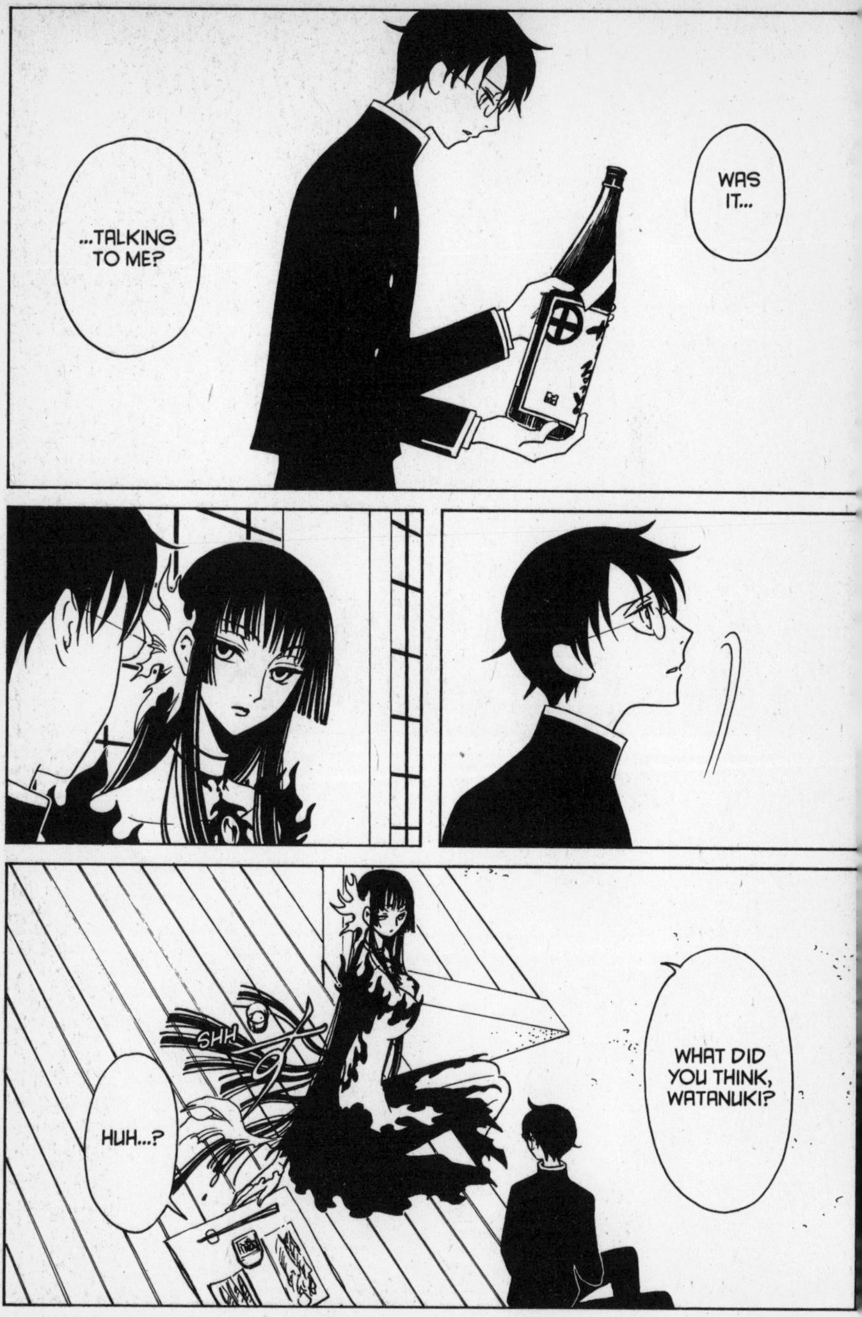
WAS IT...
...TALKING TO ME?
WHAT DID YOU THINK, WATANUKI?
SHH
HUH...?

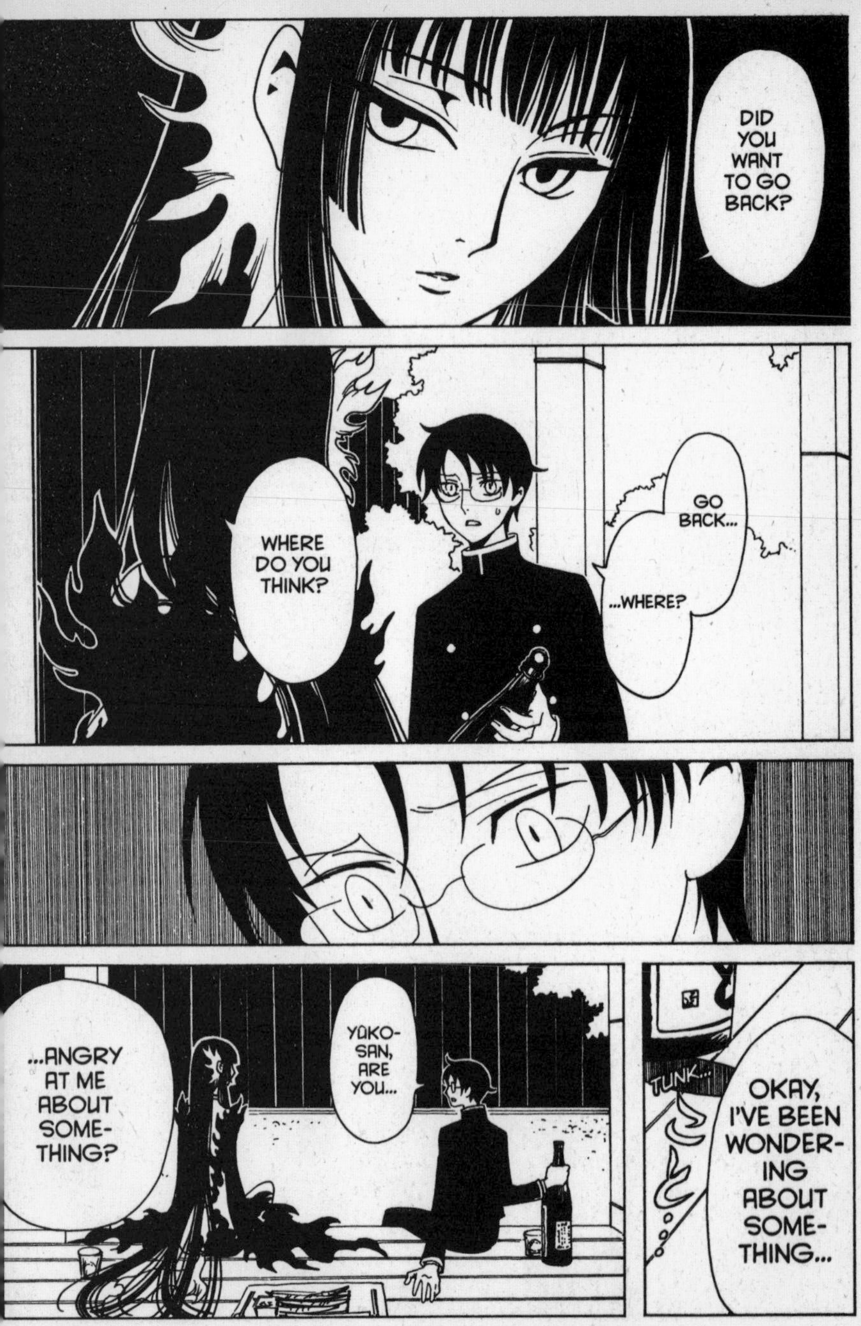
DID YOU WANT TO GO BACK?
GO BACK... ...WHERE?
WHERE DO YOU THINK?
TUNK...
OKAY, I'VE BEEN WONDERING ABOUT SOMETHING...
YÛKO-SAN, ARE YOU...
...ANGRY AT ME ABOUT SOMETHING?

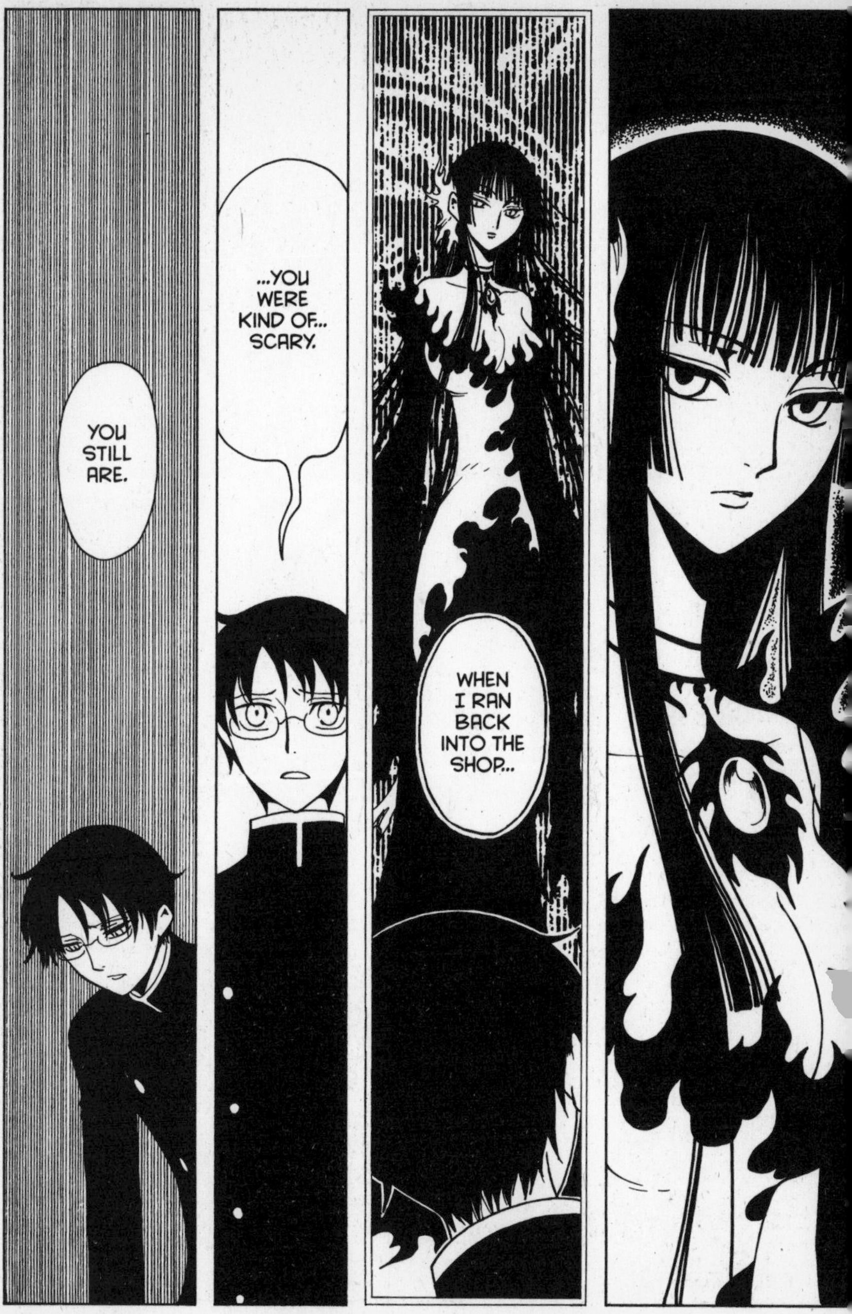
WHEN I RAN BACK INTO THE SHOP...
...YOU WERE KIND OF... SCARY.
YOU STILL ARE.

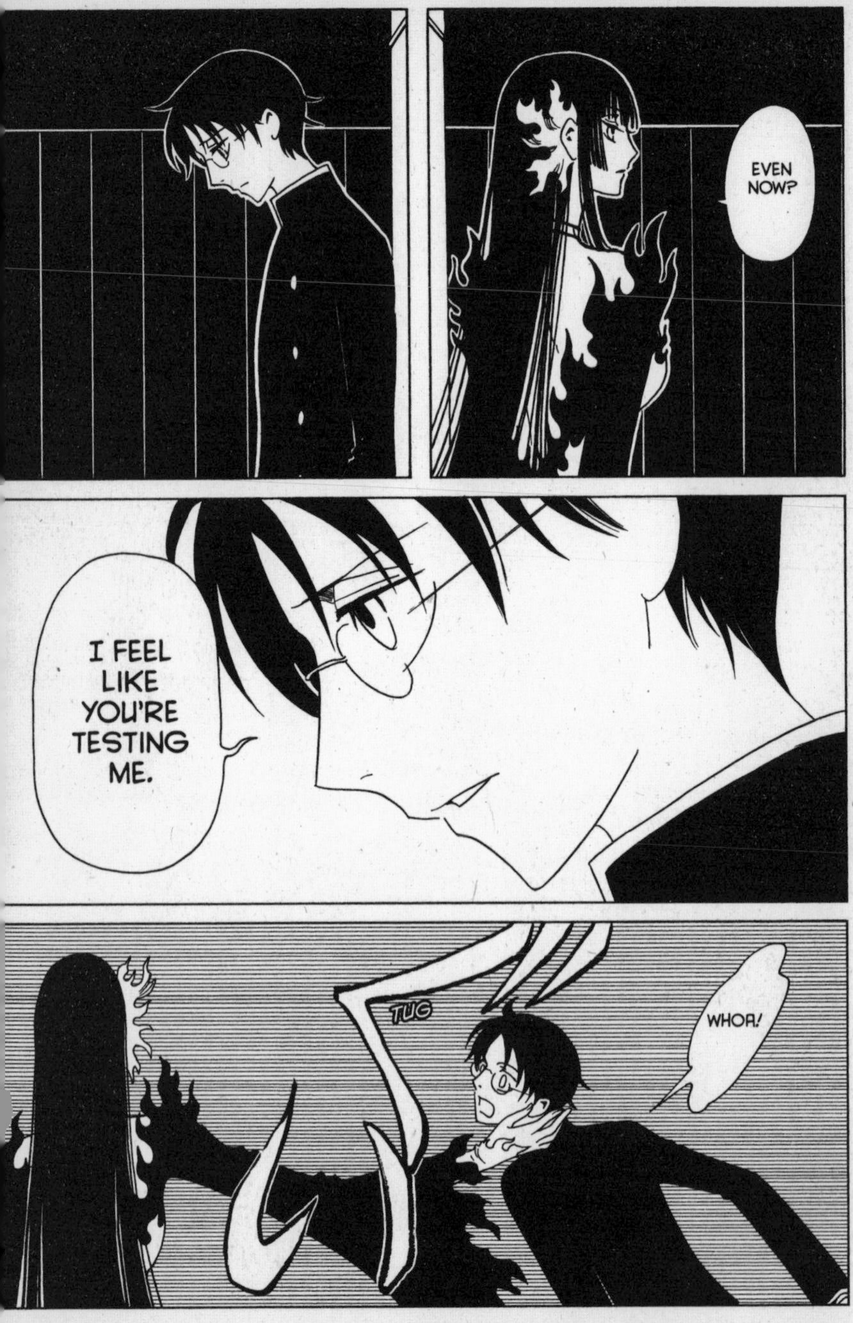
EVEN NOW?
I FEEL LIKE YOU'RE TESTING ME.
WHOA!
TUG

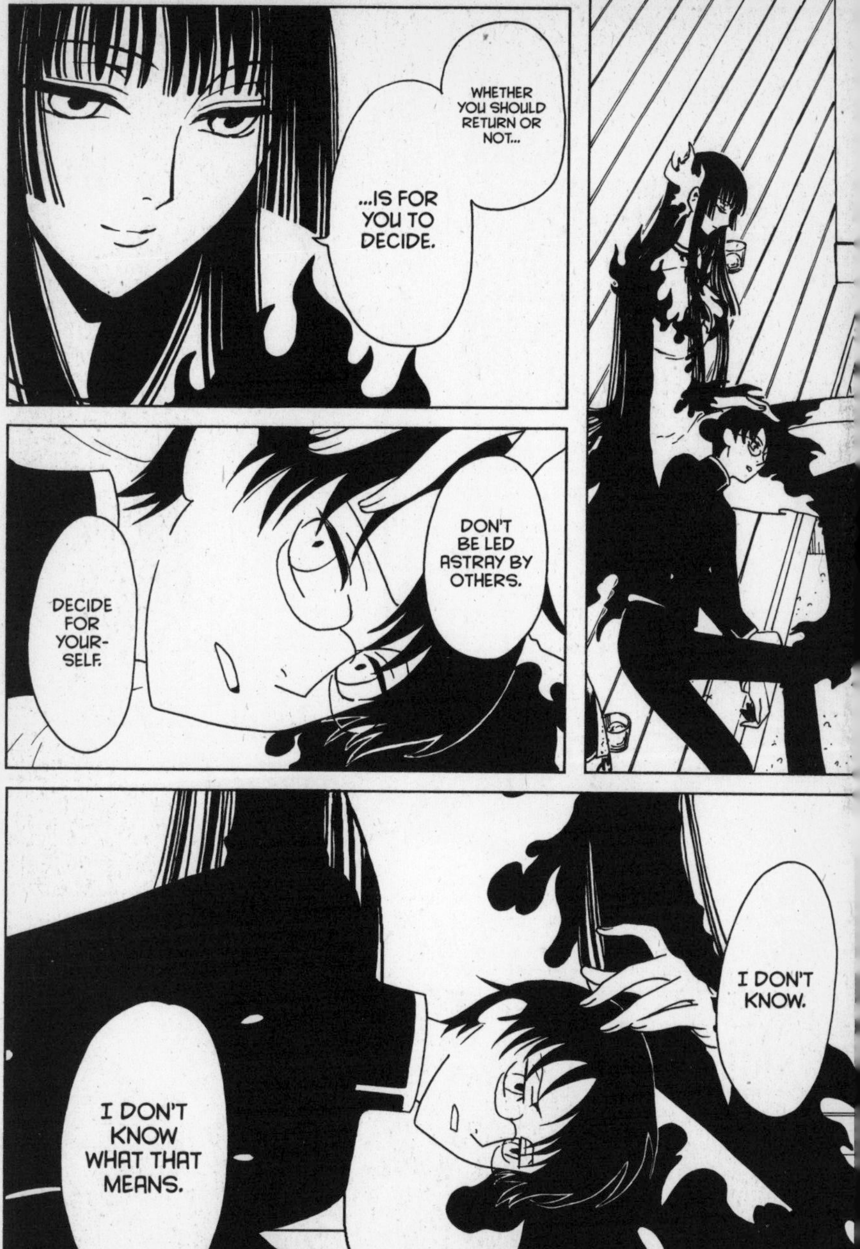
WHETHER YOU SHOULD RETURN OR NOT...
...IS FOR YOU TO DECIDE.
DON'T BE LED ASTRAY BY OTHERS.
DECIDE FOR YOUR-SELF.
I DON'T KNOW.
I DON'T KNOW WHAT THAT MEANS.

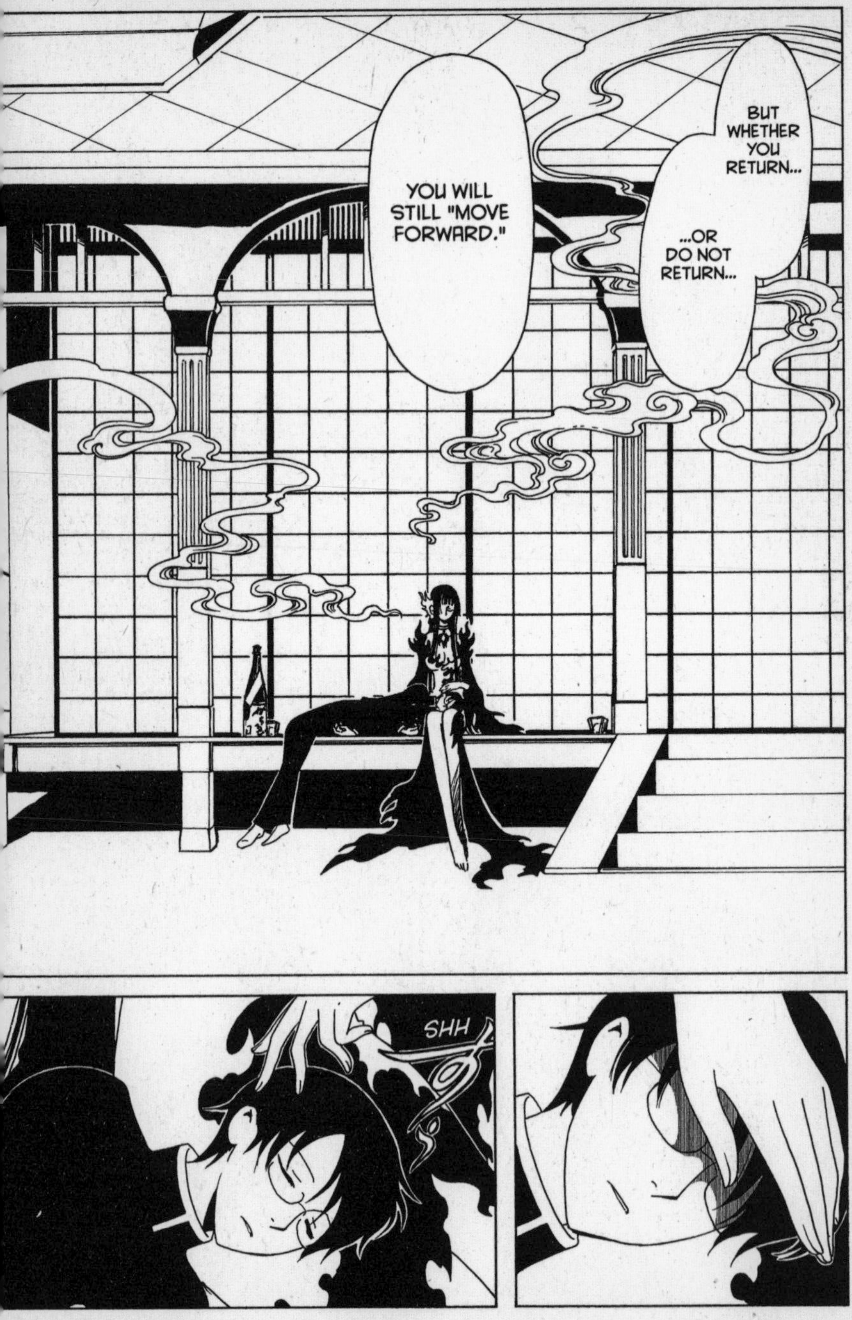
BUT WHETHER YOU RETURN...
...OR DO NOT RETURN...
YOU WILL STILL "MOVE FORWARD."
SHH

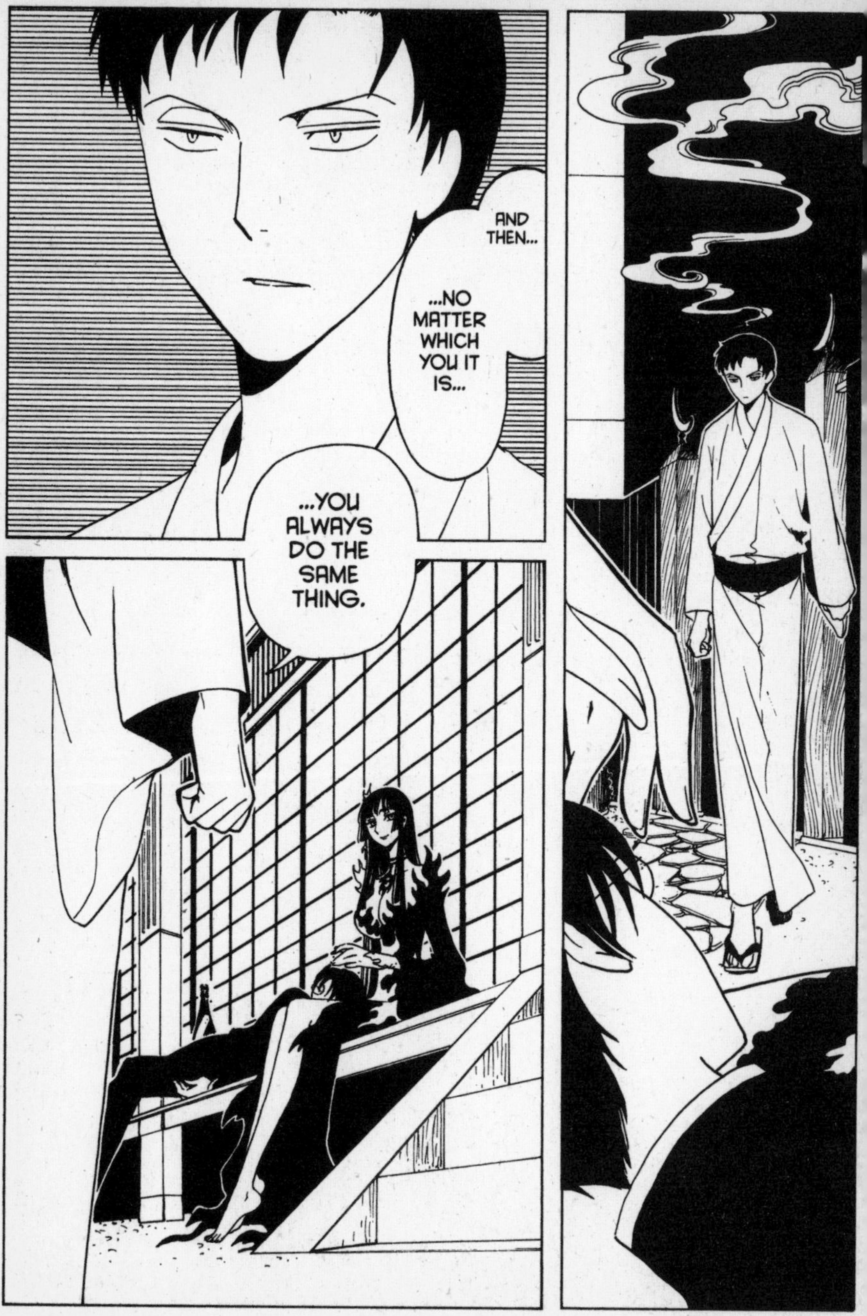
AND THEN...
...NO MATTER WHICH YOU IT IS...
...YOU ALWAYS DO THE SAME THING.

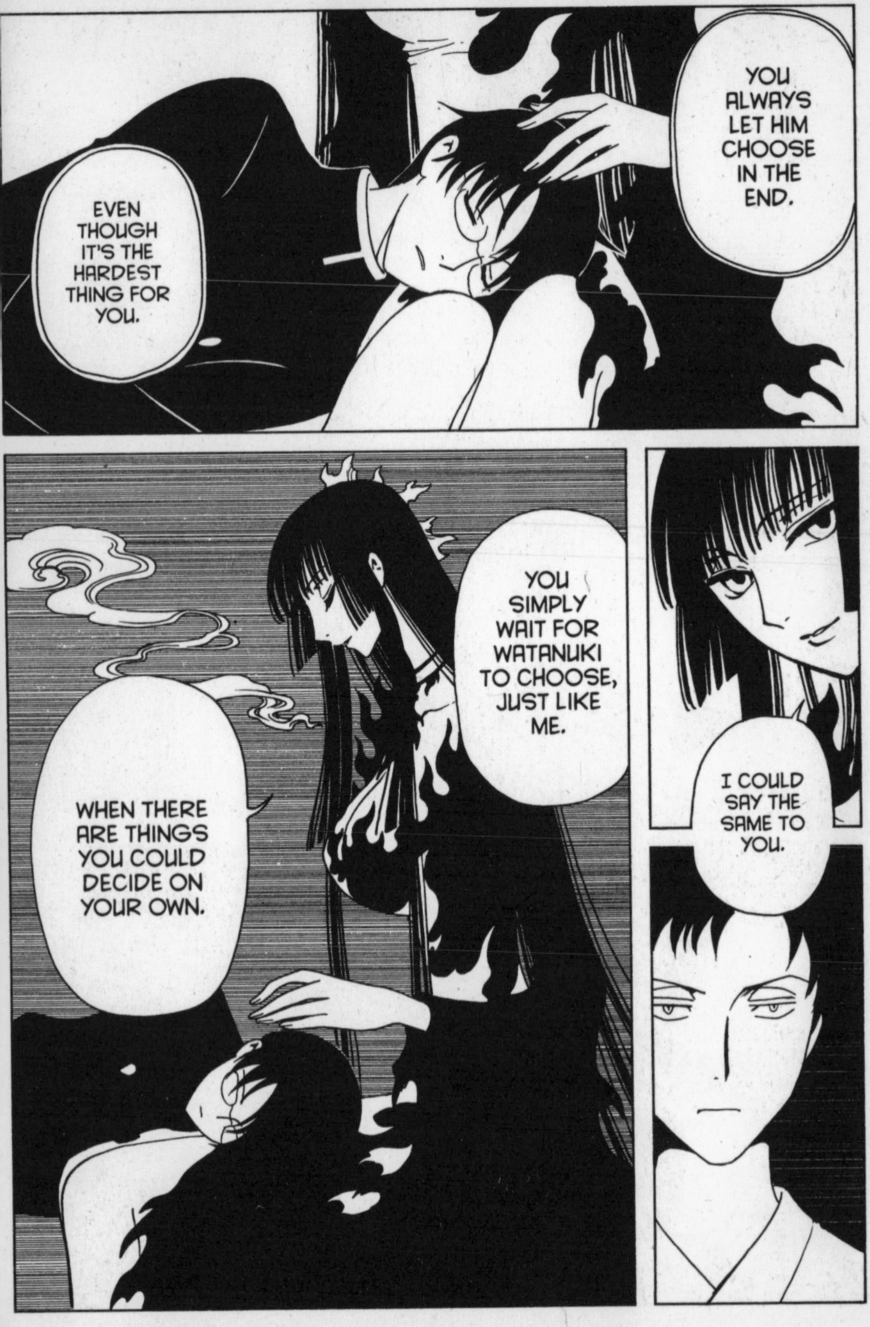
YOU ALWAYS LET HIM CHOOSE IN THE END.
EVEN THOUGH IT'S THE HARDEST THING FOR YOU.
I COULD SAY THE SAME TO YOU.
YOU SIMPLY WAIT FOR WATANUKI TO CHOOSE, JUST LIKE ME.
WHEN THERE ARE THINGS YOU COULD DECIDE ON YOUR OWN.

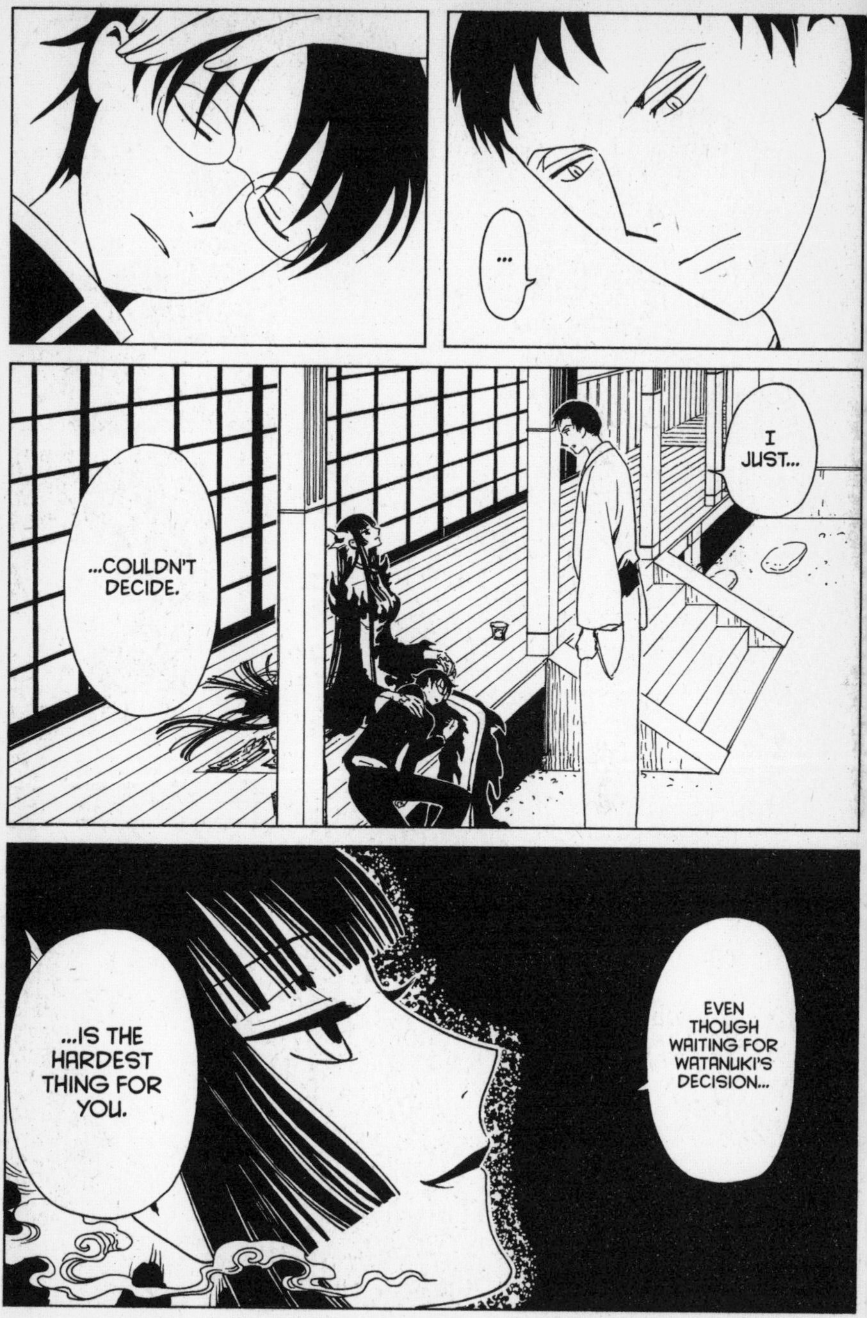
...
I JUST...
...COULDN'T DECIDE.
EVEN THOUGH WAITING FOR WATANUKI'S DECISION...
...IS THE HARDEST THING FOR YOU.

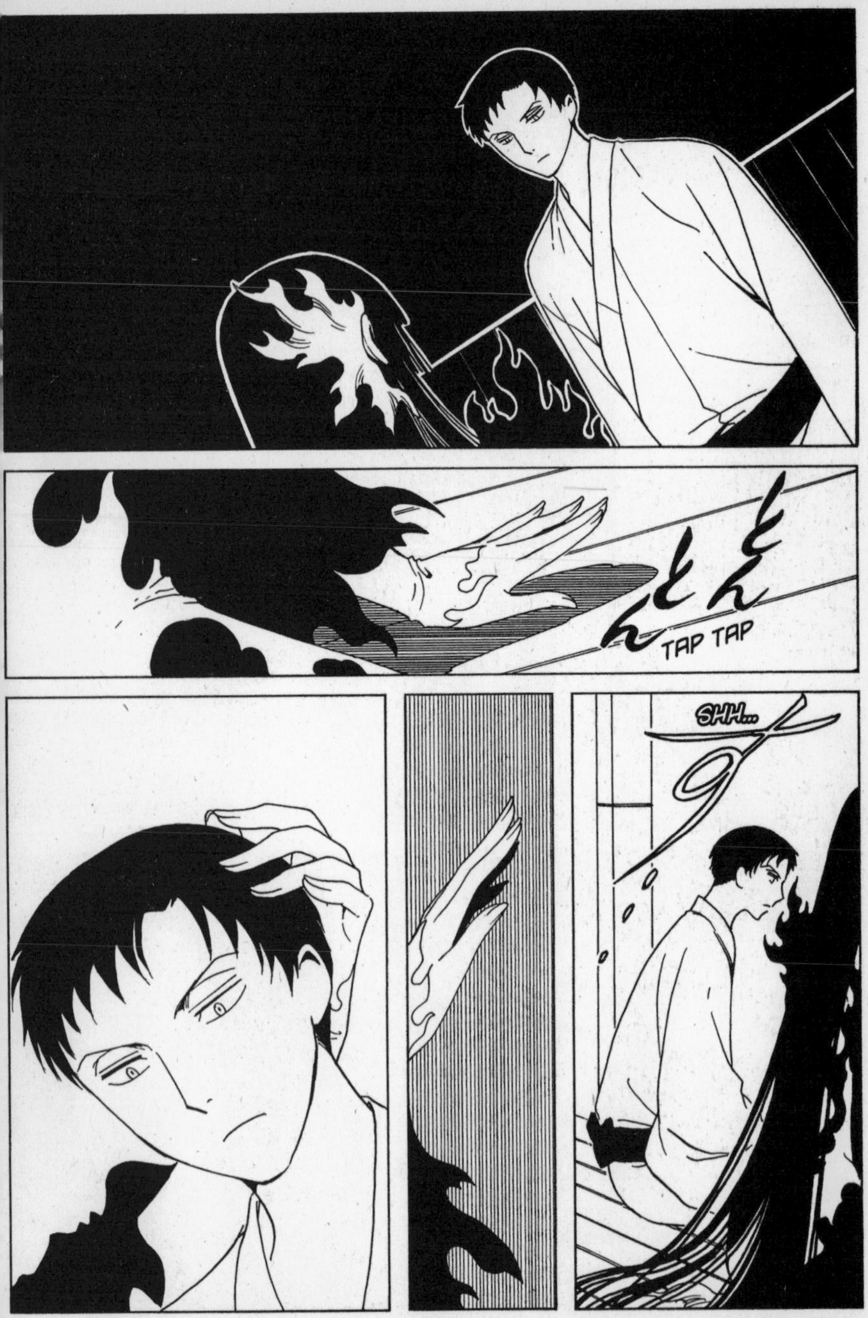
TAP TAP
SHH...

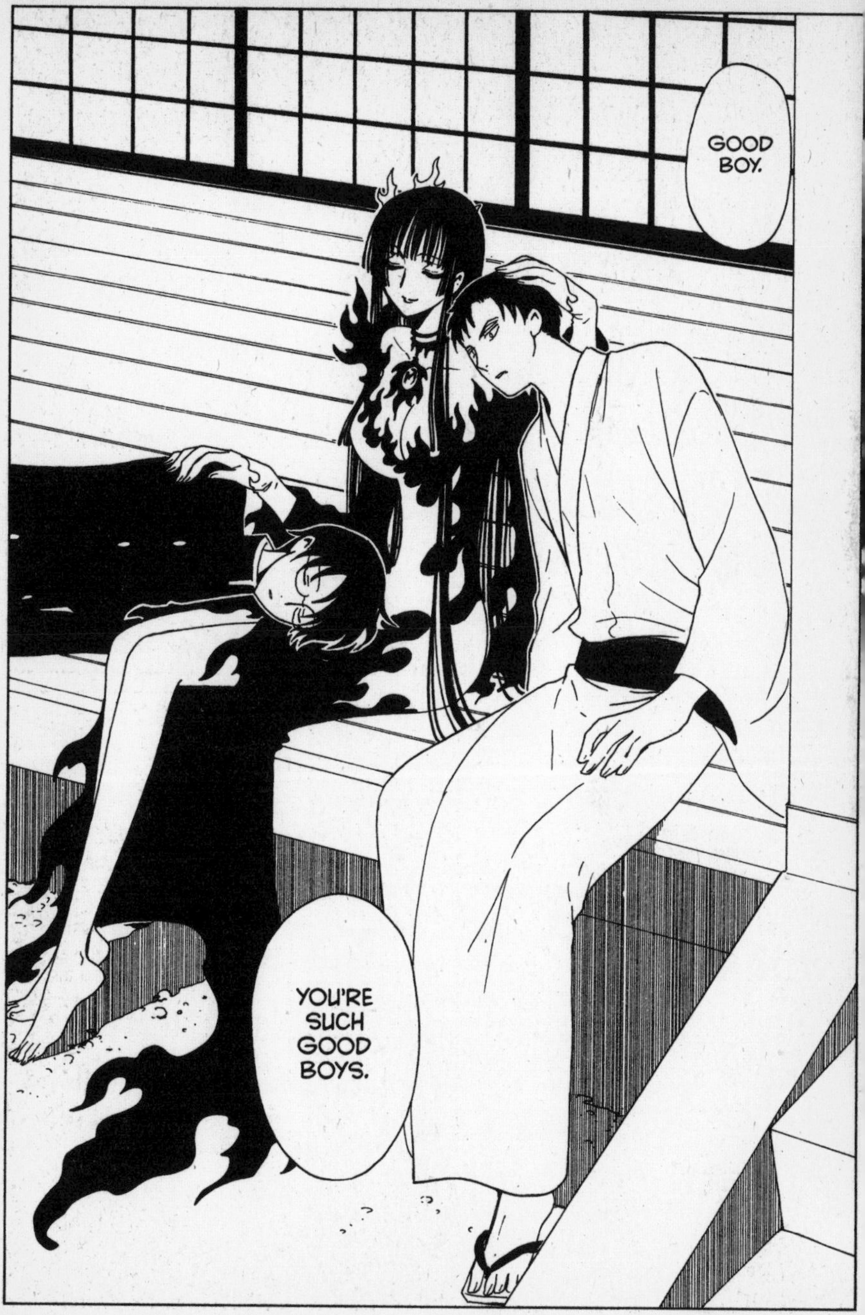
GOOD BOY.
YOU'RE SUCH GOOD BOYS.

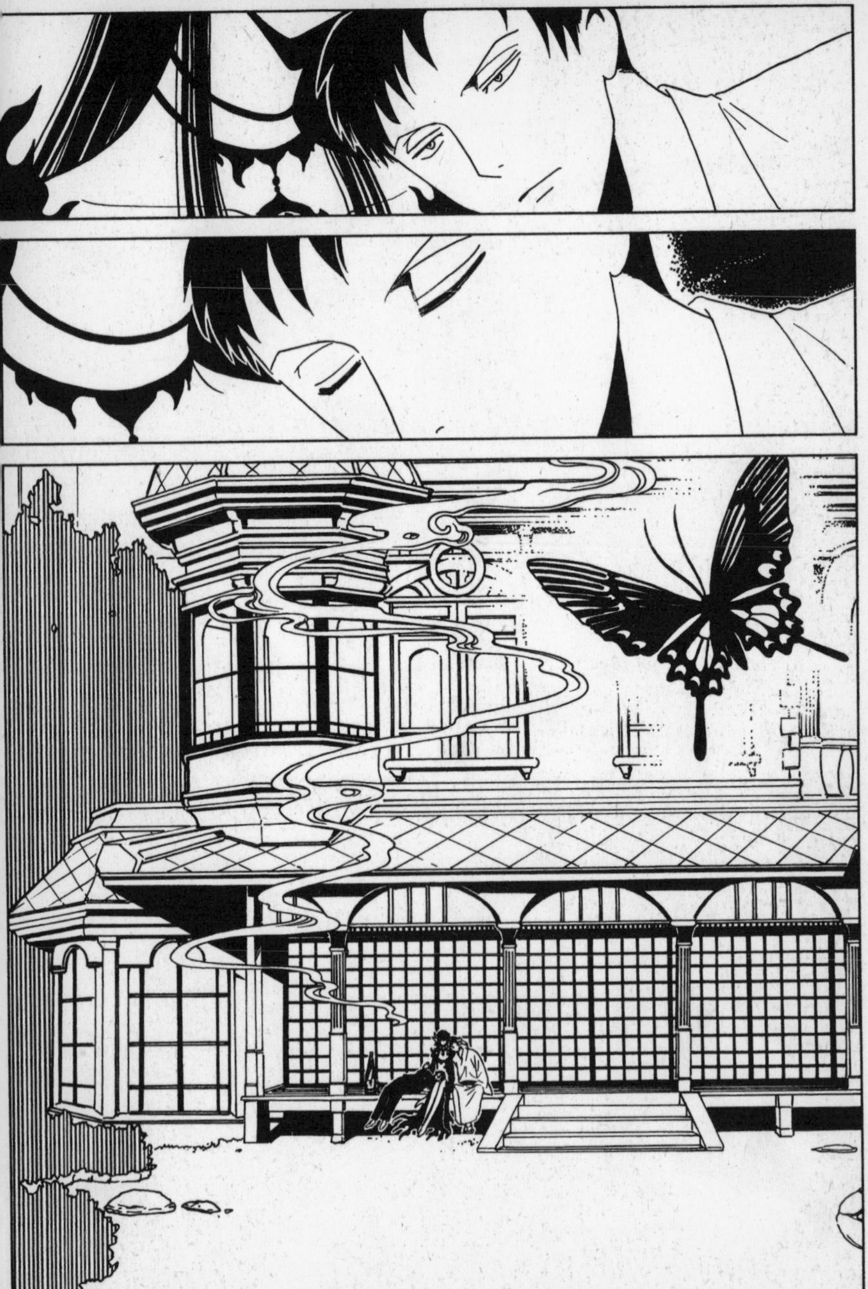

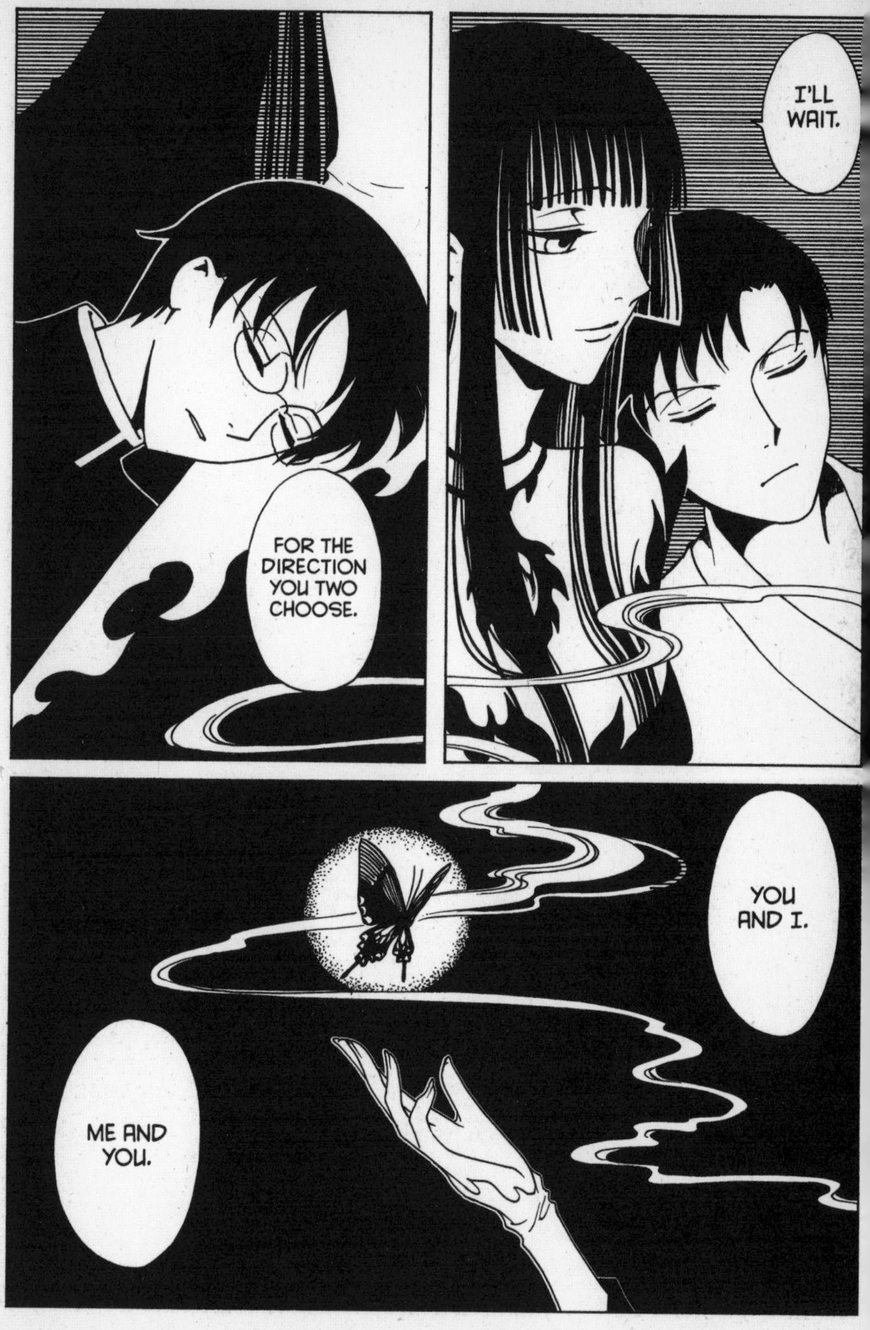
I'LL WAIT.
FOR THE DIRECTION YOU TWO CHOOSE.
YOU AND I.
ME AND YOU.

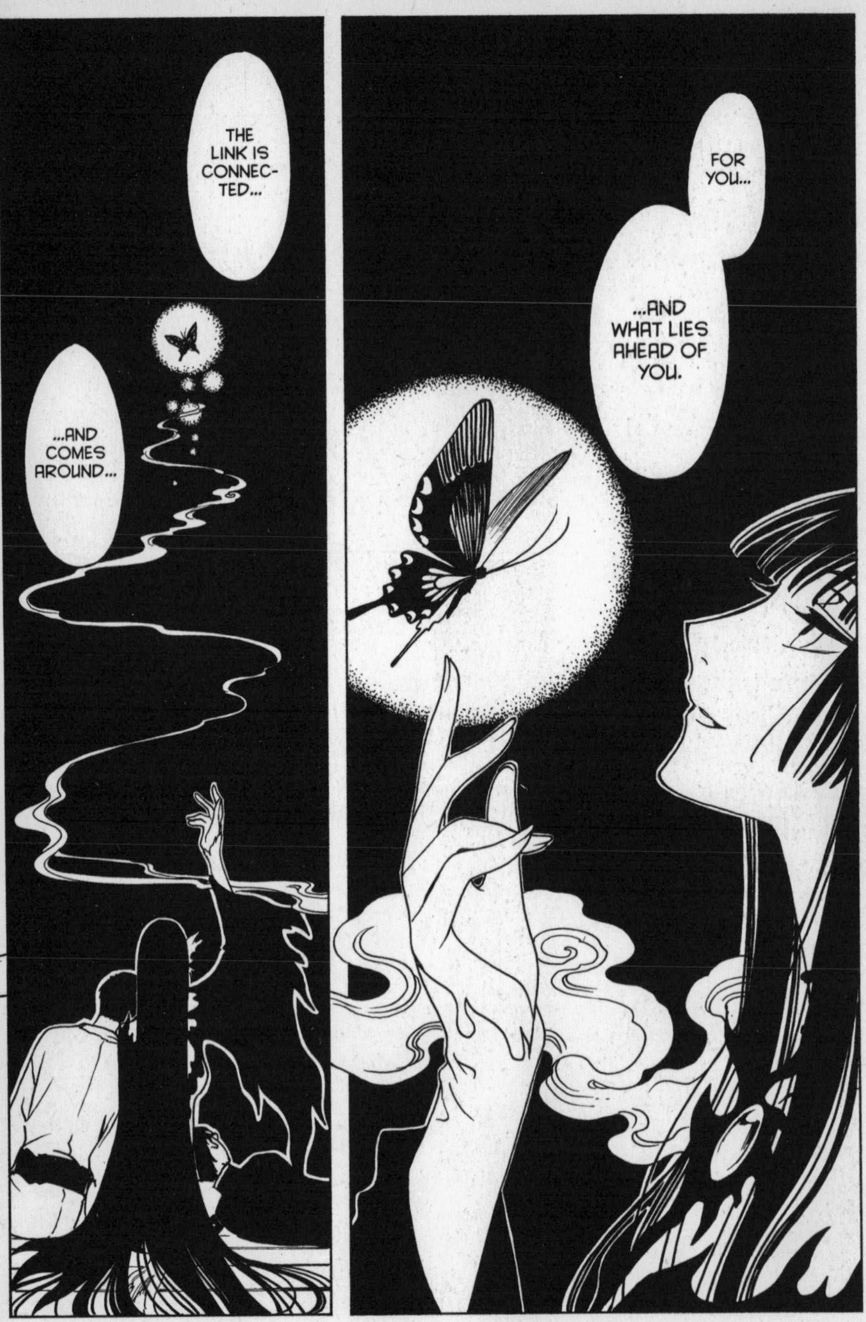
FOR YOU...
...AND WHAT LIES AHEAD OF YOU.
THE LINK IS CONNEC-TED...
...AND COMES AROUND...

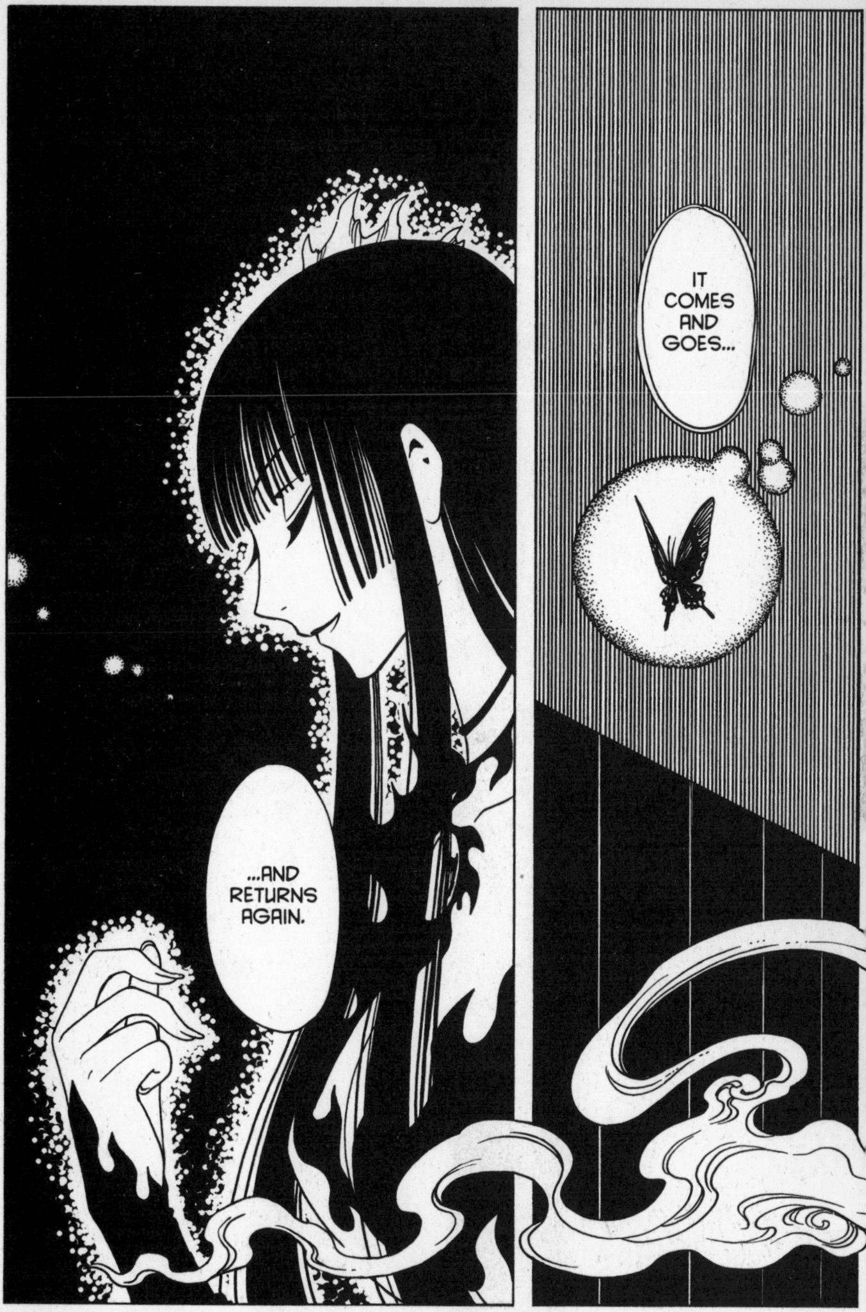
IT COMES AND GOES...
...AND RETURNS AGAIN.

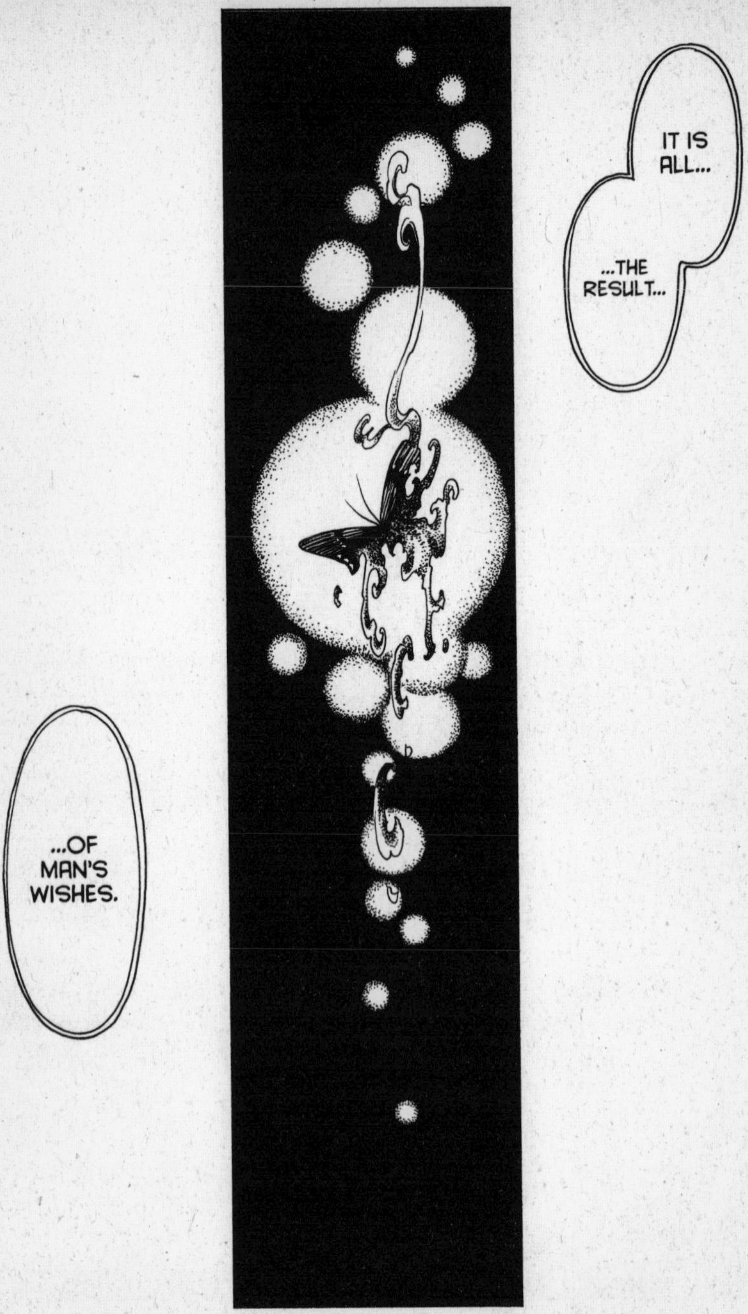
IT IS ALL...
...THE RESULT...
...OF MAN'S WISHES.

~ TO BE CONTINUED ~

Translation Notes

anese is a tricky language for most Westerners, and translation is often more art than science. For your edificaiton reading pleasure, here are note on some of the places where we could have gone in a different direction with our translation of this book, or where a Japanese cultural reference is used.

Rei

subtitle of this series is the kanji for "return," signaling a return to the series and to its roots. You'll notice that the concept of returning also appears throughout the book.

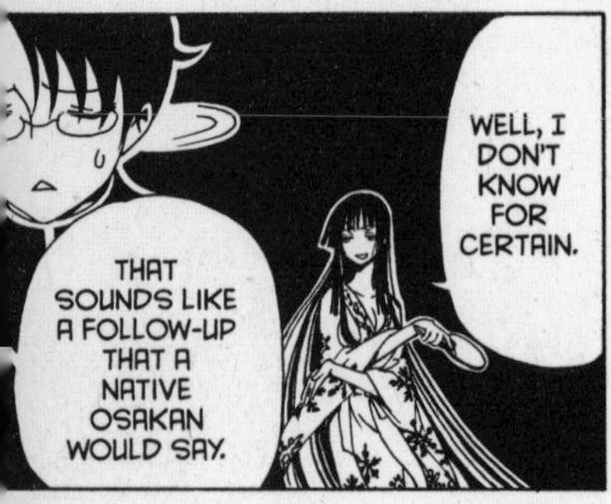
WELL, I DON'T KNOW FOR CERTAIN.
THAT SOUNDS LIKE A FOLLOW-UP THAT A NATIVE OSAKAN WOULD SAY.

Osakans, page 6 [6.3]

As the largest, most distinct regional culture within Japan outside of Tokyo, Osaka enjoys a rather colorful reputation with the rest of the country. Veterans of manga and anime are likely familiar with the presence of Osaka-ben or Kansai-ben, the particular dialect that is a popular type of characterization for colorful, larger-than-life people. The stereotypical Osakan is loud, loose, friendly and energetic. Spend enough time on the Japanese internet and you might find lists titled, "You Know You're From Osaka If..." and in almost every case, one of the entries will read: "You say 'but I dunno' after every authoritative statement."

White Day, page 8 [8.1]

A uniquely Japanese extension of Valentine's Day. In Japan, the custom on Valentine's Day is for women to give chocolates to men, either to ignify romantic interest or out of a social obligation (giri-choco). White Day was concocted as a return of interest, a holiday in mid-March in which the men give a romantic gift to the women. Note that in the example here, Watanuki and Yûko have switched roles, but the general idea is the same: one gift given is meant to be returned at a later date.

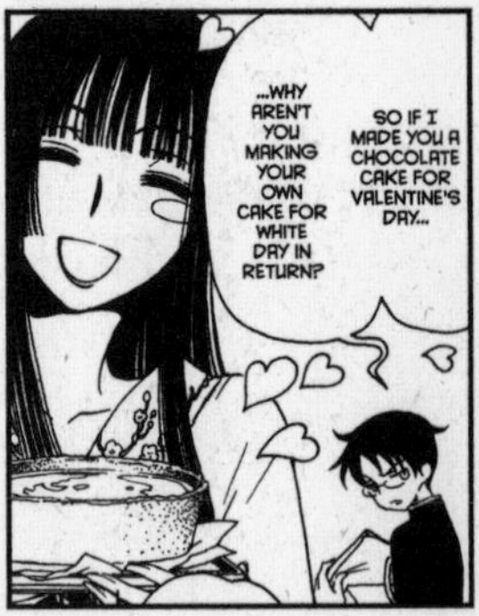
SO IF I MADE YOU A CHOCOLATE CAKE FOR VALENTINE'S DAY...
...WHY AREN'T YOU MAKING YOUR OWN CAKE FOR WHITE DAY IN RETURN?

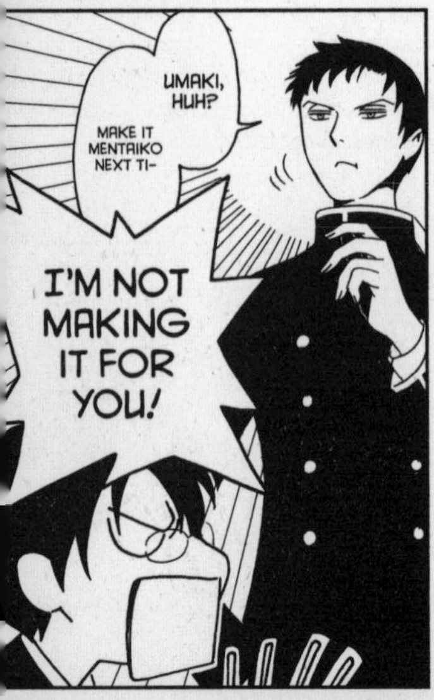
UMAKI, HUH?
MAKE IT MENTAIKO NEXT TI-
I'M NOT MAKING IT FOR YOU!

Umaki and mentaiko, page 32 [32.5]

Umaki is a dish of roasted eel that has been wrapped in a roll of fried egg, much like a typical sushi roll—the name itself means "eel roll." Mentaiko is a common side dish consisting of cod roe (eggs) that has been marinated and spiced with chili pepper. It's a popular filling for rice balls.

Yoshimoto stage show, page 46 [46.2]

In the world of Japanese comedians, nearly all of the big names are represented by a few powerful talent agencies, and Yoshimoto Creative Agency is the biggest of them all. While appearing on comedy TV shows is a huge source of popularity and fame, another outlet of the comedy industry is live shows. Yoshimoto has long held a comedic stage show called the Yoshimoto Shinkigeki that features many famous members of its stable of talent. While the form of a comedy play is rather old-fashioned in comparison to in-your-face TV shows, the Shinkigeki is a long-running tradition that enjoys solid popularity from the Japanese people and serves as a place for Yoshimoto's comedians who have lost the shine of the spotlight to continue working productively.

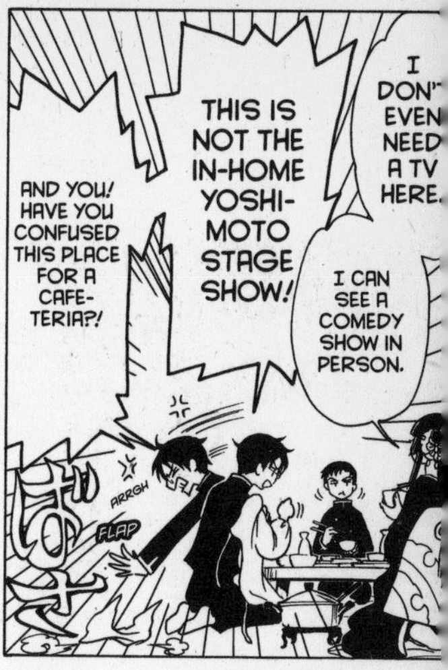
I DON'
EVEN NEED A TV HERE.
I CAN SEE A COMEDY SHOW IN PERSON.
THIS IS NOT THE IN-HOME YOSHI-MOTO STAGE SHOW!
AND YOU! HAVE YOU CONFUSED THIS PLACE FOR A CAFE-TERIA?!
ARRGH
FLAP

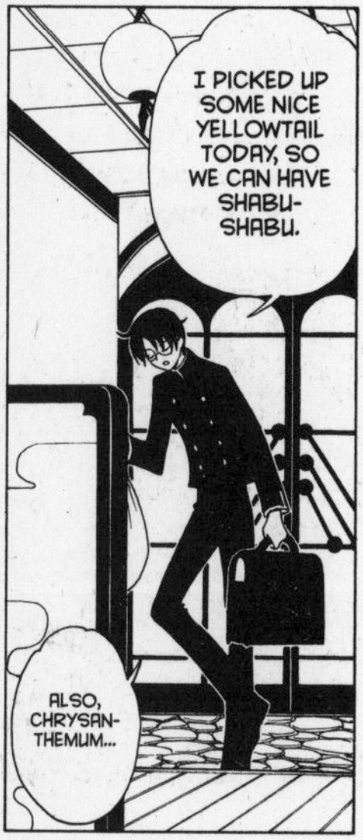
I PICKED UP SOME NICE YELLOWTAIL TODAY, SO WE CAN HAVE SHABU-SHABU.
ALSO, CHRYSAN-THEMUM...

Shabu-shabu, page 63 [63.2]

A dish of thinly sliced meat and a small pot of boiling water or broth. The me is put into the liquid to cook—the name itself refers to the splashing sound- before it is removed and dipped into a savory sauce and eaten with rice. In addition to the meat (which is traditionally beef), an assortment of tofu and vegetables is also served, with edible chrysanthemum being a popular side. While shabu-shabu is ordinarily meat, yellowtail (buri) is an occasiona alternative, which is called buri-shabu.

Saikyô-yaki and shiokara, page 119 [119.4]

Saikyô-yaki is fish broiled in saikyô miso, a sweeter variety of miso that means "West of Kyoto" after its place of origin. Shiokara, meanwhile, is one of Japan's most acquired tastes: fish or shellfish that has been fermented in its own guts and heavily salted. The resulting chunky paste is quite rich and powerful. Because of its considerable punch in a small serving, it makes for a popular appetizer at pubs to go with drinks.

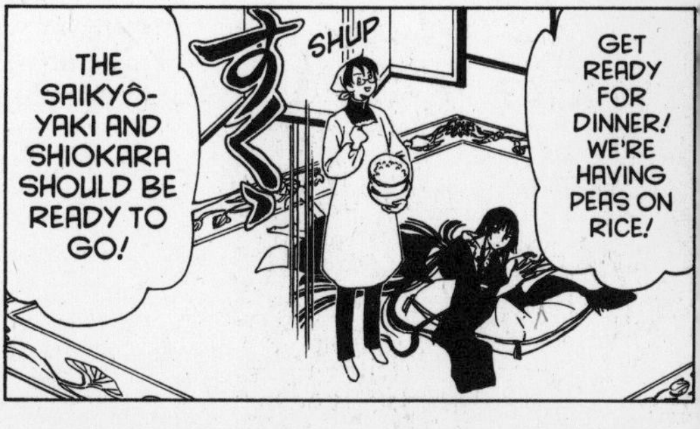
GET READY FOR DINNER! WE'RE HAVING PEAS ON RICE!
SHUP
THE SAIKYÔ-YAKI AND SHIOKARA SHOULD BE READY TO GO!

Shôchû, page 156 [156.1]

One of the most popular kinds of hard liquor in Japan. As opposed to nihonshu, which most of the West calls "sake," and is actually brewed with rice in a process that bears similarity to beer, shôchû is a classic distilled liquor made from starch—potatoes, rice or barley. The "Gararuddo" bottle is an actual brand of shôchû. The name means "to get scolded" in Kagoshima dialect. As in, drink too much and you'll "gararuddo"!

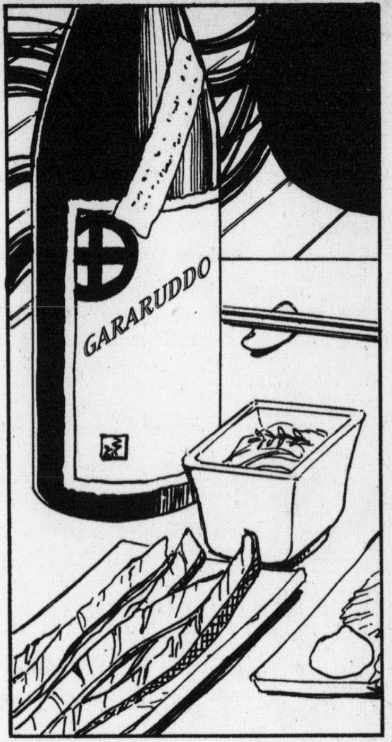
GARARUDDO

A Kodansha Comics Trade Paperback Original.

xxxHOLiC Rei volume 1 copyright © 2013
CLAMP • ShigatsuTsuitachi CO., LTD./Kodansha
English translation copyright © 2014
CLAMP • ShigatsuTsuitachi CO., LTD./Kodansha

Published in the United States by Kodansha Comics, an imprint of Kodansha USA Publishing, LLC, New York.

Publication rights for this English edition arranged through Kodansha Ltd., Tokyo.

First published in Japan in 2013 by Kodansha Ltd., Tokyo.

ISBN 978-1-61262-939-1

Printed in the United States of America.

www.kodanshacomics.com

9 8 7 6 5 4 3 2 1

Translator: Stephen Paul
Lettering: Paige Pumphrey

IT IS ALL THE RESULT OF
MAN'S WISHES.